Dowding of Fighter Command

Dowding of Fighter Command

Victor of the Battle of Britain

Vincent Orange

GRUB STREET · LONDON

Published by
Grub Street Publishing
4 Rainham Close
London
SW11 6SS

British Library Cataloguing in Publication Data
Orange, Vincent, 1935-
   Dowding of Fighter Command: victor of the Battle of Britain
   1. Dowding, Hugh Caswall Tremenheere Dowding, Baron,
   1882-1970 2. Great Britain. Royal Air Force – History –
   World War, 1939-1945 3. Marshals – Great Britain –
   Biography 4. Britain, Battle of, Great Britain, 1940
   5. World War, 1939-1945 – Aerial operations, British
   I. Title
   358.4'1331'092

ISBN-13: 9781906502140

Typeset by Pearl Graphics, Hemel Hempstead

Printed and bound by MPG Ltd, Bodmin, Cornwall

Grub Street Publishing uses only FSC
(Forest Stewardship Council) paper for its books.

Captions to back cover
Top: The Air Council in session at the Air Ministry – 23 July 1940.
Left to right: Air Vice-Marshal A. G. R. Garrod; Sir Harold G. Howitt; Air Marshal
Sir Christopher L. Courtney (Air Member for Supply and Organisation); Air Marshal
E. L. Gossage (Air Member for Personnel); Captain H. H. Balfour, M.P. (Under-
Secretary of State for Air) (Vice-President of the Air Council); Rt. Hon. Sir Archibald
Sinclair (Secretary of State for Air) (President of the Air Council); Air Marshal Sir
Cyril Newall; Sir Arthur Street (Permanent Under-Secretary of State for Air); Air Chief
Marshal Sir Wilfred R. Freeman (Air Member for Development and Production); Sir
Charles Craven (Civil Member for Development and Production); Mr. R. H. Melville
(Private Secretary to the Secretary of State for Air); Flight Lieutenant W. W. Wakefield,
M.P. (Parliamentary Private Secretary to the Parliamentary Under-Secretary of State for
Air).

Bottom: Dowding and his fighter boys, and girl. He is pictured with, left to right:
S/L A.C. Bartley; W/C D.F.B Sheen; W/C I.R Gleed; W/C M.Aitken; W/C 'Sailor'
Malan; S/L A.C. Deere; F/O E.C. Henderson; F/L R.H. Hillary; W/C J.A. Kent;
W/C C.F.B Kingcome; S/L D.H. Watkins; W/O R.H. Gretton.

for

AUDREY

in memory of her dear husband
and my good friend and mentor

HENRY PROBERT
(1926-2007)

My job was to prevent the war from being lost,
not to win it, and when my job is done,
I shall go out like a cork from a bottle

Lord Dowding

Contents

Acknowledgements

Everyone who has written on any aspect of Royal Air Force history during the last thirty years owes a great deal to the former head of the Air Historical Branch, Air Commodore Henry Probert, who died on Christmas Day, 2007. Whenever I visited London, he found me space in the Branch, encouraged my efforts, introduced me to senior officers, arranged for me to speak at conferences and (best of all) he and his wife Audrey made me welcome in their home. He will always be a five-star gentleman for me.

I am also deeply indebted to Henry's successors: Sebastian Cox, Sebastian Ritchie, and all who toil in that ever-moving Branch – not forgetting Humphrey Wynn, who escaped long ago. At the RAF Museum, Hendon, and the RAF College, Cranwell, everyone I met was kind and helpful, but I must mention Peter Elliott, Tim Pierce and Joel Hayward in particular. As always, I am grateful to archivists whom I do not know: at British National Archives in Kew, the Liddell Hart Centre in King's College, London, Winchester College, and Georgetown University in Washington DC. One archivist whom I do know, and who has been a very helpful friend for years, is Yvonne Kinkaid, of Bolling Air Force Base, Washington, DC.

Paul Baillie, Elizabeth Hussey, Kevin Kelly, Simon Muggleton, Nick Peacock and Arnie Wilson in England were all helpful. For years now, I have benefitted from the expertise of all who work in the University of Canterbury Library: this time, I thank especially Janette Nicolle, Bronwyn Matthews and Katharine Samuel. My publisher, John Davies, gives me plenty of encouragement and Errol W. Martyn has again proved a tower of strength, especially in regard to providing First World War material. I am also grateful to Trevor Richards for his advice.

Without the wholehearted co-operation of David Whiting (Dowding's stepson), who sent me valuable information and photographs, this book would certainly be much poorer. But without the skills – and tender loving care – of my dear wife Sandra it would probably not have been completed and would certainly not have reached London by electronic means.

Vincent Orange,
Christchurch, New Zealand,
11 May 2008

1

From Moffat to Upavon, 1882-1914

Wiltshire Scotsman

His full name was Hugh Caswall Tremenheere Dowding. He was a Scotsman, born in the village of Moffat, about 50 miles south of Edinburgh, on 24 April 1882.[1] A number of historians, however, insist that he was really an Englishman because his father was from the other end of Britain, latest in a long line of Wiltshire men, most of them parsons, teachers, soldiers or sailors although his great-grandfather – John Dowding – was a banker and owned a local newspaper.[2] His mother was also from southern England, but it can be argued that the boy was shaped by his first 13 years in Scotland. As a rule, we do not change much after that age, save to become a disappointment to ourselves and to those who know or even love us.

Moffat has a splendid statue of a ram, erected in 1875 and standing proudly on a rock, to honour the importance of sheep farming in the area. The image of that ram – immovable, unwilling to back down from any challenge – might also stand for Dowding. He would often have heard locals telling visitors that 'it has nae lugs'; true, but it sees clearly, just as Dowding did throughout his long life as a soldier, airman and in his last 20 years as an influential opponent of cruelty to animals. It is likely, however, that Moffat's famous Toffee Shop, an irresistible magnet for locals and visitors alike, appealed more to young Dowding – if he was allowed to spend his pocket money there.

Whether we think Dowding was shaped more by rural Scotland than rural Wiltshire, he was certainly not an *urban* man: Whitehall was never, for him, a natural home, which may help us to understand why he was so often at odds with officers who were comfortable in its corridors of power. Moffat has a sulphur spring and some of that sulphur evidently got into young Hugh's bloodstream because many of his colleagues – especially those in high office – would be shrivelled by him in later years. It was only when he was elderly and married for a second time that he became an amiable chap, easy to get along with.

John Dowding, Hugh's great-grandfather, had a son, Benjamin, who reverted to family tradition and became rector of Southbroom in Wiltshire.[3] He married Maria Caswall, daughter of a fellow-parson and grand-niece of a bishop. Hugh's father, Arthur John Dowding (1855-1932), was one of their ten children. He was educated at Winchester College, as were several of Hugh's forebears. One of Britain's oldest public schools (founded by bishop William of Wykeham in 1382), it is spiritual home to countless 'Wykehamists' who became famous in every walk of life and enjoy a reputation for being distinctive if not distinguished. Arthur was a good scholar, cricketer and athlete, cheerful and popular, who very properly became a prefect. He did well after Winchester, when he went up to New College, Oxford (also founded by bishop William, in 1379).

After brief spells of teaching in England, Arthur went to Fettes College in Edinburgh, one of Scotland's most famous schools. There he learned that wealthy local families regretted the lack of a nearby preparatory school run by gentlemen for their sons awaiting entry to Fettes. Arthur had class; they had money. So he agreed with a clergyman friend to set up a school dedicated to St Ninian that opened in Moffat in 1879. Ninian, who lived c. 360-432, was a significant choice as patron because it was he who began the endless task of converting the Scots to Christianity. He also built the first known stone church in Britain.[4]

There were nine first-day pupils, among them E. W. Hornung, creator of Raffles – gentleman, cricketer, thief – who is the antithesis of Sir Arthur Conan Doyle's immortal Sherlock Holmes in that he commits crimes instead of solving them. Willie Hornung married Doyle's sister Connie and the two authors became close friends. Like Doyle, whom he greatly admired, Hugh Dowding became in later life a devout Spiritualist.[5]

St Ninian's prospered and in 1880 Arthur Dowding was able to marry Maud Tremenheere (1855-1934), daughter of Lieutenant-General Charles Tremenheere, chief engineer in the Public Works Department of Bombay Presidency. Arthur and Maud had four children, of whom Hugh was the eldest. Then came Hilda (1884-1976), who never married. She skied well and became a fine ice-skater. During the Great War, she served with the First Aid Nursing Yeomanry in Italy. Otherwise, like so many daughters of her class and generation, she devoted her life to the family, especially to Hugh. At number three came Arthur Ninian (1886-1966), who reached admiral rank in the Royal Navy and finally Kenneth Townley (1889-1979), an articled clerk with a firm of London solicitors who joined the Royal Flying Corps in 1914, qualified as a pilot and briefly commanded a squadron in Italy. Unlike his brothers, Kenneth chose not to follow a military career after the Great War.[6]

Hugh's parents were intelligent, educated, hard-working and prosperous; morally secure, wise and firm. He was not sent away from home at a tender age, as were so many boys of his class, to cope with strange adults and a host of unknown boys. On the other hand, there are disadvantages to being the headmaster's son. When the other boys left St Ninian's for the holidays, Hugh merely moved to another room in the same house. Although Arthur Dowding was respected by his pupils, it was inevitable that his words, moods and actions should be much discussed by the boys in private, and not always reverently, but Hugh was excluded from all this normal, healthy gossip.[7]

Unstuffy Maverick

Dowding acquired the nickname 'Stuffy' when he was about 30 years old, and some of that word's meanings might reasonably be applied to him: he was indeed 'prim', as were many late Victorian gentlemen – and ladies – of the comfortable middle-classes. No-one, however, denies that he became a man of formidable personality – cold, rather than hot – with a sharp tongue and an even sharper pen. Usually, though, when dealing with subordinates or with those men and women who worked as hard as he did, he was the soul of formal courtesy. Better still, he was a good listener and as ready to back them, if he thought they had a fair case, as he was to stand up for himself in any dispute with other authorities, no matter how high. But it was mainly on the polo ground or the ski field, or with members of his immediate family, that Dowding was a jovial man. One says 'mainly' because a contemporary of his – Air Chief Marshal Sir Philip Joubert de la Ferté, who was by no means an uncritical admirer – recorded that:

> 'Out of office hours he could be an extremely entertaining companion, having a fund of good stories and a quick wit with which to tell them. This sense of humour did not, as a rule, extend into his work, and he could be extremely exacting and tiresome to his subordinates. He had, however, a great sense of justice which earned him the respect of all who worked with him.'[8]

'Since I was a child,' Dowding once recalled, 'I have never accepted ideas because they were orthodox, and consequently I have frequently found myself in opposition to generally-accepted views.' He went on to say, somewhat smugly even though with justification, 'perhaps, in retrospect, this has not been altogether a bad thing.'[9] If that is so, we might think of him as a maverick rather than stuffy: the dictionary tells us that one meaning of 'maverick' is an unorthodox person and Dowding was certainly that.

As for the 'generally-accepted views' which Dowding opposed, he had in mind those of Hugh Trenchard, widely regarded as a founding father of the Royal Air Force. Trenchard, his acolytes and many historians (not only those appointed by the Air Ministry) elevated those views into a doctrine.[10] For many years, that doctrine was blindly accepted by most ambitious officers, but never by Dowding. This resistance to conventional opinion lies at the root of his many quarrels with authority. He was also reluctant to accept a need to *persuade* opponents that he was in the right or even to *compromise* with them. Persuasion and compromise were concepts that he found difficult to accept throughout his career, especially in important matters that he had carefully studied. During the 1930s he became the RAF's most senior serving officer and disliked resistance to his decisions from Air Ministry officials who were very much his juniors in rank and service.

This exasperating maverick might best be described these days as 'Dowding of Fighter Command'. When he was tardily raised to the peerage

– as a mere baron, unlike several contemporaries who were made viscounts or even earls – he took 'of Bentley Priory' as part of his title. Certainly appropriate, but the broader title would be even more fitting, for no subsequent head of that command, now extinct, had either his authority or bore anything like his weight of responsibility for Britain's safety.

As for Bentley Priory and the grounds in which it stands, they will pass out of Royal Air Force hands in 2008. *Sic transit gloria mundi* as it always does, for nearly everyone who served at Bentley Priory when it mattered to Britain and her allies is now dead or soon will be. The decision to sell pleases those persons who propose to convert it into a housing estate, and does not distress those revisionists who like to tell us that the significance of the Battle of Britain has been grossly exaggerated. Perhaps it has, in some quarters. But they also insist that Dowding's command did not fight it alone. In fact, neither he nor the men and women, in or out of uniform, who served with him before or during 1940 ever made such a foolish claim. That year (and also the five years following) form one of those rare periods in the life of any society when a majority of its people were united by a great purpose and tried (how they tried!) to live above their ordinary selves. We have not seen the like since.

The failure of the Royal Air Force to promote Dowding to its highest rank disgraces those responsible, as scores of men and women who served with him – including many opponents – have said or written, often vehemently, in every year since at least 1943. Fortunately, the guilty men are now barely remembered and their pettiness has not prevented Dowding from being recognised today as one of the 20th Century's heroes, a man who deserves permanent honour for the vital part he played in preventing the worldwide triumph of Hitler's vile régime.

As Basil Collier, his first biographer, wrote more than half a century ago:

> 'It is scarcely an exaggeration to say that, but for Dowding, there would have been no Hurricane, no Spitfire, no radar chain, no escape for the Royal Air Force from the fate that had overwhelmed its counterparts in European countries, no avoidance of irremediable disaster.'

He was 'the presiding genius'; the 'Victor of the Battle of Britain'.[11]

He also deserves credit for selecting a man – Keith Park – who proved capable of conducting that defence during 1940.[12]

Artillery Officer

Dowding left St Ninian's in his 14th year for Winchester College. It was a world away, in distance and customs, from everything he had known. He arrived alone, after a long journey via Edinburgh and London, and remained alone, throughout his four years there (1895-9). Unlike his father – a Wiltshire man who entered that school from close range with several friends – Hugh made no mark. Useless at games; not at all a bright spark socially; barely adequate academically; never considered prefect material; and speaking, when he spoke at all, in a curious Scotch-Wiltshire accent. He did, however, become a very correct late-Victorian gentleman, taking to heart Winchester's motto, 'Manners Makyth Man'.

Quite unable to master classical Greek – essential for following his father to New College, Oxford – he decided to enter the Royal Military Academy, Woolwich, in September 1899. According to his stepson, Dowding hoped to become an engineer, a calling that would have suited his practical talents. For a boy of his class in that generation, however, his only hope of achieving such an ambition – supposing it was as fully formed then as he later claimed it had been – was in the Army. As a consequence of the outbreak of war in South Africa, the course at Woolwich was shortened to one year and Dowding was commissioned as a second lieutenant in the Royal Garrison Artillery in August 1900, aged 18. His examination results were too poor (laziness, he later admitted, was the cause) to win him a commission in the more prestigious Royal Engineers.[13]

Second Lieutenant Dowding served first in Gibraltar. In those days, he recalled in 1956:

> 'Unless one had a pony one was confined to the somewhat dreary precincts of the Rock. A second lieutenant's pay at that time was 5s 7d a day and one's mess bill came to about 3s 6d even for the most temperate. So, even with the £100 a year allowance which I had from my father, it was some months before I could save up the £15 which it cost me to buy my first pony.'

One's heart does not bleed for this young man, because such a generous annual allowance was well beyond the reach, if not the desire, of most contemporaries. Thanks to his father (and his own frugality), he was able to enjoy hunting in the nearby cork woods: 'I don't think we did much execution among the foxes, but it was great fun and got us away from the prison-like confines of the Rock.'

In the late autumn of 1901 Dowding's company was transferred to Colombo, Ceylon (now Sri Lanka), where he learned to shoot fast-flying snipe and made his first attempts at playing polo: not a game for the faint-hearted, but a social obligation for ambitious subalterns. Dowding, however, became dissatisfied with his career prospects and asked for a transfer to the Mountain Artillery. He had still to learn the outcome of his request when the company was transferred, after less than 12 months, to Hong Kong.

There he was promoted in May 1902 to lieutenant and flourished: plenty of polo, horse-racing, yachting, picnics and even mixed bathing. Racing at Hong Kong was great fun, he recalled, and entirely amateur. Every year a batch of 30 or 40 ponies was brought all the way from Manchuria, more than 1,200 miles to the north. One paid a fixed price for a pony assigned by lot. Dowding got what seemed to be a hopeless nag, which he named Panjandrum, and refused to place a bet before riding him in the first race for both of them. To everyone's amazement, especially his own, Panjandrum romped home. A drunken Canadian doctor, who backed him by accident, won $1,140 and Dowding's capacity for composure under stress received its first serious test.

Another test came in February 1904 when a Japanese attack destroyed Russian warships in Port Arthur, at the southern tip of Manchuria. The authorities feared that a Russian fleet might try to seize Hong Kong as a base for operations against Japan. So Dowding, in charge of the defending guns, got a shock when a sergeant told him that 'there was two Russians shot here this morning'. After further discussion, he learned that the sergeant had actually said 'there was two rations short here this morning'.

Dowding spent one leave in Japan, where the fishing was 'execrable, a few fingerling brown trout in a sluggish muddy stream', until they were taken to a nearby lake stocked with landlocked sea trout. Dense cloud covered Mount Fuji, preventing him from trying to climb it, and later he was introduced to nude bathing in a country inn. One of his companions, a Captain Radford, insisted on wearing trunks. 'This excessive modesty,' wrote Dowding, 'was considered diverting in the extreme and he was famous throughout the length and breadth of Japan.'[14]

Annihilating the Enemy

In the spring of 1904 Dowding got his wish to join a mountain battery and was sent to British India, to Rawalpindi, south of Islamabad in the Punjab, now part of Pakistan. He would assure his first two biographers that the next six years, taking him from the age of 22 to 28, were the happiest of his entire career. Plenty of polo and shooting, plenty of plodging through thick mud or toiling up a steep hillside, getting thoroughly wet, frozen, boiled or suffocated by dust storms. A grand life. He was not known as Stuffy in those days.

He transferred to a mountain battery at Kalabagh (about 100 miles south-west of Rawalpindi) and did all he could to stay away from that city, much preferring to rough it in remote areas. He liked seeing new country and having his own show to run, even if constant rain was a nuisance. 'Still rain every blessed day', he wrote to his parents on 15 August 1906, 'the whole place is like one vast sponge. Tennis is impossible most days, and even when we do play we stodge about in several inches of mud and beat flabby puddings across the net with racquets strung about as tightly as landing nets.'[15]

After six contented if sometimes soggy years, however, Dowding hoped to attend the Staff College at Camberley in Surrey, but his commanding officer, Major J. L. Parker, refused to recommend him. He was not serious enough, Parker thought, about his profession. Dowding disagreed – as he usually did with senior officers – and got himself transferred to a Native Battery at Dehra Dun in the Himalayas, 120 miles north of Delhi. It proved to be 'the best station at which I ever served', he wrote later. 'I see that I am writing as if I was very good at polo. As a matter of fact, I never was much good, only very keen.' He was also very keen on shooting in those days, with what success he does not say.

Dowding was at ease with Sikhs, Punjabis and Hindus, all hard-living, self-reliant men, expert gunners and ideal companions for a man of his frugal, abstemious tastes. He valued the responsibility which came his way: 'so different', he told his first biographer, 'from the lot of the junior officer in an infantry regiment.' He had to make arrangements with local authorities for camping, rations, fodder, medical services, etc, and no senior officer was on hand to help if he got into a muddle or found a road blocked or a bridge washed out.[16]

Close at hand was Mussoorie, an ideal hill station in that it lacked senior officers. Dowding was sent with his guns to join British troops at Chakrata, a few miles north-west of Mussoorie, and take part in an important exercise. It began with a day's march along a forest path, to be followed by a retreat over the same ground, assuming – for the purpose of the exercise – that they were under fire from 'a savage enemy'. That enemy was represented by two companies of Gurkhas sent from Dehra Dun.

Dowding got permission from the umpires of the exercise to begin his retreat very early, in order to get his guns into a good position from which to cover his British allies when they began their retreat. As a careful officer should, he sent out scouts to discover exactly where the enemy Gurkhas were. To his delight and surprise, he learned that they were enjoying a leisurely breakfast below an unguarded ridge: most unsoldierly. So Lieutenant Dowding deployed his troops and guns along that ridge and then went down alone to tell the Gurkhas, politely, that they had just been 'annihilated'.

They were under the command of Lieutenant Cyril Newall, an officer four years younger than Dowding who would later transfer, as he did, to the Royal Flying Corps. Later still, Newall would be preferred to Dowding as head of the Royal Air Force. In January 1941, when Britain needed every man and woman of energy and experience to help her withstand a severe crisis, it was found possible to spare Newall (then only 54) for the undemanding duty of Governor General in New Zealand. He idled away the rest of the war there and received a barony on his return to England in June 1946. He took no further part in public affairs, wrote no memoirs, made no speeches of consequence, and died in November 1963, entirely forgotten.[17]

Dowding enjoyed life at Dehra Dun so much that he was moved to make his first excursion into verse. It was inspired by an order from headquarters that units were becoming too fussy about the cleanliness of forage provided for their animals. It could only be rejected, someone in headquarters decreed, if it contained more than 2% of dirt. As would often be the case in his later life, Dowding received many decrees from on high with a bucketful of salt. His response to this one was published, to his surprise, in the *Civil and Military Gazette*. It is clearly the work of one who, in those days, was far from stuffy. Here is a sample:

'The remount of the future must
Be trained from birth to swallow dust
And then by gradual degrees
To masticate the bark of trees
And later, sticks and little stones
And bits of string and chicken bones,
Nor trust to liquids alcoholic
To mitigate the pangs of colic.

But hold, perchance Dame Nature may
Refuse this alien role to play.
She may decline to break her rule
And make a rubber-tummied mule.'

Should that happen, Dowding concluded, we must find a substitute for mules:

'Our saddles we'll prepare to pack
And limber up on ostrich-back.'[18]

Camberley Student

In 1911, after a decade of overseas service, Dowding was at last permitted to return to England with a year's leave, on reduced pay, in order to prepare for the demanding entrance examination to the Staff College. He got in 'pretty easily', having no duties to perform and the benefit of a month-long grind with a crammer at the beginning of his leave plus another fortnight with him just before the exam to get 'the latest stable tips'. He was among those accepted in September 1911 for admission in the following January and by adroit 'management of the system' contrived to remain on leave in England until then. For no good reason, when recalling these days some 45 years later, he felt rather ashamed of this triumph. 'And so I became the proud holder of what I believe to be a service record – 17½ month's leave with no element of sick leave. (Did I say proud? I don't think I am quite so proud of it now).'[19]

Dowding was now rising 30 and spent the next two years as a student. The instructors, he thought, were conscientious and well-read in the assigned texts, but 'I was always irked by the lip-service that the staff paid to freedom of thought, contrasted with an actual tendency to repress all but conventional ideas.' He also thought, even at the time, that they had two serious weaknesses. Firstly, their unshakable belief in cavalry for offence as well as reconnaissance, despite the known impact of artillery and machine-gun fire on horses and their riders. Secondly, their reluctance to recognize the dawn of air power and the influence it was likely to have on both offence and reconnaissance, to say nothing of defence.

During the summer of 1913, Dowding was attached to a cavalry regiment for a field day at Aldershot on Salisbury Plain. At an earlier field day an officer named Briggs had 'put it across' the directing staff by using his cavalry as mounted infantry. A petty revenge was carefully plotted and Douglas Haig, then General Officer Commanding at Aldershot, attended to ensure – so Dowding believed – that Briggs was put in his place. He was given the task of attacking an entrenched enemy and prevented by what were decreed as 'impassable mountains' on one flank and an 'impenetrable swamp' on the other from attempting anything clever. He had no choice but to launch a frontal attack across an open plain which, of course, failed. Haig then took it upon himself to rebuke Briggs in front of all and sundry. 'I had the greatest admiration for Briggs,' Dowding recalled, 'he went through this ordeal without the slightest loss of dignity or flicker of resentment. My admiration did not extend to Haig.'

Later, during the Great War, Dowding had his low opinion of Haig, a devout advocate of the frontal offensive, amply confirmed. On 9 October 1959, Dowding thanked Robert Wright for lending him Leon Wolff's compelling account of one of that war's longest and bloodiest battles, *Flanders Fields: The 1917 Campaign*, published in 1958. He thought it one of the most depressing books he had ever read: 'it lets Haig off rather lightly in that it shows him as a stupid, stubborn, merciless, but not a dishonest man', whereas Dowding thought him 'as crooked as a corkscrew where his personal reputation was concerned.'[20]

Flier, Skier, Stuffy

Students at Camberley worked in syndicates, each one taking a turn as commander with the rest acting as his staff. When Dowding's turn came, he found himself deemed to be in charge of six aeroplanes. The first question to answer in the exercise assigned to his syndicate was: 'Were the enemy in possession of Grantham [in Lincolnshire] or not?' He decided to send all six of his imaginary aeroplanes to find out. A senior instructor queried this decision: how did he expect his pilots to find their way from Camberley to Grantham? By following the railway lines, Dowding replied. That would not do, the instructor objected, for they would run into one another. Although Dowding then knew nothing about aviation, he refused to believe this. Typically, he decided to become a pilot himself, for he was always keen to solve problems personally, if he could.

Dowding learned to fly on a Bristol Boxkite at Brooklands in Surrey, a flying school run by Vickers. The Boxkite was a good machine in its day: an 'instant success from its flying debut at the end of July 1910 and continued in production until the autumn of 1914.'[21] He was awarded a pilot's certificate (No. 711) by the Royal Aero Club after no more than 100 minutes in the air, few of them in sole charge, on the day he passed out from Camberley, 20 December 1913. Four months earlier, in August, he had been promoted to captain after exactly 13 years as a commissioned officer.[22]

It was during these Camberley years that Dowding was given the nickname 'Stuffy' which clung to him for the rest of his career. It was also at this time that he first visited Switzerland and was infected with a life-long addiction to skiing. No-one who knew him only on the ski fields – when he was on leave with family and/or friends – ever regarded him as 'Stuffy'. When halfway up a mountain thickly covered in snow, he was always cheerful and friendly; also widely admired, for he and his brother Kenneth soon proved to be champion performers. Their sister, Hilda, also skied and was evidently a fine figure skater as well. *The Times* said of her performance at a competition in March 1914: 'Miss Dowding, although a little slow in movement, was the only competitor who seemed to have studied and acquired the essentials of good carriage.'[23]

Unlike many of his contemporaries, Dowding was not enthralled by the new marvel of flying; skiing gave him all the thrills he needed. He and Kenneth were both 'deeply bitten by the sport', he told Collier, 'and became good enough in those happy-go-lucky days to share third place in the British

Championship (such as it was).' He often went with a particular friend Arnold Lunn, hiking from hut to hut on the high glaciers. Arnold was the son of the travel-bureau pioneer, Sir Henry Lunn, and brother of Hugh Kingsmill (who dropped the 'Lunn'), a notable biographer and anthologist. Arnold earned himself a knighthood, as both a vigorous defender of the Roman Catholic church and a champion skier, who invented slalom gates and obtained Olympic recognition for the modern Alpine slalom race and downhill races. Dowding also skated a bit, 'but skating', he said, 'always took a very lowly place in comparison with skiing.' In Lunn's opinion, he had the skill, determination and courage to be a champion, 'but fortunately for his country, he chose to make the RAF his career.' Lunn recalled how Dowding was once caught in a storm on the Oberland glaciers. He realized at once that the guide 'had not mastered the mysteries of the compass', so Dowding took the lead without a word and led his friends through the storm to safety.[24]

His father did not wish him to become a full-time airman and Dowding had only learned to fly because it gave him knowledge likely to be useful to him as a soldier. Having earned a pilot's certificate privately, he was qualified to take a three-month course organized by the Royal Flying Corps at its Central Flying School near the village of Upavon on Salisbury Plain in Wiltshire, to get his 'wings'. He then intended to return to regimental duty.

For a man who liked to rough it, Upavon was just the place: most of the buildings were 'obviously temporary', wrote its historian, and 'lovers of fresh air find it here in abundance'. With some exaggeration, perhaps, the school was said to have been 'located on the top of a mountain, where it is open to every wind that blows.'[25] During the course, Dowding progressed from the Boxkite to slightly more advanced types. First, the Maurice Farman Longhorn, a blessing for novices. It was impossible for the pilot to hit anything head first, recalled Oliver Stewart: if he fell forward, 'the front elevator and outriggers took the shock' and if he fell sideways, 'corridors of wings, wire and wood' saved him. Dowding then moved on to a more advanced and powerful machine, the Henri Farman: 'Delicate, elegant, quick, with fineness in every line and every movement', before tackling the BE 2, 'designed to be automatically stable', an undesirable quality in aerial combat, as experience would shortly show.[26]

Dowding successfully completed his course on 29 April 1914 and was assessed by the commandant, Captain Godfrey Paine, RN, as very good on both Farmans, good on the BE 2, and very good at cross country flying. Overall, he was reckoned to be an 'Above average officer. Keen and able.'[27] His instructor was John Salmond, an outstanding airman who became head of the RAF in the years 1930-3; he also became a bitter, secret and devious critic of Dowding's management of Fighter Command during 1940. It was at Upavon that Dowding first met Trenchard, then assistant commandant, later head of the RAF between 1919 and 1929. He too, in collaboration with Salmond, became a bitter, secret and devious critic of Dowding.[29] Those griefs lay far in the future, but at the time he was gratified to be what his classically-educated father was pleased to call a *rara avis* (a rare bird): a gunner with wings. Even so, having earned that distinction, he gladly resumed his career on the ground.

18

2

_Life and Death on the Western Front,
1914-15_

Observing

Captain Dowding was posted to Sandown, Isle of Wight, at the end of April
1914, but on the outbreak of war in August he was required – as a qualified
airman – to serve with the Royal Flying Corps. He was then 32 years old
and his character was fully formed. He was unwilling to exchange small
talk or smile readily, or do anything else that might win arguments by other
than straightforward means. He could, and did, live without the pleasant
workplace fudgings that are so important to most of us.

Early in August 1914, he was sent to Dover on the Kent coast to organize
the departure of four squadrons joining the British Expeditionary Force.
When they had flown away, he was left with the tedious task of travelling
round the country to salvage half a dozen aeroplanes that had crashed on
their way to Dover. Persistent pestering finally provoked Trenchard (now
commanding the Military Wing at Farnborough, Hampshire) into sending
him abroad in October 1914 – but as an observer, not as a pilot. It was a snub
he cheerfully accepted, for he was anxious to get to France in any capacity.

He joined 6 Squadron, commanded by Major John Becke, flying a mixture
of BE 2cs and Henri Farmans. The BE 2c in combat 'was utterly incapable –
the most defenceless thing in the sky', wrote Stewart. 'It could not be
manoeuvred quickly enough; it had no effective gun positions; observer and
pilot were in the wrong places, and the Raf engine was never so good as the
Renault.' During the Great War, no fewer than 508 airmen lost their lives in
combat or accidents while flying in BE 2s, mostly in the years 1914 to 1916.
Only the Sopwith Camel and the RE 8 suffered a higher casualty rate and in
their day, from 1916 to the Armistice, both anti-aircraft fire and aerial
combat were far more dangerous than they had been earlier in the war.[29]

The squadron left Farnborough for Bruges on the 6th to support a
ground force attempting the relief of Antwerp; an attempt that failed,
so it moved to St-Omer. On the 9th, flying with Lieutenant Tennant in a
BE 2c, he observed what he could in the Menin-Armentières area. 'No
Germans were seen,' he reported, 'but owing to difficulty of observation
I cannot say that we did not pass any. After passing Bruges, the motor

Period map of Northern Europe as hostilities began.

failed and the machine was broken in a forced landing.'

After filing this report, Dowding was summoned to the headquarters of General Sir Henry Rawlinson, responsible for that section of the front. 'You say you saw no Germans,' Rawlinson said, 'but they're there; we know that they're there.' Dowding was unimpressed. 'Well, Sir,' he replied, 'you wouldn't wish me to say I'd seen them if I hadn't. It was a very clear day, and if there had been any Germans I must have seen them.' He was not invited to stay for tea.[30]

Dowding was in the air on most days, with different pilots, diligently noting whatever he saw: a burning farm, transport waggons, newly-dug trenches, a blown-up railway bridge, local flooding. He reported on 15 October:

> 'Fight in progress. Opposing lines north and south. Shrapnel bursting over trenches. Did not see any infantry on the move. After this point (where I made a circle to look at the fight), I lost my bearings slightly so places may not be accurate. Black-coated troops marching out of Comines to south-west, entering village but not leaving it. One brigade *at most*. Transport parked in square, roads clear. Saw Blériot monoplane. Machine broken on landing.'

He was uninjured in either of these 'broken' landings and in his usual calm way simply got on with the next day's work. The squadron moved to Ypres and then a short distance to the west at Poperinghe, where it laid out an aerodrome. They were billeted in the loft of a local inn, 'which we shared uncomfortably with some very smelly pigeons.' At least the Germans gave no trouble, except on one happy day when an enemy flew overhead at 2,000 feet and was chased away by a gallant corporal standing on a petrol tin (to reduce the range) and firing his revolver.[31]

The squadron moved again, to Bailleul, north-west of Lille, where it found a flat, well-drained field just outside a lunatic asylum for women: 'Notes used to be thrown over the wall stressing the sanity of the writers and demanding rescue.' It was now that Dowding and his comrades began to meet Germans in the air. 'I have had plenty of excitement since I have been out', Dowding wrote to his sister Hilda on 23 October. 'Two smashes without getting hurt. Peppered by "Archibald" (an anti-aircraft gun) without getting hit, two bullets through the planes one day, and today a scrap with a German biplane.'

He fired at it with his favourite rifle, but was perhaps not too surprised when it failed to crash. This letter ended with the hope that the war might stop for a couple of months around Christmas, 'so that we could all go to Switzerland', for the skiing. 'As it is,' he sighed, 'I expect we shall have to wait till next year', for surely the war will end in 1915.[32]

A Brilliant Collection of Officers

On 29 November 1914, the RFC was organised into two Wings with one squadron plus a wireless unit based at headquarters in St-Omer, 35 kilometres south-east of Calais. Dowding's squadron was placed in the 2nd

Wing, attached to the Army's 2nd Corps. St-Omer became the 'spiritual home of the RFC': countless airmen served or passed through there, for it had the largest airfield on the Western Front and housed both squadrons and support units. A generation later, the Germans also found it to their liking, for many of the fighters opposed by Dowding's defences during the Battle of Britain were based on that airfield.[34]

Although he became a pilot again after six weeks at the front, Dowding never made a name in aerial combat, even though he had been shooting (accurately, one assumes) at fast-flying birds and fast-moving animals for years. On Christmas morning, he joined 9 Squadron and early in the new year was appointed a flight commander with what was the world's first wireless squadron, based beside RFC Headquarters at St-Omer. The task was a new one, that would become of prime importance to all military organizations from that day to this. It was to work with the artillery, reporting fall of shot to a designated battery by wireless telegraphy. Although communication is now far faster and more accurate, thanks to improved devices, the need and its value remain unchanged.

The squadron was commanded by Major Herbert Musgrave, born in Australia but educated at Harrow, who had trained as an engineer, a sapper. According to Kipling, all sappers were 'methodist or married or mad'. Dowding agreed that Musgrave was 'mad'. He thought airmen had life too easy as compared with soldiers and 'made it his business to redress the balance by making us as uncomfortable as he possibly could.' Musgrave also encouraged newly-joined officers to chat easily and then, without warning, pulled rank on them. He once ordered John Moore-Brabazon (later Lord Brabazon of Tara) to have a large tent, erected with much effort, shifted 12 feet. Moore-Brabazon told him not to be silly. 'That's not the way to speak to your superior officer', Musgrave snapped. To which Moore-Brabazon calmly replied: 'senior officer, Sir'. The major, for once, was speechless.[35]

Dowding's career nearly ended during January. He flew to Paris on the 19th to collect a new Blériot. A routine task that should not have taken more than a few hours, but four days later word came from Amiens that he had made 'a bad landing with the new Blériot coming to the squadron and that the machine was a complete write-off'. He was alive and apparently uninjured, but was ordered to return to St-Omer by train because the accident was caused by 'the pilot's fainting in the air'. Not surprisingly, he was promptly ordered home for his first leave since August. Only later did he learn the cause:

'The Blériot had a rotary engine and the circular cowling led all the exhaust gas to the underside of the machine and there liberated it. The bottom of the machine consisted only of fabric and there were several considerable apertures in it. So a proportion of the exhaust gas found its way into the cockpit where it swirled about till it escaped into the open air.'[36]

The other two flight commanders, Donald Lewis and Baron James, became very well known during their short careers as pioneers in the use of wireless. They were 'splendid fellows', recalled Dowding, 'who really put wireless on a practical footing as regards observation of artillery fire.' It was Lewis who decided to 'square' his maps, and those of any battery commander with whom he was to work, so that he could signal an accurate reference, rather than saying 'just to the left' of some prominent feature or 'just above the d in Gueudecourt'; squared maps were soon in universal use.

But their machines had been standing out in the open for five months and the wing fabric had become so slack that they could hardly get off the ground. Musgrave rejected repeated requests to allow new wings to be fitted: airmen, like soldiers, should be exposed to extreme danger. As soon as Musgrave went on leave, Dowding – left in temporary command – ordered new wings to be fitted. Musgrave was so enraged on his return that he tried to have the soggy wings restored. This bizarre order reached headquarters, Musgrave was returned to the army and Dowding was confirmed in command. He later learned that Musgrave came to believe that the dangers of a creeping barrage were absurdly exaggerated. 'At the first convenient opportunity, he set out to demonstrate the soundness of his theory – and never came back. Thus perished an extremely gallant, but definitely certifiable, officer.'[37]

A good story, but not a true story. Peter Dye has found that there was more to Musgrave than Dowding told his first biographer some 40 years later. Musgrave may well have been foolish and arrogant at times, but overall he had a fine record. He was a pioneer in the development of wireless equipment suitable for aeroplanes and was made a member of the Distinguished Service Order (DSO). He did *not* lose his life while testing the effect of a creeping barrage. In June 1918, when he was 42 years old, he insisted on taking part in a night patrol. Having got into a shell hole, he was killed by a chance rifle grenade exploding nearby.[38]

According to Moore-Brabazon, the 14 officers of 9 Squadron formed 'a collection of the most brilliant officers he had ever met. All of them filled with distinction the various jobs they eventually undertook.' Among them were four subsequent air marshals – Dowding, Wilfrid Freeman, Patrick Playfair, Oswyn Lywood – and Brabazon himself was special: the first Englishman to fly from English soil, holder of Royal Aero Club Licence No. l, and a minister in Churchill's first government. Sadly, James and Lewis, who might well have gone on to fame and fortune, were killed: in July 1915 and April 1916 respectively. Bernard Smythies, the squadron's 'wireless officer' who left a valuable account of his Great War experiences, remained in the service, rose to the rank of wing commander, and lost his life in a flying accident in June 1930. He too had every prospect of reaching high rank during the coming decade.[39]

The original 9 Squadron was broken up and reformed in March 1915 under the command of Dowding – now promoted to major – as part of a 'wireless experimental establishment' at Brooklands, south-west of Weybridge in Surrey. For a man of Dowding's temperament and interests, this was an excellent appointment. He was excited by the challenges of rapid communication, a subject in which his practical direction of the work of scientists, technicians and airmen would help to create an effective air defence system from 1936 onwards. A great oak sprang, eventually, from a tiny acorn at Brooklands. Tiny it was, for Dowding found there only a single flight commander (Smythies), two civilians and no pilots. He was given two newly-commissioned officers and told to teach them to fly. For aeroplanes he had a Maurice Farman and a Blériot single-seater. Nevertheless, good work was done and in October Smythies would submit to RFC Headquarters a thorough report on the value of wireless in the field.[40]

Happily for Dowding, one of the civilians proved to be as valuable an expert as those with whom he would co-operate so successfully between 1936 and 1940. He was Mr C. E. Prince, an enthusiastic wireless amateur, who had worked before the war for Marconi, a firm pioneering the new industry. He was later commissioned, reached the rank of major, and was appointed to the Order of the British Empire (OBE). Dowding wanted to buy components needed to make efficient valve-sets, but higher authority required him to place orders and wait days or even weeks for delivery. So Prince and Dowding used to visit Marconi's offices in Aldwych, where Dowding would distract the storekeeper 'by telling him lurid tales of air battles in France, while Prince took advantage of the occasion to steal what we needed. (I hope that the statute of limitations absolves me from the consequences of this 40-year-old crime).'[41]

As a result of this initiative, Prince was able to make a single-valve set weighing a quarter of the officially-sponsored set and with four times the range. Dowding naturally recommended it to his superiors at the War Office. They rejected it out of hand. Too delicate and too complex, they ruled, for use by other than experts. Dowding challenged them to justify their decision. To his surprise and delight, they agreed. Prince went off 'into a fit of hopeless giggles' when the War Office's expert arrived, for he was a man whom Marconi had recently sacked because he proved to be useless at his job.

An aeroplane was detailed to fly round the aerodrome once the sets were tuned. Dowding and Prince were soon ready, but the opposition kept saying 'not quite ready', 'just a minute more', so they strolled across to see what was happening, 'and there was the expert sitting with his headphones on, twiddling the knobs frantically while the ends of his headphone leads were lying on the ground. He had forgotten to connect them to the set!' Eventually, the trial began and according to Dowding the Prince set outclassed the official set, but an anonymous minion in the War Office refused to change his mind. This was not the first time that Dowding found himself disagreeing with his masters, and would not be the last.

Having 'carte blanche owing to the unwitting generosity of Marconi's', Dowding and his small staff tried their hands at another procedure that would soon become of vital importance to all military organizations: air-to-ground radio-telephony. Prince installed a transmitter in the Farman and Dowding later claimed to be 'the first person, certainly in England if not in the world, to listen to a wireless telephone message from the air.' The next step was to fix up two-way communication between air and ground. Sadly, an edict from the War Office stopped him. It could not be done, the alleged experts asserted: 'I have forgotten what reason was given, but it was something silly.' Even if its use had been limited to artillery observation, wrote Dowding, its advantages over 'the slow and clumsy Morse Code' were obvious, 'but to the imaginative mind its further possibilities were almost unlimited.' Ground-to-air radio-telephony would not be adopted for another three years, when it helped the London Air Defence Area to control defensive fighters. Dowding's low opinion of some of his Whitehall masters sank lower.[42]

Commanding

Dowding was required to leave his wireless work in July 1915 and take command of 16 Squadron at Merville, 30 kilometres west of Lille on the Western Front. He was not sorry to leave Brooklands, even though he was totally absorbed by an exciting job, but he was up against what he called 'the worst side of the military machine'. Brooklands made him realize that he was not really a soldier. 'The mental laziness which makes it always easier to say No than to say Yes', annoyed him, 'because if you say Yes you will have to think, and you may make a mistake.' This attitude, he learned later, was not confined to the Army, 'but I think that Brooklands saw it in its finest flower.'

Dowding's squadron, equipped with BE 2cs and Maurice Farman Shorthorns (an improved version of the Longhorn), was part of 1 Wing, under the command of Trenchard, who had escaped from Farnborough and was soon to become head of the entire RFC in France. Trenchard told him that the previous CO had been too hard on everyone and the squadron was unhappy. There was also a growing feeling that the RFC was outmatched. By mid-1915 it was already alarmingly obvious that German airmen were skilful and determined. Many of their machines, especially the E.III version of the Fokker monoplane and the Albatros, Rumpler and Aviatik C.I biplanes, were superior to those flown by British or French crews. The 'Fokker Scourge' began in August 1915. It was a fragile machine with an unreliable engine, but faster and far more agile than the BE 2c. Better still, its pilot could fire through the airscrew. Keen young Britons, 'schooled in a tradition of hilarious contempt for foreigners', were surprised to discover how much they had to learn about aeroplanes and aerial combat.[43]

At 33, Dowding was much older than most of his air crews and they found his personality, interests, and conversation difficult to understand. He, of course, felt the same about them. They would learn, however, that while the new CO was short on easy grins and ready chat, he did what he could to improve living conditions on the ground and – no less important – backed his men against criticism by senior officers when he believed they were in the right.

The squadron occupied a small L-shaped aerodrome on the west bank of the canalized river Lys. When Dowding arrived, most of the officers were quartered in a squalid, overcrowded farmhouse. Ever the practical man, he promptly moved the mess and many of the living quarters into a more comfortable hospital barge moored in the canal. It had reasonable bunk space in separate cabins and one large cabin that served as a mess room. Writing to his second biographer, Robert Wright, on 16 September 1959, Dowding recalled how he had made himself 'very popular with my squadron (and very unpopular with everyone else) by wangling a hospital barge from the base'; we had snug cabins and a decent mess, 'while others had to pig it in dirty farm houses.'[44]

He also acquired 'a primitive contraption which provided an intermittent supply of electric light' and was christened 'Heath Robinson' in honour of the English cartoonist who drew many absurdly ingenious and impracticable devices. Dowding was not chummy, but looking after his men's comfort has always been one mark of a good officer.

At that time, fittings to enable aeroplanes to carry cameras, wireless gear and bombsights were devised locally by each squadron. Soon after Dowding took command, an inter-squadron competition was held to decide on the most useful fittings and 16 Squadron won it. Even so, bombing was as yet a primitive art. There were no bomb racks and bombs were simply dropped over the side when the sight suggested the target might be hittable. Dowding's squadron had only a single practice bomb, which had to be retrieved after every drop. Understandably, there was little enthusiasm for bombing practice until Dowding began a sweepstake. Lured by the prospect of collecting the kitty if they managed to get the bomb nearest to a target in the centre of the aerodrome, his pilots became keen aimers. Dowding had a go himself 'on a very stormy day with the machine jumping about so much that it was impossible to keep the bomb sight trained on anything for more than a second or two.' When he landed, he learned that he had 'scored a near miss on an inspecting officer from RFC Headquarters.' Eventually, some clown managed to drop the bomb in the canal and that was that.

Dowding was always irked, he later recalled, by the many quite different – and difficult – tasks expected of his pilots. For example, they must report troop movements, take photographs, drop bombs, chase away enemy aeroplanes and also carry out their essential duties of locating German guns and directing British artillery fire against them or other targets deemed important by headquarters. They had neither the time, nor the equipment, nor the necessary training, nor aeroplanes efficient enough to carry out these various tasks successfully, no matter how hard they tried.

During the battle of Loos in September 1915, Dowding flew as observer with one of his best pilots, Oscar Gould, to check a rumour that the Germans were retreating. They were not. But the occasion was noteworthy for one of the first recorded experiences – certainly the first within Dowding's knowledge – of the phenomenon known as 'icing up'. The leading edges of the wings became coated with ice and the controls could only be kept free by constant manipulation. Gould was forced to follow an ever-changing course and the compass went haywire.

After completely losing themselves and running out of petrol, they landed and were relieved to find they were not in 'Hunland', but all of 30 kilometres behind British lines. Throughout this alarming flight, Dowding behaved as a senior officer should: remaining outwardly calm, offering neither rebuke nor unasked-for advice to a better pilot than himself, and voicing no recrimination after they were rescued.[45]

Dowding commanded 16 Squadron for the last six months of 1915 and during that time it brought down only one enemy aeroplane: hardly surprising, given that most of its machines were either BE 2cs or Shorthorns of slight combat value. The unlucky German pilot of an Albatros landed safely, in British territory, on 13 September, but both he and his observer were shot by British soldiers while clambering out of their machine. Dowding was enraged by what he considered to be inexcusable murders, collected some of their belongings, and had them dropped behind enemy lines with a message saying where the men were buried. After a few days he got a grateful acknowledgement in a German message-bag. He received a letter from Germany in 1955 informing him that 'this incident had made his name a legend in the German Air Force', but this letter is now lost, like nearly all the others he wrote or received in his long life.[46]

A Blot on our Horizon

Herbert Ward, who had learned to fly at Eton, joined 16 Squadron at the age of 17 and welcomed Dowding's decision to accompany him on his first flight into enemy territory. Dowding quoted a couple of lines from Belloc, *Cautionary Tales*, and smiled when Ward was able to follow up with the next two lines. Mature beyond his years, Ward did not try to take advantage of this light moment. He quickly learned to respect Dowding for his professional approach to the dangerous work on hand and accepted that he was never going to be a jolly comrade, at least not with teenagers barely half his age.

Ward did notice, however, that two of the flight commanders heartily disliked each other and privately thought Dowding should have rebuked them: 'a curious parallel,' commented Ralph Barker, 'with his failure to intervene nearly a quarter of a century later in the Keith Park/Leigh-Mallory Big Wing controversy.' Sadly, there was no-one in the squadron bold enough to suggest a rebuke for the flight commanders. Dowding 'seldom allowed his dry style of humour to emerge from behind a barrier of terseness', reflected Ward later. 'Thus he acquired a reputation for unfriendliness.' Ward was shot down and captured on 30 November 1915, a few days before his 18th birthday. He was the first airman to escape from a prison camp, became an Anglican priest and died at the age of 90.[47]

In 1933, years before his opinion could have been coloured by Dowding's achievements in the Battle of Britain, Duncan Grinnell-Milne recorded his impressions of the major and his squadron – without, however, revealing the major's name. Grinnell-Milne, then just 19, joined 16 Squadron in September 1915. He had been educated at Cheam School in Surrey, the Royal Naval Colleges in Osborne and Dartmouth, spent a year at a German university, Freiburg im Breisgau, and was commissioned in the Rifle Brigade in 1914, where he soon earned both official and parental displeasure. An official report concluded that he had no sense of responsibility and frequently neglected his duties. In December his father wrote to the War Office complaining that the young man was 'spending more money than I desire' and wondering if a public declaration that he would no longer be responsible for his debts would harm his promotion prospects. The upshot was that Grinnell-Milne transferred to the RFC and learned to fly.[48]

On arriving at Dowding's barge, he was struck by what seemed a glum, unfriendly atmosphere. The Royal Navy, he mused, 'was not the only Silent Service. I began to wonder whether I had not by some chance strayed into a colony of Trappists.'[49] At dinner on the first evening he was introduced to Dowding. 'The major gave me a limp hand together with a tired smile.' Grinnell-Milne had then no idea of the worries heaped on a squadron commander's head, and expected a warm reception for a novice with a bad record. He returned to his seat, and 'dead silence reigned', broken only by Dowding's valiant effort to find something to say to each of his officers in turn, but 'it was always with that same tired little smile, in a quiet, rather nasal voice,' and none of those officers had the gumption to help him thaw the atmosphere.

It seemed at first to this brash young man that Dowding was an unpopular commander:

> 'And yet he was in many ways a good man. In the long run I came to esteem him as much as any member of that peculiar squadron. He was efficient, strict and calm: he had a sense of duty. But he was too reserved and aloof from his juniors; he cared too much for his own job, too little for theirs... he was not a good pilot, seldom flew, and had none of that fire which I then believed and later knew to be essential in the leader of a good squadron.'

Nevertheless, he warmed to Dowding after a rare non-duty conversation on learning that he thought Robert Smith Surtees in some ways superior to Dickens.[50] Surtees created John Jorrocks, a sporting Cockney, whose adventures – enormously popular in Victorian times – were written up in *Jorrock's Jaunts and Jollities*, which had an obvious influence on Dickens's *Pickwick Papers*. Surtees also invented Soapy Sponge, hero of *Mr Sponge's Sporting Tour*. The rackety conduct of Jorrocks and Sponge could hardly be less like Dowding's prim lifestyle and yet he enjoyed reading about them both. His façade was normally so forbidding that one relishes this brief peep behind it, to glimpse a man who liked a jolly rogue. We shall see later that Dowding greatly admired Lord Beaverbrook, a real-life jolly rogue.

One day, Dowding spoke to Grinnell-Milne about a poor landing he had made in a BE 2c. His criticisms were valid, but made so coldly that the young man resented them. Dowding then walked away, 'with long, rather high-stepping strides, turning his head inquisitively from side to side, more like a lonely bird than ever.' Another pilot commiserated with Grinnell-Milne. The major, he said, was a 'Starched Shirt', a poor pilot, 'a blot on our horizon'.[51]

In September 1915, a version of the familiar BE 2c designated BE 9 was sent to Dowding for evaluation. It had a cockpit for the observer/gunner ahead of the airscrew and hence a long way ahead of the pilot, making communication practically impossible. The BE 9 had been hawked around several squadrons, attracting many adverse comments, before it reached

Dowding and he tested it personally. Although he never claimed to be a notable pilot, he always took on dangerous tests himself. He was brave enough to fly twice what has been called 'a bizarre aircraft', on 22 and 29 September. It had a poor performance, he reported, serious engine problems and was 'an extremely dangerous machine from the passenger's point of view.' He got rid of it on 2 October and after several other pilots had flown it, the BE 9 was returned to England in January 1916 and never heard of again.[52]

In December 1915, when Grinnell-Milne wrecked his BE 2c while landing after a long flight, he discovered another side to Dowding:

'I saw the major coming up like an angry ostrich, stepping high and pecking his head at each long stride. At his side was a round little man with a monocle. The wing commander! Others followed like mutes at a well-attended funeral.'

Grinnell-Milne's flight commander explained why the landing had been a bad one. Dowding listened without interrupting, and asked sensible questions in his quiet voice, but the wing commander, after poking around in the wreckage for some time said: 'Tell me, what did the pilot – er – want to crash for?' A stupid question to which Dowding gave a civil answer. 'Oh, he was in the air for a very long time. Valenciennes and back. And he had the very devil of a scrap – chased a German all the way to Douai, made him land!' On hearing these words, Grinnell-Milne felt a burst of 'genuine affection' for Dowding: 'It was the first time in my experience that he had seemed really human.' It was also the first time the young pilot had *needed* his CO's support. The wing commander opened his eyes. Out fell his monocle, a sight never before seen. Apart from his famous eyeglass, according to Harold Balfour (who became Under-Secretary of State for Air during World War Two), he had 'a stammer, and a nose on upside down'.[53] It is a nice story and may well be partly true, except that 'the round little man' (Charles Gordon Bell) was then a mere captain. It is likely that his remark about the wreckage was an attempted pleasantry misunderstood both by Grinnell-Milne and Dowding.

Grinnell-Milne was forced down by engine failure and taken prisoner in December 1915. He managed to escape in April 1918 and after re-training was posted to 56 Squadron in September, ending his active service as that famous squadron's last CO, earning a Military Cross, a Distinguished Flying Cross and Bar. When asked who had been his CO back in 1915, he named Dowding. 'Never heard of him', came the reply. The 'Starched Shirt', as Grinnell-Milne still thought of him, was by then a general, in charge of training: 'a successful senior officer, not a bad fellow at heart'.

Ira Jones, a feisty Welshman who would earn a fine record as a combat pilot during the Great War, had a more positive opinion of Dowding. He met him when he was an air mechanic sent to 16 Squadron to receive instruction in ground-to-air communication. Dowding often sat with him, as he operated his receiver, and talked to him: 'if not as an equal, at least like a human being.'[54]

Grinnell-Milne remained in the RAF after the war, but retired in January 1926, after three years as assistant air attaché in the rank of flight lieutenant at the British Embassy in Paris. Recalled to service in August 1939, he served in France until the surrender, as air liaison officer with General de Gaulle in England, then in the Middle East, finally retiring in September 1941 to spend the rest of the war with the BBC. By then, he would have been well aware that some people had heard of Dowding, but he wrote nothing more about him. He died in November 1973.[55]

3

At Odds with Trenchard, 1916-1920

The Wrong Propellers

It was while he commanded 16 Squadron that Dowding had his first serious quarrel with Trenchard. Some of Dowding's Maurice Shorthorns had 80-hp engines and he was sent propellers intended for similar engines of lower power. He complained in vain to Wing Headquarters and then asked Trenchard himself to help. Trenchard, who had little understanding of the nuts and bolts of aviation (as opposed to uncommon political skill, a commanding personality and a voice that deservedly earned him the nickname 'Boom'), ordered Dowding to have holes bored where necessary in hubs to make the same propeller fit both engines. When the job was done, Dowding was to have an aeroplane flight-tested. This was dangerous because 'the propeller hub would be weakened by the boring of a number of new holes and if the propeller *did* break in flight it would probably cut the tail off the machine, which was a pusher and therefore had the propeller inside the tail booms and their securing wires.'

Dowding carried out the test flight himself, survived, and told Trenchard what he thought of the order. Boom backed down, gracelessly, offering no apology and blaming 'our representative in Paris' for his own mistake. He had taken the word of 'some half-baked motor salesman against mine' and had not cancelled his order as soon as he learned that he was mistaken. Dowding's 'pernickety primness' grated with Trenchard, whose 'technical stupidity' earned Dowding's contempt.[56]

Serving at Home

Dowding was recalled to England in January 1916, mentioned in despatches, promoted to lieutenant-colonel and given command of 7 Wing at Fort Grange, Gosport, in Hampshire. Fort Grange lay at the southern end of the airfield, Fort Rowner at the northern end: both were 'damp, dark semi-dungeons of red brick and mortar'.[57] He spent six dull months there:

'I remember writing round to all the better-known public schools and asking the headmasters to help us to secure suitable applicants

31

for commissions in the RFC: not necessarily the boys at the top of the school, but members of the football team and athletes and tough characters in general. This letter met with a mixed reception: some schools reponded wholeheartedly, while others (including my own old school) were less than helpful. The fact was, of course, that the RFC (in modern argot) was still distinctly "Non-U".'

It was at Fort Grange that he first attempted a task that proved too much for him (and everyone else) in the autumn of 1940: organizing an effective defence against night-raiders. 'It is to be clearly understood,' he informed the CO of 11 (Reserve) Squadron at Northolt on 7 March 1916, 'that the senior RFC officer at each station is solely responsible for ordering machines into the air' at night; not soldiers or civilians, no matter how important they were locally. Patrols were to go up whenever the weather was suitable, but men and machines must not be risked in wet, cloudy or foggy conditions.

In February he had already reported to Lieutenant-Colonel Charles Longcroft, head of 6 Brigade, that he had no machines suitable for repelling raids, and there was no guarantee that school machines, which might possibly be used would be serviceable when required. In another February letter he told Longcroft that he was short of spare parts, night landing equipment and his aerodrome needed stronger lights. 'This is one of a great number of matters,' he complained, 'that have been allowed to stand over without any attention from my various predecessors.'

His regard for Whitehall Warriors did not improve during these months. For example, he asked the War Office what action he should take, with his training aircraft, if Zeppelins appeared over his area. The reply was only too typical of emanations from that fount of authority. 'If the raid takes place over Portsmouth garrison and stable machines are available, such action as is deemed advisable will be taken by OC 7 Wing; if the raid is in another area, he will be telephoned instructions by the War Office.'

Longcroft shared Dowding's exasperation and protested to the War Office that their 70-hp Renault-engined BE 2cs were useless against any German aircraft, but especially against high-flying Zeppelins cruising over England in darkness. He was told that he would soon be getting a version with 80-hp engines: only marginally less useless, in Dowding's opinion, but nothing better was on offer.[58]

On a more cheerful note, he submitted recommendations for promotion, 'in indelible pencil because I wish to keep a copy and do not wish clerks to type.' He warmly commended several officers who went on to enjoy successful careers, among them Major Andrew Board (later an air commodore) and Captain William Mitchell (who was knighted, became Air Member for Personnel in 1937, head of RAF Middle East in 1939 and reached the rank of air chief marshal).[59]

Wing Commander

In June 1916 Dowding took command of 9 Headquarters Wing (responsible for four squadrons, under the eye of Trenchard himself) at

Fienvillers, near Doullens in Picardy. His four squadrons were 21 (equipped with RE 7s and BE 2cs), 27 (Martinsyde G.100 Elephants), 60 (Morane Bullets) and 70, flying a promising new type that Dowding had helped to get ready for operational use during his time at Fort Grange: the Sopwith One and a Half Strutter. It was so called because of an unusual arrangement supporting the upper wings. A robust and efficient two-seater, the Sopwith was the RFC's first aeroplane to have a machine gun firing through the propeller arc and the first to have a rotatable ring-mounting for the observer's gun.[60]

Dowding was shortly to get a taste of air warfare on an unprecedented scale. 'The fighting at that time,' Dowding recalled 40 years later, 'was admirably described by Alan Bott', an observer in 70 Squadron. His famous book, *An Airman's Outings with the RFC, June-December 1916*, first appeared in 1917 and was reprinted in 1987. Very heavy casualties were suffered between August and October while carrying out long-distance patrols into German air space to escort bombers or to take photographs. Few books give a better account of life and death in the air during the Great War.

British and French forces were preparing for an all-out offensive on the Somme front that began on 1 July, with massive support in the air: the squadrons of the 4th Army (of which Dowding's Wing was a part) had 167 aeroplanes on charge when the battle began. Opposing them were the squadrons of German 2nd Army, with a total of no more than 104 aeroplanes. 'In addition to its overwhelming numerical superiority, the RFC now also had technically superior fighter aeroplanes.'[61]

That being so, Dowding found the heavy casualties suffered by all the Allied squadrons hard either to bear or to understand. Sholto Douglas, an officer with whom he would later have many disagreements, wrote that Dowding had 'a concern more heartfelt' over casualties than any other commander in the RFC.[62] He never changed in this regard. Many years later, Arnold Lunn recalled him saying, 'People talk very lightly about casualties. They'll say "We only lost four pilots today." I feel as if I had lost four sons.'[63]

His wing's tasks were laid down as 'strategical reconnaissance for General Headquarters, offensive action against the enemy air service, and the long-distance bombing of enemy communications': a formidable list given the performance of the aeroplanes at his disposal. Other wings might be better equipped, but Dowding's only first-class aeroplane was the new Sopwith and when the battle began they were only just arriving in 70 Squadron. They did well in reconnaissance, bombing, and as escorts for other types, but were too few to prevent regular losses. The RE 7, for example, 'was nearly as manoeuvrable as a ten-ton truck' in the opinion of Billy Bishop, the renowned Canadian ace, 'but by no means as safe.'[64]

The Wing began its work well enough, carrying out valuable long-distance reconnaissances. Balfour, then a pilot with 60 Squadron at Vert Galant, north of Amiens, had clear memories of his wing commander at this time. He thought Dowding 'a silent, forbidding figure... difficult to approach unasked', a man who disliked team sports, funny stories and 'the gaieties of mess life'.

But Balfour also thought him a good officer. His squadron, then equipped with single-seat Morane Bullet monoplanes, formed part of Dowding's wing. Although it was based 32 kilometres away from his own headquarters, Dowding used to come over every few days to see how they were doing. Balfour once had to fly Dowding's BE 2c back to him – it had developed a fault and Dowding returned to his headquarters by car – and Balfour managed to wreck it. The engine suddenly stopped shortly after take-off. 'There was nothing to do except go straight on,' he later wrote, 'so, just clearing the road, I took a good 50 field telephone wires in my stride and finished up minus the undercarriage and festooned with broken wires in the ploughed field beyond.'

Dowding listened to Balfour's explanation and accepted it without a word of complaint or rebuke. 'Here was an example of true justice,' recalled Balfour more than 70 years later, 'from a senior to a very scared 18-year-old pilot, for which I have always felt grateful.' Everyone in 60 Squadron respected Dowding, but they did not feel affection for him: 'He was always too high for that.' This was the first of Balfour's meetings with Dowding, 'a great man'.[65]

Trenchard demanded more of 9 Wing than long-distance reconnaissance, he also required constant patrols over enemy territory. Command of the air was to be secured by flying continuous patrols of three aeroplanes each from dawn to dusk. 'Whatever the merits of this system,' Dowding recalled, 'it proved most expensive in casualties because the Germans could at will attack our small patrols in greatly superior numbers, and the casualty rate among aircrews was about 100% per month.'

Dowding was distressed about these losses, but he could not query Trenchard's orders during a major battle. He did, however, query a restriction on officers of lieutenant-colonel rank and above taking part. He was granted permission to lead a raid in a BE 2c on a target near Bois d'Havrincourt. With at least 20 machines from three squadrons airborne, it was by far the biggest raid of his career:

> 'When we were well across the lines, we were attacked by a large German formation.... My observer (my wing adjutant, Longridge) was in the front seat. We were armed with a Lewis gun which the observer could fire only backwards or sideways. He was kneeling on his seat facing backward, and I was flying straight and level to give him an easy shot at a German flying behind and to the left of us.'

Dowding's left hand was grazed by a bullet, several of his instruments were shattered, Longridge was wounded in the face, but they escaped and landed safely. More than half a century later, Dowding would leave to the RAF Museum in Hendon a souvenir of that combat, his 'control lever': it was the only memento, other than uniforms, that he kept of his long career. He and Longridge were lucky to survive, for the BE 2c had never been suitable for combat. On the Western Front by the middle of 1916, as Dowding must have realized, it was little better than a flying coffin. The flight was no more than a gallant, futile gesture, untypical of Dowding, and making no better contribution to winning the war than Trenchard's insistence on automatic aggression.[66]

Dowding thought that insistence a mistake because very heavy losses were suffered for no evident advantage. During the fighting on the Somme front, from July to December, the RFC lost 545 pilots or observers killed, wounded or captured: an average of three every day during those six months. German losses, even according to optimistic British figures, were less than half as heavy, yet Trenchard claimed that this catastrophic defeat was actually a splendid victory in that he was forcing the Germans to remain on the defensive, behind their own lines. In a memorandum written in September he looked forward to continuing the offensive more vigorously than ever, despite the fact that many of his pilots and observers were neither fully trained nor experienced in aerial combat.[67]

Trenchard's willing acceptance of heavy casualties was approved in the highest quarters. In that same September, for example, he received this chilling note from a close friend, Brigadier-General Sefton Brancker (Director of Air Organization in the War Office): 'I rather enjoy hearing of our casualties as I am perfectly certain that the Germans lose at least half as many again as we do.' This was not so and Brancker's opinion, like Trenchard's on the morale value of constant offensive, had no factual basis. Incidentally, Brancker – again like Trenchard – was an incompetent pilot and 'characteristically unashamed' of his lack of skill.[68]

History does sometimes repeat itself, for this is precisely the situation that Dowding would resist in 1940: offence for no better reason than that it was believed to offer powerful – if unspecified – advantages for morale; offence at the expense of careful training and systematic defence, both of them considered to be dull or worse, *timid*, methods of waging war. Tragically, the successors of Dowding and Park at Bentley Priory and Uxbridge in 1941 were devout Trenchardists and we shall see that many British pilots suffered under their hands for little purpose.

At the end of July 1916, one of Dowding's squadron commanders, Robert Smith-Barry (of 60 Squadron) asked him for relief – and he was not a man to accuse of timidity. They had lost many of their Morane Bullets, a very difficult machine to fly, let alone use in combat, and the replacement pilots were both inexperienced and poorly trained. He told Dowding that he could not go on sending such men into battle. Dowding agreed and told Trenchard what Smith-Barry had said. He was very angry and 'almost at once I was promoted to the rank of colonel, sent home, and never employed in the field again during the war.'

Dowding's memory here betrays him, because he was not sent home until January 1917, but there is no reason to doubt that Trenchard was indeed angry with him from August 1916 onwards. Angry or not, Trenchard was obliged to accept a measure of restraint. He told Haig on 3 August that 60 Squadron had suffered such heavy casualties that it must be withdrawn from the battle. Many years later, Edgar Ludlow-Hewitt – who became an air chief marshal, ever loyal to the 'father of the RAF' – did his best to justify that anger. 'Trenchard at this time was bearing a stupendous burden,' wrote Ludlow-Hewitt, 'persevering in his offensive policy despite terrible losses. In this he proved the greatness of his faith in his men and his own strategic vision. By this he created an "offensive" tradition which the RFC and the RAF would never lose.'[69]

These words, written after mature reflection (one presumes) by a very senior officer, admirably summarize a common mindset in the RAF which separated Dowding from a majority of his contemporaries. They try to justify 'terrible losses' by gliding swiftly over them to prate about a benefit somehow arising from them, and commending the supposed 'strategic vision' of Trenchard and those who agreed with him. Dead men may, very occasionally, 'create' an inspiring tradition, but that is more often done by live men who are well trained, sensibly led and provided with good equipment.

As for Smith-Barry, both Trenchard and Salmond came to recognize his merits and share Dowding's high opinion. Smith-Barry would become one of aviation's great men during 1917-18 for devising a system of training that saved countless lives, gave Britain a more competent air force during the last 20 months of the war, and provided a permanent framework for systematic tuition in many air forces.[70]

End of a Career?

Trenchard sent Dowding back to England in January 1917 and although he was promoted twice during that year he never again served on the Western Front. Instead, he commanded, in the rank of colonel (promoted to brigadier-general in June) Southern Training Brigade in Salisbury, Wiltshire: that part of England where the Dowdings had lived for generations. He had more than 30 units under his command, stretching from Cheshire to the New Forest in Hampshire. He had been a subaltern for 13 years and then in less than four years had become a brigadier-general: 'Thereafter, with the exception of a few months, I remained a general or air officer for 26 years: a strange, lop-sided record.'

From his headquarters in Salisbury, Dowding was able to observe the dangerous effect of Trenchard's policy of constant offensive. To make good heavy losses, some training squadrons were obliged to send partly-qualified crews off to France; they even lost their instructors. It seemed to Dowding that this could not go on and he summarized his opinions in a letter to Trenchard's senior personnel staff officer. This individual showed the letter to Trenchard, 'and that finished me with Trenchard till the end of the war and for eight years after.'[71]

In January 1918, Dowding was summoned to the War Office. Having just received a letter warmly appreciative of his efforts during 1917, he thought he was now to be personally commended, and was therefore surprised when Lord Rothermere (secretary of state for air) told him he was to be relieved of his command to make room for Smith-Barry. In Dowding's opinion, Smith-Barry was excellent as a pilot trainer, but his lack of interest in routine administration or sensible discipline made him a bad choice for Salisbury. That opinion eventually prevailed and Dowding kept his job a little longer.

He was sent to York in March 1918 as chief staff officer to the senior administration officer of the newly-created Royal Air Force in that area. It was a quiet backwater, far from the noise of shot and shell, and Dowding fretted at his lack of opportunity to play an active part in the last bloody but exhilarating year of the war. For the rest of his life, Dowding regretted that he spent so little time on frontline operations, especially in comparison with other officers who made the air force their career. It had indeed been a bloody war in the air: all told, 9,352 British and Commonwealth airmen (including those serving in the Royal Naval Air Service) were killed during the Great War – an average of six every day for more than four years – quite apart from the thousands who were wounded or spent years as prisoners.[72]

The Armistice in November seemed likely to mark the end of Dowding's aviation career, given his poor relations with Trenchard, although he was made a Companion of the Order of St Michael and St George (CMG). Better still, he was alive and so too were his brothers: Arthur, a naval officer, and Kenneth in the air force. Kenneth was appointed to command 42 Squadron in Italy in November 1917, but after only a few weeks Brigadier-General Tom Webb-Bowen, commanding 7 Brigade, decided that he was 'lacking in experience and power of command' and recommended his return to England. Kenneth went back to the law in 1919, but donned air force uniform again 20 years later and was employed on legal duties.[73]

Somewhat reluctantly, Trenchard – soon to be confirmed as head of a very small postwar air force – was persuaded by Sir Vyell Vyvyan, Dowding's CO in York, to offer 'dismal jimmy', as he called him, one of the few permanent commissions available, in the newly-devised RAF rank of group captain (equivalent to Army colonel) on 1 August 1919. Vyvyan (1875-1935) was one of the most outstanding officers, naval or air, of his generation. He reached admiral rank in the Royal Navy and transferred to the RAF on its formation in April 1918, retiring in 1925 as an air vice-marshal.[74]

Dowding, having received a letter telling him that his services would not be required by the RAF, had good reason to be grateful to Vyvyan. The admiral travelled three or four times to London to dispute that decision with Trenchard personally. Although Vyvyan is now entirely forgotten, and died before his protégé revealed greatness, he will always deserve an honourable mention in any account of Dowding's career as the man who made it possible.

Dowding was now married, since 16 February 1918, to Clarice Maud Vancourt. He first met her at Farnborough with her cousin, Major John Becke, CO of 6 Squadron, in 1914. Clarice was the daughter of Captain John Williams of the Indian Army and widow of an officer who was killed before the war when he threw himself on a mills bomb accidentally dropped by a soldier during a training exercise. They had a daughter, Brenda. Dowding and Clarice had a child of their own – a son, Derek – born on 9 January 1919. Derek was commissioned in July 1939, served as a pilot during the Battle of Britain, retired in the rank of wing commander in November 1956 and died in July 1992. As for Clarice, Dowding suffered the sickening blow of her sudden death on 28 June 1920. He then returned, with his young step-daughter and infant son to his parents' home in Wimbledon, south-west London.[75]

4

From Pageants to Palestine, 1920-1930

Physical and Mental Collapse

As head of 1 Group at Kenley (south of Croydon in Surrey) from February 1920, Dowding was responsible for organizing several of the RAF's enormously successful public relations stunts, especially the air pageants at Hendon in north London, which became an annual event as popular with all social classes as Henley, Wimbledon, Ascot and Lord's. The end of each pageant, he later wrote, 'found me in a state of complete physical and mental collapse. Nothing has ever induced in me a comparable state of prostration.' Not even the darkest days of 1940.[76]

One is at first stunned by such a claim, but Dowding was never a man to use words loosely and, on reflection, one can see why he got so exhausted: bearing in mind also the fact that by July 1920 he was a widower rising 40 with two children and had no other career prospects if he gave Trenchard a reason to recommend his early retirement. These pageants stretched everyone who had anything to do with them, in the air or on the ground, for they represented the infant RAF's best opportunity to fix itself in official and popular opinion as a going concern, one that should not be terminated – an option strongly advocated in these years by many senior officers in the Army and the Royal Navy, encouraged by cost-conscious Treasury officials. Until that happened, however, royalty (both British and continental) deigned to attend these spectacular pageants, together with persons of wealth, quality or social ambition who dance attendance on royalty, as well as those with serious influence in commerce, industry, politics and all three services. Vast numbers of spectators turned up, which was both encouraging and worrying because in every hour of every day there was a risk of a major crisis (in the timing or performance of an event) as well as the even more serious risk of a crash that might kill or injure many people. In other words, Dowding – the man in the hot seat – was given every chance to find himself incinerated.

Nothing went amiss in July 1920. On the contrary, *Flight* magazine thought that year's pageant 'by a long way the most successful aerial affair which has ever been held, in this country at least.' More than 40,000 people paid for admission to Hendon, while thousands more saw what they could from outside the aerodrome, as far away as Hampstead, and the nearest approach to an accident was a burst aeroplane tyre.[77]

However, Dowding was warned by Trenchard in April 1921 to make sure that 'big machines' did not fly straight over the heads of large crowds, as they had in the previous year. Even so, plenty of other thrills were arranged:

> 'Aerial fighting of the most realistic character, in which machines will be "shot down" in flames. Two great Handley Page bombers will be attacked by scout machines and "destroyed" as realistically as in war.'

There would also be 'an attack on, and the complete destruction of, a model village... built up from old aeroplane "scrap" and complete even to a church with quite an important-looking tower.'[78]

In March 1922 he was instructed to see that the pageant was more than simply fun for airmen and a splendid spectacle for all who watched – no fewer than 80,000 persons turned up that year. It should have 'a definite training value'. Dowding did his best to meet that sobering requirement: an exhibition of aerial photographs was arranged, smart airmen and articulate officers were detailed to act as tour guides for selected worthies who wished to examine highly-polished flying machines at close range, and demonstrations were given of loading men and guns into aircraft very quickly and then unloading them even more quickly.

But the main attraction (for airmen and spectators alike) remained competition between squadrons in formation flying and, what was always a crowd-pleaser, some thoroughly-rehearsed aerial fighting took place. Pilots and gunners joyfully fired blanks that made a realistic noise without killing anyone, followed by the destruction of 'Fort Wottnott', despite a bunch of Wottnottians in suitably non-European costumes bravely firing their antique rifles in the general direction of modern bombers.[79]

These pageants earned the RAF nothing but praise and in January 1922 Dowding got his reward: promotion to air commodore (equivalent to brigadier-general), a promotion that meant he would now be a serious contender for high command and no longer in danger of an early bowler hat (the modern equivalent of being invited to fall on one's sword).

Life was not all work, however, even in these years when it seemed that he might climb to somewhere near the top of the tree. As soon as the Great War ended, he eagerly resumed a different kind of climbing: up the ski slopes he had known so well before 1914. In 1921, he joined the Ski Club of Great Britain and helped so readily in all the dull chores needed to keep a small society alive that he was elected president for the year 1924-5. Until Britain found herself once more at war with Germany, he never failed to spend some part of every winter among Europe's mountains, even when he was serving in Iraq or Palestine.[80]

At Odds with Tedder
In October 1921 Dowding had visited Squadron Leader Arthur Tedder (later to become one of the RAF's greatest officers) at Bircham Newton,

north of King's Lynn in Norfolk. They discussed a proposal to use Bircham Newton as a base for bombing practice over the North Sea. Influenced perhaps by Trenchard, who did not regard Dowding highly, Tedder allowed a dismissive tone – for a mere squadron leader talking to a senior officer – to colour his response to the proposal. Dowding was displeased and a year later he came near to breaking Tedder.[81]

That crisis came in October 1922, shortly after Tedder arrived in Constantinople with his squadron as part of a force hoping to prevent an outbreak of war with Turkey. What became known as 'the Chanak Crisis' had erupted suddenly and Tedder was ordered by Trenchard to get his aircraft and heavy equipment shifted as quickly as possible from Bircham Newton to Constantinople. An exhausting business and one that was briefly of international importance, it was carried out expertly and diligently by Tedder and his men. But Dowding wrote to the Air Ministry on 5 October to seek 'disciplinary action' against him because he had 'deliberately disobeyed orders' by taking more spares to Constantinople than he ought to have done.

This wholly unexpected bombshell landed on Tedder's desk via his CO's adjutant, who invited him to explain. 'In view of the continual stress laid by the CAS on the vital necessity for rapidity in the erection of the first machines,' replied Tedder on 28 October, 'I did go against the strict letter of the instructions', and packed a few engine spares in two small boxes. 'Had these spares not been brought,' he continued, 'not one DH 9a could have taken the air for at least seven days after our arrival' at Constantinople.

The fact that Dowding chose to escalate such a minor incident into 'serious and entirely unsupported charges' shocked and deeply angered Tedder. He eventually received a formal rebuke from the Air Ministry on 8 December, but nothing worse. Dowding's bombshell, potentially so dangerous, had not exploded. Tedder never forgave him – and he became an increasingly influential officer from 1938 onwards. In his opinion, Dowding was a petty man, unfit for high command. Even allowing that Tedder, then a junior officer, had been alarmed by this serious threat to a promising career, the affair does indeed reveal Dowding in an unusually poor light. He had behaved in precisely the hidebound, unimaginative way that so exasperated him when he was on the receiving end. Definitely not his finest hour.[82]

Delightful, Dangerous Iraq
From February 1923 Dowding served at Inland Area Headquarters, Uxbridge, as chief staff officer under John Frederick Andrews Higgins: 'Josh', as he was known to friends, 'Bum and Eyeglass' to those who worked for him, because of his monocle and distinctive profile. He was a man with 'a sardonic sense of humour,' wrote Dowding, and 'a great grasp of detail'. He could master the contents of a bulky file in a few minutes, a gift which Dowding – who worked slowly – greatly envied.[83]

In August 1923, they observed that year's farcical 'bombing trials' in the Channel off the eastern end of the Isle of Wight. It was the third year that biplanes had 'attacked' the wireless-controlled *Agamemnon*, an ancient battle cruiser. According to the 'aeronautical correspondent' of *The Times*:

> 'The bombs released, of course, cannot be of the type actually used in warfare – the *Agamemnon* has a value still to the Fleet – but the practice bombs carried are designed to approximate in their results, from the point of view of accuracy in direction, to those which would be used in war. These practice bombs are quite light and are constructed to give a puff of white smoke on impact which can be observed and noted.'

As it happened, no-one saw anything. Not Higgins nor Dowding; not any of the other senior officers, air or naval; not the air and naval attachés of 12 powers; and not even a gaggle of journalists. But they all got wet and cold.

A few days later, on the 6th, Dowding enjoyed a far better day. He came second, of 15 starters, in a race for the Air League Challenge Cup, flying a Bristol Fighter, over a course of 100 miles between Croydon and Halton, near Wendover, Buckinghamshire. This result gave him particular pleasure and surprised many officers who thought they knew him, for he was then over 40 and had never made a name as a pilot.[84]

Then, in September 1924, Dowding welcomed his first opportunity to serve outside England and France for 13 years: as chief staff officer at the headquarters of Iraq Command in Baghdad. He went out alone, leaving step-daughter Brenda and son Derek in the care of his sister Hilda. Dowding greatly enjoyed the length and variety of his journey there: ferry to Calais, railway to Marseille, ship to Egypt, train to Haifa, car to Beirut and Damascus, bus and truck to Baghdad. Syrian car-drivers alarmed him for they whizzed without hesitation round blind corners, causing their passenger to reflect on the number of burnt-out cars visible every few miles. After Damascus, the 'road' was hard sand that swiftly turned to mud if it rained. There was at least no longer a danger of collision with a vehicle coming the other way or rolling down a steep bank, but plenty of getting totally lost, running out of petrol or water, or being attacked by tribesmen.

Hard to believe now, but in those days Iraq was regarded as a pleasant posting – once one got there – certainly for officers unencumbered by wives or children. All sports were available with delicious swimming pools nearby, jolly parties were regularly arranged at which good food and plenty of drink (alcoholic or otherwise) were available at little cost, and shooting trips (especially for duck) were often organized. There was safe travel to fascinating archeological sites, plenty of flying, and unrest among the 'natives', who were poorly armed at that time, never got out of hand and there was no fear of suicide bombers.

Aerial Control

Dowding, working under the direction of his former commander Josh Higgins, was soon introduced to the policy of 'aerial control'. This became an important issue between the two world wars. Could airmen maintain order throughout Britain's African, Middle Eastern and Asian possessions more effectively, and more cheaply, than soldiers? Trenchard persuaded successive governments that the answer was 'yes'. That answer was particularly important in Iraq for several reasons. It had been wrested from the Turks at the cost of many lives and huge expense and should therefore not lightly be given up. Also, it offered a land and air bridge across the Middle East to India as a supplement to the sea route. And, above all, it was a potential source of oil, becoming daily more vital to the Royal Navy in particular and the British economy in general.[85]

Airmen patrolled disputed or restless areas, flew political agents to meet tribal leaders, issued warnings to those who were reluctant to make agreements and as a last resort dropped bombs on or fired bullets at people, livestock and crops. Superficially, the results were impressive. Everywhere overseas RAF squadrons, with the assistance of armoured cars, were able to suppress discontent at a fraction of the cost and time taken by land operations. They also caused fewer casualties to villagers and tribesmen; and, no less important, fewer British soldiers were killed or injured. For example, 'tribal pacification' in 1927 in Mohmand country, India, by aircraft took two days, the airmen suffered no casualties and the whole business cost only 23,000 rupees. A similar operation in 1908 had taken two months, 257 soldiers were killed or wounded, and the cost was more than 18 million rupees.[86]

The doctrine seemed vindicated, though Dowding was among a number of officers who gradually became uneasy (perhaps more than that) about the casualties and destruction caused. He also doubted whether such methods would work against a European power equipped with fighters, anti-aircraft guns and its own bombers. He thought not and would be constantly agitated in the later 1930s by the difficult task of undermining the Air Ministry's excessive confidence in both the destructive capacity and impact of its bomber force on 'morale', that word which transfixed so many officers for so many years.

Even as late as September 1941, after two years in which Bomber Command had achieved little at heavy cost, an Air Staff paper had air control of virtually defensive villagers and tribesmen in mind as 'a mental model' for action against Germany, a nation with effective means of defence against British bombers. It was, the author thought, 'an adaptation, though on a greatly magnified scale, of the policy of air control which has proved so outstandingly successful in recent years in the small wars in which the air force has been continuously engaged.'[87]

Although there can be no doubt that air control caused less damage and loss of life than ground control, and thereby helped to prolong the British empire's death throes, the damage and losses were still heavy. Dowding objected, successfully, to bombing villages without giving people ample opportunity to leave, but he did not openly resist a policy that leaves a permanent stain on the RAF's record. During March and September 1932, as one example of numerous attacks, a single village on the Northwest Frontier received 213 tons of bombs. Throughout the 1920s and 1930s, strenuous efforts were made to hide the fact that delayed action bombs were often used and efforts were made to hit villages when it was known that people and their livestock were closely gathered.[88] According to Lyall, it was Dowding 'who introduced the humane policy of warning native villages by leaflet before they were bombed for real.' Although many questioned the ethics of aerial control, the fact that it was cheap ensured its continuance. Better still, as far as the RAF was concerned, it ensured the independent survival of that service.[89]

On 1 August 1924, shortly before Dowding arrived in Iraq to begin his service as a member of what James has called 'the imperial rearguard', the Air Ministry issued 'A Note on the Method of Employment of the Air Arm in Iraq', signed by the Secretary of State, Lord Thomson. As a rule, he wrote, 'defiance of the administration in Iraq and resultant disorder' are dealt with by the police; only if their resources are thought to be insufficient is an appeal made to the air officer commanding. He has operational control over all military forces in the country, using, where possible, the Iraq government's own forces. Native levies, officered by British regulars with access to armoured cars, deal with most of the problems arising in 'backward countries of poor communications and with a widely scattered population'. These ground forces, the Note emphasized, 'are known to have the air arm behind them in case of need, and this knowledge is a powerful factor for peace.' Air action is a last resort and only to be sanctioned by British and Iraqi authorities working together.[90]

The most tricky situation for Dowding personally came during a flight to Halabja, close to the frontier with Persia (later Iran), about 90 miles east of Kirkuk. His de Havilland DH 9a suffered engine failure. He waved his two companions on and managed a safe landing on a small island in a river. 'The roaring lion of the air', as Kurds described aircraft, was at least temporarily silenced.

Dowding and his mechanic, a lad of 20 named Smith, then watched a dozen mounted men, 'bristling with rifles, pistols and knives', ride down to the river bank, ford it, and advance in a rough line:

> 'I sat down upon the lower plane of the machine and told the mechanic to sit down beside me and not to move whatever happened. I laid my Very pistol – formidable only in appearance – on the plane beside me. The line advanced more and more slowly and doubtfully, and then the leader stopped and salaamed and the tension was over. The Kurds pointed to the machine and asked "Bomb? Bomb?" and I shook my head.'

Dowding and Smith were escorted to a nearby village, a collection of reed huts in which the Kurds were dwelling to escape the 'flea season' in their permanent homes. Strips of cloth were laid out near the village to tell patrolling aircraft that the local people were friendly. Young Smith proved better at chatting to them in whatever words they had in common, eked out by signs, than the gravely dignified Dowding, but he played his part in cementing relations by allowing the chief's son to fire off his Very cartridges. Rescuers appeared and by sunset on the following day Dowding and Smith were enjoying iced beers that they would never forget.[91]

Happy Days in the Mountains

During January 1925, Dowding briefly escaped on leave from the intense heat of Iraq to enjoy the intense cold of Switzerland. He and two friends carried out 'a remarkable mountaineering feat', in the opinion of *The Times*. 'Under the direction of a Swiss guide, they ski-ed down on Wednesday from the Jungfraujoch to the Concordia Hut. Next day, they made the ascent of the Finsteraahorn (14,026 feet), the highest point of the Bernese Oberland, and came back to the hut.' For their strenuous efforts, one of the party – not Dowding – suffered frostbite.[92] The feat was all the more remarkable because Dowding had never been a keen climber: 'I had never climbed anything that was not well within the powers of a reasonably athletic traction engine.'

He wrote a lively account of his Finsteraahorn climb for the Ski Club journal in 1925, warning readers that the route down 'was, I believe, invented by an almost blind goods-train shunter, after a visit to the rodeo and a heavy lobster supper.' Another piece, entitled *May in the Oberland* began:

> 'Readers may reasonably ask themselves from what institution I had escaped in order to subject myself afresh to conditions which I appeared to find so distasteful. I know, however, that I shall find many sympathisers with my view that any form of discomfort or inconvenience is preferable to work.'

It is a most entertaining piece, revealing a feckless, rough-and-ready side to his character, more suited to Jorrocks or Soapy Sponge about whom he had read so avidly as a young man. Dowding and his friends, Wing Commander Franks Robinson and Arnold Lunn: 'effected a burglarious entry into the premises of the local grocer, and proceeded to organize the commissariat on the principle that the necessities of life might go hang, provided that its luxuries are forthcoming.' As for kit, 'every member of the party forgot something, but nobody forgot everything, so we managed well enough between us.'

One of their porters dropped a 50-pound bundle of firewood on Dowding's head, which caused him to utter remarks best left unrecorded, but he took to his bed, filled himself up with aspirin, 'and awoke the next morning my usual sunny self.' The weather turned nasty and inflicted on everyone the miseries that skiers revel in, inspiring Dowding to create a verse:

> 'Ours is an ice-house, ours is,
> We who wears two pairs of trousis;
> The fire's gone out in our little shack,
> And there's no more wood in the pile at the back.
> Ours is an ice-house, ours is.'

Eventually they reached the station restaurant in a state of total collapse. No-one among the locals could understand why even Englanders were out in such weather. 'Thus ended an expedition to which I look back with mixed feelings; it had many pleasant, some painful, but very few dull moments.' Lunn later recalled that Dowding won an open race at Gstaad, 'beating first-class performers when he was nearer 50 than 40, a great encouragement to those who are inclined to believe that racing is a young man's game.'[93] We are all at least somewhat unbuttoned when on holiday, but the contrast between Dowding in uniform – correct, civil, unsmiling – and Dowding in skiing gear, when he was unfailingly cheerful and full of fun, could hardly be more extreme.

Director of Training

Trenchard was impressed by Dowding's conduct in Iraq and on 12 January 1926 he recommended to the secretary of state that Dowding be posted in May to the Air Ministry as Director of Training. It was his first seriously influential appointment, at the age of 44, and his deputy (from December 1926) was none other than Arthur Tedder, now a wing commander. On learning of this appointment Tedder told his wife: 'I can't say I relish the prospect.' He would spend the whole of 1927 under Dowding's command, but sadly no letters survive in which either man spoke of their antipathy; perhaps it mellowed into cool formality, given that both were hard workers by nature and in particular enthusiasts for training. Tedder was also, like Dowding, abstemious, careful with money (he too had a young family to look after) and relished physical discomfort when on leave, so these two exceptional officers may have found enough in common to keep them civil with each other.

Patrick Huskinson, who became one of the RAF's ablest masters of air armament problems despite being blinded in an air raid in April 1941, served under Dowding at this time. 'Tall and wiry, a tireless worker and a ruthless driver, his cold and somewhat intimidating manner, which earned him the nickname "Stuffy", hid the gentlest, the kindest and the most generous of natures. I could not have wished to be in better hands.' It was 'a national blessing', Huskinson thought, that Dowding became head of Fighter Command, but he also praised his vital role in the unspectacular organization of air force training.

In 1926, recalled Huskinson, there were no ranges in the country where airmen could learn to shoot and bomb from the air. His job was to find and buy such ranges despite vehement opposition from farmers, bird watchers, local politicians, trampers, squires and pacifists. Fortunately, he was 'magnificently supported' by Dowding and by Sir Philip Game, a member of the Air Council. After four years of effort, ranges were established at four sites, all on the east coast, one in Scotland (Leuchars in Fife), one in Yorkshire (Skipsea) and two in Lincolnshire (North Coates and Holbeach).[94]

Until August 1927, Dowding had the pleasure of serving with his brother Arthur, who had been the Royal Navy's liaison officer in the Air Ministry's Directorate of Training since July 1924. Arthur's naval career, in these years, was as successful as Hugh's in the air force: he had been promoted to captain in June 1926 and left the Air Ministry on 17 November 1927 to take command of a destroyer depot-ship, *Sandhurst*.[95]

Dowding's star was still rising and it was about this time that he earned Trenchard's grudging approval. 'Dowding,' he growled one day, 'I don't often make mistakes about people, but I made one about you,' a remark he would live to regret in 1940. Meanwhile, in the New Year's Honours List for 1928 Dowding was made a Companion of the Order of the Bath (CB), halfway to a knighthood, for his 'distinguished service' in England and Iraq. Then, in October, Trenchard recommended him for promotion in the Honours List for 1929 to the rank of air vice-marshal (major-general). 'He is apparently slow and heavy,' he told the Secretary of State for Air, but has 'any amount of intelligence, initiative and knowledge.' He does his work 'exceedingly well, and has been of great assistance to the Air Force since it was formed.'[96]

Crisis in the Holy Land

On 7 February 1929 Trenchard proposed to give him command of 'Fighting Area', a formation at Uxbridge responsible for all fighters, for a period of two years from November. Before taking up that appointment, Dowding suddenly found himself at 48 hours' notice sent to command all military forces in Palestine and Transjordan, arriving in Jerusalem on 10 September 1929. He had not visited or served in either country and knew nothing whatever about their social and religious problems, but he had served in Iraq, and it has always been assumed by the RAF that a senior 'General Duties' officer can cope with anything. His arrival was reported in *The Times* on the 12th. The 'campaign of recrimination' was now in full swing, according to that newspaper, and concerned with three allegations: atrocities, requiring the exhumation of bodies; inadequacy of measures of protection taken by British forces; and Arab complaints that Jews were being allowed to acquire arms. The Air Ministry had taken over the defence of Palestine in May 1922 and by 1925 the garrison had been whittled down to a single cavalry regiment, a company of armoured cars, and one squadron. Lord Plumer, who replaced Sir Herbert Samuel as High Commissioner in 1925, disbanded the Palestinian gendarmerie (many of them Europeans), created a new Frontier Force to serve in Transjordan, and got rid of the last regular troops. By 1929, fighting between Arabs and Jews was becoming serious, air control proved inadequate and British troops were rushed in.[97]

Trenchard had signed specific instructions for Dowding on 4 September 1929. The current High Commissioner (Sir John Chancellor), he reminded him, was titular commander-in-chief and Dowding was to be guided by him in all matters that were not purely military. Brigadier William Dobbie remained in command of British forces under Dowding and the senior naval officer in Palestine waters was a rear-admiral of whom Dowding later remarked, 'I believe he is a solo quartet': the Hon Reginald A. R. Plunkett-Ernle-Erle-Drax, whose flag flew in HMS *Barham*. As for administration, Dowding came under the general direction of the AOC, Middle East, in

Cairo. So much for essential background information, but what greatly heartened him were Trenchard's final words: 'I do not want to fetter your hands in any way, and you can count on my full support; even when I feel I must disagree with you, it will not mean that you have lost my confidence in any way.'[98]

Substantial forces were available at need: 1,000 naval officers and men aboard *Barham*, *Sussex* and *Courageous*, including six flights of the Fleet Air Arm; soldiers of several battalions; three RAF squadrons, one of them equipped with troop-carriers; armoured cars; and the Transjordan Frontier Force. Two regiments were on short notice in Malta with *Eagle* and *Royal Sovereign* poised to transport them, another squadron was available in Baghdad and more armoured cars in Aboukir. But Dowding was well aware that movers and shakers in Whitehall wished him to use his velvet glove wherever possible, and not reveal his mailed fist unless it became absolutely necessary.

A crisis was clearly brewing, if not boiling, and Trenchard spelled out for Dowding 'the general situation'. The official line was that Palestine 'could not be considered as in rebellion, but rather the disorders are the result of inter-racial feeling between Muslims and Jews.' Dowding's duty – easy to state, less easy to implement – was to calm everyone's fears and bring about a state of affairs enabling civil authorities to resume their proper function, and military forces to be withdrawn.

He was advised not to send small detachments to remote areas and 'the use of punitive columns and the burning of villages on account of past misdeeds is strongly deprecated.' Only if there was 'serious unrest' should he get the High Commissioner to agree that a particular village might be bombed, and only then after the issue of clear warnings. Every effort should be made to stop Arab tribesmen coming into Palestine from Transjordan and Syria, while at the same time he was to release as many soldiers and sailors for other duties as quickly as possible. In other words, Dowding was once again in the hot seat, as in his years of responsibility for the Hendon displays; once again he emerged unsinged and this achievement cleared his path to high command. 'I started my investigation,' wrote Dowding, 'with a completely open mind: in other words, in a state of complete ignorance of Jewish, Arab and Palestinian problems and politics.' He had a good look at the country from the air and then drove round it with an armoured-car escort.

He sent Trenchard his initial appreciation of the situation in Palestine from Jerusalem on 25 September 1929. He had only been in the country a fortnight, and had not hitherto kept abreast of events there, so his opinions, he admitted, rested on 'very slender foundations'. Palestine was quiet for the moment, but acute tension existed between Jew and Muslim following several violent acts late in August. The quiet was due to the number of troops on hand. If they were suddenly withdrawn, 'a state of turmoil' would immediately follow with 'incalculable' consequences. The problem, as Dowding saw it, 'consists of protecting the Jewish communities against Arab attack religiously inspired; also of preventing Jews, arrogant when secure, from provoking reprisals by irritating acts of aggression.'

The notorious Balfour Declaration of 1917 was the principal factor behind the unrest. It was a declaration by Britain's Foreign Secretary pledging support for a Jewish national home in Palestine while at the same time claiming to safeguard the rights of non-Jewish residents. Its 'wisdom and expediency', in Dowding's opinion, were open to argument, but it had recently been re-affirmed. The Arabs maintained, 'with a good show of reason, that a promise was made to King Hussein in 1916 that the Arabs should be self-governing' in most regions and they therefore wished to restrict Jewish immigration, which threatened to undermine their social and political influence and, above all, their land ownerships.

Looking back on these events late in 1956, Dowding believed Britain should not have repudiated her promise, made during the Great War, of self-government for Arabs if they helped to overthrow the Ottoman Empire:

> 'Everything was done perfectly legally! Rich landowners, often absentees in Syria, cheerfully sold their land to the Zionists at about three times its market value, and then the Arab peasants, who had cultivated the land for generations, were given short notice to quit without being offered any alternative tenancy or employment. And so a growing army of landless unemployed was created – the forerunners of the dispossessed thousands now in Jordan refugee camps.... It was indeed a sad situation for anyone with the most rudimentary sense of justice.'

In 1929, Europeans believed that those Arabs taking part 'in an orgy of destruction, robbery and murder' were criminals, but according to Dowding this was not the Arab view. The Grand Mufti of Jerusalem had plenty of money and encouraged them. 'In Iraq and other Muslim countries,' Dowding wrote, 'in which we have a prepondering influence' religious bequests were audited, and their expenditure supervised, by a government department, and this used to be the case in Palestine. Sir Herbert Samuel, however, handed the funds over to the Muslims when he was High Commissioner (1920-5) and the Grand Mufti now had 'undisputed control'. Dowding thought the government should reverse Samuel's decision.

The presence of Jews in the higher posts of the administration generated distrust. 'It goes without saying', though Dowding nevertheless said it, that these officials were honest and 'quite impartial in their dealings with the interests of all nationalities and religions.' Even so, it was impossible to balance their presence with a 'Muslim element' because too few of the latter had either the necessary education or powers of application.

When the outbreak began, Dowding informed Trenchard, the native police – most of them Arabs – collapsed under the strain. The British police were excellent, but too few to cope. Too few troops or aircraft were on hand, although those available did well. The arrival of fresh troops helped greatly. 'Incidentally, it may be mentioned [and would be by Trenchard to all and sundry in London] that the arrival of the first 50 men by air had a great moral effect.' Dowding then described the railways, roads, telephone

48

and telegraph systems of Palestine. These were all easy to cut or block, and the British needed their own systems, including wireless links.

The intelligence system, he said, in his driest manner, was 'capable of improvement'. Government officials 'simply did not know what was going on under their noses. They relied for their intelligence on an incredibly inefficient police force, which in turn seemed to have no sources of information except bazaar rumour.' The authorities in Palestine, compared with those in Iraq, were inept. For example, the High Commissioner eventually noticed that unauthorized persons were reading all the telegrams he sent to and received from the Colonial Office. 'This is hardly surprising,' wrote Dowding to Trenchard on 12 November, 'as the files are left lying about on a shelf in an unlocked office.'[99]

Trenchard warned Dowding on 21 November that 'ignorant people – soldiers as well as civilians' were suggesting that the Air Ministry was responsible for the unrest by insisting on the withdrawal of troops from Palestine: 'The truth is, as you know, that though we pressed for reductions we always insisted that some ground forces must be retained – until of course Lord Plumer went out there and recommended their complete withdrawal.'

Dowding was to enquire further into this and see that a commission of enquiry, sent to Palestine in September 1929 and chaired by Sir Walter Shaw, assisted by three Members of Parliament, was given the facts.[100] He did so, and told Trenchard on 7 December that he had acquired an excellent source of local information: 'a Jaffa friend, who is head of the Jaffa Shipping Board, a Palestinian by birth, a Maltese by blood, and British by nationality'; he and Dowding conversed in French. He claimed to have been in the British secret service during the Great War, 'was largely concerned in persuading the Arabs to revolt against the Turks', and Dowding recommended that he be taken on by Trenchard's successor – Sir John Salmond – to provide the RAF commander in Palestine with detailed information that might well be reliable.

These were only two of several unofficial letters which they wrote to each other at this time, both taking care that as few eyes as possible saw what they were writing, and commenting with a frankness on policies and persons that would not do in official reports. Dowding usually wrote in pencil, not trusting the discretion of the typist assigned to him, and so that he could keep his own copy of what he told Trenchard. Ironically, it was only during this brief visit to Palestine, at the very end of Trenchard's term as CAS that these two strong men, so sure of themselves, became genuinely friendly. 'I must say your private letters and appreciations are very good,' wrote Trenchard on 7 October, 'but be careful not to include political matters in letters that must be sent on to the Colonial Office; say what you like in letters to me.' The local officials are all 'very jumpy' because 'they never had anybody to keep a calm attitude in an emergency out there until you went out.' On the 17th, he wrote again. 'The atmosphere at home is that you are doing very well, and that you are the one cheerful spot. Put into your letters as much as you like on the humorous side of anything that strikes you. It is of value.'

It was with Trenchard's support that Dowding took a high line with Shaw on 11 November. The situation, Dowding told him, was so sensitive that his personal opinions must not appear in any official report in case they conflict with those later expressed by the Air Ministry. Unless Shaw agreed, Dowding would confine himself to giving him such answers as could be published 'without detriment to the service'.

Dowding had already recommended the withdrawal of one of the three battalions of regular troops and half the Army's armoured cars, but he was not yet ready to propose further cuts. The key factor, he thought, was the number of British police who could be brought in: as many as possible, bearing in mind the time it would take for them to get on top of the job. It would greatly help if they could be mounted. Perhaps a battalion of Assyrians could be raised from among those who have served in Iraq. They are Nestorian Christians, Dowding wrote, 'admirable soldiers, and pathetically loyal to the British who are their only friends, or shall I say, the only people who do not regard them with indifference or dislike.'

On the other hand, they would be unpopular with Palestinians and would be reluctant to leave their families to the mercy of Iraqis. So Dowding suggested strengthening the Transjordan Frontier Force. Their officers were keen; officials in Palestine were not. One squadron of aircraft was enough, given those available nearby, but a stronger armoured car company would be valuable. Air transport was not much use, he thought: in dry weather, lorries served well enough, while in wet the landing grounds were useless.

The conclusion to all this, he told Trenchard, was that: 'If the Zionist policy is to be imposed on the country, it can only be imposed by force; for the Arab will never believe that it has any sanction in equity.' Tension was always high, he added, citing a typical recent incident at Jaffa when a prisoner tried to escape from a policeman: 'a crowd followed; the Jews saw the crowd, shut their shops and bolted; the civil authorities got frightened and called on the troops to "stand to"; and then it all fizzled out. So you see, with people's nerves in that state anything might happen.' These words, though written long before the Holocaust and the creation of Israel, may resonate with a modern reader as a thoughtful comment on what seemed even in 1929 to be a problem without a solution.

Unrest had 'fizzled' sufficiently for Dowding to return to England late in December 1929. He had done well in a testing assignment quite outside his previous experience, but he had no wish to convert himself into a political airman. The War Office tried to regain control of Palestine's defence, 'to demonstrate publicly that air control had failed at least once', but the Cabinet ruled that the Air Ministry should remain in charge. It may be that Dowding's tireless and sensible efforts during the last three months of 1929 did something to tip opinion in favour of the airmen; those efforts certainly played a significant part in his own advance to high command. On the other hand, he is never mentioned in any of the reports published by *The Times* in 1929-30.

Near the end of his time in Palestine, Dowding was able to relax and enjoy some excellent shooting with the High Commissioner and senior officials. He had 'a good many frights', however, caused by his elderly car backfiring violently when running downhill. 'Passers-by took this to be the beginning of a new pogrom and pistols appeared as if by magic from the recesses of their clothing.'[101]

When Dowding left Palestine, all was relatively calm. Unrest would soon revive, but by then Dowding was fully occupied elsewhere. He greatly valued an opportunity to work closely and harmoniously with the overwhelming 'Boom', but otherwise was mightily relieved to shake the sand out of his shoes. Sadly, a decade later we shall see Trenchard using his potent backstairs influence to undermine Dowding.

5

Framing an Air Defence,
1914-1930

Fighter Command in Embryo
Britain had been attacked from the air for the first time on Christmas Eve,
1914, when a German seaplane dropped a bomb that exploded in a garden
near Dover on the Kent coast. No-one was hurt. By then, more than a million
Europeans had already been killed or wounded in the Great War, to say
nothing of the unfortunate horses and farm animals destroyed. Enormous
damage had also been done to public buildings, private homes and farmlands.
Nevertheless, this petty incident over Dover alarmed many who learned of it,
among them Dowding, at that time a squadron pilot on the Western Front,
because they realized that a new method of waging war had been found
against which Britain must quickly find a means of defence.[102]

When Lord Kitchener became Secretary of State for War in August 1914,
one of his first acts had been to invite the First Lord of the Admiralty,
Winston Churchill, to take on 'the protection of Britain in the air'. A year
earlier, in 1913, with German airships in mind, Churchill had publicly
declared that 'the needs of the national safety demand the best possible
measures for aerial defence.' He had therefore provided funds for the
expansion of the naval wing of the RFC into a virtually autonomous service.
When war came, Churchill anticipated by 26 years Britain's finest hour when
he drafted instructions for the deployment of aeroplanes, the installation of
guns and searchlights, the illumination of aerodromes and instructions 'for
the guidance of Police, Fire Brigade and civil population under
bombardment', adding that any bombardment 'must be endured with
composure'.

By the mid-1930s, when Churchill perceived in Hitler a deadly threat to
European peace, the continued existence of Britain's independence and
control of her empire, he had experience superior to that of all other British
politicians of the problems that would face Dowding in shaping and
managing a system of air defence. He knew and valued this austere, far-
sighted man. That is why, as we shall see, he backed him against Air
Ministry critics throughout 1940; and later did all he could to keep
Dowding employed in the RAF.

Fighter defence in Britain, as Ferris has written, 'sprang not from a marriage between "Stuffy" Dowding and radar in the 1930s, but from the First World War.'[103] Many elements in air defence were the same in both wars: anti-aircraft guns, searchlights, balloons and aircraft, all – eventually – working together and aided by early warning from a network of coastal observers connected by the most modern means available to control centres. Wireless and the telephone, used in the First World War, pointed towards those ground-air-ground communications that would become so highly developed in the Second World War. Operations Rooms, strikingly similar in layout and function, were used in both wars to co-ordinate the defenders' efforts and they faced exactly the same problems.

Some examples. When will an attack be launched? Where will it come from? Which targets will it attempt to hit? How can the range and accuracy of guns and searchlights be improved? At what height should balloons be flown? Where should these 'static defences' be sited? How can aircraft be got quickly enough into position to attack the enemy and with what weapons should they be armed?

In both wars, it was soon learned that different aircraft, different crews and different methods of control were needed to deal with day and night raiders. It was also learned that the sight and sound of defences *in action* – however uselessly from a military viewpoint – were necessary for civilian morale. Airmen and politicians alike were obliged to swallow their exasperation and accept that people needed to be cheered up and to believe that we were hitting back.[104]

Airship raids began, under the cover of darkness, in January 1915. The casualties and damage they inflicted were minute in comparison to those suffered every day on the Western Front, but they were *unprecedented* and no-one could say they would not become *devastating*. Their hidden effects were also great: loss of confidence in military and civilian leaders, loss of production in factories, delays in loading and unloading cargoes in ports. Exactly the same thoughts agitated the minds of Dowding, his colleagues and masters every day in 1940.

In April 1916 Colonel M. St L. Simon, an engineer, was summoned from France to take charge of ground defences. He organized them efficiently and had them linked by telephone to his headquarters. Lieutenant-Colonel Felton Holt was also brought home from France and he set up the first purely air defence formation: a wing of two squadrons (about 20 aeroplanes in each), truly, they were the first of the few. By the end of July 1916 Holt's wing had expanded to five squadrons and was re-named 'the Home Defence Wing'. It was the embryo of Dowding's Fighter Command.[105]

Britons learned that war now included direct attack on civilians at home, at work, in hospitals or at school, as well as men and women in uniform. They did not waver seriously before the Armistice, but would afterwards be all the readier to back the hotly-debated policies of disarmament and appeasement in the 1930s, when the danger of annihilating aerial attack seemed far greater. Across the Channel, meanwhile, German rulers learned that the much-vaunted airship was actually an inadequate weapon, even under the cover of darkness. Consequently, in 1917 Germany turned to the use of aircraft in daylight.

Raiders in Daylight and Darkness

On 25 May a raid on Folkestone on the Kent coast by 21 twin-engined Gotha G IV bombers killed or injured 290 persons. The town received no warning and not a single bomber suffered from ground or air attack during the 90 minutes that the raid lasted. The defences had relaxed since the decline of the airship menace; demands from the Western Front had drawn away many pilots and aircraft; and not least those defences had been designed to cope with night raiders. It was not easy, as John Bushby put it, 'to switch overnight from whale harpooning to mosquito swatting.'[106]

Then came the first raid on London, 13 June 1917. In perfect weather, 14 Gothas flew up the Thames and caused the highest casualties from any raid during the Great War: nearly 600 persons killed or injured. As at Folkestone, all the raiders returned home unscathed. Some three weeks later, on 7 July, 21 Gothas arrived over central London, as undisturbed as if they were taking part in a peacetime flying display. They killed or injured 250 Londoners. Nearly 100 Home Defence fighters went up to deal with them and brought down only a single bomber between them. That night, mobs ran riot in London, venting their wrath on anything or anyone who seemed German. Civilian unrest alarmed many politicians and serving officers, particularly in that year when the Allies seemed close to defeat. The unrest was not forgotten during the 1930s and played its part in strengthening appeasers of Hitler and Mussolini.[107]

These raids had a major consequence. 'One great defect in the present system,' wrote *The Times*, 'is that the air defences are under the dual control of the Army and the Navy.' The Prime Minister, David Lloyd George, set up a committee on 11 July to deal with 'Air Organization and Home Defence against Air Raids'. Its chairman was Lieutenant-General Jan Christian Smuts, an eminent South African then in London. By the end of the month, Smuts had recommended, and the government had agreed, that all defence forces – ground and air – should be placed under a single commander.

That precedent would prove of great value to Dowding 20 years later. The whole of south-eastern England came under the command of a RFC pilot (like Dowding, formerly a gunner): Major-General Edward Ashmore. Dowding's merits are incontestable, but Ashmore is 'the father of all modern air defence systems'. He devised a standardized method of reporting for all defence units, which passed information on a basic grid to the operations map table in his headquarters. His contribution to the development of air defence 'was of vital importance', wrote *The Times* obituarist in October 1953: 'he emphasized the co-ordination of each section of the defence system, linking aircraft, guns, searchlights, and sound indicators into a comprehension system.' In his book, *Air Defence* (1929), 'he pleaded for one authority, preferably the Air Ministry, to be in full charge of all air defence units, air and ground.'[108]

On 17 August 1917 Smuts recommended in a second report, accepted almost as speedily as his first, that the RFC and the Royal Naval Air Service should be amalgamated into a new command, independent of both the Army and the Navy. Two famous prophecies burned into the souls of airmen from that day to this. Firstly, that aerial operations 'with their devastation of enemy lands and destruction of industrial and populous centres on a vast scale may become the principal operations of war.' And secondly, that the enemy 'is no doubt making vast plans to deal with us in London, if we do not succeed in beating him in the air and carrying the war into the heart of his country.'[109]

Daylight raiding ended badly for the Germans in August 1917 as a result of poor weather, faulty engines, landing accidents and stouter opposition from a re-organized British defence. The Germans therefore turned to night attacks, as they did in September 1940, and Ashmore came to preside over a defensive system that had much in common with Dowding's, though without the priceless aid of radar. His means of communication between observers, gunners, searchlight crews and air crews were also fewer and slower.

Londoners responded in much the same way as they (with their sons and daughters) did in 1940. If they could not get out of town, or into solidly-built cellars or rooms below street level or into public or private shelters, they headed for the safety of the underground railway platforms and set up camp for the night with bedding, hot drinks, sandwiches and cheerful songs, especially when journalists, cameramen, parsons and politicians called by. Although the deaths, injuries and damage caused by night raiders were nothing like as great as prewar experts predicted, the loss of production was. There was also, in the minds of many employers or members of the government, a fear that the morale of the working classes would collapse and provoke demands for an end to the war on terms that would satisfy only the Germans and their Allies.[110]

Deter or Destroy?

In 1917, as in 1940, many Britons were not content with an effective defence. They wanted revenge: to read about British bombers blasting the homes of German civilians as well as making attacks on targets of military value. Trenchard agreed and persuaded himself that the effect of bombing on morale was much greater than any material damage it caused. Here we see the first appearance of a doctrine that came to dominate the strategic thought of a majority of British airmen for many years. It asserted that defence should be based on a force of bombers, not fighters; a force so powerful that it would deter an aggressor. But if deterrence failed, these bombers would then hit enemy cities far harder than the enemy could hit British cities. The doctrine depended on a conviction that *every bomb counted*: in wrecking factories, disrupting public services, destroying houses, killing workers or soldiers home on leave, destroying livestock and crops; ultimately, in undermining morale to a point where a majority of enemy citizens would oblige their government to make peace, or at least desist from bombing.

It was not realized by Trenchard or by those who accepted his opinions that numerous bombs would cause no significant damage at all, even if they exploded, which many did not. Those bombs that did cause harm might generate such anger against the bombers that morale actually improved, or hardened resolve to endure the attack (which comes to the same thing) and, if possible, strike back.

The belief that every bomb counted also led to complacency about methods of navigation, identification of particular targets, accuracy of bomb aiming and increasing the size and explosive force of bombs dropped. No special effort was made to improve any of these, poor as they were during and for long after the Great War, because the mere act of dropping them in enemy territory was believed to achieve the result desired. The Trenchardists were also convinced, during and for long after the war, that a formation of bombers would not be disrupted, scattered, or shot out of the sky by a combination of enemy fighters, ground gunners and searchlights.[111]

Also, just as the Soviet Union would find in 'General Winter' a most valuable ally against German invaders in 1941, so too – in both wars – the British would be greatly helped by their weather: always unreliable and sometimes cloudy, wet or cold. Germans also had good reason to thank their own weather gods for reducing the impact of British bombing.

These weaknesses in a doctrine taught in every RAF unit with a devotion that any priest of any religion would admire were not recognised, tested, or remedied between the wars. Consequently, the Air Ministry's pride and joy – an allegedly effective deterrent bomber force – would in fact perform very badly for years after the Second World War began. If the Air Ministry's defence force, designated 'Fighter Command' from July 1936 with Dowding at its head, had performed equally badly, the war might well have been lost. He was a notorious heretic, but an influential one, and determined attempts to burn him at the stake (metaphorically, of course) failed, until the worst of the crisis had passed.

By the time of the Armistice in November 1918, those responsible for Britain's air defence system had become aware of most of the problems and had found adequate answers – given the small number of lightly-loaded raiders and the essential help given to defenders by bad weather and faulty navigation. The outstanding unsolved problem was how to get earlier warning at longer range of an impending attack and thereby permit defending fighters to get airborne and into a good position to attack intruders. Between 1918 and 1934, no solution to this problem was found, but this hardly mattered in those years, because the war to end all war was now over and Britain was in no danger of aerial attack.[112]

Improving a System

The first serious attempt to restore and improve Britain's wartime air defence system began in 1923. The Steel-Bartholomew plan of that year was designed to defend Britain against conflict with her recent ally, France. The same three needs were emphasised that had been of anxious concern during the Great War and would still be causing Dowding daily anxiety in 1940. Firstly, the need for a chain of command to secure full and swift co-operation from the system's service and civilian components. Secondly, the search for some reliable means of getting early warning that raiders were coming. And thirdly the equally pressing search for rapid communication of two kinds: between ground and air and between aircraft in the sky. There were to be 35 bomber squadrons and 17 of fighters, a proportion the Trenchardists stuck grimly to for many years. The whole force, bombers and fighters, were to be under a new formation, the 'Air Defence of Great Britain' (ADGB) and was to be ready for action by 1928.[113]

Civilian volunteers of both sexes, all ages and every level of education, united only by their willingness to help, their patriotism, their realization – first brought home to them during the Great War – that there were no non-combatants in wartime, became an integral part of the air defence system. After the Armistice, Ashmore's network of ground observers had been disbanded. Attempts began to reconstruct it in 1924. A force of volunteers manned nine posts between Romney Marshes and Tunbridge Wells with the village post office in Cranbrook, Kent, as control centre.

Promising results were obtained and the system was therefore expanded to cover Kent and Sussex. In 1925, the Home Office sanctioned the creation of an 'Observer Corps', extending around south-eastern England from Hampshire to East Anglia. The whole system was handed over to Air Ministry control in 1929. By that time, there were 100 posts divided into four groups. Ashmore seated the plotters in these groups around a table, each plotter connected by telephone to a 'cluster' of three posts, and placing counters on the table in accordance with reports coming over his earphones. A teller, seated at a prominent position overlooking the table, transmitted the general picture to ADGB headquarters.

The Observer Corps, which became 'Royal' in 1941, was 'the most cost-effective air defence element'. Apart from a small nucleus of full-time paid officers, the vast majority were unpaid volunteers. Before and throughout the war, they finished their day's work and then walked, cycled or bussed to a lonely, windswept or waterlogged post where the equipment consisted of a table, a telephone, a pair of binoculars, a simple contraption for measuring the bearing and height of aircraft passing overhead and some means of making tea. Because all radar stations faced out to sea, the Observer Corps was the only source of notification once intruders had crossed the coastline. It also provided valuable information about friendly or enemy aircraft crashing near the posts, thus enabling police, military, fire and ambulance services to take necessary action as quickly as possible.[114]

The Rise of Keith Park

John Salmond, head of ADGB with Felton Holt as his chief of staff, moved out of the Air Ministry to Hillingdon House in Uxbridge, north-west of London, on 31 May 1926 and set Holt the task of finding him a staff. Holt recruited Keith Park, at that time a squadron leader home on leave from Cairo, in August and put him in charge of 'Operations, Intelligence, Mobilization and Combined Training'. According to Park, ideas about air defence that were set down on paper in 1926-7 had not changed significantly when war came a dozen years later. For this he gave the chief credit to Holt and Ashmore, who drew upon their experience of defending London in 1917-8. Fighter sectors, searchlight belts, anti-aircraft zones and balloon barrages were all created – though only on paper. Even so, Park always insisted that Fighter Command existed in fact, if not in name, long before its formal creation in 1936. It was in 1924 that Fighting Area began to work at problems of air defence and achieved notable successes in communications, material, organization, and intelligence.[115]

In November 1927, after 15 months at Uxbridge, Park was given command of 111 Squadron, equipped with the Armstrong-Whitworth Siskin IIIA, a now largely forgotten biplane fighter that nevertheless pointed the way towards the famous monoplane fighters of the Battle of Britain. It did so because it was the first fighter taken into squadron service of postwar design; the first with an all-metal airframe; and the first provided with high-pressure oxygen, a short-wave radio-telephone transmitter and receiver, a supercharged engine, plus a parachute and a heated flying-suit for its pilot. In its day, the Siskin was a fast, efficient fighter, comparable to any then flying.[116]

'Treble One', already a famous squadron, introduced Park to the possibilities of modern fighters not only in daylight but also in darkness because he and his pilots pioneered the RAF's long quest for an effective night fighter. Ten years later 111 Squadron would be the first to get the Hawker Hurricane, a monoplane that gave excellent service throughout 1940 (and also did well in other theatres for the rest of the war). On leaving the squadron in March 1929, Park was posted to the headquarters of Fighting Area for air staff duties and came under Dowding's command from January 1930, when he returned from Palestine. They served together until September, when Dowding left for the Air Ministry.

Park was appointed station commander at Northolt, near Uxbridge, in January 1931 and by August 1932 he had had six years in frontline home defence posts. For some reason that seemed excellent to the Air Ministry's personnel department, he would then spend the next five years far removed from fighters. But at last, in December 1937, he returned to the fighter world when he was appointed to command Tangmere in Sussex.

Only five months later, however, the Air Ministry decided to despatch him to Palestine for no good service reason, and to send a certain Arthur Harris, who had no particular interest in fighter problems, to Bentley Priory as Dowding's chief of staff. Fortunately for Park, for Britain and for Harris himself, Harris objected. He was newly re-married and both he and his young wife wanted to go to Palestine. Cyril Newall (a competent staff officer, recently elevated above his ceiling to CAS) gave way and reversed the postings. A decision lightly made and lightly reversed, it had immense consequences. Had Harris gone to Bentley Priory, his lack of a fighter background would probably have prevented Dowding from recommending him to command 11 Group in April 1940. Even if he had been appointed, Harris would not have matched Park's natural flair, honed by long experience, for managing a wide variety of fighter operations and talking easily to men under his command. Similarly, the conduct of Britain's bomber offensive would certainly have been different without Harris; no other officer is likely to have achieved the degree of authority which he gradually assumed after February 1942.[117]

Fighting Area

During 1929 and 1930, Fighting Area had carried out combined exercises (with bombers, searchlights, anti-aircraft guns, the Observer Corps and army units), as well as arranging its own exercises in daylight and darkness. New aircraft types were brought into service and equipment of all kinds was tested. Operations rooms began to be staffed by specialists, proposals to introduce plotting tables were approved and negotiations were in train with the Post Office to lay land lines. Receivers were installed at ADGB headquarters and transmitters at Fighting Area. Arrangements were in hand for circuits to link them with coastal observer posts. An 'Air Defence Landline Telephone Scheme' was under consideration, the wireless telegraphy organization was being revised and tested, and radio telephony was planned for fighter squadrons.

All these were matters of daily concern for Dowding during the first eight months of 1930; matters that he did not lose touch with during the coming six years as a very senior Whitehall Warrior; matters that then absorbed him totally throughout more than four years as first head of Fighter Command.[118]

Some of the air exercises, he recalled bitterly, were ridiculous. In August 1930, for example, he was required to command 'Red Colony', with his headquarters in Cranwell, Lincolnshire; 'Blue Colony' (under Sir John Steel) was based in London and the aerodromes of Kent:

'Farcical conditions were created by the directing staff, in which an impassable range of mountains existed in Essex, and Bedford was a neutral country whose frontier must not be violated. This left a corridor about 20 miles broad through which air attacks must pass. So the first thing I did, without telling anyone else, was to collect half a dozen wireless tenders and string them across the corridor about 15 miles south of Cranwell. So on the first day, my fighters were able to intercept every bombing raid coming up from the south.'

The result was that his fighters were always in the air, waiting to receive the enemy, as would be the case on so many days during the Battle of Britain, a decade later. Dowding had been clever, but not clever enough to defeat the umpires. In every combat, they judged that Dowding lost two fighters for every bomber shot down. It was clear that he could not win against umpires who had such a high opinion of the bomber, even such vulnerable machines as the RAF could muster at that time. So he fitted one of his fighters with wireless, ordered it to follow the bombers back to base, and when they were neatly parked on the ground to re-fuel and re-arm, inform Dowding. He then sent his fighters to 'annihilate' them as completely as he had eliminated Newall's Gurkhas nearly 20 years earlier. The umpires could find no reason to deny him victory, but they were much displeased. The exercise, a total farce, was nevertheless reported, uncritically and in loving detail, by *The Times*.[119]

In later years, Dowding would frequently insist that whatever achievement he was credited with during his time at Fighter Command was only made possible with the help of many assistants, in and out of uniform. But it may be that the indispensable condition, the *sine qua non*, for those achievements was the RAF's independence.

Had Britain's aviation remained in Army and Navy control in 1918 or been returned to that control after the Great War, it is likely that air defence would have been assigned a lesser role, as simply another part of the air arm, such as artillery spotting, battlefield reconnaissance, close support of ground troops, fleet and convoy escort or the protection of ports. The Army might have equipped itself with efficient aircraft to co-operate with soldiers, but the Hurricane and Spitfire were specifically designed to shoot down enemy bombers and any escorting fighters. They proved to be of limited value when attempting to support land forces or damage ground targets. Such fighters depended for most of their effectiveness on a radar system developed solely to meet a need to defend the country against aerial attack, which was what in the end, they got.

6

Life in the 1930s:
An Aircraft Revolution

A Disaster in Waiting

In August 1930 Dowding received news of a splendid elevation: to the RAF's ruling body, the Air Council of the Air Ministry, with responsibility for supply and research. He took the place on 1 September of his old mentor, Josh ('Bum and Eyeglass') Higgins, who had retired at his own request in order to become chairman of Armstrong Whitworth Aircraft.[120]

Almost at once a decision of Dowding's played a part in permitting a spectacular tragedy, when he agreed to issue a certificate of air worthiness for a newly-completed airship, the R.101. She departed from Cardington in Bedfordshire on 5 October, en route to India, but had made good only 350 kilometres in very bad weather when she struck a hillside at Beauvais, about 70 kilometres north of Paris. She exploded and of the 54 persons on board, 48 were killed, including Lord Thomson of Cardington, Secretary of State for Air, who was determined to make a brief, but spectacular, visit to Karachi before flying home for an imperial conference in London. He had been the driving force behind the whole airship programme. A 'fanatical believer' in airships, he had no technical background or aeronautical knowledge, 'and found it all too easy to override his experts whenever their doubts were opposed to his personal ambitions.'[121]

The bodies were brought home to lie in state in Westminster Hall on 10 October and enormous crowds filed through the hall to pay tribute to the dead. A memorial service was held in St Paul's on the same day and another in Westminster Cathedral for four Catholic victims. Afterwards, all the bodies were buried at Cardington 'in a common grave'.[122]

One may wonder now, though neither the court of enquiry nor the press did then, why such an important decision lay in the hands of an officer who knew nothing whatever about airships: nothing about their design, construction, equipment or performance. The RAF in 1930 may well have been the best flying club in the world, but it was a very small club and alarmingly short of expertise in many areas of aviation. Remarkable progress would be made during the 1930s by Dowding and a handful of other officers (greatly helped by many scientists, some civil servants and a few politicians), but in 1930 it is difficult to think of another senior officer, from Salmond (CAS) down, who was any better qualified than the unqualified Dowding to decide whether to allow R.101 to attempt the demanding task of flying safely to and from India.

Thomson had encouraged the building of R.101 and pressed hard for the fatal flight to begin. Dowding was aware of intense pressure to permit it, and accepted optimistic technical reports. 'I was wrong,' he later admitted, 'not to insist on much more extensive trials and tests.'[123] A public enquiry was conducted by Sir John Simon, sitting alone. A lawyer and Liberal politician, he would become foreign secretary in 1931. He had two assessors sitting with him, Moore-Brabazon (Dowding's colleague in 9 Squadron in 1915) and Charles Inglis, Professor of Mechanism and Applied Mechanics at Cambridge University. The attorney-general, the solicitor-general and a lawyer representing the widow of the airship's captain also took part.

Proceedings began on 28 October and concluded, with intervals, on 12 December. The logs for the last trial flight were destroyed in the crash, but Dowding had been on board and gave an account of what happened: 'all the officers,' he told Simon, 'were quite serene.' He had approved curtailing that trial at the request of Wing Commander R. B. Colmore, Director of Airship Development, provided that Major G. H. Scott (Assistant Director), who had commanded R.100 on her flight to Montreal and back, was satisfied with the airship's behaviour. Josh Higgins, Dowding's predecessor, had privately assured him that Colmore 'could never err on the side of rashness'. Dowding had suggested to Colmore that as there had been no full-power test on the trial flight, it should be done as soon as possible on the actual flight, so that the airship could return to Cardington if anything seemed amiss.

This was not done, but even with hindsight it seems that Dowding's conduct was both prudent and realistic. He knew nothing of the doubtful procedures followed throughout the course of R.101's construction, and there was no-one in the Air Ministry able or willing to advise or warn him. Simon's report was published in April 1931 and concluded that several factors, especially gas leakage and bad weather, but not faulty construction, caused the crash. The report carefully avoided blaming anyone.[124]

Writing about this disaster in 1956, Dowding was anxious to make it quite clear that:

'No direct pressure was ever exercised on me to sanction the departure of this new airship without extensive trials, but of course I should have been very unpopular if I had vetoed a journey on which such important hearts were set, after being in my new saddle for only a few weeks.... I was not sufficiently self-confident to set my individual opinion against that of the technical experts whose advice was available to me.'

Not that he wanted to override those experts. As he candidly admitted, at the time the venture 'seemed reasonable to me' and he had spent 16 hours aboard R.101. Looking back, of course, he thought there should have been more trial flights. The 'greatest mistake', in his opinion, was to begin the journey to India in such bad weather, heavily loaded, and flying very low. 'Here was this great ship, over 700 feet long, longer than many a golfer can hit a golf ball, staggering along in a gale only 2-300 feet above the high ground near Beauvais.' If an up-current raised the stern or a down-current depressed the bow, the ship lacked sufficient altitude to avoid disaster. Similar trouble, wrote Dowding, was experienced with early submarines, 'which on occasion dived into the mud before the stern could be lowered sufficiently to cause the vessel to ascend.'[125]

Douglas Robinson, an eminent airship historian, summarized the depressing saga of the R.100 and R.101: 'an incredible tale of vision versus governmental muddling and indecision; of genius advancing the state of the art and of inexperience creating an airship that would have been grounded had she not been constructed by a government department.'[126]

Neville Shute Norway, who later became a famous novelist, helped to build R.100, a far superior airship that flew safely to and from Canada between late July and mid-August 1930. He too described this sorry tale at length, sharply criticizing everyone who had anything to do with the design, construction, equipment and inadequate testing of R.101. 'The first-class brains in the Air Ministry, the high executive civil servants at the top,' wrote Norway, were responsible for the disaster:

> 'If just one of them had stood up at the conference table when the issue of the certificate of airworthiness was under discussion, and had said – "This thing is wrong, and I will be no party to it. I'm sorry, gentlemen, but if you do this, I'm resigning" – if that had been said then or on any one of a dozen previous opportunities, the disaster would almost certainly have been averted. It was not said, because the men in question put their jobs before their duty.'

That is perhaps so, but in Dowding's case it may fairly be said that he acted responsibly by taking part in the airship's only trial flight and accepting the expert opinion of those who built her.

On 13 October 1930, barely a week after the disaster, Salmond wrote to Dowding, asking him to investigate the possibility of R.100 making another long-distance journey, to match the publicity which a German airship, *Graf Zeppelin*, would enjoy from a proposed flight to the Middle East. 'I am *personally* anxious that R.100 should do the trip to Egypt this winter,' wrote Salmond, 'if the winter journey to Ismailia presents no more danger than a journey to Canada.' Dowding replied on the 16th, firmly refusing to consider his request: quite apart from the loss of so many airship experts, it would take months – and cost a great deal of money – to get R.100 ready for such a venture.[127]

Memories of the disaster were kept green for Dowding – as well as for the families of the victims – during the next few years. First came a memorial service on 11 October 1930; then a lengthy enquiry, fully reported in the press at home and abroad; then the unveiling of a memorial tablet at Cardington in August 1931; the laying of the first stone of a memorial at the crash site in October 1932; and finally the unveiling of that memorial a year later. Never again did he accept 'expert' opinion if he could possibly make his own test.[128]

The Schneider Trophy

In 1912, Jacques Schneider – a member of the French family of armament manufacturers – had an imaginative bronze trophy created. It showed a sea nymph kissing a wave, and was to be competed for by seaplanes. His hope was to foster maritime aviation, which then lagged behind aviation on land. This far-seeing act 'started perhaps the most emotive series of air races ever held and led to more technical development of the fixed-wing aeroplane and piston engines,' plus greatly improved fuel, than any other development before the appearance of jet propulsion.[129]

A Sopwith Tabloid had gained Britain's first victory in 1914 and a Supermarine Sea Lion won the trophy again in 1922, but Italian and American machines then triumphed until 1927 when the S.5, another Supermarine design, won. By then, international rivalry was intense and great national prestige was deemed to be at stake. Whichever nation could win three races in succession (not in total) would get to keep the trophy permanently. The S.5 won in 1929 and its successor, the S.6b, completed the hat-trick in September 1931. In the opinion of some, the final victory was a hollow one because no rival machine got to the starting-line and so S.6b had merely to fly round the course. On the other hand, the absence of competition was not caused by the British and they did in fact win the trophy five times. It became, and remains to this day, a proud British possession.

There were many who wished to continue the competition, it being such a spectacular commercial and popular success, with a new trophy at stake. Dowding, however, strongly opposed this. Partly because it was such an artificial race, partly because it put excellent pilots at unnecessary risk, but mostly because he thought designers and manufacturers should put their experience of airframes and engines into more useful work by developing land planes.[130]

Decades later, on 1 June 1966, Dowding wrote to Sholto Douglas about the Air Ministry's desire to keep the competition alive. He resisted this proposal because the fastest float plane in the world had *absolutely* no value as a combat machine: it could only fly from sheltered waters in light wind conditions. He said he wanted to invite private tenders from two firms to cash in on the experience gained in aircraft construction and engine performance to order 'two of the fastest machines which it was possible to build, with no restriction except landing speed (which was then necessary for grass aerodromes).' His plan was accepted. 'The result of this,' he told Douglas, 'was the emergence of the Hurricane and the Spitfire, which the Air Staff very sensibly pounced on as they emerged from the egg, fitted them with eight guns and put us for the time being ahead of the world in fighter aircraft.' If the RAF had been equipped with biplanes, 'which were the Air Staff requirements at the time', we could not have coped in 1940 with far faster German bombers, let alone German fighters.[131]

Fear of the Bomber

Aircraft development before the mid-1930s was handicapped not only by shortage of money, the mania for airships and preference for familiar designs, but also by the notorious 'Ten Year Rule'. In 1919, Lloyd George – then Prime Minister – had told the service chiefs that they need not anticipate a major war within the next ten years. In 1928 they were told that the ten years' freedom from major war began anew each morning. This dangerous edict was only revoked in 1932.[132]

At that time (and, indeed, for the rest of the 1930s), memories of the last war so dominated the thinking of politicians and population alike that re-armament 'was tardy, ill-conceived, and in general unrealistically minimized (especially for the army).' Added to this was 'a simplistic trust' in the League of Nations. During the 1930s, it was widely recognised in British ruling circles that Britain had everything to gain and nothing to lose from the abolition of the use of aircraft for warlike purposes. If such an abolition could be achieved by international agreement, the British Empire would return to the position it had enjoyed for centuries before the invention of flying machines, when the heart of the empire was virtually safe from assault and the communications binding it together were guarded by unchallenged sea power. It was not until the end of 1936 that the government finally accepted that an international agreement against aerial bombardment was impossible.[133]

In discussions on defence throughout the years 1934-9, the War Office and the Admiralty were ambivalent about the danger of aerial bombardment. They underplayed it when discussing re-armament, partly to strengthen their own cases for funds, but perhaps mostly because they did not believe the Air Ministry's claim that airmen would decide the next war. At the same time, the Admiralty was concerned about the threat of attacks on merchant shipping, which carried essential raw materials and food to Britain, and the War Office was much exercised about the fate (and still more, the morale) of civilians of the working classes in the event of aerial attack.

As late as January 1936, Sir Archibald Montgomery-Massingberd (head of the Army) argued that 'air limitation', if not absolute prohibition, was of 'infinitely greater importance to our security than the production of superior air forces.' And in November of that year, Sir Samuel Hoare (civilian head of the Admiralty) urged the government to seek an international agreement to restrict air warfare. Debate continued in 1937-8. A committee, headed by Sir William Malkin of the Foreign Office, studied the whole question of air power – and how to restrict its use in warfare.[134]

During 1938, the Cabinet was made aware that Fighter Command was, as yet, unable to guarantee Britain's security, even if its new-fangled aeroplanes and its new-fangled radar system justified all the hopes – and money – being poured into them. Worse still, some in the Cabinet were beginning to realize that Bomber Command was impressive only in theory; in practice it was utterly incapable of deterring Hitler by threatening a heavy blow against vital German targets. The Luftwaffe, however, might well have the power to destroy vital British targets. 'We thought of air warfare in 1938,' recalled Harold Macmillan (a senior member of Churchill's government, 1940-5; Prime Minister, 1957-63), 'rather as people think of nuclear warfare today.'

Lionel Charlton, for example, a retired air commodore – who presumably understood such matters – published a book, *War over England*, in 1936 in which he explained how the country would be conquered in two days:

> 'First a small force of aircraft attacked the annual Hendon Air Show, killing two-fifths of all British pilots and all the air force leadership and 30,000 spectators; then further attacks on London disrupted electricity, water supply and the docks. The *coup de grâce* was delivered with a gas attack on London and Paris which brought immediate surrender.'

Few people thought Charlton's fears wildly exaggerated. The Committee of Imperial Defence, a notably sober assemblage, supposed in that same year, 1936, that a well-aimed attack against 'our people' from the air 'might well succeed'. The Air Ministry advised the committee to expect 20,000 casualties on the first day of another war and 150,000 by the end of the first week.[135]

Many influential persons believed that air power actually *improved* prospects for peace because its use to enforce policy was too appalling to accept. If war did break out, aircraft would achieve a rapid, decisive victory and spare millions a renewal of the horrors of the Great War. They believed, in short, in the 'knock-out blow', a blow as much to morale as material. Effective defence was impossible, given the size of the sky, the speed of bombers and the long hours of darkness. Air power must therefore concentrate on pre-emptive or counter-attack – in either case, massive and immediate – to win a brief, but deadly, race before civilian morale collapsed at home. Consequently, re-armament should concentrate on bombers, not fighters. In peace, they would deter; in war, they would bring a swift victory. Such beliefs were very strong throughout Whitehall as well as in the Air Ministry.[136]

In 1932, Stanley Baldwin, leader of the Conservative Party, was right to say that 'the bomber will always get through'. At least four more years would pass before the RAF could even begin to hope that the bomber *might* often be intercepted.[137] On 24 October 1933, Lord Londonderry (Secretary of State for Air) reminded the Cabinet that Britain's production of military aircraft had been halted in 1932, as a result of the 'Armaments Truce' of November 1931. Although that truce ended in February 1933, production remained at a standstill, 'in spite of marked inferiority in air strength as compared with other great powers'.

On 27 July 1934, Dowding escaped from all his Whitehall worries to spend a happy day at Cranwell as 'inspecting officer' of cadets on the occasion of their 'passing out' and heading off to join their first squadrons. Except when he was on leave, preferably with skis on his feet, as we have seen Dowding did not come across as a jovial man, ready to chat easily with all and sundry.

For a day at Cranwell, however, among keen young airmen in a lovely setting, he thawed perceptively. He enjoyed the 'steadiness and accuracy' of the cadets on parade; the quality of their efforts in workshops and in the air; and their enthusiasm for games. He regretted that some cadets were not interested in aeronautical engineering, as it was fundamental to our technical service. He therefore passed on to these cadets, soon to be junior officers, advice which had greatly benefitted him when he flew regularly, advice which he still followed: 'take every opportunity of working with your own crew on your own machine whenever inspections, repairs or overhauls have to be carried out, and as you become more senior, keep yourselves abreast of technical developments.'

He ended by urging these young men to realize that they were now in greater danger of an accident then when they first took up flying:

> 'Statistics show very clearly that the most dangerous time in a pilot's career is just at the time when he thinks he knows all about flying, and nobody can teach him anything, and that is the time when you are most likely to be caught out.'

He certainly did not want to put anyone off flying. All he asked was that these newly-qualified pilots should have a 'healthy respect' for their aeroplanes; keep an eye open for other aircraft in the sky; and 'fly every day, every hour, that you possibly can, and never give up flying so long as you remain in the service.'

A sad footnote to this happy day: Dowding presented the Sword of Honour to Paul Ashton, born in Cape Town. Ashton was posted to 1 Squadron at Tangmere, promoted to flying officer in January 1936, and killed in a flying accident at Hawkinge on 23 May. He was 22 years old. And now an even sadder statistic: of 1,095 cadets who passed through the college before 1939, more than half (555) did not survive the war.[138]

Parity

In March 1935, Hitler told Sir John Simon (foreign secretary) that the Luftwaffe already had parity with the RAF and was now aiming for parity with the French. The Air Ministry, with good reason, doubted this claim, but pressure for rapid expansion increased. The resulting Scheme C reversed the Air Ministry's traditional emphasis on quality rather than quantity, for it was required to increase frontline strength even though this meant ordering aircraft known to be useless as fighting machines.[139]

The word 'parity' began to be used constantly in those British circles where military action, defensive or offensive, was an ever-more anxious concern. How many aircraft has Germany (and perhaps Italy) today? How many will they have next year? How many in five years? And can we, the British (and perhaps the French) match those numbers? A hectic, even hysterical, race began to regain or maintain numerical parity with whatever the Germans *said* was their frontline strength: never mind the quality, count the numbers. For the Air Ministry, this meant bomber strength. Fighters were considered to be of little use as compared with a bomber counter-strike force. Although fighter numbers were increased in four successive air re-armament schemes authorized between 1934 and 1937, aircraft designated as bombers increased much more.[140]

What mattered more than mere numbers, however, and what was even more difficult to discover, was how many serviceable combat aircraft the Luftwaffe possessed, aircraft with fuel, guns, bombs, spares, competent ground crews and qualified pilots available today and ready to replace tomorrow those who must inevitably be killed or seriously injured in accidents as well as combat.

Churchill had already taken up this subject in his unique manner. Words, for him, were never a means of conveying information or advancing an argument, but high-impact bullets, intended to overwhelm friends and enemies alike. As early as November 1934, he assured the House of Commons that in seven to ten days of intensive bombing, 30-40,000 Londoners would be killed or maimed and three to four million would flee the city. In fact, throughout the whole of the Second World War no more than 147,000 Britons were killed or seriously injured by aerial weapons considerably more potent than those available in 1934.

Churchill constantly exaggerated the scale of the danger facing Britain. For example, in September 1935 he predicted a German Air Force of 2,000 aircraft by October 1936 and a possible production rate of 3,000 every year thereafter. Actually, the Luftwaffe's total strength in September 1939 was barely 4,000. Until 1938, Hitler had in mind operations against Poland and France, with an assault on the Soviet Union to follow; only in that year did he begin even to think of an attack on Britain. This fact, had they known it, would have bewildered most Britons, who took it for granted that they must be Hitler's prime target. Another fact: the Luftwaffe was never capable of decisive – as opposed to destructive – bombing of British targets. But it would have been capable in 1940, in the absence of a defeated Fighter Command, of sinking even the largest and most powerful naval vessels. That is what some historians believe; others do not; no-one can know who is right, but Dowding and his colleagues were unwilling to see the Royal Navy exposed to the risk.

Such is the pass to which the failure of Dowding's Fighter Command might well have brought Britain. Her government, with or without Churchill at its head, would have been obliged to accept Hitler's terms for occupation. Initially, that occupation would have been as superficially endurable as that of France, the Low Countries and Scandinavia (including, before long, Sweden). Later, as the German war machine turned eastward, it would face an opponent as fanatical and ruthless as itself. Consequently, the occupation of all states in western Europe, including Britain, would have found themselves pressed harder for supplies and labour, both male and female; and British Jews, Gypsies, Communists and other undesirables, would have found themselves part of the 'final solution'. Resistance, in the absence of any prospect of outside help, would have been useless as well as suicidal.

From 1935 onwards, however, with Churchill leading the charge, discussion of the air threat and demand for parity was conducted in Britain in alarmist, not analytical, terms. His exaggerations had a double effect: stimulating air re-armament, but also inducing 'diplomatic paralysis'. Until Britain had a bomber force sufficient to deter Hitler, it would be dangerous to confront him. This fear governed Prime Minister Chamberlain (and the Chiefs of Staff) during the crises of September and October 1938. As for fighters, Dowding had only a handful of Hurricanes at that time and precisely three Spitfires, one of which had broken down. Only the appearance of an effective radar screen, plus Hurricanes and Spitfires in growing numbers during 1939 gave confidence to Dowding and those of his colleagues responsible for home defence.[141]

New Types of Aircraft

In the early 1930s, Britain's aircraft industry was surviving on the smell of an oily rag: repair and overhaul contracts doled out by the Air Ministry, with an occasional order for a new type. The work force was small and production procedures were governed by such rigid construction practices that it took at least five years for a new biplane to progress from drawing-board to squadron service. There was a 'ring' or 'family' system, whereby a small number of firms were fed most contracts. The system kept them alive, in years when few military aircraft were required, and when re-armament opened the way for expansion, they responded vigorously – with essential help from the automobile industry. Until 1934, the monthly output of any aircraft firm lay between three and eight machines; by September 1939, the industry was producing hundreds of machines every month, although too many of them were obsolete types.[142]

Dowding was one of a few senior officers, politicians and civil servants who were becoming uneasy at that time about Britain's defences. They made a simple calculation of the time taken by a twin-engined monoplane bomber to reach a city from the coast, and the time taken by a biplane fighter (nothing more modern was yet available) to reach that bomber's altitude from a ground start. The answer was depressing, even granting two unlikely suppositions: one, that the fighter would immediately find the bomber, and two that its feeble armament of two machine guns would be sufficient to destroy it, even though the bomber was likely to be carrying for its defence more than two machine guns. That left standing patrol as the only feasible, but none too promising, answer. To maintain such a system around the clock, however, would take far more aircraft, pilots, ground crews, spare parts and fuel than any government could afford. Determined and expensive attempts to get useful early warning from 'sound mirrors' proved to be a total failure.[143]

The RAF's annual air exercise in August 1934, like all those before it, was a fiasco. The 'attackers' carried out mainly night attacks against London with a prophetic choice of Coventry as the chief provincial target. In these attacks, not only was the Air Ministry itself deemed to have been wrecked, but only two of the five – repeat, five – bombers were intercepted. Critics were not pleased to learn that five was as many as the 'defenders' could even hope to intercept.

Three important consequences followed. Firstly, Dowding and a number of other senior officers were formed into a sub-committee of the Committee of Imperial Defence and ordered to study air defence. Secondly, Churchill, already publicly voluble on the German danger, now focussed his attention specifically on air defence. And thirdly, Albert Rowe, assistant to Harry Wimperis (Director of Scientific Research in the Air Ministry), wrote a memorandum after reading the files on air defence and said that unless science found some new weapon or method, then the next war would be lost if it started at any time in the next ten years.[144]

As the officer responsible for the RAF's supply, Dowding soon realized that dramatic improvements in the design, construction and production of airframes and aero-engines were necessary. He gave a high priority to eliminating wood from aircraft construction. This was because unseasoned wood was unsuitable, and the supply of seasoned wood – mainly imported from abroad – would certainly fall if there was another war. 'This led to many troubles with metal parts,' he remembered, 'owing to fatigue failures, inter-crystalline corrosion, torsional vibration, etc., but we learned from our experience.' As well as the change from wood to metal, retractable undercarriages, variable-pitch propellers, high-octane fuel, enclosed cockpits and improved radios all appeared from 1935 onwards.[145]

It is difficult now to believe how rapid and how complete was the change from slow biplanes to fast monoplanes. All very exciting, as Dowding doubtless relished in his discreet way, but also very costly. For example, a Hawker Hind single-engined biplane cost £1,650 in 1934. A decade later, the Avro Lancaster four-engined bomber cost £17,000.[146]

Britain's frontline fighters in 1934 comprised nine squadrons of biplanes. At that time, they might have coped with any likely opponent, but Britain's 'bomber' and 'army co-operation' forces were a motley assortment of unpromising types. At sea were a few stately flying boats of limited combat value. Collectively, these aircraft were markedly inferior to those coming into service elsewhere in Europe, the United States and Japan.[147]

Dowding was well aware that airframe design and engine development went together like bacon and eggs. Airframes were produced by 13 firms and engines by four: Napier, Rolls-Royce, Bristol, and Armstrong Siddeley. All 'were completely dependent' on decisions made by Dowding and he, in turn, relied heavily on advice from two permanent civil servants: John Buchanan (specialist in airframes) and George Bulman (engines). Unlike serving officers, they knew what they were about, having been properly trained in the aviation industry and they were not circulated, as serving officers were, into and out of unrelated positions at home and abroad every three years.[148]

The improvements over which Dowding presided coincided with fears that another major war was more than likely, as Hitler had now achieved absolute command in Germany from July 1934 onwards. Even though he had no scientific or technical training, Dowding now confirmed, as his wireless experiments of 1915 suggested, that he had a rare capacity – at least among senior RAF officers – for grasping scientific and technical principles. He gave practical support to the work of experts, service or civilian, both on the ground (radar, radio, the layout and staffing of operations rooms) and in the air (aircraft design, engines, armament and equipment). His insistence on experiment and trials often led him into conflict with those who lacked his determination to develop a comprehensive air defence system.

The Bristol Bulldog and Hawker Fury I were top of the range in 1930-1, giving way to the Fury II, Hawker Demon and Gloster Gauntlet in 1934-5; to be followed by the Gloster Gladiator (1937-41), the RAF's last, fastest and most heavily armed biplane fighter with four machine guns, and then came the first monoplanes. By 1940, despite financial, structural and political handicaps, the aviation industry was the world's largest producer of aircraft. It was greatly helped by a system of fixed-price contracts negotiated before large-scale production began, based on estimated costs plus a percentage for profit.[149]

Eight-gun Monoplanes

Dowding had been advised by aviation experts that the biplane was superior to the monoplane because for a given wing area the biplane was lighter and stronger than the monoplane, and the lower head-resistance of the monoplane did not compensate for its other handicaps.

'So I said, "All right, then: why didn't you choose biplanes for the Schneider Trophy?" And indeed if it had not been for our Schneider Trophy success, we should have started the 1939 war with nothing faster than the Gladiator, from which the German bombers could fly away in derision.'

By 1937-8, Britain had fallen 18 months behind the best fighters flying elsewhere, 'but even at its technical nadir,' thought John Ferris, 'Fighter Command's aircraft would have whipped any German bombers attacking across the North Sea.' As we shall see, those bombers had serious limitations, but slow biplanes armed with at most four machine guns would not have found them easy targets.[150]

A study by Wing Commander (later Air Commodore) Arthur Thomson in 1932 recommended that the next generation of fighters be provided with eight guns, firing 1,000 rounds a minute. Thomson had served as a flight commander in 16 Squadron under Dowding's command during the Great War and he endorsed his study. His work was confirmed in 1934 when Squadron Leader Ralph Sorley argued, with Dowding's backing, at an Air Ministry conference that such an armament would be needed to destroy a modern armoured, metal bomber. Thomson would have made his mark during World War Two, but on 28 August 1939, when head of 3 Group in Bomber Command, he walked into the turning propeller of a Wellington after examining the bomb bay.[151] As for Sorley, he later recalled that the number of guns was by no means the only point at issue. He wrote:

'Wing installation involved departures from current thought and practice. Guns in the wings dispensed with the complication of interrupter gear previously necessary to fire through the propeller [arc]. This offered saving in weight and complication, and enabled the guns to fire freely at their own rate instead of a mechanically restricted rate.'

Even so, there were arguments against Dowding's decision. Fuselage-mounted, synchronized guns continued to be used by the fighters of most nations in World War Two because they did not need to be harmonized to converge at a certain distance. As a recent study concludes, 'It always remained a controversial subject'. Although many British pilots expressed a preference for the concentrated armament of the Messerschmitt Bf 109, a much superior German fighter, the Focke-Wulf Fw 190, had both wing and fuselage armament.[152]

As Lyall has written, 'It is impossible to disentangle Dowding's influence from the work of his department generally, or from industries that were already due for a bumper harvest,' as re-armament got under way. Part of Dowding's job was 'to sift the wheat and chaff from this harvest.' He did not 'pioneer' the monoplane fighter, which was being developed in several countries. But he did encourage Hawker and Supermarine to submit designs in 1933 of what became the immortal Hurricane and Spitfire fighters.[153]

It was then believed, wrongly, that the high speed of the monoplane fighter would permit its pilot only a single pass at a bomber. Neither he nor his machine would be able to tolerate the twists and turns, the rapid deceleration and acceleration, required for old-fashioned dog-fighting. He would faint and/or the wings would fall off. Consequently, maximum damage must be caused during the one pass possible and so eight machine guns were specified: four times the armament then usual in a British fighter. Sydney Camm's Hurricane flew for the first time on 6 November 1935 and Reginald Mitchell's Spitfire appeared on 5 May 1936.

The Hurricane was of conventional, fabric-covered tubular steel construction: easy to build, able to withstand considerable battle damage and quickly repaired, but its fabric burned readily. Although many more Hurricanes than Spitfires fought in the Battle of Britain, it was the end of a line, a design with so little potential for further development that the performance of the last Hurricane was not greatly superior to that of the first. Even in 1940, its single-engined German opponent outclassed it.

The Spitfire, by contrast, was of the latest stressed-skin metal construction: difficult to build, less able to withstand battle damage and not easy to repair, but it was less ready to burn. It was the start of a line, a design with so much potential for further development that it was still in production after the war and the performance of the last Spitfire was incomparably superior to that of the first. Even in 1945, it matched the best German single-engined fighters. Its most serious weakness, obvious from 1941 onwards when it was used on missions across the Channel, was its short range. Jettisonable fuel tanks seriously impaired its performance and were in any case not available in Dowding's day.

The first production Hurricane flew in October 1937 and by the outbreak of war the type equipped 18 squadrons. In August 1938, the first

Spitfires arrived for 19 Squadron and there were nine Spitfire squadrons when the war began. These aircraft put the RAF in the forefront of fighter development.[154]

But Dowding gradually became aware that many pilots were poor judges of distance. They regularly opened fire at far too great a range, and even those who got close to their targets found that rifle-calibre bullets were not necessarily lethal. Numerous German bombers reached home safely even though they were thoroughly riddled, sometimes by as many as 200 bullets. The 20-mm cannon, firing explosive shells, was the answer, but one of Dowding's greatest disappointments in 1940 was to be the failure, despite strenuous efforts, to get reliable cannons fitted to his fighters.[155]

7

Life in the 1930s:
Research and Development

Testing Weapons

Dowding was promoted to air marshal (lieutenant-general) in January 1933 and achieved further distinction in June when he was made a Knight Commander of the Order of the Bath (KCB).[156] During that year, he attended an armament demonstration at Martlesham Heath, near Ipswich in Suffolk. As had long been his custom, reinforced by bitter memories of the R.101 disaster, he was determined to see for himself what was going on, rather than rely on reports sent to him by alleged experts. He boarded a two-seat Hawker Hart day bomber to test the various weapons on offer. He selected the Vickers 'K' gun, which then superceded the drum-fed Lewis, standard equipment since the Great War. After further development, the Vickers became a reliable, efficient, free-mounted gun and remained in service until the appearance of multi-gun turrets.[157]

Dowding had been invited to meet Sir Hugo Cunliffe-Owen, chairman of the British-American Tobacco Company, in 1934. He showed Dowding photographs taken in Germany of rockets designed for use in aircraft against air or ground targets, asking him to keep in mind the danger to his staff in Germany if word got out about these photographs.

Realizing at once the immense importance of this information, Dowding sought permission from his Air Ministry colleagues to begin his own development programme. Permission was refused on the grounds that the Army was in charge of such matters. So with 'grim forebodings' he handed this project over to his military opposite number. From time to time, Dowding attended firing tests at Portland Bill, the tip of a peninsula off Dorset on the south coast. They all failed, and after two or three years of negligible progress, the programme was cancelled, but Dowding did not learn this until 1937 when he prevailed upon Henry Tizard to use his influence to get the programme restarted and conducted with a great deal more enthusiasm. Rockets that could be carried under the wings of fighters did become formidable weapons against armoured vehicles and shipping by 1943, but Dowding believed they could have been available at least two years earlier.[158]

In November 1934, Dowding met senior executives of the aircraft industry and complained about 'Britain's backwardness in comparison with the very great progress which has been made recently by some other nations.' He therefore advocated the creation of a new Air Council member to take charge of research and development and was himself appointed to that position in January 1935, giving up supply and organization to Newall. From this time on, Dowding was responsible for the first monoplane fighters and bombers. The most important aero-engines, the Rolls-Royce Merlin and the Bristol Hercules, also appeared. Fundamental changes in procurement procedures were made, when several motor-car manufacturers agreed to manage new aircraft factories built at government expense.[159]

An 'Air Fighting Development Establishment' (AFDE) was created, with two permanent fighter squadrons and the frequent loan of bomber flights, 'for the principal purpose of studying tactics', and devising equipment to suit those tactics. Dowding noted, after the air exercises in August 1935, 'how valuable these practical experiments are, and how misleading arguments can be when they are based on theory alone.'[160]

Dowding and Edgar Ludlow-Hewitt (then Deputy CAS) had discussed bomber specifications during 1934. New types were needed, they agreed, to incorporate recent improvements in airframe design and engine power, but both men realized that Britain was suffering from a shortage of skilled manpower, civilian and service, to build, fly and maintain advanced aircraft and their increasingly expensive equipment. The Air Ministry had quietly sent its Director of Technical Development to the United States to learn what he could about American methods of designing, producing and equipping large aircraft. It had to be a quiet mission because Dowding and Ludlow-Hewitt knew that the Americans led the world in these fields, and also that many British politicians, industrialists and citizens going about their business in factories, offices, pubs and at home were reluctant to believe that this could be so.[161]

In June 1935, Lord Weir, a successful businessman and air power enthusiast, went to the Air Ministry as adviser to his friend Sir Philip Cunliffe-Lister (later Lord Swinton), the new Secretary of State for Air. Later that year, Weir was made a member of the influential Defence Policy and Requirements Committee. With apprehension about Hitler's Germany mounting, Weir became very concerned at the many years passing between design and production of aircraft. He argued that aircraft design had now become such an exact science that there was no longer any need for building prototypes.

Dowding disagreed, emphatically. Performance, in his opinion, could not be predicted from paper calculations, although he well understood – and so did Swinton – the need to get new types into service far more quickly than in the past. Until very shortly before the outbreak of war, however, Dowding would be exasperated by the several reasons given to him for delay: small factories, insufficient skilled labour, rigid craft demarcation, tight finance, continuous Air Ministry requests for modifications and – not least – everything to do with airframes and engines seemed to be in a state of permanent change. However, Swinton did order aircraft directly from the drawing-board and was responsible for the so-called 'shadow factory' scheme: a reserve capacity in the motor-car industry for aircraft production if the threat of war became extreme.[162]

In November 1935, Dowding found himself beside Swinton and Weir confronting the formidable Lord Nuffield, motor magnate and philanthropist. Nuffield, who owned an aero-engine factory, currently developing Wolseley engines, complained about the lack of support he got from the Air Ministry. Dowding, not easily overawed, answered back: hitherto, he said, Nuffield's engines had been too small for service use (as the great man was obliged to admit), but if and when more powerful engines were proposed, Air Ministry support would be seriously considered. Nuffield offered to build American Pratt & Whitney engines under licence: a proposal that attracted Dowding, but Swinton and Weir turned it down, on political rather than technical grounds. A prolonged public squabble followed, but in 1938 – after Swinton and Weir had gone from the Air Ministry – Nuffield agreed to construct a huge factory at Castle Bromwich, near Birmingham, for the production of Spitfires at a far greater rate than the small Supermarine factory could manage. We shall see later though, that Spitfires only emerged from Castle Bromwich after Lord Beaverbrook ordered Vickers-Armstrong to take over the factory.[163]

Writing in 1956, Dowding admitted 'a very serious error' in attempting to develop crash-proof fuel tanks for the new monoplanes. 'I blame myself for my lack of clear thinking.' Only afterwards did he realize that experiments carried out at the Royal Aircraft Establishment (Farnborough, Hampshire) were confusing 'the quality of being self-sealed to bullet holes and the quality of being crash-proof': the former could be achieved at a fraction of the cost of the latter in weight and bulk. 'During the Battle of Britain, I had bitter cause to regret my obtuseness while we strove frantically to remedy the fault.'[164]

As for ground defences, such anti-aircraft guns and searchlights as still existed were leftovers from the Great War. Some improvement had been made in ground-to-air radio-telephony, but exercise after exercise showed that successful interception of approaching bombers by guns, lights or fighters was a matter of luck. With regard to night defence, the situation was *worse* than it had been in 1918, given the facts that bombers could now fly faster, higher, farther, carry heavier loads, had better navigation and aiming equipment, armour to protect crew members and engines, and more defensive machine guns.

Naval Aircraft

Antagonism between airmen and seamen over numerous issues, especially over control of the Fleet Air Arm, was a fact of life throughout Dowding's career. From 1918 until 1937, the FAA was part of the RAF, which trained its pilots and ground crews. The RAF was responsible for the design and production of aircraft for the FAA, but from 1930 onwards Dowding tried to convince the Admiralty (which paid for them) that it was getting exactly what it asked for. Unfortunately, as Admiral Sir Caspar John later wrote, 'The Admiralty was not competent to say what it wanted and the

Air Ministry was not competent to advise.'[165]

The antagonism was real, even though neither service gave serious thought to the quality and number of naval aircraft produced nor paid attention to what other powers, in particular the United States and Japan, were devising for use at sea. Much of that antagonism was merely petty, common enough between branches of armed services in peacetime with too much time on their hands. Basically, however, the RAF and the Royal Navy were competing for resources that are always scarce, except during wartime, in order to carry out their duty to defend the homeland and destroy its enemies. For both sides, in other words, the FAA was a useful pawn.

Sir Arthur Longmore, head of Coastal Area (soon to be Coastal Command), submitted a report on 30 March 1936 to the Air Ministry on the state of the FAA and Captain Boucher, RN, wrote to Churchill in April on that subject. He spoke of a lack of training facilities, the dislike of RAF officers at serving afloat, conflicting systems of discipline, the Air Ministry's failure to supply the FAA with adequate aircraft, and poor relations between the Air Ministry and the Admiralty. In May, Churchill advocated handing the FAA over to the Navy and Oliver Swann, a retired air vice-marshal with a naval background, agreed: dual control 'will not stand the test of war'.[166]

In July 1937, Sir Thomas Inskip (Minister for the Co-ordination of Defence), backed by Prime Minister Chamberlain gave the pawn to the Admiralty. Delight in one quarter of Whitehall was matched by fury in another, in both cases largely instinctive: our team has won or our team has lost. Ellington, then in his last days as CAS, had supposed the issue still undecided until he met Trenchard at a garden party and was angrily abused for losing the pawn. Although Boom was long out of office, his influence remained strong, but not strong enough, fortunately, to prevent a sensible solution to an issue distracting both services from more important matters. The Admiralty argument for control of ship-borne aircraft was accepted, but not its demand for control of shore-based aircraft, which remained in Coastal Command.[167]

Dowding knew that most senior naval officers in his day were at heart like Admiral Tom Phillips, who would be killed in his beloved battleship while confidently sailing in hostile waters without air cover, more than four years after the FAA came into unfettered naval control. Brighter seamen than Phillips were already aware that a carrier-borne air arm was an essential weapon, but the war was well advanced before the Royal Navy came close to matching the number and quality of aircraft working with the fleets of Japan or the United States.[168]

Dowding was responsible between 1930 and 1936 for developing machines for service with the Royal Navy, and to that end was supposed to work closely with his opposite number at the Admiralty, the Controller or Fifth Sea Lord. This was 'the least satisfactory' part of his work at the Air Ministry because the naval staff could never be persuaded to agree to a specification accepting the principle of 'one aircraft, one task'.

He did not mean that no aircraft could be used outside its primary role, but the naval staff insisted on combining three roles in one specification, such as fighter-spotter-reconnaissance, and then complained, loud and long, because the resulting machine was slower than anything used by the RAF. 'They said that we took all the best machines and gave the duds to them,' Dowding recalled, 'whereas they had got only what they had insisted on having. As recently as 1956 this old accusation was voiced in a debate in the House of Lords. Luckily, I was present and was able to state the facts.'

Two outstanding duds were built by Blackburn in the late 1930s and responsibility for their specifications lies with the Admiralty, not the Air Ministry. Both were single-engined two-seaters, the Skua (a dive-bomber) and the Roc (a fighter provided with a turret, like the Defiant, but also with forward-firing guns). Too big, too slow, and too clumsy, their operational lives were mercifully short and they saw out their days as trainers and tugs.

Two other duds for which the Admiralty was solely responsible came from Fairey: the Albacore biplane (delivered from March 1940) and the Barracuda, a mid-wing monoplane which entered service in January 1943. Like the Blackburn duo, neither compared favourably with contemporary Japanese or American aircraft in naval service. The Admiralty ordered a third Fairey machine – the Fulmar, based on the Battle – that at last proved to have value in reconnaissance and some even in combat, though slow and clumsy. Equipped with eight 0.303-inch machine guns (in a few cases with four 0.50 guns), it served for a couple of years from August 1940.[169]

There was much heated debate in service circles during the late 1930s about whether aircraft could sink warships. Some rather perfunctory trials were carried out, which suggested that American reports of destruction achieved were exaggerated. Dowding, typically, suggested that the Admiralty and the Air Ministry test, not talk: 'instead of sitting round a table and arguing what *would* happen *if* such and such a thing were done, but it was strangely difficult to get staffs to see things in this light.'[170]

'Looking back today,' wrote Captain Stephen Roskill, RN in 1976, at the long controversy over control of the FAA, he concluded that the Air Staff was 'unjustifiably rigid in their indivisibility of air power argument,' and the government ought to have knocked heads together no later than 1935. Once the decision had been made, however, the Air Ministry accepted it 'with reasonably good grace' and did its best to help strengthen naval air power.[171]

Some naval officers, unfortunately, were unable to let the quarrel die. For example, Sir Herbert Richmond, a retired admiral and life-long opponent of independent air power, complained publicly as late as November 1942 that the Air Ministry had supplied the FAA with ineffective types before the war. Dowding felt obliged to reply, in a piece for the *Sunday Chronicle* on 29 November 1942: 'the Admiralty got precisely the types which they specified and demanded,' he wrote. 'They insisted on a plurality of roles for each type, and such hybrids as the torpedo-spotter-reconnaissance aircraft were foredoomed to inefficiency before pencil was laid to drawing board.' Most admirals, Dowding concluded, 'were obsessed by the idea of *fleet action* and the role of naval aircraft was completely subordinated to this conception.'[172]

Re-orientation

Until 1934, a strong popular repugnance in Britain against the very idea of warfare combined with an equally strong popular sentiment in favour of international disarmament and a prolonged, severe economic depression to ensure that ADGB remained weak. At the end of June, however, Hitler eliminated the Brownshirt leadership (and other opponents, real or imagined) and it became clear that confict with Germany was a possible, if unwelcome, prospect. The British government therefore decided to expand the RAF as both a defensive and an offensive weapon.[173]

During the winter of 1934-5, several plans for this expansion were drafted. One factor common to them all was to re-orientate the defensive alignment so that it no longer faced south-east to France but east to Germany. The new alignment had also to consider the increased radius of action possessed by bombers, which meant that London was no longer the only major city threatened. In 1935, a Re-Orientation Committee (under Brooke-Popham, now head of ADGB) proposed an aircraft fighting zone, containing 25 squadrons, reaching from Portsmouth in the south to Middlesbrough at the mouth of the Tees in the north. That zone would be flanked on the east by a narrow outer artillery zone. London would retain its inner ring of gun defences. Thought was given to the need for camouflage, smoke screens, air raid warnings and the control of BBC broadcasts.

But fear of war, hopes for peace and shortage of money jointly ensured that in 1935 the government only sanctioned for completion in 1940 the southern part of this new alignment. Under a revised expansion plan, known as Scheme C, there would eventually be 70 bomber and 35 fighter squadrons. This amounted to such a huge force that the decision was taken to divide it into two commands. Thus ADGB disappeared in July 1936, replaced by a 'Bomber Command' (under Sir John Steel) and a 'Fighter Command' under Dowding.[174]

Fostering Radar

When Dowding had gone to the Air Ministry in 1930, the only hope of intercepting raiders before they reached London lay in standing patrols, but, as explained earlier, these were too costly in wear and tear on machines, pilots and ground crews to be a practical answer. Failing such patrols, could some means be discovered to assist eyes and ears? Concrete sound-mirrors were tried and found wanting. In July 1935, for example, Dowding and an entourage visited Greatstone, a site north of Dungeness on the Kent coast. When all was ready for a demonstration of the detection of approaching aircraft, the local milkman, with his horse and cart, inadvertently provided the only clear sounds that anyone could hear.[175]

Fortunately, something rather more useful was shortly to be discovered. Albert Rowe's memorandum, mentioned earlier and written in late 1934, stating that unless science found some new weapon or method, the next major war would be lost, had greatly impressed Harold Wimperis. On his initiative, a Committee for the Scientific Study of Air Defence was set up under Henry Tizard, with Professors A. V. Hill (founder of Operational

Research during the Great War), Patrick Blackett (one of Britain's leading physicists), Wimperis and Rowe as members. Its first meeting was held on 28 January 1935, by which time Wimperis had discussed the problems with Robert Watson-Watt of the National Physical Laboratory. Could electromagnetic radiations bring down intruding aircraft? No, he replied, but it should be possible to detect and locate those aircraft.

In late January 1935, Watson-Watt's report, composed in partnership with his able assistant, Arnold Wilkins, was laid before the committee. Dowding was asked to seek approval for spending serious money on trials. If the scientists could convince him, he replied, he would do as they asked. The sequel was one of the most influential scientific demonstrations ever held in Britain.[176]

A trial was arranged at Weedon in Northamptonshire in late February 1935, using a continuous beam from a radio station six miles away, at Daventry. The pilot of a Handley Page Heyford bomber, Squadron Leader Robert Blucke (commander of the wireless and electrical flight at Farnborough), was instructed to fly back and forth between Daventry and a point 20 miles distant, keeping close to the centre of the beam. Echoes from the transmission were discernible at ranges up to eight miles. Dowding was delighted with the success of the experiment: 'I can now have all the money I want, within reason.' This was no exaggeration because he made £10,000 available: a sum equivalent to £1,800,000 in the money of 2008.[177]

Wimperis was also delighted. 'We now have in embryo,' he wrote to Dowding on 4 March, 'a new and potent means of detecting the approach of hostile aircraft, one which will be independent of mist, cloud, fog or nightfall.' Certain that the project had a future, Dowding pressed for money to finance further work and an experimental station was set up at Orfordness, near Bawdsey Manor, on the Suffolk coast: a suitable site because it was flat and isolated. The manor, together with 180 acres around it, was bought by the Air Ministry for £23,000 (£4,140,000 in the money of 2008).

It is already clear, then, that a massive investment of scarce resources was being made available to back the judgement, on evidence that was as yet scanty, of Dowding and a handful of scientists. The Air Ministry, so often criticized in these years, has never been praised for these bold decisions that contributed so much to Britain's salvation in 1940. Thanks to that money, and those who had the spending of it, radar became 'the catalyst of defence science'. In short, Watson-Watt gave it birth; Tizard supported it; and Dowding grasped it.[179]

As well as the scientists and Dowding, Lord Swinton (Secretary of State for Air, 1935-8) played an important part in developing the new device. The Treasury had authorized the initial building of five stations, and a total of 20 were proposed. At this point, it is worth noting that the Treasury, often criticized for stinginess, regarded a strong air force 'as the cheapest and most effective way of meeting the German challenge.'

Finding suitable positions was no easy matter: they had to be accessible to heavy engineering work, with soil suitable for carrying steel masts 350 feet high; convenient for electric supplies, secure against sea bombardment; and must not 'gravely interfere with grouse shooting' by local landowners. By April 1939, there were 11 stations in working order, providing early warning along the south coast as far west as Portland and up the east coast as far north as Dundee.

Apart from the physical problems of building these stations however, there was the difficulty of finding and training staff to operate them. With some initial reluctance, voiced by Park among others, it was decided to recruit women. By 1940, not only would the system have collapsed without them, but they were daily demonstrating the essential skill, concentration and sensible judgement.[179]

After years of stagnation, the intelligent, hard-driving Swinton generated a refreshing spirit of urgency in some of Whitehall's comfortable offices. He played an important part in helping to prepare Britain's defences. Some examples: ordering modern monoplanes; encouraging Dowding to make radar the centrepiece of his system; setting up a 'shadow factory' organization; and initiating a dramatic expansion in the RAF's training programme for pilots, engineers and radio/radar operators. Unfortunately, his decision to accept a peerage in November 1935 proved a serious handicap because it removed him from the House of Commons and by May 1938 he had been fatally undermined and Chamberlain sacked him.[180]

Dowding strongly approved of all Swinton's initiatives, and also his decisions regarding uniforms. The useless, uncomfortable and time-wasting puttees were at last abandoned and airmen were now provided with tunics not unlike those of officers, over a shirt with a collar and tie. As a senior officer, Dowding no longer had to wear riding boots, as if he were about to mount a horse rather than climb into a cockpit – or more often than he would have preferred, sit for long hours with other officers at a table covered with reports and proposals.[181]

Churchill claims much for his own contribution, primed by Frederick Lindemann, his close friend and scientific adviser. Radar depended on rapid communication of data to centralized control rooms and swift deployment of fast fighters to intercept raiders: neither Churchill nor Lindemann helped in these areas. Churchill was indeed invited to join a Cabinet sub-committee on defence in June 1935 and agreed, provided Lindemann was included on the Air Ministry's technical committee under Tizard. Unfortunately, Lindemann and Tizard became bitter enemies and Lindemann was forced off the Air Ministry committee in 1937.

According to Churchill, professional jealousy was the main reason, but in fact Lindemann – 'a man of great intellect and deep prejudice' – was arrogant, opinionated and (far worse) frequently mistaken: he pushed ideas that would have caused 'chaos' in the radar research programme, greatly disrupting its integration into a system of air defence. For example, he vehemently advocated aerial mines, dropped by parachute or fired from the ground, wires suspended from balloons and infra-red detection. A great deal of time and money was wasted on these and other ill-conceived ideas, but it was only in June 1939, after a visit to Bawdsey Manor, that Churchill overcame his instinctive backing for whatever Lindemann decreed on any technical subject and supported sensible radar research. But when he became Prime Minister, Churchill at once found Lindemann a sinecure in the government as 'Paymaster General', had him made 'Viscount Cherwell' and listened as avidly as ever to his opinions, expressed in simple words that Churchill could understand.[182]

Many people in Britain and Germany knew something about radar, but in 1940 only one battle formation had 'an operational expression of radar which enabled decisive tactics to be based upon it' and that was Fighter Command. Tizard was the main reason for this: 'the only scientist of whom it may justly be said that he did more than any other individual to achieve victory in a decisive battle.' Tizard, an Oxford scientist in 1914, had joined the RFC and explored many aeronautical problems, earning the confidence of airmen by his eminently practical approach, including learning to fly himself. Throughout the inter-war years, he occupied key positions in aviation research.[183]

Within six months of the trial at Weedon, aircraft could be detected at a distance of up to 40 miles, but it only became possible to fix their position and line of flight if two stations spotted them and worked out bearings. The potential value of this breakthrough was obvious, so work on sound mirrors was abandoned and the first batch of five stations, all provided with tall steel masts, began to be built north and south of the Thames estuary. In July 1936 Dowding ceased to be immediately concerned with developing the new system and instead became its chief potential user.[184]

Hough and Richards remind us that in Watson-Watt's opinion there were other officers who grasped radar's possibilities 'and gave support more quickly than Dowding'. No doubt; but he never claimed to be the only man responsible for bringing this wonderful device into existence and making of it a practical aid to national defence. One may observe here that most radar historians find plenty to criticize in Watson-Watt's methods and decisions. The fact remains, as Hough and Richards find themselves obliged to admit, that it was under Dowding that radar was successfully incorporated into the air defence system. 'He was a convinced, though far from uncritical, supporter from the early days, and without that support the radar chain would never have been in place to play its outstandingly important part in the Battle.'[185]

Put simply, the invention of radar in 1935 revolutionized fighter tactics. Formerly, because accurate intelligence was lacking, patrols and sweeps were the only means of seeking and finding enemy aircraft. The value of air defence seemed lower in the early 1930s as bomber loads, navigational aids and speeds increased. But radar promised to give unprecedently early warning: if it worked as hoped, there would be no need for standing patrols, wearing out engines, wasting fuel and tiring crews.

But a radar-based system was to take a lot of time and effort during the years 1935 to 1940 before it was anything like reliable. Only one station existed in 1937 and it could not give accurate information regarding the number, range, height or direction from which intruders were approaching. Even later it could not detect intruders below 3,000 feet and a new system (Chain Home Low: CHL) had to be hurriedly set up. Radar was still an oracle, and the information it gave had to be interpreted by intuition and experience.[186]

An excellent example of the development of 'forward interception', as it began to be called, was seen in the success of the Biggin Hill experiments, prior to the building of a chain of radar stations.[187] By the spring of 1937, the lessons of Biggin Hill were clear. 'Provided that the sector operations room could be supplied with the positions of bombers at one minute intervals, correct to within two miles,' according to an official signals history, 'it should be possible to direct fighter aircraft to within three miles of them. This was sufficient to ensure interception in average conditions of visibility.'

Dowding attended a meeting at the Air Ministry on 21 April 1937 and reported, on behalf of the Biggin Hill sector commander, success in devising and testing the techniques of interception. These would now be introduced to all other sector stations. Tizard, said Dowding, found the results achieved so far exceeded his expectations. Some experts thought the Biggin Hill experiments premature, but according to the official signals historian, if these experiments had not been initiated in July 1936 'it is doubtful whether Fighter Command could have been adequately prepared for the Battle of Britain.'[188]

8

At Fighter Command, 1936: Saving a Destitute Child

Big Man, Big Job
In July 1936 Bomber, Fighter, Coastal and Training Commands were formed and Dowding was appointed first head of Fighter Command. Given the fact that his name is now indelibly linked to that command, it is interesting to note that before his appointment he thought the re-organisation unwise: it would reduce the CAS's authority and give him the difficult task of deciding between the demands of bombers and fighters.[189]

The re-organization certainly benefitted the new Fighter Command. It was given an opportunity 'to press ahead with sophisticated techniques of air defence, an opportunity of which everyone from Dowding downwards took full advantage.' On the other hand, Bomber Command benefitted far less from radar, and also failed to learn as quickly as it should have 'how vulnerable bombers would prove to be in daylight against modern fighters.'[190]

The changes mark a clear rejection of Trenchard's opinion that a commander should control all types of aircraft in his area. When war came experience in North Africa and the Mediterranean suggested that Trenchard was right, perhaps because command eventually fell into the hands of Tedder, one of the RAF's greatest officers. Meanwhile, at home, Dowding was empowered to build a force that had only a single task and no capability for any other. It was a job that demanded a close focus; or, as Lyall put it less kindly, 'rather narrow single-mindedness'.[191]

He got the job because, wrote Ferris, 'he was a big man for a big job.' The creation of a new headquarters, and the support he got from the Air Ministry – greater than he or his later admirers liked to admit – enabled him to build on a system of air defence devised during the Great War, revived, and steadily improved ever since 1924. Between 1925 and 1940, according to Ferris, 'the RAF always had the world's largest and most advanced fighter defence system. It learned all the right lessons of the First World War and it was always able to handle any and every strategic bombing force which might have attacked the United Kingdom.'

Dowding learned to understand the system; he laboured to improve it; he had plenty of skilled help; and never claimed to have *invented* it. He had a sure grasp of training, research, supply and development problems. Unlike many senior officers, he was keenly interested in air defence. He had always resisted Trenchard's obsession with offence and argued that 'security of the base' must come first.[192]

Fighter Command currently rated below Bomber Command, in Air Ministry thinking, but just at this time radar, a promising means of getting early warning of intruders, was becoming a practical proposition and equally promising monoplane fighters, far faster and far more heavily armed than any known biplanes, were also becoming a practical proposition. In other words, some senior Air Ministry officers would have realized only a few months later that this command might have a brilliant future. Dowding had a good record, but many Whitehall Warriors thought of him as indeed 'stuffy', with a grim manner unlikely to inspire boisterous young fighter pilots. He was surely close to retirement and this exciting new command should, they believed, have been entrusted to a younger, more cheerful officer.

The job, however, was his for the next three years (unless he made a total cock of it) and he arrived in July 1936 at Bentley Priory, outside the village (as it then was) of Stanmore, north-west of London. Typically, he turned up on his own, in civilian clothes, looking more like an unpromising applicant for a cleaning job than the all-powerful new commander. He wandered in and out of the large building's many impressive rooms in the company of a deferential but puzzled sergeant, finally chosing a small one for his office that had a splendid view – on a clear day – across open country as far as Harrow School.[193]

For some time, according to his step-daughter Brenda, he commuted across London from Wimbledon, until the Air Ministry found an official residence for him, Brenda, his son Derek (now 17) and his sister Hilda: 'Montrose', in Gordon Avenue in Stanmore village. 'If mother had lived,' Brenda recalled, 'I believe he would have enjoyed the social side of life associated with his job, because she was always so full of fun and wanted to be involved.' When war came, Brenda was employed in the code and cypher section at Bentley Priory and like her 'Dad' (as she called him), Aunt Hilda and the rest of the family, fretted over Derek's chances of being killed.[194]

Meanwhile, back in August 1936, Dowding learned that his brother Arthur, then commanding HMS *Furious*, an aircraft carrier, had been promoted to rear-admiral (equivalent to air vice-marshal, two-star rank). Arthur had been a navy man for 36 years and according to his record of service was consistently regarded as a capable, reliable and hardworking officer, though sometimes criticized for being rather slow. He was particularly praised for his liaison work at the Air Ministry. Although Arthur held important positions for the rest of his career, he never became nationally important. Sadly, it seems he left us no letters to or from his brother and though he lived until November 1966 no historian invited him to reflect on Hugh's character and achievements or tell us anything about their other brother, Kenneth, or their sister Hilda.[195]

On 18 December 1936, Dowding was invited for a second time to address those cadets at Cranwell who were just about to 'pass out' to their squadrons. He began by praising them, for keeping their workshops and aircraft so clean and for defeating Sandhurst at both rugby and soccer. He then reminded them that their new commanding officers would expect Cranwell-trained men to be first class, on the ground as well as in the air. 'As I am preaching a sermon, I will give you a little text, taken from the epistle to the Corinthians: "Know ye not that a little leaven leaveneth the whole lump." This refers to you – see to it that you are good leaven.' With regard to their flying, he repeated his warning of July 1934, telling these new pilots that they were now at a dangerous stage of their careers: skilled enough to believe they were crash-proof, but not yet experienced enough to know that a careless or foolish action could snuff out their careers in a moment.

Dowding thought 'we old stagers' who learned to fly on machines with little reserve of power, had an advantage over such young men in that they did not kid themselves that they had enough power available to get out of any trouble. 'If you have a healthy respect for your aeroplane, and remember that there are others in the air besides yourselves, you will be all right.' He ended by urging them never to get drunk, to avoid undue criticism of equipment or superior officers, and work hard for entry to the Staff College and subsequent promotion.[196]

On New Year's Day 1937, Dowding received his last promotion: to air chief marshal (equivalent to full general or admiral). By then, he was well aware that he had been given what Peter Townsend called 'a destitute child'. A well-bred child, certainly, but in need of a great deal of tender loving care, if it were to grow up big and strong:

> 'The most crying need was for operations rooms at all commands and stations with tables on which courses of all aircraft, hostile and friendly, could be tracked.... There was absolutely no establishment for the manning of any operations rooms. In the silly little exercises which were sometimes held in the long evenings of summer, the unit commander himself acted as controller.... Next, there had never been any attempt... to represent our own bombers leaving and returning to the country. Everything on the table was assumed to be hostile.'

Very few 'friendly bombers' were provided for exercises and then only under the strictest rules; Dowding's own fighters were also closely restricted; there were no all-weather runways; and the Observer Corps was made up entirely of volunteers who took part in exercises if and when they could get off work.[197]

Serious Service in Prospect

Dowding's appointment was followed by the greatest building boom in RAF history. The first five radar stations were set up and brought into service by 1938, with many more to follow. Observer Corps posts were erected and linked by telephone and teleprinter lines to the filter room at Bentley Priory. Operations rooms, which controlled the groups into which Dowding sub-divided his command, were built and more such rooms created on the principal sector airfields which controlled the fighter squadrons. Sector airfields needed to be able to disperse and shelter aircraft from attack and also to ensure serviceable landing and take-off areas. The need for dispersal led naturally to the creation of satellite landing grounds. All-weather runways and perimeter tracks to dispersal areas were needed – as Dowding demanded of the Air Ministry during the winter of 1936-7 and got its agreement in March 1939! Numerous blast shelter walls were put up and air raid shelters built.[198]

Dowding had taken a close interest in the equipment of Britain's proposed new monoplane fighters ever since May 1935. He received regular reports from Sorley, who examined mock-ups during that year, confirming that both designs promised well.[199] But even a year later, although a Spitfire and a Hurricane were shown at Hendon, all the machines taking part in the display were biplanes. In June 1937, when the last display was held, only one or two monoplanes were to be spotted among a host of biplanes. On that occasion, Dowding offered a message about the display's value to readers of *Flight* magazine. It had appeal, he wrote, as a spectacle; it improved the RAF's efficiency; it enhanced its reputation with foreigners; and it made money for various charitable purposes, especially the RAF Benevolent Fund.[200]

Fair enough, but no-one knew better than Dowding that the aircraft on view that year were not good enough if war broke out. The situation only began to improve in 1938. Instead of the famous display, local 'Empire Air Days' were held at the end of May. Hurricanes, Spitfires and the Vickers-Armstrong Wellington – an excellent medium bomber – appeared, but so also did the Fairey Battle (supposedly a light bomber) and the Boulton Paul Defiant (supposedly a fighter).

The Battle and the Defiant were both single-engined machines, of modern all-metal construction. They were powered by the same Rolls-Royce Merlin engines that served the Hurricane and Spitfire so well. They were skilfully designed, attractive to the eye, and much admired. But that was in peacetime. As combat machines, they were among the most disastrous in aviation history. The Battle was slow and far from agile; it had a crew of three, carried a light bomb load, defended itself with two machine guns (one firing forward, one to the rear) and was virtually unarmoured. The Defiant was also slow and unagile, but far worse was the amazing decision to equip it with a heavy four-gun turret firing to the rear and give it no forward-firing armament. Consequently, in the event of war, its unlucky pilot had to place his machine in the worst possible place in the sky: below and in front of any aircraft he wished his gunner to engage. The pilot, unable to see what either his gunner or the enemy were doing, could do nothing to help the one or thwart the other. And yet these death traps were built in huge numbers. Battle production, amounting to more than 3,000 aircraft, did not end until January 1941. As for the Defiant, it was still being built in 1942 and altogether Boulton Paul turned out no fewer than 1,060.[201]

Hough and Richards admit that the Battle and the Defiant 'did not properly justify themselves': a criticism they could hardly have put more mildly. It may be that Dowding shares some of the blame for helping to bring these and several almost equally useless twin-engined bombers into service, among them the Handley Page Hampden and the Armstrong Whitworth Whitley, but his opponents were formidable. Richard Fairey, for example, regarded Air Ministry criticism of his decisions as intolerable, refused to farm out work to other companies except under extreme protest, and was very keen to build a larger version of his useless Battle.

He, and other manufacturers were indeed parochial, but the Air Ministry, for its part, lacked business expertise. Dowding, and all other officers temporarily at work in the Air Ministry, were out of their depth – inevitably so – when dealing with the aircraft industry. Roy Fedden, of Bristol, visited Germany in 1937 and returned convinced that a single controller of aircraft production in the Air Ministry was essential: someone 'to cut out once and for all the soul-destroying procrastinations and pin-pricking delays with which the whole organization is at present hidebound.' Yet Britain's aviation industry outperformed Germany's, once war began. It is, wrote Ritchie, 'a veritable success story compared to the chaos in Germany'.[202]

Even so, the British produced many inadequate machines. Harris had a low opinion of the Hampden: apart from the fact that its engines were reliable and it was available in large numbers, he dismissed it in his usual sweeping way as 'typical Handley Page junk'. When war came, no fewer than half of all Hampdens used on operations would be lost (714 out of l,433): more than 3,000 crew members were killed, injured or captured, and for all their courage and determination these men caused no serious damage either to German industry or morale, although they did useful service as minelayers in the North Sea.

The Whitley's record was no better: a poor design, inadequately equipped, it caused more harm to its crews than to the enemy. Nevertheless, some 1,800 would be built. The eventual appearance of a twin-engined bomber of quality (the Vickers-Armstrong Wellington) and two efficient four-engined bombers (the Handley Page Halifax and the Avro Lancaster) was, in Smith's opinion, 'a triumph of muddling through'. From a British point of view, fortunately, there was even more muddling on the other side of the hill.[203]

In January 1937, Christopher Courtney (Deputy CAS) was invited to Germany. He took with him Strath Evill, who later became Dowding's right-hand man at Bentley Priory, and a couple of Air Ministry intelligence officers.[204] Erhard Milch, second only to Goering in the new Luftwaffe's hierarchy, showed the Englishmen his latest bombers and gave them information – much of it accurate – about their construction and performance.

Then, in October, Milch and a party of German airmen paid a return visit. Swinton and Newall greeted them warmly and the RAF band played Nazi marches in their honour. The Germans visited bomber and fighter stations and were even shown round some of the 'shadow' factories, currently turning out motor-cars, but ready to produce aircraft if war came.

Milch was received by Dowding for lunch at Bentley Priory and suddenly silenced the amiable babble customary on such occasions by asking: 'How are you getting on with your experiments in the radio detection of aircraft approaching your shores?' Dowding, never afraid of silence, offered Milch his stoniest gaze. Other officers were obviously flustered, to Milch's delight. No need to be coy, he said, 'We have known for some time that you are developing a radar system. So are we, and we think we are a jump ahead of you.' The British system helped Dowding to withstand the Luftwaffe's attack, but some years later the German system would prove just as effective against British and American bombers.[205]

Debates in Parliament in March and May 1938 generated severe criticism of the government. Most squadrons were still equipped with biplanes, there were only 28 Hurricanes in service and not a single Spitfire had yet been delivered to squadrons, although contracts for construction had been placed in 1936. Essential equipment was also lacking. From the viewpoint of defence, according to an official history, 'it was extraordinarily lucky for us that we did not go to war' in late 1938. Of 406 'mobilizable' fighters on 1 October, 238 were obsolete and the reserves position was 'catastrophic'. Britain would be short of modern fighters, especially Spitfires, for another year.

Churchill had been a member of the Air Defence Research Subcommittee of the Committee of Imperial Defence since July 1935 and took the closest interest in every item of RAF equipment. He received a steady flow of detailed information from concerned officers about deficiencies. Group Captain Lachlan MacLean, for example, sent him a seven-page report on the inadequate state of 3 (Bomber) Group in September 1938, when he was in command. If Britain had then gone to war, that group 'would have had to conduct operations with an unsuitably equipped and inadequately trained force, working from ill-prepared and defenceless bases, and depending on a fundamentally defective organization.'[206]

Shortly before the war began there was still not a single aerodrome in Fighter Command with all-weather runways, as opposed to fields liable to be either dusty or muddy. For three weeks during Dowding's first winter at Bentley Priory (1936-7), aircraft were unable to take off from Kenley or land there and yet Kenley was a vital link in the chain of sector stations guarding London. Runways had been opposed by Air Ministry officials on the absurd ground that they were difficult to camouflage. Dowding had to waste valuable time before convincing his masters that safe, speedy take-off and landing mattered more than attempting a disguise that was only too likely to deceive his own pilots, many of whom were inexperienced. There were also senior officers who thought 'the landing area should be a vast expanse of specially-grown grass on carefully-tended flat land.' As late as 1938, recalled Balfour (Under-Secretary of State in Churchill's government), 'the Air Staff declared there was no need to plan for hard runways.'

The situation would have been worse had Dowding not won what has since become a famous argument at a technical conference called to consider specifications for the new fighters:

'I said that I wanted bullet-proof glass for the windscreens. I remember that a gust of laughter swept round the table. I said, "if Chicago gangsters can have bullet-proof windows for their cars, why can't my pilots have bullet-proof windscreens?" Tests showed that the extra weight was by no means prohibitive. I have no idea how many lives were saved by this; the important thing was the confidence engendered when flying into the return fire when attacking bombers from behind.'

On Dowding's initiative, fighters gradually received vital equipment: as well as bulletproof windscreens, more powerful radios, armoured seats, constant-speed airscrews (which greatly improved take-off speed, rate of climb and maximum ceiling), self-sealing fuel tanks and an electronic device allowing radar operators to distinguish them from enemy fighters.[207]

The 'shadow' programme was important and so too the pricing system which encouraged firms to produce as many aircraft or as much aircraft material as possible. In 1935, the aero industry made 893 aircraft for the RAF, but by 1941 that figure had increased to over 20,000. The greatest rate of expansion came after Hitler's annexation of Austria in March 1938. In Germany, on the other hand, Goering set low targets to avoid upsetting factory managers and workers whose complaints would reach Hitler's ears: the Fuehrer liked to believe that his folk were already striving as hard as possible to make Germany great again.

In Britain, 'important' aircraft (bombers) were ordered from companies considered reliable and 'low priority' aircraft (army reconnaissance and maritime operations) from 'suspect' companies. When re-armament began, several aircraft types were being produced merely to keep firms alive. Moreover, it was difficult for officers rotated into and out of the Air Ministry to get a grip on the problem. When the war began in September 1939, the British aircraft industry was producing no fewer than 59 designs: dissipating effort and wasting scarce resources, especially engines. Moreover, some types were obsolete when brand new, such as the Whitley bomber.[209]

Bombers or Fighters?

Sir Thomas Inskip, appointed Minister for the Co-ordination of Defence in March 1936, suggested that Dowding say how many squadrons, anti-aircraft guns and searchlights were needed to make Britain safe in the event of attack, setting aside the problem of supplying these. In early 1937 a committee chaired by Dowding prepared an 'ideal' scheme to counter the threat of German attacks during or after 1939. 'Passive defences' (balloons, searchlights, air raid shelters, etc) were obviously vital, but it was realized that no system could ensure complete safety. He asked for 45 squadrons, 1,200 heavy guns (plus light guns) and nearly 5,000 searchlights. He would also need hundreds of barrage balloons and the help of a large Observer Corps.[209]

The scheme remained no more than a pious intention until 'business as usual' was abandoned in early 1938. Only later in that year was the provision of fighters given priority over building bombers. Dowding himself made the point that a successful air offensive would become necessary if the war were to be won, but only a successful air defence would ensure that Britain avoided defeat and gained time to prepare for that offensive. Although the scheme was accepted 'in principle', a government reluctant to believe that Hitler was not merely a rabble-rousing politician who could be appeased by nicely-judged concessions, approved action only for an 'intermediate' stage. Nevertheless, more fighter squadrons were created, the Observer Corps expanded, air raid shelters were built, and appeals made for citizens to train as voluntary firewatchers.[210]

Bombers still mattered more than fighters, as far as most senior Air Ministry officers were concerned. During exercises in the 1920s and 1930s, defensive fighters were accorded only half the 'killing power' of twin-engined bombers. These Whitehall Warriors produced this remarkable decree: 'the fighting value of a good formation of bombers is higher than that of the same number of single-seat fighters; as an arbitrary figure, the fighting value of the bomber is assessed as two and that of the fighter as one.'

Even more remarkable was this conclusion from an exercise in 1930 that was still regarded as sound years later. Although the 'Redland' defenders were deemed by the umpires to have destroyed large numbers of the 'Blueland' attackers, victory was nevertheless assigned to Blueland. Why? Because Blueland's 'policy of commencing the operations by practically ignoring the existence of the enemy air force,' and concentrating on its own attacks, 'was fully justified by the results.'[211]

There was a 'fundamental tension' at work within the RAF and Dowding's disputes from 1930 onwards with the Air Ministry clearly illustrate it. If methods of air defence were improving in Britain, might they not also be improving in Germany? As Overy wrote, 'To admit that there was a defence against the bomber was to question the whole basis upon which an independent air force had been built.' Devout Trenchardists were gradually compelled, as they observed the practical achievements of the defensive system presided over by Dowding, to accept that a Luftwaffe attack might be beaten off. At the same time, however, they held to their belief that a British attack on Germany would not be beaten off.[212]

They clung to this foolish line in part because most British airmen had been provoked, by opposition from the other services, into what Smith described as 'apocalyptic utterances on air power' that they were now reluctant to abandon. This led them to claim that 'in order to achieve the breakdown of the enemy economy and society, it was unnecessary to defeat the enemy air force.' Fighter defence, except perhaps for the most significant targets of national importance, was therefore believed to be a waste of resources. Trenchard and his disciples always held that the RAF must have twice as many bombers as fighters. The opinion had some merit in theory, but in practice the bombers produced – and the crews provided for them – were totally inadequate until well into World War Two. Dowding, who had the good fortune neither to attend nor teach at an RAF staff college, did not succumb to this nonsense. As Slessor, one of the RAF's foremost bomber champions put it, 'Our belief in the bomber, in fact, was intuitive – a matter of faith.' But faith without works, so the Bible tells us, has no value.[213]

If air warfare had been left to senior officers in the Air Ministry, opposed only by Dowding, some politicians (Swinton, Inskip and Churchill in particular) and a few scientists (led by Tizard) who developed radar and created a system to pass its information to fighter pilots, 'there would have been no Battle of Britain because there would not have been enough fighters on our side to wage it. The RAF side of it would have taken the form of dropping small bombs somewhere within ten miles of badly-selected targets in Germany.'

In their attacks on German targets between September 1939 and February 1942, Bomber Command lost far more aircrew, for no significant advantage to Britain, than Fighter Command did during the three months of the Battle. It is certain, Sir David Hunt believed, that 'if the Germans had won complete control of the air they would have been able to invade, as they did Crete in similar circumstances.' As for the majority of senior officers in the Air Ministry, who were so pleased to see the back of Dowding: 'They would spend the rest of the war attempting to do in Germany exactly what the Luftwaffe had signally failed to do in Britain in 1940.'[214]

Defence on the Ground

Guns and searchlights were provided by the Army, though controlled by Dowding. When he went to Bentley Priory, there were only 60 usable guns and 120 searchlights in the whole country. The guns were obsolete and replacements were unlikely to appear for years. The Observer Corps, intended to report the movements of aircraft after they had reached British soil, covered only part of the vulnerable east coast. The corps had a full-time commandant, but posts were manned by part-time volunteers and nothing had yet been done to increase their number, or even to ensure that they would be available in the event of war.

Dowding chaired a meeting in Whitehall Gardens of the Home Defence Committee of the Committee of Imperial Defence on 29 October 1936. It was an important group of senior soldiers, sailors and airmen and they all agreed that Britain needed more anti-aircraft guns to protect vulnerable military and naval bases, aircraft factories and airfields as well as factories of every kind and those who worked in or depended upon them. Dowding thought the danger to Britain from modern, high-performance, streamlined monoplane bombers attacking from high levels was greater than that from dive-bombers: these were essentially short-range battlefield weapons and would be unable, he thought, to withstand attack by faster and more agile defending fighters. The committee met regularly and considered many problems, including how to prepare an 'ideal' system of air defence.[215]

In the event of war, Dowding thought, the main danger would be an attempt by the enemy to demoralize the population of London; its defence 'should be treated as the priority issue'. After London, he continued, should come Manchester, Leeds and Sheffield. Guns and searchlights would be as essential as fighters. It would never be possible to cover every potential target, but given the flexibility of an enlarged and properly equipped and trained fighter force, with good facilities for re-arming and re-fuelling, it should be possible to protect most major targets. Apart from the 21 squadrons earmarked for home defence, he concluded, Britain possessed four more squadrons assigned to a 'Field Force', should one be sent across the Channel. The Field Force itself would not sail for a fortnight or so after the outbreak of war, and he suggested that if this country was seriously threatened it might not even leave at all.[216]

A New Emphasis on Fighters

Dowding wrote to Ellington, CAS, on 2 November 1936 about the armouring of opposing bombers against fire from astern. 'If the enemy adopt this practice', he thought, our new fighters would be 'comparatively ineffective' and we would have to consider the use of 'an explosive shell'. As for armouring British bombers, he raised this issue at a recent Fighting Committee meeting and the experts assembled there, he told Ellington, 'said it couldn't be done – the experts always do. I think it *must* be done, if only to find out how likely it is that foreigners will do it.' He therefore suggested, as he so often did, systematic experiments, using old bombers loaded with dummy crews and guns firing away to discover how effective machine guns and cannons were at various ranges.[217]

A few days later, on 14 November 1936, Ellington told his deputy, Courtney, that 'Every fighter is a loss to the striking force – the true defence against air attack.' It was an opinion widely held in the RAF, one that would add significantly to Dowding's difficulties in shaping an air defence. As Mason observed, for every visit Ellington paid to a fighter station, he called on three bomber stations. The issue came up at a Home Defence Committee meeting a few days later, on 23 November. George Pirie, Deputy Director of Operations, announced that the Air Ministry had agreed to provide 21 fighter squadrons, 68 bomber squadrons, and would be reluctant to change this proportion. A week later, Douglas assured Courtney that bombers would not need to be escorted by fighters. Courtney agreed. They could not have been more wrong, as airmen of all nations would learn during the coming war.[218]

The Abyssinian, Spanish and Rhineland crises of 1936 had revealed the RAF's unreadiness either for defence or offence in Europe. Scheme C for its expansion was therefore replaced by Scheme F, the first which promised to put the services on a sound war footing. Although the government had approved expansion for all three services, it had also ruled that there must be no interference with industry, saying in effect: 'yes, we need Hurricanes, Spitfires, tanks, warships, guns and rifles urgently, but if you prefer to carry on making private cars or washing machines, feel free to do so.' The services were therefore *obliged* to compete fiercely to get their orders taken and completed. The ferocity of this competition was redoubled by the decision that the Treasury set aside a total sum for military expansion and dole it out according to the strength of demand made. This decision required air power advocates to go over the top: to put forward air power as a self-sufficient, war-winning weapon; to argue against the preparation of an army to serve in France; and to argue against strong naval forces in the Far East.

Thus Harris (Deputy Director of Plans in the Air Ministry) argued in February 1937 that the only practical deterrent to a continental tyrant was a stronger bomber force than he had. Britain should rely on Bomber Command. It was already an efficient, clinical weapon – he really seems to have believed that – infinitely preferable to 'morons volunteering to get hung in the wire and shot in the stomach in the mud of Flanders.' Those who doubted such half-witted bombast, remembering the limited impact of bombing, both German and British, during the Great War were easily answered: bombers were now bigger, faster, flew higher, further, found their targets more easily and dropped heavier bombs more accurately. Bombers had proved themselves in Spain and China. Numerous books described their efforts in deliciously horrifying detail. A famous film, *Things to Come*, made in 1936 from a prophetic tract by H. G. Wells, summarized common fears: there would be no early warning, ground defences would be useless, destruction would be immense and panic widespread.[219]

Chamberlain became Prime Minister in May 1937 and in June told the service ministries to work out the cost of completing present programmes and postpone any plans for further expansion. In effect, 'grab today because the bank closes tomorrow'. On the basis of new estimates of the size of the Luftwaffe, the Air Ministry put forward Scheme J to be ready by the end of 1939. There would be no fewer than 1,442 bombers, all supposed to be capable of bombing targets in Germany from British bases. They would not need continental bases and no British soldiers need cross the Channel. Only 532 fighters (in 34 squadrons) were required, even though the Home Defence Committee of the CID had reckoned 45 squadrons would be the 'ideal' number.

Enter the good fairies. First, Sir Maurice Hankey, secretary of the CID. When asked by the Cabinet in October 1937 to give his advice on strategic priorities, Hankey placed the RAF first in the role of defence and deterrence, the Navy second and the Army third. Hankey also thought that the RAF should spend more of its money on fighters, rather than bombers.[220]

Then came Inskip, Minister for the Co-ordination of Defence, an able and fair-minded conciliator who was already unpopular in the Air Ministry for 'giving away' the FAA. He now made matters worse, in Air Ministry eyes, by producing a memorandum in December 1937, drafted for him by Hankey, in which he argued that the RAF's role was not to *deliver* a knockout blow, but to *resist* it. He would be demonized by generations of bomber enthusiasts as no more use than 'Caligula's Horse'.[221] The case for victory through air power alone was far from proven, despite years of blather from Trenchardists, and Britain must be able to confront Germany with the risk of a long war, in which superior British staying power would bring victory. Her advantages included financial, as well as moral strength; the Navy's capacity for blockading the continent and safeguarding the import of food and supplies, plus the likelihood that sooner or later the United States would join in on the Allied side. That being so, Inskip continued, there was no need for the RAF to have as many long-range bombers as the Germans. The need was rather for a system of effective defence against aerial attack to secure Britain as a base for a later growth of offensive power (dependent on the Army) and economic pressure (dependent on the Navy).

The government accepted Inskip's opinion and rejected that of the Air Ministry, as voiced by Newall. Inskip and the government, the Trenchardists said, preferred fighters to bombers because they were cheaper; but without the extra fighters provided at Inskip's insistence, the Luftwaffe might well have triumphed in the summer of 1940. Thanks to Inskip, the problems of defence and offence were clearly separated. Defence, and therefore fighters, must come first. Bombers must be reserved and improved in a host of ways – speed, range, bomb load, armament, armour and cockpit equipment – before a serious offensive could even begin.

Actually, the 'Inskip Doctrine', as Smith called it, was a two-part gamble in the light of British and German aviation in 1937: one, that Dowding's system would in fact provide effective defence and two, that the Luftwaffe would not be able to cause anything like the devastation in Britain that many in the government and the Air Ministry feared. 'Fighter defence would assume the kind of priority in pre-war preparations that coastal defence had always had in the past, while the air offensive would supplement the naval blockade in the long haul to victory that would follow.'[222]

In attempting to strengthen Britain's air defences, Dowding would also benefit from the creation of an Auxiliary Air Force. When that experiment began, he said at Hendon on 28 March 1938, pessimists thought such squadrons would prove useless in a crisis. They were actually 'great assets to the first line', and personnel put in far more hours, on the ground as well as in the air, than they were required to. Most of them were not regulars: pilots, gunners, mechanics, armourers, wireless operators and clerks earned their living in every walk of civilian life. They learned service duties from a nucleus of regulars. Flying and other training was done at weekends, on two evenings a week, and at an annual camp. Dowding had 'not been idle' in pointing out to the Air Ministry 'the disabilities under which some of the squadrons laboured, and the unfairness of the conditions.' But remedies, he believed, were in train.[223]

Given the government's refusal to frame a military policy, as opposed to refereeing inter-service squabbles, its reluctance to direct industry to military production and its eleventh-hour decision that air defence must come first, naval power second and the army third in funding, it followed that the size, training and equipment of an army for the continent were all grossly inadequate. The disastrous campaign in France, in other words, was the price paid for a successful defence in the Battle of Britain.[224]

Necessary Arguments

Dowding never minced his words in arguments with Air Ministry officials. He felt he must not, for the good of the country, and he thereby upset many officers and civil servants, who were unable or unwilling to recognize the extreme danger posed to Britain by Hitler's aggression:

'I have been asked if I could not have settled these disagreements with the Air Ministry by more frequent personal visits, and it may be that a just criticism lies behind this question. It is probably a defect in my character, but I have found that a stage in personal relations can be reached where more harm than good is done by verbal discussions. I was senior to everyone at the Air Ministry with whom there could be anything to discuss, and it was not pleasant to have one's recommendations turned down by somebody who had quite recently been one's subordinate.'

The weakness in these concluding words is obvious. Dowding's opinions were often wise or correct, but his rank conferred no guarantee that such would always be the case: he seemed reluctant to accept that an air commodore, or even a mere squadron leader, might sometimes be wiser or more correct than a distinguished air chief marshal.

It would have been easy enough, Dowding admitted, to remain on good terms with the air staff, if one had been content to accept every ruling without question, but the home defence organization had been allowed to lapse into a state of 'grave inefficiency' and he was continually fighting to remedy the situation while there was still time.

Sometimes his opponents were poorly informed or merely obstructive out of an instinctive regard for established procedures, but often they were themselves victims of government policy. Treasury controlled all purse strings and firmly believed until the spring of 1938 that rearmament must not be allowed to interfere with normal trade, a belief strengthened by a very proper determination to avoid war if at all possible.[225]

Most senior Air Ministry officers were becoming increasingly irritated by Dowding's constant objection to their decisions. He, for his part, was no less annoyed by their reluctance to communicate with him. On 22 October 1938 he wrote to Douglas, reminding him that as long ago as 25 June he had sent him a long letter about aircraft types proposed for Fighter Command. After two months he got a note from Robert Saundby to say he would be getting a proper reply shortly. He did not and neither did he get a response to two letters sent to Douglas in September – and now it was late in October. 'I know the Air Ministry is preoccupied,' he told him, 'it always is about something, but surely it is wrong that in four months it should not have been possible to deal with the very important matters raised in my letter of 25 June.' Douglas got around to offering a non-reply a week later: Richard Peirse, Deputy CAS, would respond shortly, said Douglas. Nothing, it seems, in those balmy pre-war days could galvanize the Air Ministry into dealing promptly with Dowding's serious concerns.

On 28 November 1938, for example, Dowding wrote to Peirse about building all-weather runways at Filton, north of Bristol in Gloucestershire:

'I am convinced that we must have these runways at almost all fighter stations, if we are to be able to operate fighters by day and night during a wet winter. I have pressed this view on the Air Ministry for the last two years. The initial cost of the runways will,

Top left: In 1879, Dowding's father set up a preparatory school in Moffat for the sons of gentlemen awaiting entry to Fettes College in Edinburgh. He named it in honour of St. Ninian (c. 360-432), who began the task of converting Scots to Christianity. Dowding, born in Moffat, was a pupil there (1888-95), before his parents sent him to Winchester College. The school was converted by the RAF Association into a home for disabled ex-airmen in 1988 and re-named Dowding House. *Whiting Collection.*

Top right: No other surviving picture shows Dowding smiling so happily. He had only just started his education, in his father's school, and the prospect of Winchester College, very far from home, had not yet blighted his young life. *Whiting Collection.*

Inset, above: Dowding was sent to Winchester College in 1895, aged 13. Three years later, when this photograph was taken, he was still small, solemn and lonely. Unlike his father, he made no mark there. Useless at games; not at all a bright spark socially; merely adequate academically; and speaking, when he spoke at all, in a curious Scotch-Wiltshire accent. He did, however, become a very correct late-Victorian gentleman, taking to heart the college motto, 'Manners Makyth Man'. *Winchester College Archives.*

Middle: Dowding had one sister, Hilda (right), and two brothers, Arthur and Kenneth. She skied well and became a fine ice-skater. Hilda served with the First Aid Nursing Yeomanry in Italy during the Great War. She never married and like so many daughters of her class and generation, devoted her life to her parents and three brothers, especially Hugh. She made a home for him, his stepdaughter Brenda and his son Derek, until 1951, when Hugh re-married. *Whiting Collection.*

Bottom: Dowding's brother, Arthur, reached the rank of vice-admiral in the Royal Navy, served as superintendant of HM Dockyard at Devonport throughout the war and was knighted (KBE) on 1 January 1945. For a few months in 1926-7 the brothers, always close, served together in the Air Ministry.

Top left: Kenneth, Dowding's youngest brother, was a solicitor who joined the RFC in 1914, qualified as a pilot and briefly commanded 42 Squadron in Italy in November 1917. But his brigade commander decided that he lacked experience and powers of command and returned him to England. Unlike his brothers, Kenneth chose not to follow a military career after the Armistice, but he returned to the RAF in 1939 and was employed on legal duties. As with Arthur, so too with Kenneth and Hilda, none of their letters survive and no historian ever asked them about Hugh. *Whiting Collection.*

Top right: Dowding learned to fly on a Bristol Boxkite while a student at the Army Staff College, Camberley. He was awarded his aviator's certificate after no more than 100 minutes in the air, few of them in sole charge, and was thereby qualified to ta a three-month course at Upavon on Salisbury Plain early in 1914 organized by the Royal Flying Corps. At that time, he intended to remain a gunner, but w required to transfer to the RFC on the outbreak of war in August. *Whiting Collection.*

Bottom: A Maurice Farman Longhorn, the first machine that Dowding learned to fly at Upavon. It was 'a blessing for novices', recalled Oliver Stewa because it was impossible for the pilot to hit anythin head first: if he fell forward, 'the front elevator and outriggers took the shock' and if he fell sideways, 'corridors of wings, wire and wood' saved him.

Left: After the Longhorn, Dowding moved on to a more powerful machine, a Henri Farman, in front of which he is photographed here. *Whiting Collection.*

bove: Dowding (6th from left, 2nd row) earned his 'wings' at Upavon between January and April 1914, where
was reckoned to be a very good pilot and an above average officer, keen and able. It was here that he first met
renchard (assistant commandant, far right, 2nd row) John Salmond (his instructor, absent from this photo)
d Wilfrid Freeman (a fellow-pupil, 3rd from left, 2nd row). All three became bitter critics of Dowding during
)40. *Errol W. Martyn, via John Grech.*

Top: Dowding commanded 16 Squadron on the Western Front from July 1915 to January 1916. This photograph was taken at Beaupré Farm in 1915. *National Archives, London.*

Bottom left: In July 1916, Dowding, then a Lieutenant-Colonel in command of 9 Wing on the Western Front, was permitted to lead a raid by 20 BE 2cs on a target near Bois d'Havrincourt. By far the biggest raid of his career, it achieved nothing and ended with both Dowding and his observer wounded. More than 50 years later, he left his 'control lever' to the RAF Museum at Hendon, the only memento, other than uniforms, that he had kept of his long career.
Whiting Collection.

Bottom centre: At the end of July 1916, Major Robert Smith-Barry (CO of 60 Squadron) told Dowding that he could no longer send inexperienced, poorly-trained pilots into battle on Morane Bullets, an aeroplane difficult to fly, let alone use in combat. Dowding agreed and Trenchard was reluctantly obliged to concur. Smith-Barry devised a system of training in 1917-8 that saved countless lives and provided a permanent framework for systematic tuition in many air forces.

Bottom right: Trenchard sent Dowding back to England in January 1917 and although he was promoted twice during that year – to colonel and then to brigadier-general – he never again served on the Western Front. He commanded Southern Training Brigade until March 1918 from a headquarters in Salisbury, Wiltshire, and was responsible for more than 30 units, stretching from Hampshire to Cheshire.
Whiting Collection.

op left: Clarice, Brenda and Derek. Clarice's first husband, by
whom she had a daughter Brenda, was accidentally killed before
the war. She and Dowding married in February 1918 and their
son Derek (a Fighter Command pilot in 1940) was born in
January 1919. Clarice died suddenly on 28 June 1920, but
5 years later – so Dowding came to believe – she often appeared
to him, still full of fun and laughter. She told him of healing work
that he had done, forgotten when he awoke, in concentration
camps, bringing blessed sleep to sufferers. *Whiting Collection.*

op right: In 1912, Jacques Schneider started a famous series of
r races that concluded in September 1931 with Britain's third
successive victory, when Supermarine's S6B simply flew
unopposed round the course. Despite this tame ending, the Air
Ministry wanted to keep the contest going, but Dowding insisted
that the improvements made to airframes, engines and fuel be
now applied to land-planes. And so were born the Hurricane and
Spitfire, without which the Battle of Britain would have been lost.

Bottom: After the disaster which was
waiting to happen. Dowding, recently
appointed to the Air Council, agreed to
issue a certificate of air worthiness for a
newly-completed airship, R.101.
On 5 October 1930, she set off for India in
very bad weather, but struck a hillside at
Beauvais, about 70 kilometres north of
Paris. She exploded and of the 54 persons
on board, 48 were killed, including
Lord Thomson, Secretary of State for Air.
Dowding knew nothing of the doubtful
procedures followed during R.101's
construction, but later admitted that he
should have insisted on more trial flights.
Never again did he accept 'expert' opinion
if he could test the matter himself. *Flight.*

Right: On 27 July 1934, Dowding escaped from his Whitehall worries to spend a happy day at Cranwell as inspecting officer of cadets just about to 'pass out' to their first squadrons. He presented the Sword of Honour to Paul Ashton, born in Cape Town, who would be killed in a flying accident at Hawkinge on 23 May 1936; he was just 22 years old. Of 1,095 cadets who passed through Cranwell before 1939, more than half (555) did not survive the war. *Cranwell Archives.*

Below: Dowding went to Bentley Priory in Stanmore village, north-west of London, as first head of Fighter Command in July 1936. Typically, he turned up alone, in civilian clothes. He chose a small room for his office that had a splendid view – on a clear day – across open country as far as Harrow School. *Bentley Priory brochure.*

Top left: Dowding returned to Cranwell in December 1936 as inspecting officer. By then, he was even more acutely aware of the number of fine young pilots who were killed or injured in avoidable accidents. 'Please don't believe that you are now crash-proof,' he told them; 'respect your aeroplane, remember that there are other pilots in the sky; never get drunk and don't criticize your superiors' – this last piece of advice he was himself reluctant to follow from start to finish of his long career. *Cranwell Archives.*

Top right: A fine body of devout appeasers of Hitler's Germany, properly dressed for a day's slaughter of birds at some time in the 1930s. Geoffrey Dawson, editor of The Times, 1912-19 and 1923-41 on the left; Neville Chamberlain, Prime Minister, 1937-40 in the centre; Edward, 1st Earl of Halifax on Chamberlain's left. *Rowse, All Souls and Appeasement, frontispiece.*

Bottom left: Dowding was surprised as well as angered in 1937 when he learned that he had been passed over in favour of Sir Cyril Newall, whom he regarded as an amiable lightweight, to succeed Ellington. The same three founts of wisdom – Trenchard, Salmond and Freeman – who plagued 'Uncle Ted' soon turned on poor old Cyril'. He endured increasing criticism from these and other quarters and virtually disappeared during his last five months in office, June to October 1940. *Flight.*

Bottom centre: Sir Edgar Ludlow-Hewitt, head of Bomber Command from September 1937 until April 1940, when 'CAS [Cyril Newall] gives me the boot': a rare decisive act. Ludlow thought Trenchard's insistence on constant offensive in wartime proved his 'strategic vision' and was entirely justified. Dowding was one of a minority of senior airmen who disagreed and would have left the RAF in 1919 if Admiral Sir Vyell Vyvyan, his CO in York, had not persuaded Trenchard to offer 'dismal jimmy' (as he called him) a permanent commission in the newly-created rank of group captain. *Flight.*

Bottom right: Sir Edward Ellington (CAS, 1933-7) was widely regarded by senior officers in all three services and by those civil servants and politicians obliged to work with him as a liability. 'Uncle Ted' was apparently kindly and fair-minded, but he never flew in combat and saw active service only as a soldier. Three RAF heavyweights (Trenchard, John Salmond and Freeman), all sure of their own merits and judgment, came to despise him and a fourth, Jack Slessor, would tell the head of the Air Historical Branch in 1975 that he had been 'a disaster'. Ellington had the thankless task of explaining to Dowding that he had been passed over as his successor.
RAF Museum, Hendon, PC 71-19-87.

Right: Dowding pressed hard for the expansion of the Observer Corps from 1936 onwards, encouraged its first full-scale call-out two years later, and when war began strongly supported a proposal that observers be paid. Given that radar's value ceased at the coastline, essential work was done from that point on in tracking, plotting and reporting aircraft. Eventually, more than 30,000 men and women were employed, full or part time, 24 hours a day, seven days a week, until May 1945. This is the Watford operations room in 1940, with plotters receiving reports from a network of posts and passing information on to 11 Group headquarters.

Below: On 6 September 1939, three days after Chamberlain's mournful announcement that Britain was now at war with Germany, the king and queen visited Dowding at Bentley Priory. Never the most cheerful of hosts, except on a ski field, they found him glummer even than usual. Two Hurricanes had just been shot down by Spitfires and a third by ground gunners. This 'Battle of Barking Creek' suggested that something was seriously wrong with the defence system. Fortunately, Dowding and his colleagues were allowed eight quiet months for practice before serious fighting began. *Whiting Collection.*

of course, be high, but (apart from the fact that they are an operational necessity) they will pay for themselves hand over fist in ten years because this eternal tinkering with the drainage of aerodromes will not be necessary.'[226]

Nothing was done during the next year, until a fourth fighter group was formed to cover south-west England and Wales. Filton was then out of service for months, while the work was done.

Even as late as January 1940, some Air Ministry departments were still wrapped up in their cosy cocoons. Harris, then head of 5 Group in Bomber Command, and no admirer of Dowding except that he shared his exasperation with Whitehall Warriors, complained bitterly about the supply and organization departments. All his requests went 'meandering through a maze of offices' and were subjected to 'endless scrutiny, delay, obstruction, idle chatter and superfluous minuting by whole legions of departmental subordinates, some of whom quite obviously haven't the vaguest idea what it is all about.'[227]

9

Improving a System,
1937-1938

Passed Over

Dowding learned on 4 February 1937 that he had been passed over for the RAF's highest office, chief of the air staff, which would fall vacant in September when Sir Edward Ellington retired.[228] He would then be 55 and it may well be argued that so young a service, in the throes of a technical revolution, needed young blood in command. The argument was given added force by those who observed Ellington in office. He not only turned 60 during 1937, but was widely regarded by senior officers in all three services and by those civil servants and politicians obliged to work with him as a liability. 'Uncle Ted' was apparently kindly and fair-minded, but he never flew in combat and saw active service only as a soldier. Three of the RAF's most eminent officers – Trenchard, Salmond and Freeman – openly despised him and a fourth, Slessor, would tell the head of the Air Historical Branch in 1975 that he had been 'a disaster'.[229]

The nod went to Cyril Newall: hardly 'young blood', for he was less than four years younger than Dowding. The other serious candidate was Edgar Ludlow-Hewitt, who was four months younger than Newall. Although a Trenchardist, he was a shrewd, experienced and widely-respected commander who would probably have made a better fist of the heavy burdens of CAS than the amiable lightweight Newall, who seems to have collapsed under the strain during his last five months in office. Trenchard, Salmond and Freeman soon became as bitterly opposed to 'poor old Cyril' as they had been to 'Uncle Ted'. One must note, however, that sweeping condemnation – except of each other, of course, and a handful of likeminded officers – came easily to that particular trio.

If Dowding had been appointed CAS, to take over in September 1937, he would have left Bentley Priory after spending little more than a year in a most demanding task. By then, he was only just beginning to understand its problems, far less solve them. Even so, he was clearly ready to abandon a big job that it already seemed he was suited for, in order to take on a bigger one for which he was less well suited. Whoever succeeded him at Bentley Priory would still have been trying to get a grip on those problems a year later, when Munich opened almost all eyes to the scale of the crisis facing Britain. Even without hindsight, it was wise to leave Dowding at Bentley Priory until July 1939, when his three-year term expired.

Sir Christopher Courtney, head of Reserve Command, had been selected to replace him, but on 28 June 1939 (the day after his 49th birthday) he suffered a broken knee-cap in an aircraft accident. A month later, had he been uninjured, he would have been ensconced at Bentley Priory and, presumably, still there throughout 1940. According to John James, Courtney's accident 'is one of the few recorded instances of justice being done by blind providence to men of worth.'[230] In the opinion of Maurice Dean, a senior civil servant in the Air Ministry, Swinton seriously considered appointing Courtney as CAS, a man 'whose brilliant intellect and attractive personality made a strong appeal', before taking the safe option. Had that happened, or had Courtney gone to Bentley Priory, only a handful of historians would even have heard of Hugh Dowding.[231]

Dean thought well of Newall, who seems to have been a capable administrator with a pleasant personality. Unfortunately, he learned nothing from the Luftwaffe's effective conduct of operations during the Spanish Civil War, and even asserted that its adroit support of ground forces was a gross misuse of air power. He therefore resisted demands for similar support of British and French soldiers in the event of, and then in the face of, the German invasion of France. Amazing as it may seem, for a man in his position, Newall quite failed to realize that his short-range, lightly-loaded bombers would only be able to damage (let alone destroy) German targets if they operated from bases in France. When German forces occupied the Channel coast, and the Luftwaffe prepared to attack targets in southern England, he still thought it best to employ bombers against what he called 'strategic' targets (factories, oil tanks, railway junctions, etc) far behind the front lines. Douglas, then working closely with him, thought he was 'an absolute bag of nerves' by 1940. 'He worked at his desk at the Air Ministry during the day, and had a cell underground where he used to work and sleep at nights. He never left the place.'[232]

Strenuous efforts were made from May 1940 onwards to get rid of Newall, backed by Trenchard, Salmond and Beaverbrook. A memorandum composed by an Australian-born officer, Wing Commander Edgar Kingston-McCloughry (a member of the Air Ministry's Directorate of War Organization) and circulated anonymously, castigated Newall as 'a weak link in the nation's defence'. He was, according to Kingston-McCloughry, a man of 'inadequate mental ability, limited practical experience, weakness of character and personality, and lack of judgement and foresight'. Everyone who mattered read the memorandum, and though Newall was not relieved of his command until October he faded from view after May, leaving Douglas in virtual command. Incidentally, the memorandum also criticized Dowding, calling Fighter Command 'a one man show' led by a man with 'inadequate mental ability and a very slow brain'; he was a 'complete non-co-operator with authority' and treated his staff badly.[233]

Meanwhile, on 1 February 1937, Ellington had written to 'my dear Ludlow' to give him the bad news. 'As I told you a long time ago, I had hoped that you would succeed me, but the Secretary of State [Swinton] has decided otherwise.' Ellington did what he could to sweeten the pill: Ludlow-Hewitt was to succeed Sir John Steel as head of Bomber Command. 'You will find it a less exacting job than mine and strictly between ourselves I may tell you that I think you might have found the present Secretary of State somewhat irritating': a revealing comment, for Swinton is generally regarded as one of very few shining lights among Britain's rulers in the 1930s.[234]

However, the personal grief felt by Dowding turned out to be a national blessing because he had all the qualities needed at Fighter Command and none of the smooth amiability so highly prized in Whitehall. He may, in time, have come to recognize that as CAS he would have been a square peg in a round hole, but in February 1937 a whole range of emotions, among them shock and resentment, threatened to overwhelm him. He fired off an immediate reply to Ellington's letter next day, 5 February:

'Thank you for letting me know your plans. I trust that I may be permitted to continue to serve until I have completed a year in my present rank. On November 2nd I wrote you a letter about the armouring of bombers and attack of armoured aircraft by fighters; and I gave you some further comments on the subject at an interview in December. I did this at a time when I had reason to believe that I should be your successor and should in due course find myself responsible for the equipment of the Air Force. In the altered circumstances I have no *locus standi* for pressing my views, and I would ask you to disregard my papers, except in so far as you may be convinced of their soundness.'[235]

Ellington replied temperately on the 8th. You speak of 'my plans', but the selection of a CAS, as Dowding – so recently a member of the Air Council – ought not to have needed telling, was a matter for the Secretary of State. He was not obliged to consult the current CAS or anyone else and even if he did, need take no notice of the advice he got. Ellington continued, again making a point that Dowding understood perfectly well, when in control of his emotions, that an air chief marshal would be employed until he reached the age of 60, so Dowding would certainly complete at least a year in his current position, unless he wished to retire. Ellington went on to hope that Dowding would continue to serve, 'at any rate for two or three years', and saw no reason why he should not continue to express his opinions as forcefully in the future as in the past. Incidentally, he ended, would he be prepared to take on the job of Principal Air Aide-de-Camp to the King?[236]

Although this letter helped to calm Dowding, he now dredged up another grievance. His reply, on 9 February, began with words that surely brought a wry smile to Ellington's face. Dowding claimed to have always had 'rather a contemptuous pity' for passed-over officers complaining about their lot and had no intention of joining their ranks. Nevertheless:

'It seems to me in the highest degree undesirable that it should be possible for a civilian minister to select the future head of one of the fighting services without seeking the advice of its existing chief. His knowledge of the service and its personalities must necessarily be sketchy and his own position is ephemeral, depending as it does on the favour of the Premier and other political considerations.'

The service members of the Air Council should refuse to accept this situation, he argued. As for his own plans, Dowding told Ellington that he was anxious to complete at least a year in his current rank because it would greatly improve his pension. He remained 'keenly interested' in organizing his operations room, introducing radar and moving the Observer Corps onto a war footing, but hoped the new CAS would not find it 'embarrassing' to have a subordinate senior to himself. As for the position of Principal Air ADC, he would be greatly honoured to accept it, if offered. Dowding was only the fifth officer to be so honoured, following Trenchard, John Salmond, Ellington and Brooke-Popham.[237]

Ellington gratefully ended this distressing correspondence on 11 February by reminding Dowding of some facts of life:

'The selection of CASs and Chiefs of Staff is an evil, if it be an evil, of long standing. Henry Wilson [CIGS in 1918, murdered by the IRA in 1922] told me 15 years ago that he did not know who was to be his successor until he saw it in the papers and was never consulted. The Secretary of State decides whether he will consult anyone and the decision is his. That was the case when you were a member of Council and Geoffrey Salmond was selected and also when I was selected.'

The decision had nothing to do with 'my plans', Ellington repeated, and assured Dowding that Newall would want him to stay on. He refrained from reminding him that Frederick Bowhill, then Air Member for Personnel, had told Dowding on 10 March 1936 that his appointment to Fighter Command would be for three years, a perfectly normal length of tenure.[238]

Dowding recovered his balance, helped by heaps of demanding work, but the exchange did nothing to persuade Ellington (or anyone else who learned of it, including subsequent historians) that he should have got the top job. Dowding was deeply gratified in June 1937 to learn that he was to be appointed to the Royal Victorian Order in its highest class, with the Grand Cross (GCVO). This distinction, unlike all other awards and decorations, was in the sovereign's personal gift and conferred only on those who had performed some 'personal service' to him or her. It marked Dowding's admittance to society's highest level, for the Chapel of the Order was an exclusive 'royal peculiar' (exempt from outside jurisdiction) in the Savoy, central London, and a religious service for members was held every four years in St George's Chapel at Windsor. Very few airmen had hitherto been admitted, as Dowding must have known; and he would also have known that 'the establishment' could hardly have done more to soothe his hurt – justified or not – at being passed over for CAS.

The reasons for his elevation were his role as Principal Air ADC to the new king, George VI, and his work as chairman of the Hendon Air Display in 1937.[239] Dowding – now back on an even keel – told Swinton and later Ellington that those who did good work at the displays should be awarded the Air Force Cross (AFC). He specially commended Flight Lieutenant E. M. ('Teddy') Donaldson, reminding Ellington that, 'At the present moment it is very difficult for anyone to get an AFC who is not serving at Martlesham or Farnborough' and has the opportunity at those places to help in experimental work of all kinds. Donaldson *did* get an AFC; he and his brothers would earn far greater distinctions when war came.[240]

Fighter Tactics

Meanwhile, on 7 May 1937, Dowding had lectured on fighter tactics to officers at 11 Group headquarters in Uxbridge, raising numerous points for anxious debate throughout Fighter Command for years to come and giving the pilots in his audience plenty of food for thought. Here are some examples. What was the most effective distance at which to open fire? Should machine guns be thought of as a precise rifle or an imprecise shotgun: that is, angled so as to hit a small area very hard or to hit a larger area less hard? He answered this question himself: pilots were not expected to hit enemy aircrew in the head, but to spray their fire throughout the fuselage. During the Battle of Britain, however, the better pilots preferred the former option, finding that enemy bombers could withstand a great deal of puncturing by rifle-calibre machine guns. Would synchronized attacks by two or more fighters be possible? How dangerous was return fire from the rear-gunners of enemy bombers? How much armour should fighters carry and where best should it be placed? How should enemy formations, small or large, flying high or coming in at low levels, be challenged? Would two-seater fighters offer significant advantages over single-seaters?[241]

At this time, Dowding accepted the opinion later expounded in the *Manual of Air Tactics* in 1938 that 'manoeuvres at high speeds in air fighting is not now practicable because the effect of gravity on the human body during rapid changes of direction at high speed causes a temporary loss of consciousness.' Monoplane fighters would therefore be unable to engage each other and must focus on shooting down bombers. This could best be done by formations of three fighters, flying in a tight vee. In fact, when war came, the tight vee ensured that two out of every three pilots spent more time vigilantly watching their leader, in order to avoid collisions, than they did searching the sky for enemies.

It would only be during the Battle of Britain that Dowding's pilots gradually learned from Luftwaffe experience in the Spanish Civil War: four fighters, in two pairs, proved to be a far more efficient formation than the vee of three fighters. In the German system, 'Each pilot searched inward, as well as to his front, scanning the hemisphere of sky beyond and behind his partner for any sign of the enemy'; all four were poised to attack at any time, whereas in the British system only the leader of the vee was.[242]

Dowding and his staff had a better understanding of the likely course of fighter combat than most Air Ministry officers. For example, Slessor (often regarded as one of Whitehall's more thoughtful Warriors) suggested in 1936 that the RAF needed only a few single-seat fighters for air defence, since a two-seat fighter offered a better chance of shooting down bombers. As late as June 1938, an Air Staff note on 'Employment of Two-seater and Single-seater Fighters in a Home Defence War' attracted a minute written by Donald Stevenson (Deputy Director of Home Operations) in which he argued vigorously for the *Defiant* over the Spitfire and Hurricane. Dowding objected even more vigorously and, mercifully, successfully.[243]

Douglas (Assistant CAS), Stevenson and others were strongly in favour of two-seater fighters. At that time, Douglas thought single-seaters were 'practically restricted to attacks from directly astern' and wished to equip no fewer than nine of Fighter Command's planned strength of 38 squadrons with two-seaters. Bearing in mind his experience in the Great War, Douglas was convinced that 'for work over enemy territory a two-seater fighter is best'. Dowding disagreed and was in any case reluctant to see any of his fighters employed 'over enemy territory'. As he told the Air Ministry on 20 June 1938 he was 'not at all keen' on intercepting bombers far out to sea because the pilots of any fighters shot down would probably be drowned, whereas they might well survive if shot down over land.[244]

In June 1938 Douglas had informed him that he must form nine squadrons of Defiants for no better reason than that 450 were already on order. They had been ordered in the mistaken belief that they would emulate, as Ludlow-Hewitt (head of Bomber Command) told the Air Ministry, 'the tremendous success of the Bristols in the last war'. For some unfathomable reason, Ludlow and other senior officers quite overlooked the well-known fact that the Bristol Fighter had relied primarily on its forward-firing guns, as has every other successful fighter produced anywhere in the world since the dawn of aviation.

Most senior officers in the late 1930s had served in the Great War and it is amazing that some of them had forgotten this elementary point. Douglas, who always had a very high opinion of his own merits, later claimed to have been 'a well-known fighter pilot and an expert on air fighting when in its infancy'. Neither claim will stand close scrutiny. He did indeed serve throughout the war – as did many of his contemporaries – in combat or training or command duties, but he met with virtually no success in aerial combat. He certainly failed to shoot down five enemy aircraft: the minimum qualification for 'ace' status. In this respect, among others, his record bears no comparison with that of Park, for instance, whose tactical handling of the Battle of Britain he felt qualified to criticize so relentlessly in 1940.[245]

As for Stevenson, he ignored the fact that the Defiant, carrying two men and a heavy turret, weighed at least half a ton more than the Hurricane, equipped with the same Merlin engine. He somehow persuaded himself that the Defiant was 'slightly faster'. It was, in fact, markedly inferior at every point of comparison: level speed, rate of climb, manoeuvrability; above all, in capacity for inflicting damage on enemy aircraft or resisting destruction by conventional fighters.

Stevenson was quite mistaken, thought Dowding, in his thoughts on tactics: fighters could easily attack bombers from areas other than dead astern, but it was the mindset of Stevenson (and others) in the Air Ministry that revived for Dowding bitter memories of the shocking mismanagement of Britain's air power in 1916. 'I hate the implication' of Stevenson's note, which suggests that 'the wasteful and bloody policy of the Somme is to be perpetuated, whereby tiny formations of fighters were sent out day after day to be continually subjected to anti-aircraft fire, and to be attacked in superior numbers whenever the enemy chose to do so.'[246]

In response to growing doubts about the wisdom of the turret-fighter concept, Stevenson informed Dowding in June 1939 that he was to have six, not nine, Defiant squadrons. Dowding remained unhappy. He was now, he said, 'faced with the necessity of placing the Defiants where they will do the least harm', and sensibly proposed to use them solely for training, where they would have had real value, but the Air Ministry was reluctant to cut its losses so drastically. In the event, only two squadrons were actually formed for daytime use and suffered appalling casualties during both the French campaign and the battle following. Unfortunately, so many had been built and taken into service that as many as 13 squadrons were formed for use in darkness. They achieved little and during 1942 the survivors gave useful service as target tugs, as far as possible away from the Luftwaffe.[247]

A few days after his 7 May lecture, on 24 May 1937, Dowding spoke to students at the RAF Staff College at Andover in Hampshire. He woke them out of their comfortable doze by considering how it would be possible 'most quickly to lose a war'. That would happen if Londoners panicked under aerial attack or if Britain's imports of food were cut off. We could be defeated in less than a fortnight if these two disasters came together. Fighter Command, however, would prevent them. 'Imagine, if you can,' he said, 'that I am dictator of a European country.' He would attempt to 'paralyse' an enemy air force, keep it paralysed and then, at his leisure, 'adopt any of the methods of frightfulness which are most likely to bring victory in the shortest possible time.'

Britain's defences may prove efficient, he told the students – who were now, presumably, actually listening – but we cannot win a war unless our bombers systematically destroy those of the enemy, his reserves, factories and fuel supplies. As for Fighter Command's task, we cannot know when or in what force the enemy will attack and so our preparations are very wide-ranging. We must protect not only London but also our factories, private homes and docks, our ports and convoys of both ocean-going and coastal ships from warships and submarines as well as aircraft. These will be difficult tasks, he freely admitted, because we cannot be everywhere all the time. Dowding then went on to outline the defensive system, emphasizing the importance of the Observer Corps, and adding:

> 'There is another means of obtaining information about the enemy's approach. I regret that I cannot give you much information about this system because its existence is very secret, and I must specially ask all present here today not to refer to the existence of this organization which has been christened RDF.'[248]

Operations Rooms

In 1937 it was hoped that the radar system would comprise about 20 detecting stations scattered around the southern and eastern coasts of Britain from the Isle of Wight to the Firth of Forth. Every aircraft approaching the country within that area would be detected, if the system worked properly, by at least two stations. A means of collating their reports, identifying friendly aircraft, allotting a number to each enemy aircraft (or formation of aircraft) and passing the information simultaneously to every operations room was needed. The term 'filtering' was given to this activity. Dowding centralized filtering at Bentley Priory in a room adjacent to his operations room. Ultimately, the two rooms would form part of an underground 'operations block'. A massive rectangular crater was dug to receive them, and duplicate (or 'stand by') rooms were provided elsewhere for use in case of emergency.[249]

Operations rooms at the headquarters of formations down to station level, in which the positions of both hostile and friendly aircraft could be plotted on squared maps, would need to be manned continuously, day and night. But such rooms did not exist at all headquarters, let alone stations, and nothing had been done about continuous manning except when exercises were in progress – and these exercises were notoriously unrealistic. Artificial restrictions were imposed on the forces taking part and, as Dowding observed, no attempt was made to plot outgoing or incoming bombers not deemed hostile for the purpose of the exercise.[250]

All operations rooms were eventually laid out on the same pattern. On a dais sat the senior controller, flanked by assistants and liaison officers. All places on the dais were provided with communications to squadrons, to aircraft in the air, and to all other units and headquarters to which messages needed to be sent. Wireless operators sat in cubicles behind the dias in contact with airborne fighters. Radio cross-bearings of sector aircraft were plotted and the results passed to the main operations room. The senior controller could see at a glance plots of hostile raids as well as the movements of his own fighters, the state of the local weather, and the state of readiness of his squadrons. He could even see how much petrol and oxygen his airborne fighters had left.[251]

An informal arrangement was made between Albert Rowe and Squadron Leader Raymund Hart (who both had distinguished careers ahead of them in radar research) for a small group of scientists to move to Bentley Priory in the event of war. Hart began a long association with radar development at Bawdsey, where the first radar station was built. He took part in experiments at Biggin Hill, where the basis of a modern air defence system was laid. In particular, Hart 'was responsible for injecting the service requirements – as opposed to the scientific ideals – into the creation of a practical system.' He advocated filtering, whereby information from a number of radar stations was compared and turned into a picture that was intelligible to controllers, who had to decide what to do with their aircraft. 'Although the highly-centralized filter room system' was Hart's particular brain-child, he knew that a centralized system was vulnerable 'and always pressed for decentralization which could only come about as the standard of information from the individual radar stations became intelligible on its own account.'

Hart foresaw, more clearly than Dowding, a time when information taken directly from the cathode ray tubes at radar stations, rather than from filter rooms, might lead to quicker interception of intruders. Nevertheless, he worked closely and amicably with Dowding in evolving airborne radar and in setting up GCI stations, both of which were vital in achieving interceptions at night.[252]

A team moved to Bentley Priory for the summer exercises of 1939 under Eric Williams, a young science graduate from Birmingham University, to observe the working of the filter room and proved so helpful that Dowding asked for it to be attached permanently. At the same time, a second group – under Geoffrey Roberts, formerly a post office engineer – was sent by Rowe to observe how group controllers were handling the information provided by the radar chain. They concentrated on techniques for controlling aircraft during an actual interception attempt. Robert invented an automatic plotting device, the 'fruit machine', which converted range and direction into a grid reference far more quickly and accurately than even the most skilled operators could use a manual converter. Thanks to Dowding's support, dozens of these machines came into service during 1940.[253]

Roberts's team was also attached to Bentley Priory by September under Harold Larnder, a radio engineer who had wide experience in communications work all over the world before joining the staff at Bawdsey in 1935. Larnder was a godsend to Dowding, for he was able to get on equally well with both civilian scientists and RAF officers, and had the personality needed to get a group of ambitious, self-confident individuals pulling in the same direction.

The unusual step of appointing civilians to a military headquarters was taken because radar was so new and knowledge about what it could do was increasing almost daily. It was therefore essential that its progress be constantly monitored by those who best understood it. When war came, the group (named 'Fighter Command Operational Research Section' in 1941) comprised engineers, physicists, a biologist, a minerologist who understood about gun harmonization, graduates in English and Geography, a statistician and several botanists.[254]

Keith Park arrived at Bentley Priory in July 1938 as Dowding's second-in-command. He and Hart worked together on operations room problems: Hart on the equipment, Park on the practical layout. Hart had been attached to Bawdsey research station in 1936 to supervise radar training and to act as a link between the scientists there and command headquarters. He convinced Park that the plotting on the general situation map was too elaborate. For example, were the indicated aircraft friendly or hostile? Were there duplications caused by reports from two or more radar stations or Observer Corps posts? Park therefore introduced a second table on which could be displayed a clean, filtered, plot once queries had been resolved. Only this filtered plot should be passed to the main table. Dowding rejected the idea of a second table when Park suggested it to him, but he and Hart decided to set it up secretly in the basement. When Dowding realized 'his general situation map seemed to be much more readable and his operations room far more quiet and well-regulated', he was convinced.[255]

Petrol, Training and Accident Problems

Dowding wrote to 'Dear Ludlow' on 16 September 1937 about one of the aggravating problems distracting him from the higher purpose he and his masters had in mind for safeguarding Britain from the possibility of German aggression. He had visited Usworth, near Newcastle in Northumberland and found 607 Squadron, lodging at a Bomber Command station, in a hopeless position with regard to its essential petrol supplies. He was told it took four days to get petrol from the Shellmex installation [near Thornaby in north Yorkshire]. Shellmex would not deliver less than 1,200 gallons or multiples of 1,200 gallons at a time, but the squadron had only two tankers and was obliged to spend hours filling barrels. The squadron, like several others, needed ready access to its own storage tanks and the whole command was woefully short of tankers. Solving, or trying to solve, such basic problems never figures prominently in any account of Fighter Command's preparations for war and yet they consumed a great deal of Dowding's time and energy.[256]

Another problem concerned training. On 22 February 1938 Dowding sent his training report for the year 1937 to the Air Ministry. He was greatly concerned about a large number of new pilots coming into the command and an extreme shortage of experienced flight commanders to look after them. The Hendon Display, for all its advantages in keeping the RAF in the public eye, imposed a heavy burden upon all ranks, especially in 11 Group, and Dowding feared it was becoming 'something of an ever-swelling monster'.

It was also a great waste of time, from the point of view of useful training. For example, in June 1937 three modern Gloster Gladiator biplane fighters had 'attacked' a couple of ancient Vickers Virginia twin-engined bombers, painted bright red to make an 'artistic contrast' – so the press enthused – with the clear blue sky. After fooling about for some time, the bombers dropped eight dummies by parachute: 'these made as pretty a picture as ever', when they floated neatly across the aerodrome. Other events were only marginally more realistic, and there can be no doubt that the enormous crowd – at least 190,000 people – went away happy. So did Dowding, putting aside his grave concerns about the future for once, because it was on this occasion that the King invested him with the insignia of a Knight Grand Cross of the Royal Victorian Order.[257]

Turning his attention away from such trivial matters, Dowding thought there was a need for more armament training camps and more opportunity for realistic training, above all in firing practice at moving targets, when squadrons went there. Fighting tactics were in constant need of revision, as more and faster monoplanes came into service and pilots learned how vastly superior they were to the old biplanes. But everyone's work, Dowding emphasized, was held up by a shortage of modern aircraft, of dual control aircraft, of flying aids and, not least, of sealed runways: many grass airfields became too soggy to use in wintertime. On a happier note, he found the expansion of the Observer Corps satisfactory and personnel becoming more accurate in their identifications and estimate of altitude, but more work was needed to improve co-operation between aircraft on the one hand, and anti-aircraft guns and searchlights on the other. It was a very thorough report and detailed comments on the points raised were made by a host of Air Ministry officials.[258]

His report in September on a combined training exercise carried out in August 1937 had been more critical. There was 'a lack of reality' all round in both bombing and interception, and the night bombing results were 'deplorable', but he again praised the efforts of the Observer Corps.[259]

A few months later, on 1 April 1938, Dowding wrote again to Ludlow-Hewitt about accidents, a matter that increasingly worried both commanders as monoplanes came into service that were not only faster, but also full of equipment demanding more careful handling – including remembering to lower retractable undercarriages when landing – than the familiar and simpler biplanes on which pilots learned to fly. The service had a dreadful accident rate these days caused, Dowding thought, by 'a careless and casual attitude towards the dangers of flying and a lack of method in handling the extremely complicated mechanism with which the pilot is now equipped.'

He wrote again to Ludlow-Hewitt on 23 April to point out a marked discrepancy in the accident rate between Fighter and Bomber Commands. In the last 24 months, Bomber Command had had 231 cases of mishandling engine controls, plus no fewer than 478 forced landings due to pilots losing their way. In Fighter Command, by contrast, there had only been 19 mishandling cases during the last 12 months and 33 forced landings, 13 of them by university students under training. Dowding did not cite these statistics in order to gloat and told Ludlow-Hewitt that the discrepancy was probably because fighters were simpler and smaller machines than bombers; they also had short-wave RT sets capable of giving homing directions. He personally studied every accident report and had issued, since the formation of Fighter Command, numerous instructions about coping with bad visibility, avoiding dangerous manoeuvres, and the need to wear properly fastened sutton harness and a parachute at all times.

He had 'the highest admiration' for 'the inexperienced boys' trying to fill these duties:

> 'But the fact remains that they cannot possibly have the knowledge and experience to supervise and control the flying education of numerous other pilots even less experienced than themselves. I feel that we have been very patient under this handicap for the last two years, realizing that the primary requirement in any expansion must be the training of new pilots, but this state of affairs no longer obtains; so many pilots have been trained that there are not enough machines for them to fly, and they have become a serious embarrassment to service units.'

He then came to the point. Ludlow-Hewitt, he wrote, could count on his full support in telling the Air Ministry that the time had come to end the monopolization of experienced pilots by training establishments and send more of them to squadrons.[260]

On 17 May 1938 Newall sent Dowding a table showing his estimate of likely combat losses if war broke out. Dowding replied on 10 June. You make 'a gross over-estimate of the casualties likely to be incurred by home defence fighters in air fighting,' he told Newall. 'It may represent a fair figure for field force fighters, if they are used in the same prodigal fashion as obtained on the Western Front' during the Great War. Newall, ever a man to prefer a quiet life, wisely ignored this barb and made no reply.[261]

On 26 May, no doubt prodded into action by the Secretary of State, Newall warned Dowding against undue co-operation with France. Staff conversations, wrote Newall, were shortly to take place, but were only to cover 'administrative arrangements' if British aircraft were ever sent across the Channel. He was most anxious that Dowding should not encourage the French to discuss war plans. No mention was to be made of radar, Fighter Command's organization or operations rooms, explosive ammunition, aircraft or engine production figures, aircraft reserves, or indeed of anything whatever that might possibly suggest effective co-operation between Britain and France in the event of war against Germany.[262] This dismal letter confirmed Dowding's belief that Britain stood virtually alone in the event of German aggression. There could be no question of the air forces of Britain and France offering anything approaching a joint challenge to Germany in the air or on the ground until some time after an invasion had actually begun. Meanwhile, Dowding reasoned, he must work even harder at extending and strengthening Britain's defences.

10

Strengthening Fighter Command, 1938-1939

Removing Dowding: Round One

Dowding had been appointed head of Fighter Command for a term of three years in July 1936, so he had no reason to be surprised in June 1938 when Newall privately reminded him that he was to be replaced in the following July. An official confirmation of this decision was sent to him on 4 August. To offset this disappointment, even though it was one long foreseen, there was good news for the family in that same month of June 1938: his brother Arthur was made a Commander of the Order of the Bath (CB) and learned in July that he was to be appointed admiral superintendent of the naval dockyard at Devonport from September.[263]

Sadly, there now began a saga that caused Dowding much heartache, lasting throughout the fearful crisis of the Battle of Britain, because the Air Ministry could not decide, once and for all, after Courtney's accident ruled him out of employment for several months, whether to keep Dowding on or find him another position.

Dowding had always had a low opinion of his masters in Whitehall, whether in the War Office or in the Air Ministry, and by the later 1930s he was by no means alone in the latter opinion. For years senior officers of the Army and the Royal Navy, civil servants and politicians elsewhere in Whitehall had been exasperated by the muddle, indecision and conflicting statements regularly emerging from the Air Ministry's various offices. In Churchill's opinion, based on years of close observation, an opinion supplemented by a steady stream of information coming from disaffected RAF officers, 'jealousies and cliquism' were rampant in 'a most cumbersome and ill-working administrative machine'. As long ago as July 1934, a retired air commodore, Peregrine Fellowes, had complained to Churchill about the serious lack of 'practical knowledge of flying' among senior officers at the Air Ministry. 'Many senior officers,' he said, 'seldom flew even as passengers.'[264] There the matter rested, until the early months of 1939.

Dowding had written to his masters in the Air Ministry on 27 June 1938 after a meeting of the Air Fighting Committee. At that meeting, he said pilots of single-engined fighters needed no protection from enemy fire beyond that of their engines and bullet-proof windscreens. He was wrong, he now thought: pilots might be hit in the chest or throat unless an extra metal plate was fitted above the engine. He returned to this subject in October: we must do more, he said, to protect pilots from injury or death in the event of fire in their own petrol tanks.[265]

Next day, 28 June, Dowding offered 'Some Notes on the Protection of Vital Points Against Low-Flying Attack by Aircraft' to members of the Home Defence Committee of which he was chairman. It was a large and important committee, including senior officers of all three services. Unlike many Britons – servicemen, civilians and especially politicians – he saw no special threat to Britain from the Luftwaffe, least of all from its dive-bombers, as long as they were based in Germany: they lacked the range to cover so great a distance, out and home, and deliver a heavy load of bombs. Moreover, German bombers must reach British targets unescorted, for their fighters were all short-range, and therefore they would be at the mercy of British fighters, operating from bases close to any targets the Germans threatened. He urged everyone present to resist 'a tendency to attribute superhuman qualities to the enemy's bomber pilots.' At this and other committee meetings Dowding discussed with members his problems with guns, searchlights, balloons, the radar chain, observers and emphasised the difficulty of carrying out practical trials of any weapons in peacetime.[266]

Weaknesses in the System
The home defence exercise in August 1938 revealed many weaknesses in the system that Dowding was trying to devise. Radar stations did not always find the friendly aircraft they were trying to help, and would therefore struggle to pinpoint enemy aircraft doing their best to evade the defences. Operations rooms were understaffed and those men and women working there needed more experience, shorter shifts and better ventilation. A means of separating friendly from enemy signals had not yet been found. Many more telephone links were needed and also an underground operations block at Bentley Priory.

Dowding spoke at length, and with unusual passion, about the difficulty of finding an effective IFF (Indentification Friend or Foe) device at a conference in Bentley Priory on 11 October 1938. This had been a serious weakness clearly recognised, but unsolved, during the Great War. Without such a device, any air defence system could be overwhelmed by the need to intercept every approaching aircraft, on the assumption that it might be hostile. Also, mistakes in identification resulted in friendly aircraft being attacked while returning to their bases from anywhere overseas.

Eric Williams was set to work on this problem at Bawdsey by Albert Rowe and by March 1939 had apparently found a solution. He demonstrated it to Dowding on the 4th, who was both relieved and delighted. An automatic identification signal, he reported to the Air Ministry, showed up clearly on radar screens; it would be cheap and easy to install and operators would be able to tell friendly from enemy aircraft. It became known as 'pipsqueak' because of the high-pitched squeak it transmitted for 14 seconds in every minute. However, it took much longer than Dowding hoped to perfect and then to produce a device that would become 'a centrepiece of the increasingly complex air defence system', and it only became acceptably reliable on the very eve of the Battle of Britain. By the end of February 1940, no more than 258 aircraft, mostly bombers, were carrying the device, but by October virtually every RAF aircraft was fitted with it. During this testing time, Dowding had asked the experts to find some means of destroying pipsqueak if the aircraft carrying it crashed in enemy territory. They did so, much to his relief, because otherwise it was likely that the Germans would learn how to duplicate its response to radar signals.

Although these and other vital improvements were made either before September 1939 or during the months allowed by Hitler for practice, there were failures: among them, the ability to assess accurately the altitude of intruders. Another of great concern to Dowding was the slow introduction of Very High Frequency (VHF) air-to-ground telephones. Reliable communication between fighters, ground controllers and direction finding was essential to the system. High Frequency (HF) equipment had to be used, even though it was neither as good nor compatible with VHF. Work went ahead on a superior TR 1130 VHF radio, but adequate supplies were not available until mid-August.

Behind all these worries about equipment, Dowding was constantly concerned about finding and training personnel to use it. This was a problem never solved during his time at Bentley Priory – nor, indeed, for long afterwards. Here lay a basic weakness in his system. There simply had not been sufficient time to recruit and train enough men and women to use equipment that was at what we nowadays call 'the cutting edge'; those charged with training duties were themselves finding either that new devices appeared regularly or that unforeseen snags arose when attempting to use relatively old devices. Throughout his time at Bentley Priory, Dowding always welcomed an opportunity to discuss these and other vital issues with the scientists and technicians working in great secrecy at Bawdsey. He was greatly impressed by their understanding of defence problems and their determination to solve them.[267]

At Odds with Bomber Command

Air Ministry theorists had for years waxed eloquently about the capacity of bombers to win any future war, but they did nothing useful to translate persuasive theories into effective practice. For example, by what means would bomber crews find and then hit their target either by day or by night in bad weather over unfamiliar territory? Actually, they could not do it even over familiar territory. During a night exercise in 1937, two-thirds of a bomber force failed to find the very large and fully-illuminated city of Birmingham. Matters did not improve: during 1938 and 1939, numerous bomber crews simply got lost. If they did learn to find a target, how accurate were bomb sights? Would the bombs dropped be heavy enough to cause serious damage? How certain was it that they would explode? And would incendiaries serve better than high explosives?[268]

These were all matters of constant concern to Dowding. He was preparing an effective defence of Britain, but he was acutely aware of the fact that if war came, an effective *offence* would also be required. In other words, his fighters would, he hoped, prevent defeat, but they could not deliver victory.

On 28 July 1938, a few days before the home defence exercise in August, Dowding complained to Park that he had been 'badly held up' last year by not receiving details of what the bombers had done 'and when I did get these reports they were incomplete and inaccurate.' The exercise was intended to test the efficiency of both Bomber and Fighter Command over two days, but failed to do so. It was pointless, he said, to have 'friendly' and 'enemy' aircraft working from the same aerodromes. The efforts of radar operators and Observer Corps personnel promised well, although they lacked experience and their working conditions were poor, but the defence system was short of anti-aircraft guns and searchlights. Aircraft must be more widely dispersed on aerodromes even though this made life more difficult for ground crews, and lights in bomber cockpits were too easily visible to attacking fighters. Controllers still had no means of distinguishing between friendly and enemy aircraft.[269]

Bomber Command's reluctance to co-operate enthusiastically in home defence exercises vexed Dowding. On his behalf, Park wrote unusually bluntly to Ludlow-Hewitt in December 1938. He criticized the absence from Ludlow-Hewitt's instructions regarding monthly exercises of any mention of the need to test fighter groups in the control of their sectors and squadrons, neither, he maintained, was any awareness shown of the need to test radar and air-raid warning systems. His list of objectives, Park noted, was concerned solely with his own command.[270]

After an exercise in January 1939, Park wrote to two bomber group commanders, pointing out to one that he had attached an out-of-date map of the area covered by radar stations to his operation orders, and to the other that he was evidently unaware of the area covered since only two bomber raids used it. The relevant information had been sent from Bentley Priory to command headquarters, but not forwarded to the groups.

In May 1939, Park wrote again to Ludlow-Hewitt on behalf of Albert Rowe, in charge at Bawdsey. Rowe wanted a copy of bomber raid schedules two or three days before the August exercise. He could then send men to the radar stations concerned with tracking them and study the results. But Ludlow-Hewitt's staff officers were unable to cope with this obviously important request, even though it was made in good time. Such slackness, contrasting sharply with Fighter Command's alertness under Dowding, was normal in Bomber Command, even though it was always regarded in the Air Ministry as the élite force. However, it would not be until April 1940 that Ludlow-Hewitt was sacked – a rare act of decision by Newall. Not 'relieved', not 're-assigned', not let down gently by any other consoling euphemism, but sacked. As he himself put it, when he heard the bad news on 15 March, 'CAS gives me the boot.'[271]

Even the simplest matters had baffled his staff. As an exasperated Dowding told Park on 24 May 1939:

'I am a much misunderstood man! I have never asked that "one particular type of aircraft" shall be used to represent friendly bombers.... My point is that *all* aircraft of any particular type shall be friendly or *all* enemy.'

Otherwise, of course, confusion was certain. Park tried to explain this to Norman Bottomley, his opposite number at Bomber Command, the next day without success. Dowding yielded as often as he dared in an effort to exact genuine co-operation, but he got none. For example, during exercises bombers must start their approach from 100 miles out to sea, if the fighters and the radar system were to have realistic practice, but Ludlow had no confidence either in the minimal navigational skills of his crews or in the reliability of single-engined 'bombers' and refused to allow them to fly more than ten miles from British coasts.[272]

Primed by Dowding, Park wrote again to Bottomley on 31 May with masterly politeness hiding extreme exasperation. It was generally agreed, said Park, that in the event of war the Germans were unlikely to employ bombers one at a time against inland targets. Would Bomber Command therefore stop using single aircraft in the exercises? In our opinion, retorted Bottomley, that is precisely what the Germans *would* do. Although it beggars belief that a responsible senior officer could hold such an absurd opinion, Bottomley presumably amended it after the outbreak of war, for he was not sacked, but went on to fill important positions, eventually retiring as an air chief marshal – the same rank that Dowding achieved.[273]

Dowding wrote to Ludlow-Hewitt on 20 June 1939, enclosing a copy of a letter from Trafford Leigh-Mallory (head of 12 Group) about the cancellation of a joint Fighter/Bomber Command exercise on 1 June. One of Dowding's staff officers had gone to Hucknall, north of Nottingham, to attend the exercise and was astonished at the cancellation. 'Will you consider instructing your Groups,' Dowding asked, 'not to cancel exercises in anticipation of bad weather, but to wait until the time when raids are due to depart?' This was the second time 5 Group had cancelled, unilaterally and prematurely. It was commanded by an air commodore, one William Callaway, who was replaced in September by a rather more dynamic character, Arthur Harris. Callaway only learned that he had been sacked when Harris marched into his office: a not untypical example of sloppy organization in the Air Ministry.[274]

Neville the Unready

'The time of anxiety is past,' said King George VI on 2 October 1938, reading words written for him by the Prime Minister, Neville 'the Unready' Chamberlain, 'and we have been able today to offer our thanks to the Almighty for His mercy in sparing us the horrors of war.' The nickname of King Aethelred II (968-1016), is *unraed*, which actually translates as 'lacking in counsel', but those words, as well as 'unready', serve just as well for a prime minister of impenetrable arrogance, whose closest advisers were (in Churchill's words) 'time-servers and careerists'. Between them, they fecklessly exposed their people to invaders. At a dinner party in late 1938, the question of Hitler's false assurances came up. 'Ah,' replied Chamberlain, 'but this time he promised *me*.'[275] As prime minister, he had insisted on conducting foreign policy personally even though he had no knowledge of foreign people or places. His arrogance matched his incompetence, for he had no-one with him to take notes at his meetings with Hitler and, unable to understand German, was wholly reliant on whatever Hitler's interpreter reported that either man said. The fact that Hitler regarded Chamberlain and all who served him as 'arseholes' played its part in confirming his belief that Britain would never seriously oppose his aggression.[276]

On 30 September, Chamberlain had signed an agreement with Hitler in Munich to dismember Czechoslovakia. 'The real triumph' of that agreement, he declared in the House of Commons on 3 October, was to have 'averted a catastrophe which would have ended civilization as we have known it.' Not everyone in Britain agreed, and neither did those Czechs and Poles who later fought so valiantly and skilfully in Fighter Command and in Britain's armies.[277]

However, it has to be said that the crises with Germany over the fate of Czechoslovakia in September and early October found Britain's air defences woefully unprepared, thanks in large part though to Chamberlain and his colleagues. Arnold Lunn recalled spending a night with Dowding during September. 'He was gloomy about the ability of the French to hold up the Germans', if war came, and was therefore greatly relieved by news of the settlement.[278] At that time, Dowding had 29 squadrons nominally fit for service of the 45 thought essential to meet a potential crisis in six month's time, March 1939. None of them were equipped with Spitfires and only five with Hurricanes – which at that time were useless above 15,000 feet because their guns froze.

Dowding did learn, however, in September that 100 octane fuel – imported from the United States – had been approved for his fighters, though none was released until as late as May 1940.[279] Both Hurricanes and Spitfires (when they came into service) were to be fitted with constant speed airscrews and these changes, taken together, greatly improved performance. Five squadrons had the most modern biplane fighter available (the Gladiator, armed with four machine guns). The rest had to make do with older and less well-armed biplanes. All lacked the performance and armament needed to match the latest German monoplane fighters in combat, but Dowding knew that these could not escort bombers to and from British targets, as long as they flew from bases in Germany. He was more concerned about the fact that no barrage balloons were yet in place, few searchlights were yet available and only one-third of the promised heavy anti-aircraft guns.

As for the offensive arm, Bomber Command was in a far worse state than Fighter Command despite all the words lavished for so many years by so many officers on its deterrent power. If Britain had gone to war with Germany in the autumn of 1938, as a number of eminent historians have argued, Dowding could have raised about 565 fighters, most of them obsolete biplanes. No part of his system was yet ready for a major challenge, but he had a reasonable hope that those biplanes would at least disrupt bomber formations and shoot some down before his monoplane fighters came along to give more effective help.

Bomber Command, however, would have achieved nothing useful if called upon to attack German targets in late 1938. It was equipped with 1,100 machines designated as 'bombers', but few of them could have reached even western Germany, with a light load of bombs, from British bases, unless they ignored the neutrality of the Low Countries. If based in France, some damage could have been done, but such a transfer was unrealistic, for a host of logistic as well as political reasons.[280]

By now, Dowding had foreseen that attacks would be made on his aerodromes and wondered what would happen to fighters dispersed around them. In his usual way, he urged a test and after long argument was allowed to have 30 obsolete Bristol Bulldog fighters spread in a circle on Salisbury Plain. They were attacked for a week in July 1938 by various bombers from high and low levels, with large and small bombs, incendiaries and machine-gun fire.[281] At the end of the week, Dowding composed a report more devastating than the bombing: 22 tons of high explosive bombs, 1,000 incendiaries and 7,000 rounds of machine-gun fire had destroyed three Bulldogs, damaged one beyond repair, left 15 with minor damage and 11 completely unharmed. These shockingly bad results indicated that dispersal alone might give fighters a fair chance of survival, unless the Luftwaffe proved to be more accurate than Bomber Command. The test also demonstrated the appalling gulf between theory and practice in RAF doctrine with regard to bombing.[282]

During October 1938, Dowding had a report compiled on the organization and operation of his command during the recent crises. Park drew attention to several weaknesses: shortage of fighter squadrons; lack of a sector organization either in the south-west or in the far north of Britain; a poor serviceability rate because spare parts for modern fighters were as yet in short supply; and a need for unskilled labour to work as guards or to repair bomb craters or to fill ammunition belts. In addition more balloons, anti-aircraft weapons, searchlights, radar stations and radio equipment were also needed, together with intensive training in making efficient use of these. Dowding added a need for more Observer Corps posts and personnel, plus guarantees of time off from their normal work and better pay, and asked for many more land lines and attempts to camouflage vulnerable targets.[283]

In October 1938 Rowe told Dowding that significant progress had been made since August by radar stations in counting aircraft approaching from seaward. Until August, he said, they could only distinguish between one and more than one. They were now capable of doing better, but progress was handicapped by the lack of large numbers of aircraft to use in trials. Since Dowding thought such trials very important, Rowe hoped the Air Ministry would arrange for sufficient aircraft to be provided.[285]

Improvements in the System
The defence of ports and naval bases was a particular worry because there were so many of them, all important for military or economic reasons. Dowding wrote to the Air Ministry on this subject in February 1939. In

England, he maintained, Chatham [in Kent, on the Medway estuary] was the most vulnerable port 'because it is situated in the middle of what will probably be one of my most active sectors.' Dover, Harwich, the Humber, Tees and Tyne were all, he thought, easier problems to solve. 'Portsmouth is probably more important than any of the foregoing from the naval point of view, but it is less of a problem from the general aspect of air defence.' Plymouth was likely to be safe, but it was clear that 'an extensive programme of work lies before us.'

Dowding therefore recommended a stronger Admiralty presence on the defence committee and also someone to speak on behalf of Coastal Command. In April 1939 the committee discussed the defence of the Royal Navy's bases at Scapa Flow in the Orkneys and Rosyth (on the north bank of the Firth of Forth, nearly opposite Edinburgh), also Northern Ireland, especially the Belfast docks. All were likely targets, all remote from the centres of Dowding's power. Finding what would be needed (airfields, fighters, pilots, ground crews, observers, radar equipment and personnel to operate it) would stretch, perhaps overstretch, the Air Ministry and his defensive system.[285]

Another improvement that Dowding had constantly in mind concerned his fighters. Good as the basic designs were, he was well aware that much could be done – in armament, armour, more powerful engines – to make them even better weapons. He wrote to the Air Ministry about them on 25 July 1939. He had had a Hurricane and a Spitfire tested at various heights and found, as he expected, that the performance reported by experimental stations was not matched by aircraft received for squadron service: 'expert pilots,' he said, 'handling fighters under ideal conditions, will always get results that have to be scaled down by squadron commanders working under operational pressure on airfields with less skilled pilots and ground crews.'

A four-day exercise held in early August 1939, when Dowding's 'Westland' opposed Ludlow-Hewitt's 'Eastland', was written up by the aeronautical correspondent of *The Times* with breathless enthusiasm. It was in fact the largest and most realistic of all peacetime exercises. The 'defensive machinery over fully one-third of England', he wrote, would be tested by no fewer than 500 bombers. Both commanders hoped local authorities and private civilians would co-operate by not turning on their lights each evening, but there was no compulsion to do so and many did not. The enemy bombers would approach their targets from a distance of up to 100 miles, 'and find the land beneath is nothing but a pool of darkness', just as they would if war had been declared; in fact, lights were burning everywhere.

'The scales will be weighted in favour of the defence' because the enemy will know 'that his movements are being watched, his courses checked, guns laid on him, and fighters sent up to destroy him'; and a balloon barrage will make low level or diving attacks extremely dangerous. Some 600 searchlights will be at work and twice as many members of the Observer Corps as were available in 1938 will be on duty.

By the end of the exercise, improvements had been made. Filtering was working, Observer Corps reports were being co-ordinated with radar tracks, low-level radar stations had been built, radio communication with aircraft was better. At least in daylight and even in bad weather, the defensive system promised well. Dowding made his first wireless broadcast on the eve of war, discussed the exercise, and said he was satisfied with the results. 'I confidently believe that serious air attacks on these islands,' he said, 'would be brought to a standstill in a short space of time.' If launched, as he did not say, from German bases.[286]

Park later recalled what he always considered one of Dowding's outstanding achievements as head of Fighter Command: his capacity for delegation. There was strong resistance, Park thought, in the years 1938-40 among some staff officers at Bentley Priory to the idea that instead of direct control its operations room should focus on broad direction, inter-group reinforcement and the dissemination of information. In defence exercises, it upset these officers to learn that they should not interfere, even though the same picture appeared on the command's plotting-table as on tables at group headquarters. Dowding wisely insisted that tactical control could not be exercised from Bentley Priory, nor even, at times of hectic activity, from group headquarters. He encouraged the widest possible decentralization of authority to act. Park agreed entirely and worked tirelessly to improve the command's methods and organization.[287]

Park rejected a suggestion made by Douglas Bader (whom we shall meet later) to Peter Townsend, one of the Battle of Britain's most famous pilots and author of an excellent account of it, *Duel of Eagles* (1970), that the battle should have been controlled from Bentley Priory. It was a suggestion, Park thought, that revealed only too clearly Bader's ignorance of the defence system not only in 1940 but a generation later, when he had had ample time to study it. As Park said, Bentley Priory had a demanding strategic role, controlling the entire system: that is, the radar chain, the Observer Corps, barrage balloons, guns, searchlights, the supply of fighters, pilots and ground crews for the whole command, rotation of squadrons into and out of the front line, and liaison with other services, the Air Ministry and government ministers. Not least, Dowding was responsible for deciding when and where to have air raid warnings and the all-clear sounded. Group commanders had the tactical role, to conduct the actual fighting. No individual, at Bentley Priory or anywhere else, could have maintained tactical control of more than 50 squadrons on a front extending around all Britain's southern and eastern coasts. Swift, effective response, Park recalled with feeling, to a bewildering variety of challenges through long hours of daylight and darkness, was difficult enough from group headquarters even though they were trained and equipped to provide it.[288]

Although Dowding delegated tactical control of fighter operations to his group commanders, he kept – or tried to keep – control of everything else in what has often been called the Dowding system. He was a micro-manager. For example, the filter room at his headquarters controlled information from all radar stations (except for a few in northern Scotland). In 1939 and 1940, this filtered information was sent to the operations room next door. Only after Dowding (or the senior watch officer) had assessed the situation on the operations room map were group headquarters informed and allowed to decide which sector was best suited to deal with it. This degree of centralization was necessary, Dowding believed, because only he could decide which group or groups should be involved, and only he could give air raid warnings. But it became increasingly difficult to handle all filtering in one room.

Dowding's insistence that he retain control over all aspects of the radar chain was supported by the Air Staff in late 1939, when rejecting a recommendation by the Tizard committee to allot radar tracking to a separate command. That change was urged by Joubert, who had been given a special responsibility for radar by the Air Staff in October 1939 and persuaded Newall early in the new year that the creation of filter rooms at group headquarters would greatly improve the interception rate. A 'fiery confrontation' followed on 12 January 1940 when Dowding was 'ambushed' by Newall, Joubert and other senior Air Ministry officials, who gave him no advance warning about the subject of the meeting. They forced him to agree to change filtering procedures to allow raid plots to pass more quickly down the chain, and also to allow plots from CHL stations to pass directly to nearby sectors.

But Dowding would not allow filter rooms to be established at group headquarters and on 31 January challenged the Air Staff either to back him or sack him: 'the Air Council have the right to tell me what to do, but should not insist on telling me how to do it, so long as I retain their confidence', and he refused to discuss the matter further. Newall and his colleagues backed down, but the issue would not go away.[289]

Some members of the CID assumed that Britain would supplement the small number of soldiers offered to her allies on the continent with substantial air power, but Swinton – and his successor – scotched that notion. 'The primary object of our Air Striking Force was the defence of the United Kingdom.' Bases in France or Belgium were required only as launching pads for raids on Germany.[290]

The Munich Crisis provoked Scheme M, eighth and last of the prewar expansion schemes, intended for completion in March 1942. It provided for 1,360 genuinely 'heavy' bombers (four-engined Short Stirlings and Handley Page Halifaxes, also the twin-engined Avro Manchester, later re-modelled into the four-engined Lancaster). If all went well, they might be able to begin serious bombing in the second half of 1941, but only enough of these expensive machines were to be ordered to prevent workers being laid off. Scheme M placed 'a new emphasis', wrote Kingsley Wood (Swinton's successor as Secretary of State for Air) on 'strengthening our fighter force, that force which is designed to meet the invading bombers in the air.'[291]

The Air Staff proposed to spend no more than £45 million pounds on fighters, despite this 'new emphasis'; the bomber force was allocated £175 million.[292] The Air Ministry's adoption of the 'false doctrine' that strategic bombing was a war-winner in itself blinded the service to other uses of air power: escort fighters, anti-shipping forces, air transport, close air support 'and very nearly Fighter Command'. As a consequence, the RAF was in no position to intervene effectively in the Battle of France. That failure was 'the pay-off for all that the RAF had ignored about army support between the wars.'[293]

Wood rejected complaints, voiced by Trenchard and his supporters, that the RAF was set to become too defensive-minded when it should be concentrating on all-out offence. He explained Britain's weakness to fellow-Cabinet members in unusually blunt terms on 25 October 1938:

> 'We must face the facts that our ground anti-aircraft defences, guns, searchlights and balloons cannot be made up to the full scale for some time to come, and that our arrangements for passive defence and the organization to fit the country to withstand air attack, though they have made marked progress in the past few months, have not as yet reached a very high standard.'[294]

Inskip had begun this critical shift in two reports (December 1937 and February 1938) 'from a belief in a costly bomber offensive as the core of British defence policy,' in Smith's words, 'to a stress upon the importance of cheaper fighter defence.' Inskip had become convinced by late 1937 that Britain could not match the Luftwaffe in numbers, so Germany had to be faced with the threat of a long war. In practice, this meant priority for Fighter Command because only when the base was secure could a telling offensive be mounted. He was therefore bitterly criticized by the Air Ministry's Trenchardists and it is certainly true that the word 'cheaper' appealed mightily to him and other members of the government. But the fact remains, as Dowding frequently and forcefully observed, that many more fighters were to come to him after Munich than had been thought sufficient before.[295]

Ever since its continued independence was confirmed during the 1920s, the RAF had ordered twice as many bomber as fighter types on the ground that offence was vital to defence. But the 'essential minimum' required for defence was gradually raised from nine squadrons in 1922 to 30 in 1936 and 53 on the outbreak of war in September 1939.

By October 1938 communications by telephone or teleprinter between all parts of the command were incomplete and the radar chain covered only part of the east coast. Only 50 heavy guns were available and ammunition was in short supply, but the next 12 months would see Fighter Command grow much stronger. Hurricanes and Spitfires began to reach squadrons; guns were delivered; radar stations were built, equipped and brought into service, especially those intended to detect low-flying intruders; and communications were extended and improved.[296]

Dowding spoke at a dinner for members of an observer group in Coventry on 14 February 1939. He was reported in the *Midland Daily Telegraph* as saying:

> 'A proper war will not consist of digging deep holes in the ground and going into hiding in cellars. I am not one to minimize air raid precautions, particularly in the matter of fire services, but I think the politicians have allowed the nation to get an altogether wrong idea

about modern air war. I believe the fighter has sixty to four the best of the bomber.'

The last of these words greatly disturbed Newall, a devout bomber champion, and he therefore wrote to Dowding on the 23rd to ask for an explanation. On what basis did he suppose the odds against the bomber were as high as 15-1?

Dowding replied next day. He had been anxious to emphasize the value of the Observer Corps and also to combat 'the excessive pessimism' of so many Britons. His reference to politicians had in mind Baldwin's remark about 'the bomber will always get through'. He spoke without notes, but doubted if he said 60-4; more likely 6-4, although he believed the fighter had a much greater superiority than that. His main point, he said, was that people did not realize how severely bombers would suffer if they attacked Britain. 'I said that there was no greater pacifist in the country than myself, and prayed from the bottom of my heart that no war might come; but if it did come it would be a good one from the home defence point of view.'[297]

And so it would prove, if only by a narrow margin, at least in daylight. In February 1939, after discussion with Dowding, Park sent four copies of a new set of instructions, 'Fighter Command Attacks, 1939', to the Air Ministry. They were intended to assist new squadron pilots learn standard attacks upon bombers flying in formation. They assumed that increased fire-power, as eight-gun fighters came into service, permitted decisive effect to be achieved at greater ranges. Both Dowding and Park, however, insisted that these instructions were not to be regarded as *drills* to be followed thoughtlessly. Pilots must use their initiative in combat. Good teamwork would be important and pilots must learn to take advantage of blind areas in enemy bombers, of cloud cover, use the sun as a shield whenever possible and above all seek to surprise the enemy. But such detailed precautions were laid down by the Air Ministry to prevent accidents that effective attacks were not even practised. Day attacks could only be made in formation at specified safe heights; all aircraft were to avoid cloud; pilots were not to change their aim after starting an attack run; and they were not to lose sight of other aircraft, either in their own formation or in that under attack.[298]

Leslie Gossage, commanding 11 Group, wrote to him in March 1939 to say that he had been asked at the Staff College if *annihilation of a few* was not preferable to the command's emphasis on the *interception of many*. Dowding replied that his intention was to match machine with machine. If too many fighters were sent up, they would be caught on the ground re-fuelling and re-arming when a second wave of bombers came in. But if too few were sent up, they risked defeat. Unfortunately, ideal tactics could not even be practised because most squadrons had not yet had their monoplanes long enough to be familiar with them as flying machines, let alone as weapons of war. Also, as Gossage was well aware, too few target aircraft were provided by Bomber Command to offer realistic interception opportunities. All very discouraging, but Dowding ended his reply on a positive note: training in small units brought out those men who had leadership qualities and they would be worth their weight in gold if war came. [299]

11

Preparing for War, 1939

Removing Dowding: Round Two

During February 1939, the question of Dowding's departure from Bentley Priory came to the fore as he neared the end of his three-year appointment. On the 24th Newall telephoned him to say that a paragraph was shortly to appear in London's *Evening Standard* about his 'retirement', as opposed to leaving Fighter Command for another position in the RAF. Responding to enquiries for more details, the Air Ministry then announced that in fact no change would be made in 1939. A decision that must have puzzled Christopher Courtney, who had been selected to replace Dowding at the end of June, when his three years were up. It was only on the 28th of that month that he suffered his afore-mentioned accident and he was presumably poised, until then, to move into Bentley Priory. One hopes that Newall told him of the change of plan before the accident that in any case put him out of the running. Newall's message was the first intimation Dowding received that he might be remaining at Bentley Priory after 30 June.

Puzzled and angry, Dowding immediately wrote to Kingsley Wood, now Secretary of State. During the past two years, he said, he had suffered 'very cavalier' treatment at Air Ministry hands. He had been given to understand, while a member of the Air Council, by Ellington, Salmond (his predecessor as CAS) and the Air Member for Personnel (Bowhill) that he would be the next CAS. Ellington then told him that he had been passed over, offering no reasons for the decision, adding that it was not his to make and he was unable to intervene. Dowding replied that he had no patience with disgruntled officers and accepted the decision. He was, however, advised that he could stay in service until he reached the age of 60 (in April 1942). 'I can say without fear of contradiction,' he continued, 'that since I have held my present rank I have dealt with or am in process of dealing with a number of vital matters which generations of Air Staff have neglected for the past 15 years.' In summary, he had demanded that the Observer Corps be placed on a war footing; he had seen to the manning of operations rooms; sought a solution to the difficult problem of distinguishing friendly

122

from enemy aircraft; agitated for improvement to aerodromes; and set up an adequate air raid warning system. All this work had been carried out despite 'the inertia' of the Air Staff.

Moreover, that staff had frequently made decisions concerning Fighter Command without consulting him. Among them, failing to back an attempt to develop a radar chain over land; interfering in plans for an underground operations room; and resisting proposals regarding air-to-air radar, night fighting tactics, the installation of cannons (rather than machine guns) in fighters, the development of rockets, etc. In conclusion, he wrote, 'I am not keen to carry on fighting the Air Ministry.'[300]

Three weeks later, with no reply forthcoming, Dowding wrote again, on 19 March. He was unwilling to stay on, he wrote, without a formal assurance that he had Air Council support. This letter provoked Newall into sending him one of his lumbering notes next day. 'In view of the importance of the efficiency of the Fighter Command,' he wrote, 'and the desire to avoid the coincidence of crises and changes in the higher appointments in operational commands, it has been decided to ask you to defer your retirement until the end of March 1940.'

This decision was a consequence of a recommendation from Portal (Air Member for Personnel) on 23 May 1939 that Courtney should not take over at Bentley Priory until 1 April 1940. Many historians have rightly sympathized with Dowding over his suffering at the hands of the Air Ministry's inept personnel management, but one should spare a thought for Courtney too. However, all would come right for him. He never got to Bentley Priory, but in January 1940 it was decided to appoint him Air Member for Supply and Organization, a very important position, but one that had nothing to do with the use commanders made of their aeroplanes. He handled it diligently and competently throughout the war and was eventually promoted to the rank of air chief marshal, the same rank that Dowding achieved.[301]

Newall would later write to 'My dear Dowding' on 30 March 1940, the day before he was due to retire. 'Even at that time of disturbed and uneasy peace your Command was of the very greatest importance and since then war has intervened with a consequent increase in your responsibilities.' He therefore asked Dowding to stay on for a few more weeks, until 14 July. It would be 'undesirable' for a change to be made when 'we may be on the verge of intensified air activity', but even if Britain is experiencing this 'activity' on that date, you must then retire. The RAF 'will greatly regret the conclusion of your active duties in the Service.'[302]

One wonders what Newall supposed would happen on 15 July that was not likely to happen before that date. Dowding naturally agreed to stay on and equally naturally asked for the name of his successor. This was not vulgar curiosity; there would be much for that man to know before he took over at Bentley Priory and no-one could brief him more comprehensively than Dowding. No answer came. Courtney had by then been safely stowed in the Air Ministry, but surely there were other officers available of ability, energy and ambition whose pleasant manners would have brought harmony between Bentley Priory and Whitehall? Apparently not, because on 5 July

Newall changed his mind again and asked Dowding to stay on until the end of October. Once again, one wonders what Newall supposed was going to happen on 1 November. Whoever was ear-marked to succeed Dowding should surely have been posted to Bentley Priory no later than the beginning of October. This was not done.

Thoroughly exasperated by all this dithering, Dowding wrote at length to Newall on July 7, succinctly summarizing the saga to date, concluding:

> 'Apart from the question of discourtesy which I do not wish to stress, I must point out the lack of consideration involved in delaying a proposal of this nature until ten days before the date of my retirement.'

This was the fifth retirement date he had received and though he would have been content to leave in July 1939, he now wished to stay on, 'because I feel that there is no-one else who will fight as I do when proposals are made which would reduce the defence forces of the country below the extreme danger point.'

Meanwhile, Archibald Sinclair (leader of the Liberal rump in the House of Commons and now Secretary of State for Air) received a well-merited rebuke on 10 July from one of Whitehall's few men of quality:

> 'I was very much taken aback the other night [wrote Churchill] when you told me that you had been considering removing Sir Hugh Dowding at the expiration of his present appointment [he is] one of the very best men you have got, and I say this after having been in contact with him for about two years. I have greatly admired the whole of his work in the Fighter Command, and especially in resisting the clamour for numerous air raid warnings, and the immense pressure to dissipate the fighter strength during the great French battle. In fact, he has my full confidence.'

He should remain in office as long as the war lasted, thought Churchill, and might very well be promoted to take over from Newall.[303] Sinclair – a politician with pleasant manners who knew nothing about aviation – reluctantly set aside the wishes of senior Air Ministry officers and agreed at once to Dowding remaining in command of Britain's fighters, 'upon whose success in defeating the German attack upon our munition factories during the next three months,' wrote Sinclair, 'will almost certainly depend the issue of this war.'

On 13 July 1940, Newall sent Dowding a long letter including an apology which he accepted. But Newall spoiled any good effect of these words by saying that he 'was glad to have your support' regarding the despatch of fighters to France. These words angered Dowding because he believed – wrongly, as it happens – that he alone had opposed their despatch. Dowding then wrote to Sinclair on the 14th. He had dined the previous evening with Churchill, who assured him of his confidence and his wish for him to remain indefinitely on the active list.[304]

Several men who knew Sinclair and Newall thought little of them. For example, Stanley Bruce (Australian High Commissioner in London) wrote on 10 June 1940: 'While a perfectly nice person, I do not think Sinclair is much good or has any particular force and drive.' Bruce met Beaverbrook on 2 July and later wrote: 'We were in complete agreement that Newall had not the fighting weight necessary for the position of CAS.' A week later, on 10 July, Bruce told Sinclair that he had always had 'the gravest doubts' about Newall's capacity. Referring to the disastrous French campaign, recently concluded, he added: 'the difficulty in getting decisions was an indictment of Newall, who was after all responsible.' Sinclair, himself a feeble man, could only reply that Newall was 'a first-class staff officer'. No doubt he was, but rather more was required of a service chief in wartime. Sinclair went on to say that Newall would be removed, if he was found not to be up to the job: this of a man who had then been CAS for nearly three years![306]

The next twist in the long-running saga of what might be called 'the Battle of Bentley Priory', what Dowding would later refer to as 'the shopfull of bowler hats which had been held over my head', came on 10 August, when Churchill gave Sinclair an even sterner rebuke:

> 'I certainly understood from our conversation a month ago that you were going to give Dowding an indefinite wartime extension, and were going to do it at once. I cannot understand how any contrary impression could have arisen in your mind about my wishes. Let me, however, remove it at once and urge you to take the step I have long desired. It is entirely wrong to keep an officer in the position of Commander-in-Chief, conducting hazardous operations from day to day, when he is dangling at the end of an expiring appointment. Such a situation is not fair to anyone, least of all to the nation. I can never be a party to it. I do hope you will be able to set my mind at rest.'

Within 48 hours, both Newall and Sinclair had unwillingly recognised the force of Churchill's unanswerable arguments, bowed to his cogently expressed wishes, and told Dowding that he was to stay in office. One does not doubt that they meant what they said, when they said it, but both men belonged to a generation that was familiar with the Bible. They knew what Sirach (Ecclesiasticus) had written as long ago as 180 BC: 'the race is not to the swift, nor the battle to the strong... but time and chance happen to them all.' These facts of life, they believed, linked to Dowding's abrasive personality, would offer an opportunity to get rid of him sooner or later.[306]

Barrage Balloons

After Munich, Dowding had taken a close interest in the question of whether or not to use hydrogen-filled balloons as part of his 'passive defence'. Following several meetings in the Air Ministry chaired by Dowding it was decided that a Balloon Command should be formed (under Air Vice-Marshal Owen Boyd) on 1 November 1938, subject to Dowding's operational control and based at Bentley Priory as soon as possible. The advantages and disadvantages of balloons were thoroughly thrashed out.

On the one hand, despite the efforts of their keepers – known irreverently as 'balloonatics' – they broke away in storms and careered across the country, tangling with electric and telephone lines, sometimes even bringing down aircraft. But when flown at low levels, where guns and defending fighters were least effective, they would deter all but the boldest enemy pilots.

On the other hand, at least 450 would be needed to protect London alone; getting them up and down quickly would call for a large labour force as well as trucks fitted with powerful winches; and only trial and error would reveal where best to fly them and co-ordinate their presence with gun fire and aircraft movements. Their real value, in Wykeham's opinion, was psychological: a visible sign, floating overhead, to the man and woman in the street that the RAF was doing something to protect them.[307]

By the end of the war's first day, 3 September 1939, 624 balloons had been flown in response to the war's first air raid warning and 19 were destroyed by bad weather. Dowding ruled that they were to be flown at all times, throughout the country, except when the local barrage commander decided the weather was too bad and except near aerodromes, where a station commander could rule that they were interfering with flying.

Whatever its value, Balloon Command remained at the bottom of the supply chain – for equipment, personnel, telephones, etc – even though factories, ports and all large cities were soon clamouring for their own barrages. By May 1940, with Dowding's discreet encouragement, Boyd was vigorously castigating a legion of Air Ministry officials in terms that Dowding could not have bettered himself. 'If a greater trust were put in my judgement as to my requirements and a greater appreciation shown of the need for haste,' Boyd wrote, 'we would get along better. There is a tendency, dangerous at a time of war, to query demands and to rely too greatly on figures of which the interpretation cannot be known beyond my headquarters.'[308]

Observer Corps

Balloons formed an unsung part of Dowding's defensive system, and although more notice has been taken of the Observer Corps, its contribution to Britain's avoidance of defeat in 1940 remains undervalued. But not by Dowding. He pressed hard for its expansion from 1936 onwards, encouraged its first full-scale call-out two years later, and when war began strongly supported a proposal that observers be paid. Given that radar's value ceased at the coastline, essential work was done from that point on in tracking, plotting and reporting. Eventually the whole country, except for north-west Scotland, was covered, with posts spaced from six to ten miles apart, and more than 30,000 men and women were employed, full or part time, 24 hours a day, seven days a week, until May 1945.

It was difficult, especially in the early days, to tell friendly from enemy aircraft and mistakes were made: most famously in plotting the planet Venus at 30,000 feet. Another problem was the handing over of information from one post to another. As with the radar chain, the long months of the 'Phoney War' (phoney only in regard to attacks on Britain) offered a vital opportunity for constant, serious practice. After the battle began, observers reported where and when bombs had been dropped, they spotted aircraft crashing and parachutes carrying airmen, British or German, to safety. Coastal posts were often able to report attacks on shipping.

One problem never solved was what to do about bomber formations that split up, because of bad weather or fighter attacks: how were the raiders, their formation now broken up, to be reported? Dowding sent an officer to 11 Group headquarters to help with this problem, and members of his scientific research section to work with the major Observer Corps centres. He was well aware of the strain on observers during enemy raids, when they were obliged to remain on duty even though they knew that their own districts – quite possibly their own homes – were being bombed. He commended their efforts regularly, and so did his successor at Fighter Command.[309]

Radar Interceptions

Rowe of Bawdsey reported encouraging progress in radar interceptions on 16 June 1939 and on that day Dowding went aloft at Martlesham, near Woodbridge in Suffolk. He flew with a scientist (E. G. Bowen) and a young pilot named Smith in a Fairey Battle to monitor that progress from the sharp end, as it were. The end nearly became a deal sharper than he expected, because Smith made a very bad landing. 'We put down with a dreadful thump,' Bowen recalled, 'half way across the field and skidded to a halt. It turned out later that we had broken a tail frame and that the tail wheel had collapsed. We limped back to base with awful grinding noises coming from the rear of the aircraft.'

Apologies were offered, but Dowding – 'who had a fearful reputation as a disciplinarian' – was unruffled. 'I always say,' he told the apprehensive pilot, 'that the most important thing is to land the right way up.' After lunch, he talked to Bowen for two hours about the problems of night fighting. We would need, Dowding argued, a two-seater (pilot and radar operator) with a long range, heavy armament and reliable contact with the ground in order to direct the aircraft home at the end of a patrol. Most Air Ministry officials at that time thought only of single-seat, single-engined fighters and Bowen 'had never heard such a clear and definite analysis of the fundamentals of night fighting.' According to the official signals history, he 'showed great foresight' in advocating further tests with Bristol Blenheims, pending the arrival in service of the Bristol Beaufighter which would be, everyone hoped, a much superior aircraft.[310]

Dowding attended a conference in the Air Ministry on 28 June 1939 to consider interception problems. Although Douglas was chairman, several scientists had been invited to attend and were able to give substance to the discussions. Dowding, briefed by those scientists, said that the work done at Biggin Hill had been most successful. He had based his policy of giving the command's sectors three DF stations each as a result of experiments carried out there. He also said that he was now getting radar detection at ranges up to 60 miles from British coasts, but at that distance his operators could not distinguish between friends and possible foes. Tizard, present at this meeting, was acutely aware of the problem. He discussed it with Dowding whenever he visited Bawdsey.[311]

Tim Pile

On 28 July 1939 an Irish-born soldier arrived at 'Glenthorn', a large house near Bentley Priory, to command the Army's anti-aircraft and searchlight defences in support of Fighter Command. He proved to be that rarity in Dowding's life (except on ski-fields): a colleague who became a friend. He was Lieutenant-General Sir Frederick Pile, known to both family and friends as 'Tim'. Back in 1905, a major's wife had asked him for his Christian names: 'Frederick Alfred', he replied; 'Nonsense,' she said, 'It is Tim from now on.'[312] And so it was.

He and Dowding, a former gunner himself, hit it off at once. Both had enjoyed their service in India, where they learned to love horses, shooting and polo. 'We have a unified command', wrote one of Pile's senior officers. 'Stuffy Dowding is solely responsible for ADGB.... My chief goes to see him practically every day, and the wheels go round like oiled clockwork.' Dowding, wrote Pile:

> 'Was the outstanding airman I met in the war. A difficult man, a self-opinionated man, a most determined man, and a man who knew more than anybody about all aspects of aerial warfare.... He was a good friend to me on many occasions, and history will undoubtedly record his great contribution to Allied victory.'[313]

Every morning, punctually at 10 am, Pile would arrive in Dowding's office 'and for an hour he would walk about, lecturing me on every conceivable subject.' He treated all visitors to his walking monologues and Pile particularly relished observing him doing the same to the Queen. Like Pile, she was quite unable to stem the flow, 'and could only wait until he had finished, by which time everyone was a good deal behind the clock.'[314]

When Pile took up his command, he had 695 heavy anti-aircraft guns at his disposal, many of them obsolete; according to the latest plans, he was supposed to have 2,232. He was also very short of light guns and searchlights; in addition, too many of the men assigned to Anti-Aircraft Command were unfit, in every sense, for prolonged, demanding service.[315] Although guns of all kinds were being produced or bought from overseas with some urgency during 1939, Pile got few of them. Many had to go to France with the British Expeditionary Force (BEF), but more went to the Royal Navy. In December 1939, the Admiralty demanded 255 guns to protect fleet anchorages, at a time when the London area had only 96 and the Rolls-Royce aero-engine factory had to manage with eight. There was nothing either Dowding or Pile could do, because the allocation of gun defences lay in the hands of the Deputy Chiefs of Staff Committee, 'some of whose decisions defied rational explanation'.[316]

Because of the excellent aircraft recognition training that Pile insisted upon, there were very few 'friendly fire' incidents in 1940. Anti-aircraft fire gradually became more effective. On the outbreak of war, Patrick Blackett – one of radar's fathers – did valuable work on the improvement of bomb-sights for a year until he transferred to Anti-Aircraft Command as Pile's scientific adviser. Pile thought him 'an ideal man for the job'. He assembled a team of young scientists as an 'operational research' team, some from the United States (working at gun sites in the guise of civilians) to analyse the performance of gun batteries. The work proved of great value in improving the ratio of 'shots per bird'. Pile and Dowding were sorry to lose Blackett to Coastal Command, although they understood why that command needed his help in the desperate battle against U-boats.[317]

One benefit from the Dunkirk evacuation was that Pile had plenty of gunners from June onwards: an important point, given the need by September to man the defences around the clock. But he was short of everything else. On 10 September, with Dowding's approval, he ruled that his gunners must fire at *all* aircraft flying over central London and the RAF must keep out of the way. They hit few bombers, but they did force them to fly higher – and the noise of a constant barrage consoled the people as well as politicians and civil servants.[318]

Re-organizing the Defences

On 14 August 1939 Dowding wrote to Newall about the proposal to form a fourth fighter group to cover south-west England and Wales. He had at first been reluctant to agree: both the Army and the Observer Corps would have to re-organize and he himself was already short of everything needed to make his existing groups fully efficient, but he was now persuaded that 11 Group could not be expected to cope with yet more responsibility. He then treated himself to a therapeutic moan:

'All the sailors in Portsmouth are, of course, convinced that the harbour and dockyard will be the focus of all German attacks, but then the same thing is true of almost everybody in the country. All the inhabitants of Stanmore, for instance, think that the balloon depot will be the primary objective of the Germans, and that they will be killed by bombs which miss the depot; and it is the same everywhere.'[319]

Dowding later wrote to the Air Ministry on 2 February 1940 to say that the defences of south-western England and Wales were in 'a very embryonic condition'. In spite of repeated reminders, nothing was done for three months. Then, having resisted his recommendation that runways be built at Filton, north of Bristol, the Air Ministry changed its mind, thereby putting Filton out of service until the work was completed. Colerne, east of Bristol, was the designated replacement, but it had no grass at present. 'Although these are the facts,' he told Joubert, who had raised the question of defending the south-west with him, 'I do not suggest that you broadcast them.'[320]

Dowding had asked Park in November 1939 if Duxford should not be moved into 11 Group, but Park thought the groups would be better balanced if it stayed in 12 Group and Dowding accepted his opinion. Unwittingly, they had made a decision that would cause them much grief. If Duxford had gone to 11 Group, Douglas Bader (a pilot based at Duxford who would greatly impress Leigh-Mallory and other senior officers with his courage, skill and confident opinions) would have come under Park's direct command during the Battle of Britain. He would then have been in the frontline, as he craved, getting his fill of action, and would have had no need to advocate those faulty 'big wing' tactics that Leigh-Mallory and others used to telling effect in undermining Dowding and Park.[321]

12

The Other Side of the Hill, 1933-1940

Hasty Improvisation

'All the business of war,' said Wellington, 'and indeed all the business of life, is to endeavour to find out what you don't know from what you do; that's what I called "guessing what was at the other side of the hill."'[322]

What did Dowding or those who advised him know about the Luftwaffe in the years 1933 to 1940? They knew it was growing fast – but how fast? – and they supposed it would one day – but when? – become at least as formidable as the Kaiser's air force. During the Great War, that air force had caused serious, though not intolerable, damage and casualties in Britain, but in that war it had bases west of Germany, in the Low Countries and France. Surely that would not be the case in a new war? Not if France proved as powerful as many Britons hoped.[323]

If bombers were to attack targets in Britain from bases in Germany, Dowding could reasonably hope to repel them, with the help of his radar chain and reporting system. Dowding believed that German bombers would not be escorted all the way out and all the way home by fighters, for they were short-ranged machines. There was no such animal, he believed, as a long-range, single-engined fighter – unless it was provided with drop tanks, about which he seems to have known nothing.

He was, however, perturbed by reports in 1939 that the Germans had a fighter that was twin-engined, powerfully armed, and might indeed prove to have the range to serve as a bomber escort: the Messerschmitt Bf 110. As it happened, that fighter failed in daylight, though it later proved to be a very effective night fighter. He expected French airmen to prove as gallant, skilful and well-equipped as they had been during the Great War. No doubt they would resist invading Germans and also intercept some of the bombers sent to attack Britain and disrupt the formations of the rest. Overall, then, although Dowding had plenty to worry about in the later 1930s, he had good grounds for supposing that Britain's situation – in the air, at least – was no worse than serious.

The Luftwaffe had made good use of the Spanish Civil War as a far more practical 'exercise' than anything available to Dowding or his colleagues during the late 1930s. German engines, airframes, weapons and radios all failed at a greater rate than predicted by the authorities, and the need for ample spares became clear to those on the frontline, if not to the top brass in Berlin. As well as these logistic lessons, valuable tactical lessons were also learned, in particular the value of the 'finger four' formation, and as a result operations in Poland, Scandinavia, the Low Countries and France were conducted with skill and efficiency.[324]

However, Hitler had made no plans before July 1940 to invade Britain, whereas Dowding (and some other Britons) had been anxiously pondering the many problems of aerial defence since at least 30 June 1934, when Hitler's victory over the Brownshirts confirmed his mastery of Germany. Consequently, the German offensive in the Battle of Britain, unlike the attacks on Poland and western Europe, was a hasty improvisation. That was a key reason for the Luftwaffe's failure, just as the fact that Dowding commanded a carefully-prepared defence was a key reason for the RAF's success.

As Horst Boog wrote: the Luftwaffe assault only began on 13 August, thus giving the British seven weeks after the fall of France to test their defences. No coherent strategy emerged on the German side. For example, should Britain be invaded? Should she be isolated by eliminating the Soviet Union (her only potential European ally)? Or by seizing Gibraltar and/or the Suez Canal? And would she agree to make peace on German terms?[325]

Dowding's Opponents

Whatever disagreements Dowding had with Air Ministry officials, civil servants, aviation executives and politicians, they were nothing compared to the misery that would have been inflicted upon him if he had been a German air commander. Between them, the Luftwaffe's four most influential leaders – Hermann Goering, Erhard Milch, Ernst Udet and Hans Jeschonnek – would have done their cunning and/or ruthless best to ensure that he did not rise to the top. If by some freak of chance or Hitler's favour he did, they would have neutered him. Hitler, being unpredictable except in his fixed policy of keeping underlings at each other's throats, might have backed Dowding from time to time, but he could never have become the favourite that Albert Speer did. Why not? Because on duty he could be as grim, humourless and single-minded as any Prussian, entirely out of sympathy with the guttersnipes who haunted Hitler's court. Off duty, he was devoted to skiing, a sport the Fuehrer detested. And Dowding would not have been prepared to sit about for hours listening to repetitive monologues when there was work to be done. Speer, despite his personal closeness to Hitler and his exceptional capacity for management, was often thwarted by underlings.

Hitler had granted command of the Luftwaffe to Goering, for years one of his closest, most popular and laziest acolytes (except when he perceived a threat to his place in the Nazi hierarchy). Actually, as *Reichsmarschall* – a six-star general – he was the highest-ranking officer in the world. The historian Richard Overy has dismissed him as 'a soap-box orator hoisted to power on the backs of disgruntled peasants and shopkeepers by courtesy of bankrupt and timid conservative politicians.' There was more substance (not only physical) to Goering than that. He was ruthless and corrupt, but also intelligent and personable, as allies and opponents often learned during the Hitler years and as Allied interrogators found (to their discomfort) at Nuremberg in 1946, once he had been detoxicated. He was not, fortunately for Britain, a professional airmen in the Dowding class.[326]

Goering lacked the steady application and technical knowledge needed to realize the potential of German air power himself. Better still, from a British viewpoint, he promoted men whose political reliability far surpassed their grasp of aviation problems, and did everything he could to undermine the authority of men working diligently and sensibly to ensure that only the most efficient aircraft types were produced in quantity. He detested all technicalities more advanced than those that had served him well enough during the Great War, when he was a brave and determined fighter pilot. Worse than his own ignorance of radio (let alone radar) and worse even than his belief that the United States could produce nothing more useful than razor blades and refrigerators, was his contempt for those who were better informed. Radar, for him, was 'simply a box with wires'. He had a way with words, though. On 1 March 1939, he announced that 'fear of the German air force, the mightiest in the world, had prevented the war-agitators from barring the way of the peace-loving statesmen to our Fuehrer and to a just understanding.'[327]

Albert Kesselring and Hugo Sperrle, commanding the two air fleets closest to Britain, had only informal contacts with each other or with Goering to decide how best to conduct a unique campaign. They were to use air power alone to force a powerful opponent to surrender. If Britain did not surrender, the Luftwaffe – having achieved aerial superiority – would either sink or drive away the ships of the Royal Navy and so permit well-trained and well-equipped solders to be ferried safely across the Channel to overwhelm such resistance as poorly-trained and poorly-equipped soldiers might offer.[328]

Another lucky break for Britain is the fact that Luftwaffe intelligence never formed an accurate understanding either of how the radar-based defence system worked or its crucial importance to Fighter Command. These failures help us to understand why the Luftwaffe did not win the battle. Britain's growing understanding of how radar could be made an integral part of a defence system was a closely-guarded secret, but nothing could be done to hide the tall masts of the chain of stations being erected along all the southern and eastern coasts.

The Germans had begun research into radar as early as 1929, long before the British. General Wolfgang Martini (head of signals for the Luftwaffe) used an airship, the *Graf Zeppelin*, to carry radio equipment and operators and sail slowly – at no more than 60 knots – along Britain's east coast in May 1939 to discover what purpose the tall masts served. Dowding's radar chain tracked her every move, but the experts aboard Martini's 'flying laboratory' – searching in the wrong radio spectrum – failed to learn anything useful: largely because the British equipment was cruder and less powerful than the Germans expected. A second venture early in August fared no better. 'Neither side realized,' wrote Derek Wood, 'that the opening round of the air war against Britain had been fought and lost by Germany.' Had the airship revealed how effective the radar system was, a serious attempt would undoubtedly have been made to wreck it a year later.[329]

Nevertheless, Martini felt sure that the masts were part of an early warning system and urged Goering to destroy the radar stations before launching a major strike at Fighter Command's airfields. Goering agreed, reluctantly, and on 12 August 1940 five stations were attacked and damaged, but only one – at Ventnor, Isle of Wight – was put out of action, though not for long. Although these and later raids caused Dowding serious concern, he was mightily relieved to observe that the Luftwaffe – thanks to Goering's lack of interest – made no systematic attacks on the chain. Nor did the Germans make deliberate, persistent attempts to jam radio transmissions, as Dowding and his scientists had feared they would. And finally, although the Luftwaffe made heavy attacks on sector airfields during the last days of August and the first days of September, causing severe damage, it failed once again to *persist* and thereby put those airfields permanently out of action.[330]

Hitler had instructed Goering in 1938 to plan the production of 20-30,000 aircraft a year, but in 1940 only 10,200 were built and no more than 11,700 in 1941, despite the fact that nearly 40% of all military expenditure went on the Luftwaffe. German victories early in the war were not a result of aerial superiority: in September 1939, Britain and France had more aircraft between them than the Luftwaffe. There was no long-range planning, no strategic thinking 'and the Luftwaffe,' as Williamson Murray wrote, 'increasingly became a force that reacted to day-to-day political and operational pressures.' Production programmes were poorly organized and therefore extremely wasteful of precious raw materials. From start to finish of the war in Europe, the Luftwaffe was short of spare parts and in order to get three aircraft ready for take-off often had to 'cannibalize' a fourth: a practice that was already having a serious impact on operational ready rates during the Battle of Britain, an impact that became more serious after that battle was over. The Germans had no equivalent to Britain's Civilian Repair Organization. Most damaged aircraft had to be transported by road and rail from the combat area to workshops in Germany. This had not been a major problem in short campaigns – in Poland, Scandinavia, France and the Low Countries – but it became an increasingly severe handicap from the summer of 1940 onwards.[331]

Goering failed to make clear to Hitler the low state of German military production. This attitude was passed on down the hierarchy. It was in everyone's interest to claim high levels of achievement and avoid accurate estimates. Likewise, in intelligence on the economic performance of Germany's enemies. In 1939, according to Overy, Goering convinced Hitler that Allied air strength was less than Germany's, whereas Britain had already achieved parity in output and was well organized for defence.

At the height of the Battle of Britain, German fighter production reached an average of 178 a month; British output was 470. When Albert Speer (Hitler's armaments minister from February 1942) was in Spandau prison, he looked back on the years 1939-41 as a time of 'incompetence, arrogance and egotism'. It was an appraisal that, had they known of it at the time, would have astounded Dowding, for he and many others assumed that the Germans were efficiently organized for war.[332]

True enough, but Dowding – as well as numerous able Britons in all walks of life – was right to suppose that the Nazi war machine was as powerful as they feared: and as powerful as men of Dowding's calibre could have made it. Only fools underestimate their enemies. It is no valid criticism of Dowding if postwar experts, sitting comfortably at home or lecturing students, can argue persuasively that Britain was not in deadly danger in 1940.[333]

On 10 July 1940, as Smith wrote, 'no-one in the know in Britain could have any grounds for complacency about what was to happen.' Throughout the year, the Air Ministry consistently exaggerated RAF victories, but it also exaggerated the size of the Luftwaffe, so one failing cancelled the other. Moreover, there was no bomber force capable of making a significant impact on German air potential through counter-attack. If Dowding was right to believe that Fighter Command could avoid defeat, 'then the Air Staff was simply wrong about the basics of air power', and had been for many years.[334]

France *did* collapse, to the surprise of everyone, including the Germans. The British Army *did* perform very poorly until late in 1942 and even then depended on American support in men and material for the successes it achieved. No-one supposed, at the end of 1940, that the apparently invincible German Army would shortly attack the Soviet Union and fail to overthrow its cruel rulers. And the British bomber offensive *did* fail completely until 1942. It suffered terrible casualties until the last days of the war, and even with massive American assistance, its important contribution to victory came only in 1944.

There was indeed a 'narrow margin'[335] between survival and defeat in the summer of 1940. Despite the skilful, devoted efforts of Dowding and every member of Fighter Command on the ground or in the air, Britain's survival depended ultimately on the 'narrow margin' by which the dynamic, patriotic Churchill came to power and the vapid appeaser Halifax did not.

Goering would make cruel and unjust jibes throughout the Battle of Britain to field commanders who were performing admirably in difficult circumstances. He issued self-defeating orders, such as the one requiring fighter pilots to stick close to slow-moving bombers and thereby make themselves vulnerable to attack by British fighters with height and speed advantage. Sometimes his comments were mind-boggling for a man who had once been a combat pilot. For instance, he urged pilots not to panic if they heard a Spitfire coming up from behind. 'I wanted the ground to open and swallow me up,' said the squadron commander. '*Donnerwetter*, the ignorance! In a plane's cockpit you can't even hear your *own* machine guns.'[336]

All might have been so different for the Germans if Walther Wever, the Luftwaffe's first chief of staff, had not killed himself in a simple aircraft accident in June 1936. Wever, 'described by all who knew him as a general of genius', was unique in enjoying the respect of both Goering and Milch, Secretary of State in the Air Ministry, and head of Lufthansa. Had he lived, Wever might have prevented the increasingly bitter personal clashes between Goering and Milch which led, soon after his death, to the disastrous appointment of Udet as head of the Luftwaffe's technical office and chief of supply and procurement.[337]

Udet had been a brilliant combat pilot, second only to the immortal Richthofen among German airmen. Between the wars, he became a famous stunt pilot, and until the last year of his life was a witty, skilful cartoonist and an ardent partygoer. Everyone liked Udet, but the aviation industry in Germany as everywhere else was a dangerous jungle for the unwary. It needed an iron hand to control it. Instead, it was presented with a most acceptable velvet glove. Udet remained in office for more than five years, until November 1941, when he committed suicide.[338]

In short, as Matthew Cooper has concluded, all four of the men who dominated the Luftwaffe at the outbreak of war lacked the qualities and experience necessary for high command. Three were civilians and two unsuited for any office of high military responsibility. All found co-operation with others difficult and all were fired by personal animosity to one or more of their colleagues. The varied merits of Dowding, his colleagues and opponents might well have ensured that Britain avoided defeat in 1940-1, but they were helped more than any of them could have guessed by rivalries, misjudgements, incoherent organization and a lack of sensible planning by those on the other side of the hill.[339]

Strategic Bombers
Wever had been an advocate of the four-engined bomber for use in the event of war against either Britain or the Soviet Union. The absence of such a weapon would be keenly felt from 1940 onwards. Prototypes of a Dornier Do 19 and Junkers Ju 89 were flying in 1936, and it has often been argued that with sensible development and production, the Luftwaffe could have had the world's first strategic bomber force by 1940.[340] Cancelling those prototypes was a perfectly sensible decision, provided Hitler never intended an attack on Britain or the Soviet Union. Big bombers were obviously more costly than medium bombers, from every point of view: precious materials, skilled labour, construction time, hangar space, maintenance hours, and crew size. Hardly battlefield weapons, they would have been of little use over Poland or Scandinavia, though their absence might well have embarrassed Hitler if France had not folded so rapidly.

Contrary to some claims, everything needed to build a powerful heavy bomber force was available in Germany. One sees this from the numerous projects so lightly begun and so casually continued throughout the war, few of which produced any reliable aircraft in squadron service. Add to this enormous waste the unbelievable squander of resources on flying bombs and rockets – whitest of the war's many white elephants – and one may conclude that a thoughtful plan, vigorously implemented, would have put heavy bombers and escort fighters with drop-tanks into the air. Milch had the capacity to devise and carry through such a programme. Employed by

Churchill, Roosevelt or Stalin, he would have done so, for all three proved more ruthless than Hitler when faced with servants who failed to perform. By 1941, if not before, Goering would have been told to concentrate on those tasks which brought out the best in him: stealing pictures and other treasures, showing a jolly face to the people and cherishing the Reich's wildlife.[341]

By operating from German bases, heavy bombers would have been able to form up out of sight of radar. They would then have been able to approach targets in Britain from many directions, thus dispersing Dowding's defences, and drop more destructive loads than the twin-engined machines actually used. Well armed and armoured, they would have been even more difficult to shoot down. But once Weaver was dead, the Luftwaffe became a close support air force. As such, it gave superb service in several land campaigns, but a prerequisite for the conquest of Britain – perhaps also for the overthrow of Stalin and his cronies – was a strategic bomber force. Working under the protection of a strong fighter force, it might well have completed in daylight and darkness during a long campaign over Britain in 1941 the devastation begun during the second half of 1940. Then, in 1942, the Lufwaffe could have turned eastward to attack not only the aircraft and tanks of the Soviet Union, but also the factories where they were made and the barracks where a huge labour force was housed.

In 1939, Udet decided that a strategic bomber force was needed after all, and Heinkel came up with an excellent design, but it was ruined by the crass decision to couple its four engines in two pairs and strengthen the airframe so that it might make diving attacks. Milch called the Heinkel He 177 'a dead racehorse' and for once Goering agreed with him. 'I don't think you can even get out the spark plugs,' he said in September 1942, 'without dismantling the entire engine!' By then, thousands had been ordered; hundreds built; but only a handful actually flew. When the engines did not catch fire, the wings came off. Or vice versa. The Luftwaffe's only effective four-engined bomber was not used over Britain in 1940. The Focke-Wulf Fw 200 Condor, a converted airliner, caused the British great concern by its efforts over the Atlantic in partnership with U-boats, a concern that would have been multiplied had it been less fragile and available in larger numbers.[342]

Many of the twin-engined bombers actually used by the Luftwaffe were 'first generation' designs of the mid-1930s and ready for replacement by a second generation of superior types by 1940: a generation that could only have appeared had Hitler supposed his Reich was committed to years of war. One bomber, the Junkers Ju 86, of which much had been expected, took no part in the Battle of Britain. Two others, the Dornier Do 17 and the Heinkel He 111, suffered heavily, while the Junkers Ju 87, a single-engined dive-bomber, proved dangerous only to its crew. In the opinion of Captain Eric Brown, RN, an expert pilot, it was an excellent weapon, if carefully escorted. If not, 'It was big enough and slow enough to present an ideal target to the humblest tyro among fighter pilots and it must even have come high in popularity with anti-aircraft gunners.' The Junkers Ju 88 was the sole first-class bomber used in 1940, and posed a serious threat to

Dowding's defences, but there were too few of them and they too carried only a light load.[343]

The Heinkel Fighter

In order to protect its bombers in the Battle of Britain, the Germans needed a long-range, heavily-armed escort fighter. They believed they had such a fighter in the Messerschmitt Bf 110. Although it had the range and fire-power needed, it lacked the essential agility and acceleration to cope with Dowding's fighters. But a single-engined, single-seat fighter capable of doing precisely that, in partnership with the excellent – but short-range – Messerschmitt Bf 109 existed. Fortunately for Fighter Command (and Britain), that fighter was never brought into service.

The Heinkel He 112 was one of four contenders at a competition held in October 1935 to choose a fighter for the Luftwaffe. It and the Messerschmitt Bf 109 outclassed the other two. Both flew with the same engine – ironically, a Rolls-Royce Kestrel V – which greatly assisted fair comparison. The Bf 109 was cheaper and easier to mass produce and got the nod. After the rejection of his fighter, Heinkel undertook a complete structural overhaul, producing in the Heinkel 112B a virtually new aircraft. It first flew in July 1937 and was faster than the latest model of the Bf 109. The Heinkel should have been taken into squadron service, not instead of but as well as the Bf 109. Like the Hurricane and Spitfire, they would have complemented one another. In range, robust construction, weight of armament, reliability of undercarriage and ability to carry drop-tanks (these could have been provided), the Heinkel had a distinct advantage. In agility and high altitude performance, the Bf 109 was superior.

The German mistake was to prefer the heavy, clumsy Bf 110 to the Heinkel. Optimistically designated 'the destroyer' by Goering, it served indifferently as a fighter, bomber escort and ground attacker. Only in a role for which it had never been intended – that of night-fighter – did it achieve success. So far from partnering the Bf 109 against the Hurricane and Spitfire, the 'destroyer' needed an escort itself.[344]

Although the He 112 would have done well as a frontline fighter, its successor – the Heinkel He 100 – would have performed better still. Drawings were complete by the end of May 1937 for an aircraft originally designated 113. Fifteen of the D model were built between March and September 1939. Despite outperforming its Messerschmitt equivalent, it was not taken into Luftwaffe service. Its airframe was closely tailored to the Daimler-Benz 601 engine, but production of that engine was almost totally absorbed by the Bf 109 and the destroyer. The German Air Ministry, at that time happy with Messerschmitt's duo, instructed Heinkel to concentrate on his twin-engined bomber, then in mass production even though its performance was unremarkable.

Soviet and Japanese delegations visited Heinkel in October 1939 to examine the 100D. The Soviet delegation included Alexander Yakovlev, designer of the Yak-1, which had appeared earlier that year, and purchased six examples of Heinkel's fighter. Yakovlev made good use of them in designing improved versions of his own aircraft, notably the Yak-9 (in large-scale production by August 1942) and the Yak-3 (which appeared a year later). As for the Japanese, they bought three 100Ds and a DB 601 engine. With these to inspire them, they produced the Kawasaki 'Hien' (Swallow), named 'Tony' by the Americans. In early 1942, the Swallow was tested against a captured Curtiss P-40E and an imported Bf 109E. It proved markedly superior to both and would serve with distinction for two years as the standard Japanese Army Air Force fighter.

Meanwhile, a few 100Ds were used by the Germans for propaganda photographs in a variety of markings, to give the impression that they were in large-scale production. Described as 'Heinkel 113s', they deceived Allied intelligence for a long time. They were frequently reported in action during the Battle of Britain, when in fact not a single one took part. The laugh, however, was really on the Germans. This formidable fighter, serving instead of the so-called destroyer, might well have converted the narrow margin by which the Luftwaffe failed in 1940 into a victory with incalculable consequences.[345]

The Focke-Wulf 187 *Falke* (Falcon) was a twin-engined single-seater that promised far better than the Bf 110 and in partnership with either the Bf 109 or the Heinkel 100 would have severely taxed Dowding's pilots. The Falcon's 'handling characteristics proved to be superb,' wrote Smith and Kay, 'the machine possessing a turning circle superior to that of many contemporary single-engined fighters, plus exceptional climb and dive performance.' Although Dowding never knew it, he had good reason to be grateful to Goering, Milch, Udet and Jeschonnek for their procurement decisions.[346]

Inadequate Intelligence

The Luftwaffe's intelligence service had been formed as recently as January 1938 and Goering put it under the command of one Josef Schmid. He was neither a pilot nor a technician, nor trained in intelligence work. He knew no foreign languages, had never been outside Germany and was a confirmed alcoholic. On the other hand, he was a devout Nazi and agreed with all Goering's opinions. Schmid proved as incompetent in his vital job as did Goering and Udet in theirs. Schmid's poor work, consistently approved, cost the Luftwaffe dear during and after the Battle of Britain. 'Seldom can one department,' wrote Tony Mason (an air vice-marshal turned historian), 'have produced so many misleading reports in such a short space of time with such disastrous consequences.'[347]

He and other intelligence officers had little status: they were required to take on other duties, such as troop welfare, propaganda and censorship to fill up their days. Worse still, the Third Reich had numerous intelligence services, civilian as well as military, co-operation between them was non-existent and men who were wise or ambitious made sure that assessments fitted in with the opinions of those further up the hierarchy. The fates of Helmuth Felmy and Paul Giesler, successive heads of Air Fleet 2 in 1939-40, were in all their minds. Felmy produced a report early in the war accurately revealing many weaknesses in Luftwaffe organization and equipment and stating that an air attack on Britain was likely to fail. The report offended

Goering and Felmy was sacked; Giesler replaced him and promptly came to the same conclusion. He too was sacked and thereafter Goering was usually told what he wanted to hear.[348]

Neither Schmid nor his masters had any information about the rates of production or repair of Britain's fighters, nor any specific knowledge of the defence system. Schmid produced an appreciation of British strengths and weaknesses on 16 July 1940 that is a model either of mistaken information or silence on matters of importance. He had no awareness that German strength in air crews had never been great and was now seriously damaged by strenuous operations in Poland, Scandinavia and western Europe. No critical appraisal was attempted of either the twin-engined Messerschmitt Bf 110 fighter or the Junkers Ju 87 dive-bomber. No allowance was made for the fact that all the bombers were lightly loaded or the fact that the excellent Messerschmitt Bf 109 had only a very short range and there were nowhere near enough of them. Basically, it was never realized that the contemptible appeasers of the 1930s were no longer in power. In the final words of Evelyn Waugh's splendid novel, *Put Out More Flags* (1942), words spoken by a Whitehall Warrior of high place but low calibre: '"There's a new spirit abroad," he said. "I see it on every side." And, poor booby, he was bang right.'[349]

The most useful contribution to Luftwaffe intelligence about Britain was in fact made by Milch in 1938. He simply wrote to a London bookseller, on German Air Ministry notepaper, requesting several copies of a detailed analysis of British industry. The books were duly delivered and formed the basis of Schmid's assessments. It never occurred to him that there had been significant changes since then.[350]

Gambling on a Quick Victory

In September 1939, the Luftwaffe – in common with Germany's other services – had behind it barely six years of development, covert and overt. In other words, Hitler risked what became a worldwide war before his armed forces were ready. The longer he waited, however, the stronger he believed his enemies would become. He had a choice, he thought, in 1939 between a quick war now or preparing for a longer war from about 1943 onwards. The Luftwaffe's frontline strength of just over 4,000 aircraft in 1939 was no more than one-sixth of the strength planned for the end of 1942. Its quality as well as its strength would by then have been greatly improved. But so too would the quality and strength of the Luftwaffe's rivals, actual and potential.

The gamble on a quick victory was taken and nearly came off. Nevertheless, despite spectacular successes during the first 11 months of the war, the Luftwaffe's losses in well-trained men and frontline material were heavy and, even more seriously, 'a predominantly tactical air force' was not suited for 'an independent strategic air offensive overseas'.[351]

Between 10 May, when the assault on western Europe began, and 31 July, when the attempt to drive Fighter Command out of the sky had barely begun, the Luftwaffe suffered horrendous casualties: 2,630 aircraft downed and numerous well-trained air crews lost. An even heavier rate of loss of men and material followed from August onwards. Worse still, Goering was fed nonsense about British losses and airfield destruction that he believed. The Luftwaffe actually lost more men and machines during the six weeks of the campaign in France than during the first six weeks of the Battle of Britain, but by late September it was reduced to no more than 276 serviceable Messerschmitt Bf 109s against 665 serviceable Hurricanes and Spitfires.[352]

Even so, Cox thought, the Luftwaffe might well have defeated Fighter Command:

> 'It should have been used, first, to destroy the Chain Home radar towers, a simple task because only nine, all flimsy and highly conspicuous, guarded the coast between Southampton and Dover. The blinded RAF fighter airfields should then have been overwhelmed by round-the-clock bombing. And finally, if the British still showed resistance, their naked cities should have been deluged with high explosives and incendiaries.'

Everything was attempted, but not in a logical order and without persistence. A combination of over-confidence and poor intelligence led to an ill-directed campaign. There should have been a constant focus on defeating Fighter Command in the air and on the ground, including aircraft factories. Other targets would then have been at the Luftwaffe's mercy.[353]

13

The Practice War, 1939-1940

Time to Learn

At 11.15 am on the morning of Sunday, 3 September 1939, Prime Minister Chamberlain mournfully confessed in a radio broadcast that his illusions were at last shattered and Britain was now at war with Nazi Germany. He nevertheless clung to office for another eight months, hoping that somehow or other the war might end without serious fighting except in faraway places. Moments after his broadcast ended, air-raid sirens wailed out over London and other cities. They did so in response to a message from Dowding's operations room, sent in accordance with standing instructions that any approaching aircraft not positively identified as friendly must be assumed to be an enemy. This aircraft, in fact, was friendly: coming from France, but the French had neglected to tell their allies that it was coming. From that day until the middle of 1940 Dowding was inadvertently granted by Hitler eight precious months in which to improve his entire defensive system and subject it, for the first time, to constant and realistic practice; eight months of what was, for Fighter Command, a vital 'practice war'. Throughout those months, a small number of German aircraft carried out raids, laid mines and attacked shipping. It was nothing like a full-scale assault, but it was continuous, gave valuable practice to pilots and ground crews, and allowed Dowding's scientific and technical advisers excellent material from which to assess performance and recommend improvements in both equipment and procedures.[354]

One day in early September, Dowding visited 43 Squadron (equipped with Hurricanes) at Tangmere. 'It was just as the airfield was being camouflaged by spraying the grass with soot,' recalled Peter Townsend, one of the squadron's pilots. 'Aloof and silent, Dowding regarded us sadly; we looked more like chimney sweeps than fighter pilots.' He knew, none better, how hard life was likely to become for such brave young men who were only just mastering their powerful new fighters. No doubt Dowding would have managed a smile had he known what a blessed practice period lay ahead.[354]

A major scare came on 6 September, when everything went wrong with

142

tragic consequences: many hostiles were supposed to be over the Thames estuary, but none were engaged and two Hurricanes were shot down by Spitfires and a third by ground gunners. This was what later became known, with a black humour common in wartime, as 'The Battle of Barking Creek'. The king and queen visited Dowding at Bentley Priory on that very day and found him an uncommonly distracted host. Years of hard work had produced nothing but a shambles: what would have happened if in fact several hundred German bombers had launched the full-scale onslaught that many feared at the very start of hostilities? A breakdown in the radar system was responsible, no hostiles were anywhere near British territory at that time, but the jolt to the self-confidence of Dowding and everyone who learned of the affair must have been severe.[356]

After six days of war, with Britain spared the expected onslaught, Dowding told his group commanders that 'since the Germans haven't attacked, we must stand down from this high state of alert or risk staleness and ill health.' The first actual brush with the Luftwaffe did not come until 16 October, when nine bombers attacked warships anchored at Rosyth, on the north bank of the Firth of Forth in Scotland. Given prior notice that a raid was coming by radio intelligence, the attack should have been intercepted in good time, but the local radar station broke down at a critical moment and several ships were severely damaged. Two squadrons of Hurricanes eventually appeared, shot down a couple of bombers and chased the rest away, but the early warning system had failed again.

As soon as Dowding learned the details, he asked the Air Ministry to appoint a committee under Tizard (who had been selected by Newall as his scientific adviser) to look into what was going wrong with the radar chain. Watson-Watt, still in charge, was unable to make the leap from conducting a small research programme to managing an ever-expanding operational system. Whatever his other talents, he had no organizational skills. Consequently, there were few spare parts available and no means of acquiring them promptly and in quantity. The committee recommended the creation of what became 60 Group from February 1940, a command responsible for maintenance, construction, development and training, under a senior officer, subject to Dowding's oversight. Watson-Watt was left to get on with what he was good at, basic research.[357]

By the end of 1939 there had already been several 'friendly fire' incidents. Dowding wrote to Rear-Admiral Hugh Burrough at the Admiralty on 29 October and again on 19 December about his fighters being shot at by the guard ship at Ramsgate on the east coast of Kent. Some anti-aircraft gunners were also at fault, his own fighters sometimes fired at British bombers and he assured Burrough that he well understood why such incidents occurred, but he would like all naval authorities to pay more attention to aircraft recognition.

On 22 December a court of enquiry held at Drem in East Lothian, Scotland, ruled that bombers and coastal patrol aircraft must identify themselves to fighters when returning to British bases. Dowding disagreed. 'This is an intolerable doctrine,' he wrote on 21 January 1940, 'and I am surprised that responsible officers should have set their names to it.'

Fighters must always be sure that their target is an enemy before opening fire. For once, Douglas and the Air Ministry agreed wholeheartedly with Dowding.[358]

By November 1939, Dowding was working harder than ever, but he refused to panic. On the 12th, for example, he sent a long letter to General Sir Walter Kirke, at the headquarters of Home Forces. Various military authorities had asked how best they might co-operate with him in the event of invasion or raids by parachute troops. The Germans, Dowding wrote, 'have been extraordinarily successful in keeping us in a constant state of panic,' in all sorts of ways.

> 'The invasion scare is, of course, the wildest of the lot. We kept back tens of thousands of men who were needed in France in the last war, to deal with this bogey. Invasion was unlikely enough then, but now, with the development of air power, the probability of its being even attempted appears to me to be infinitesimal.'

However, he continued, if we are ordered to consider the prospect, we must – but the rest of his letter is flippant. It reminds us not to be too certain that Dowding was in fact 'stuffy'. For example, there was some 'vague idea', he wrote, that the Observer Corps might see the invaders first and give the alarm. 'This is, of course, not the case. The first news that the Observer Corps would get of the invasion would be in the morning papers.'[359] Readers might like to compare this response to the prospect of invasion with that expressed by Salmond to Trenchard on 11 May 1940 (see Chapter 14).

At a meeting of the Air Fighting Committee on 12 February 1940 Dowding wanted more 'tactical courses' for fighter pilots: flying skills were of little use without combat skills. He also 'wished to emphasize the point that the primary job of fighters was to shoot down bombers, not to fight other fighters.' This point would need to be made, time and time again, by Dowding and Park during the coming summer. Those who advocated the use of 'big wings' (to be discussed later) were reluctant to accept this point.[360]

On 3 March Dowding gave his group commanders a cold blast. Since September last, he wrote, he had on several occasions felt obliged to criticize the conduct of sectors at night. He had delegated tactical control to groups, but operations room staff must keep in touch with what sectors were doing and how they were doing it. He looked forward to the time when all controllers were so expert in their duties that queries from command to group and from group to sector were rare, 'but that time is not yet'.[361]

Leigh-Mallory's Inadequacy

One week after an exercise in August 1939, Trafford Leigh-Mallory (head of 12 Group) had submitted his report. Two points alarmed Park. Firstly, a low-level raid caught some of Leigh-Mallory's sectors by surprise and caused him to put up standing patrols for their protection. Park thought Leigh-Mallory had overreacted, diverting too many fighters to local defence from their major task of intercepting bombers threatening vital industrial targets. And secondly, his operations room was actually evacuated for ten minutes during a night attack. Dowding promptly directed Leigh-Mallory to ensure that in future no operations rooms, group or sector, were to be evacuated unless so damaged as to be useless.

This was not the first time that Dowding's attention had been drawn to Leigh-Mallory's inept handling of his group. For example, as long ago as October 1938 he had sent Park a memorandum about the air defence of Britain north of London. It was based on the startling assumption, as Park told Dowding, that Britain would continue to be defended by slow lightly-armed biplanes rather than by fast heavily-armed monoplanes. It emphasized local defence at the expense of area defence, and showed no appreciation of the advantages gained by the extension of the searchlight area and improved wireless communication. To implement his plan, Leigh-Mallory asked for 29 of the command's 41 squadrons, leaving only 12 for London – the most vital area – and none at all for the rest of Britain.

Dowding agreed with Park. The memorandum, he told him, 'shows a misconception of the basic ideas of fighter defence.' It does indeed, and Dowding should there and then have sought Leigh-Mallory's replacement. It is impossible to understand Dowding's failure to act, a failure that would later play a large part in costing both him and Park their jobs. Far worse, Dowding's failure in this vital aspect of his job exposed many pilots to death, injury or capture as a result of Leigh-Mallory's misjudgements, especially after the Battle of Britain when he took Park's place at 11 Group.[362]

During September 1939, Dowding asked his group commanders not to issue special *group* orders in addition to *command* battle orders. They must remember, he wrote, that squadrons would be moved about to deal with changing situations and it was important that they should not find themselves in a group where unfamiliar orders were in force. He had in mind 'special action orders' issued by Leigh-Mallory on 5 September and told him to cancel them. He did so, but on the 26th issued instructions to his sectors about the disposition of their squadrons that Park asked Dowding to rescind. If Leigh-Mallory had his way, said Park, Digby and Wittering would be overcrowded, re-fuelling and re-arming would be slowed, and adjoining sectors underworked and weakened.

Dowding again agreed. He wrote an important letter to Leigh-Mallory in which he carefully set out his thoughts on command: 'I have delegated tactical control almost completely to groups and sectors, but I have not delegated strategic control, and the threat to the line must be regarded as a whole and not parochially.' Apologies were offered, accepted, and the incident closed. But keeping Leigh-Mallory in line with the other group commanders proved to be an endless task and one that defeated Dowding. He had good cause to seek his removal from 12 Group long before the Battle of Britain began, but his patience did not run out until after his power to get rid of Leigh-Mallory had evaporated. Dowding's failure here is the strongest of several reasons why he lost his command in November 1940.[363]

During a conference with group commanders and technical experts at Bentley Priory on 19 January 1940 there was much anxious discussion about procedures at radar stations. Dowding 'emphasized the need for beginning with only the simplest exercises in order that personnel should not be discouraged by apparent failures of the system, which were in fact due to inadequate experience.' Leigh-Mallory had nothing to add on this subject, but he later suggested that commanding officers of Blenheim squadrons be promoted to wing commander rank and thereby relieved of daily flying duties. Dowding was displeased: 'he would not agree to that for a moment; the CO was the man the squadron looked up to, the man who led the squadron;' he could not be a mere office-wallah. He preferred Park's suggestion of finding a flight lieutenant as second-in-command who had the competence to take on much of the squadron's administrative work.[364]

The Strength of Fighter Command

On 16 September 1939 Dowding wrote to the Air Ministry about the strength of his command. He had protested vehemently against the 'ominous tendency' among senior officers to refer to the need to balance the claims of one command against those of another, relying on the traditional (though untested) dogma that attack was the best form of defence. This was the first in a remarkable series of letters which set out 'with a clarity and fire unusual' in official correspondence his opinions. These letters were composed, as Collier observed, with 'devastating logic, sometimes with bitter irony, always with a smouldering eloquence born of deep conviction' in opposition to 'the great half-truths of strategic dogma' bred into most RAF officers.[365]

In the summer of 1939, it was reckoned that Dowding would eventually have a force of 57 squadrons, of which five were assigned to trade protection or the defence of Northern Ireland, leaving 52 for home defence. Two were allotted to Scapa Flow, four to the Air Component of the British Expeditionary Force (BEF), reducing his force to 46. In fact, on 3 September he had 35 at his disposal, 21 staffed by regular, 14 by auxiliaries in what he considered 'various states of efficiency'. Only 22 were equipped with Hurricanes or Spitfires and 13 with useless Blenheims, Defiants and Gladiators. Ranged against them, the Air Ministry thought the Luftwaffe had 1,650 bombers. Actually, it had only about 1,000 on hand: a gap that did not unduly concern Dowding, so long as they operated from bases in Germany.

On 12 August 1939, in an attempt to convince the British people that they were safe from aerial attack, Dowding was invited to make his first BBC broadcast. He summarized the success of a recent large-scale exercise, and even admitted that 'various new methods' had been tried with good results. 'I am satisfied with our progress, and I confidently believe that serious attacks on these islands would be brought to a standstill within a short space of time.' Three weeks later, on 3 September, when war had actually begun, Dowding broadcast again. He expected 'every nerve would be strained to increase the defence force up to the strength laid down by the Air Council themselves.' His words were heeded, because the Air Ministry came to accept intelligence estimates predicting a Luftwaffe with over 2,000 bombers by the late summer of 1940 and 3,000 by the spring of 1941.[366]

True, four squadrons had long been promised to a planned expeditionary force, but he supposed they would not be sent across the Channel until home defence was assured. Those four squadrons had originally been of Blenheims, but 'in a fit of honesty', wrote Malcolm Smith, that 'he probably lived to regret', Dowding substituted Hurricanes instead. He was shocked by a decision to send them overseas at once and even more shocked by orders to put six more squadrons on a mobile basis by January 1940. He was assured that these would not follow unless this could be done without endangering Britain's safety and replied: 'I know how much reliance to place on such assurances.' Fewer than two Hurricanes were being built each day and it would be April before three a day were appearing. Intensive operations would wipe out his force: a tap would open 'through which will run the total Hurricane output.' We must be far stronger at home, he insisted – as he would, over and over again, during the coming year – if we ever propose to use our bombers offensively, so that we can withstand German reprisals.[367]

He was told on 21 September that his command would reach its planned strength, perhaps by March 1941, but meanwhile he was likely to lose six squadrons in addition to the four already committed to France. It would be 'mutually helpful', the letter concluded, if he would attend a council meeting on the 26th.

Dowding replied on the day before that meeting. He was 'much disappointed,' he wrote, to receive that letter and hoped to be able to show 'that the Air Council under-estimate both the danger in which we stand and their power to mitigate it.' That danger was imminent and would not await our convenience until March 1941, he argued. No doubt the pressure to send the four squadrons to France was irresistible, but the consequence will be pressure to keep them up to strength – and to send more. He continued:

'Your letter seems to infer that the aiming of a knockout blow at France is a somewhat remote contingency. If I may say so, I think that this is almost certain to happen.... My trouble is that my Hurricane squadrons at home are likely to disappear before next spring through consumption in France, even if no serious attacks are made on this country.'

There was also much anxiety until 9 March 1940 about Bentley Priory's vulnerability to bombing. On that date newly-completed rooms underground were fitted out for filter and operations decisions. Dowding was delighted to report to the Air Ministry that the changeover of 167 telephones was completed in two and a half minutes. The internal telephone exchange, comprising 250 extensions and 70 exchange lines and private wires, was carried out in one minute. 'It was just like that in the first war,' he later mused: 'people got on with jobs that would have taken ten times as long in peacetime – and didn't stop for tea or to fill in forms.' However, in a letter to the Air Ministry on 1 June 1940 Dowding deplored the lack of

VHF equipment that forced him to abandon that superior form of fighter communication. Only by reverting to HF throughout the command could a workable R/T organization be maintained.[368]

Absolute Priority for Home Defence?

According to Maurice Dean (a senior civil servant in the Air Ministry) the suggestion that Dowding faced 'a grossly inept Air Ministry is of course pure moonshine'. Two serious historians, Hough and Richards, argue the point more thoughtfully. They believe it is 'nonsense' to suggest that senior officers in the Air Ministry obstructed Dowding. 'It is certainly true,' they admit, 'that Dowding now waged a vigorous, sustained and absolutely justified campaign' to strengthen his command, but Whitehall Warriors believed they must plan and act for the whole service and not favour one command over another. Dowding himself had spent six years in Whitehall and was familiar with that point of view. He was convinced, however, that massive air raids on British targets were likely in the near future, to be followed by an invasion if they wrecked his defensive system, and therefore the Air Ministry's concern for *balance* – in effect, for continuing to nurture Bomber Command – put Britain's survival as an independent nation at grave risk.

As long ago as 1953, Denis Richards neatly summarized Dowding's point of view:

> 'Dowding looked neither to left nor right.... Before his eyes there was the spectre of an overstretched fighter force vainly trying to plug the gaps and slowly wilting under the inexorable pressure of overwhelming numbers; and after that, of ports choked with sunken shipping, of aircraft and arms factories pulverized into rubble, of London undefended and burning, of the whole Allied cause collapsing from the paralysis of the British nerve-centres.'

Believing that prospect to be only too likely, Dowding could not compromise, as most of us wish to do, sooner or later, when involved in a serious argument: in his well-informed opinion, it was a matter, literally, of life or death.

Writing in 1989, Hough and Richards expressed the belief that officers serving in Whitehall and those commanding in the field understood their competing claims perfectly well because they were the same men at different stages of their careers. It is a superficially persuasive argument, but in the academic world, for example, there have always been those who find administration suits their talents and ambitions more fully than teaching or research. So too a certain kind of officer has always found life more suited to his abilities and interests in the Air Ministry, the War Office or the Admiralty than at the sharp end in Britain or overseas. Such an officer manages to stay in Whitehall, or at least to return there at regular intervals. Whitehall remains his spiritual home and his actions, even when he is far away, are in accord with what he knows will be approved in London's seats of power.

Ellington, Newall, Douglas and several of their colleagues had no recent command experience and made gross errors of judgement not only in ordering Battle and Defiant aircraft (dangerous only to their crews), but worse still in insisting upon using them on operations. The Air Ministry's top brass amply justify Churchill's contempt: 'I wonder whether the existing brain power of the Royal Air Force is at all adequate to its staff work,' he wrote in August 1935, 'or to the study of the decisive strategic problems involved.' He found it difficult to believe in later years that Air Ministry standards might have improved, allowing it to consider 'the problems of defence in a manner comparable to the two older services.'[369]

Dowding's masters were rightly alarmed at the prospect of attack on aircraft factories and he was doing his best to protect them, as he wrote on 25 September 1939:

'But these precautions will not save the industry if our fighter strength at home is allowed to reach a low ebb. The best defence of the country is the fear of the fighter. If we were strong in fighters we should probably never be attacked in force.... If we are weak in fighter strength, the attacks will not be brought to a standstill and the productive capacity of the country will be virtually destroyed.'[370]

Hitherto, he had been assuming unescorted bomber raids and he believed that even his current strength would be enough to deal with them, but the neutrality of Belgium and Holland was likely to be violated soon and enemy fighters would then be able to escort bombers based much closer to British targets. On this point, Dowding was in unwitting agreement with General Helmuth Felmy, head of the Luftwaffe's 'Special Staff Britain', who had warned Goering in September 1938 that none of his bombers or fighters could operate meaningfully over Britain from German bases. Fortunately for Britain, as we have seen Felmy fell out with Goering in January 1940 and was sacked. He seems to have been a most able commander and his departure was a hidden bonus for Dowding.[371] These matters were anxiously discussed at further meetings with Douglas as chairman: Newall, as usual, was either absent or silent.[372]

On 13 October 1939 Dowding did his best to sweeten relations with the Air Ministry: he gratefully acknowledged the Council's consideration of his requests and arguments and regretted that he could not accept its opinions. He then came to the point, one that he made repeatedly during the coming year:

'I must put on record my point of view that the home defence organization must not be regarded as co-equal with other commands, but that it should receive priority over *all* other claims until it is firmly secured, since the continued existence of the nation, and all its services, depends upon the Royal Navy and the Fighter Command.'

The Air Staff disagreed, and as Cecil James observed, offered no comment. It is difficult to see, he added, 'what could have been said without entering upon a long controversy on the nature and application of air power.'[373]

Protecting Coastal Shipping

During the war's first winter, Dowding faced two major worries. One was the difficulty of defending coastal shipping against aerial attack, the other was a constant fear that his fighters would be taken away for purposes other than home defence. As for the first worry, arming merchant ships was a possible answer, but few guns or trained gunners were available and they would not prevent high-level bombing. To help him meet this danger, he was assigned four 'trade protection squadrons', equipped with Bristol Blenheims. These twin-engined light bombers could, at a pinch, be adapted for use as fighters. Dowding rightly regarded them as unsuitable either for coastal defence or shipping protection and after some debate they were transferred to Coastal Command where, of course, their value remained just as marginal. The problem therefore remained. The most that could be done was for Dowding to ask his fighter squadrons to be especially vigilant when convoys were passing through high-risk areas. He soon realized that this active duty gave valuable training to everyone concerned, on the ground as well as in the air.[374]

Even before the war began, it was obvious that shipping on the southern and eastern coasts of Britain would be vulnerable to attack. Much traffic could have been diverted to the west coast (further from German bases), but apparently not all. Merchant ships were therefore required to sail in convoy, escorted by naval vessels equipped with anti-aircraft guns, and steer as close as possible to the British coast in order to stay within range of defending fighters. Even so, ships could be attacked, and often were, before those fighters could intervene.

Standing patrols seemed to be the answer, but they were anathema to Dowding. His entire system was designed to avoid the wear and tear on pilots and aircraft of standing patrols. There were also the difficulties of locating convoys when they were forbidden to break radio silence and the danger of fire from escort vessels, which regarded all aircraft as enemy whatever pieties about identification were agreed in Whitehall. Worst of all was the danger of being caught by German fighters at a fatal disadvantage: that is, low down and moving slowly, in order to keep the convoy in sight.

In early November 1939, the Luftwaffe carried out several successful attacks on shipping in the Thames estuary and the Straits of Dover. As many as 28 merchant ships were sunk or damaged during that month within 40 miles of British coasts. Dowding resisted convoy protection as a Fighter Command duty. Coastal Command and the Fleet Air Arm, he believed, should bear that burden. Unfortunately, in the early years of the war they were too poorly equipped to do so.[375]

On 25 November Dowding replied to a suggestion from Newall that he might do more to guard Britain's coasts in darkness. 'You realize, of course,' Dowding wrote, well aware that Newall was, as usual, out of his depth, 'that contact made at night over sea by standing patrols is purely fortuitous and that standing patrols actually decrease the probability of making interceptions because of the confusion which is caused on the RDF.' Without airborne radar, such patrols merely wasted fuel, used up engine hours and risked pilots' lives. However, 'pending reconsideration of your wishes,' Dowding would obey in good weather. Newall withdrew his unhelpful suggestion.[376]

Protecting Troops on the Continent

The other worry was the need to provide fighters to help protect any British troops sent to France. Whenever Dowding asked if he was likely to lose fighters for troop protection, he was reassured. In early 1939, however, the government decided that it must send four Army divisions to France in the event of war, accompanied by an 'air striking force' that included four fighter squadrons, and told the French that more might follow: all this without a word to the head of Britain's air defence system.[377]

In December 1939 the British air forces in France proposed a programme of patrols for two of 11 Group's squadrons that could only be carried out if they operated from French airfields and if a servicing wing was set up there for them. Dowding refused to agree. The squadrons might operate over France, he allowed, but they must return to their bases in England each evening. It soon became clear, however, that bad weather and the need to re-arm and re-fuel made a French base essential. Dowding recognised the thin end of a wedge here. Should Germany launch an offensive in the west, Britain's fighter force would be drained away to France. As a result of his efforts to co-ordinate British and French fighter cover over Channel convoys, he was keenly aware that French air defences were primitive and her fighter force inadequate.[378]

That opinion was confirmed in February 1940 when the Air Ministry forwarded to Dowding a report on recent tactics written by General Harcourt, commander of the French fighter units. Despite active patrolling, Harcourt admitted, his pilots made few interceptions because they lacked a radar system linked to a ground-to-air and air-to-air wireless network. He stressed the importance of fighters keeping together during their approach to enemy formations: 'an attacking force which dashes into battle without a co-ordinated plan and proper control' would achieve little. Dowding could not have put it better himself.[379]

In early 1940 Dowding had 57 squadrons on hand. However, the demands of defending coastal convoys off the east coast of Scotland required him to base fighters north of Dundee, where they could make no contribution to his more important task of defending the aircraft factories on which the air defence system depended. Even more alarming was the fact that he could get no assurance that more squadrons would not cross the Channel should serious fighting break out in the west. By mid-February 1940, the number of Hurricanes and Spitfires in store and ready for immediate despatch to squadrons had fallen to 16.

By April, a temporary halt in the re-equipment of existing units with new aircraft seemed the only way to avert a situation which would leave all the squadrons dependent on the machines already available. And yet, a few days later, in the aftermath of the German invasion of Scandinavia, and aware that a powerful strike against the Low Countries and France was imminent, the Air Ministry agreed to form three more squadrons and proposed to consider on 10 May the formation of a further four.[380]

Fighter Command simply could not defend British troops on the continent as well as preparing an effective defence at home. Ever since May 1939 Dowding had been forwarding to the Air Ministry monthly statements of the 'mobilizable' squadrons in his command: effective numbers available, state of re-equipment, progress in training, shortage of spares and tools. Between the outbreak of war and 1 February 1940, he reported, 18 new squadrons had begun forming, but only two were fully equipped – with obsolete Gladiators. The other 16 were all short of armament, wireless or other essential equipment.

Dowding followed up this report with a letter on 10 February 1940 provoked by news that three squadrons might be required for service in Scandinavia. These new liabilities had been incurred since September 1939: six squadrons sent to France, four more earmarked to follow them, four set aside for trade protection under Coastal Command control, two for a new sector, two for Wick (in the far north of Scotland with more likely to be sent there), two to help protect the Aberdeen coast and a new sector formed at Middle Wallop in Hampshire to protect south-west England and Wales. He feared that in practice 'apprehension of attack may have the same effect as actual attack' on his strength.

Overall, Fighter Command was weaker than it had been when the war began and sending three squadrons to Scandinavia would weaken it still further. Worse still, he foresaw that these squadrons would soon need to be reinforced if serious fighting began. 'I do not under-estimate the importance of attempting to deny the Swedish iron ore supply to Germany,' he wrote, but a letter on the subject sent to him by Slessor (Director of Plans) certainly over-emphasized it. For some reason which Dowding could not fathom, Slessor asked him to destroy the letter. Not being in the habit of suppressing official communications, Dowding refused to do so, but on reflection, decided to humour Slessor because he had on hand more important bones of contention with Whitehall Warriors. 'It is not within my province to discuss whether we are likely to win the war by stopping the Swedish ore supply to Germany,' Dowding concluded, 'but it is my duty to point out that we may lose it by opening yet another source of dispersion and wastage of our fighter resources.'[381]

Improving Radar
The opening of the first low-looking radar stations on 1 November 1939 – known as Chain Home Low – was a vital addition to the system. Hitherto, there had been no practical means of detecting low-level intruders and yet it was clear to Dowding, and everyone else concerned, that the Luftwaffe would use this method of attack. His system was saved by a team of War Office researchers at Bawdsey who were working on a means of detecting ships approaching the coast. The rotating antenna they used, sweeping the sky just like a lighthouse lamp, happened to pick up low-flying aircraft as clearly as

ships off shore. The urgent building of a string of stations began. As with IFF and many other features of the defence system, on the ground and in the air, 'the practice war' offered Dowding, and everyone who worked with him, a vital interval in which to get ready for a serious challenge.[382]

From the time of Munich onwards, as Zimmerman has written, 'Dowding decided that whatever the deficiencies in the technology, something was better than nothing.' His men and women must use whatever they had. If it failed, they must at least understand what was wrong and so be better prepared to make good use of its successor. From April 1939, he directed that the radar system go into full operation, 24 hours a day. It was 'simultaneously undergoing construction, upgrading, expansion, experimentation, training, operational testing and operations.'

Dowding closely supervised all exercises and set up several conferences at which ideas about how to improve the system were debated between senior officers of his command with Air Ministry and War Office officials, as well as Bawdsey's scientists and technicians. He personally made two major reforms. The first concerned reports by inexperienced members of the Observer Corps of large numbers of raiders approaching, when in fact most of them were friendly or even civilian aircraft. This led to an 'utterly chaotic' display on control room maps, so in June 1939 Dowding ordered that all Observer Corps information be ignored unless it reported a raid already identified by radar. The second reform was the creation of a 'Lost Property Office' to keep track of raids that had accidentally disappeared from control room maps, which sometimes happened when raiders crossed group or sector boundaries.[383]

In early 1940, Dowding had to accept that the results of fighter control were disappointing. The problem lay in filtering, defined as 'the assessing of a probability'. Accurate work in this area depended on experience and many of the ablest turned out to be women. In December 1939 Park had told Dowding that his group and sector controllers were regarding radar as totally accurate 'black magic', when it was not. Their over-reliance on it, he said, was 'our fault' because we had not pointed out its limitations.

Dowding agreed to circulate a note on the 13th. The chain of coastal stations between the Isle of Wight and Aberdeen, he wrote, had been hastily erected with 'scratch equipment', now being replaced. There were still gaps in the coastal coverage and stations could not pick up aircraft flying below 1,000 feet. Group and sector controllers were to bear in mind these important limitations: range and position were only accurate to within about one mile; height was accurate to within plus or minus 1,000 feet over the Thames estuary, 2,000 feet elsewhere; up to three aircraft could be accurately counted, but more than three could be as many as nine and more than nine could be any number over nine; and finally the time lag was about 90 seconds from the sighting by a radar operator to the plot appearing on group and sector tables. As late as 8 March 1940 Dowding would write that radar is 'very capricious and unreliable, but it is better than nothing, as being the best evidence we have of what is going on over the sea.'[384]

Sir George Lee, Director of Communications Development in the Ministry of Aircraft Production at Harrogate, wrote to Dowding on 2 July

1940. 'In this present emergency I hope you will consider yourself free to make as much use of Larnder's team as you may find practicable.' Dowding assured him that he was very happy with Larnder and his colleagues: 'they turn their hands to anything they are asked to do. The other day they got me out a series of graphs on wastage which were most helpful.'[385]

Help from British Bombers
In September 1939, the RAF had 536 frontline bombers. With such a small and weak strike force on hand, there could be no question of mounting that strategic offensive about which the Trenchardists had written and spoken so eloquently for so many years. Raids on shipping in ports were attempted with an embarrassing and costly lack of success and leaflets – not bombs – were scattered far and wide over western Germany (and inadvertently over neutral states). Given the effectiveness of German fighters and anti-aircraft weapons, Bomber Command was forced to make a rapid change from a day offensive, which proved to be well beyond its capability, to a night offensive, for which it was even less well prepared. Target-finding became more difficult than ever, and would for years remain so.

On 12 October 1939, Ludlow-Hewitt wrote to Dowding about a proposed attack on the Ruhr: 'we have no experience of the rate of casualties likely to be experienced in low attacks of this sort over a well-defended area.' His force was 'very small' and he was reluctant to sacrifice a large part of it in a single operation, 'however successful'. The Air Ministry had advised him to seek Dowding's opinion. A low-level attack, replied Dowding, on a heavily-defended area was 'an unfavourable proposition' and it might also run into a balloon barrage. 'Of course, if the German balloons are no better than ours, it would not much matter if you did.' This cold comfort killed the idea.

Seven months later, however, on 14 May 1940 – day five of the German invasion of the west – Dowding backed a proposed attack on the Ruhr even if it led to reprisals.[386] Dowding wrote to Peirse (Deputy CAS) on that day, sending a copy to Portal, the new head of Bomber Command. Peirse had invited the commanders-in-chief to consider whether or not to open an air offensive against Germany. That was before the German offensive in the west began on 10 May. Dowding's opinion now, 'for what it is worth', was that we should attack German oil resources at once, preferably by night for several reasons. Firstly, the attack might slow down the enemy's mechanised columns. Secondly, 'we should hope to draw on this country air attacks which would otherwise have been delivered on Continental targets, thus further relieving the pressure.' And thirdly, if we are to bomb oil stores, it would be best to do it when they are full and not drained away to permit attacks on British targets.

Dowding wanted his command 'to pull its full weight in this battle; but I want to do so by shooting down Germans in this country and not by being used as a reservoir for sending reinforcements to France.' The Hurricane tap was now turned fully on, 'and you will not be able to resist the pressure to send Hurricanes to France until I have been bled white and am in no condition to withstand the bombing attack which will inevitably be made on this country,' once that happens. He therefore advocated an immediate onslaught against oil targets. Portal agreed and said so to Peirse.[387]

Bomber Command's attempt to be offensive would have had some prospect of success if the RAF had possessed a fighter provided either with drop tanks or internal fuel tanks sufficient to allow it to escort bombers to and from German targets. Unfortunately, the Air Ministry had never shown interest in drop tanks and refused to believe that an effective long-range fighter was technically possible. Dowding disagreed and said so to Douglas in March 1940. Douglas curtly rejected his opinion. Such a fighter, he decreed, after much discussion but no actual testing, 'must be inferior in performance to the short-range fighter ... the escort fighter was really a myth.' British bombers were therefore left unescorted to do what they could to ease the pressure on Dowding's defences throughout 1940. For all their gallantry, they suffered heavy losses and achieved little. It would be years before the opinion of Douglas – strongly backed by Portal – was shown by the Americans to have been mistaken.[388]

Dowding had sent a paper to Ludlow-Hewitt on 30 March about how best to attack bomber formations escorted by fighters. This would be the case if the Germans conquered the Low Countries and were able to use bases there for raids on Britain. Dowding supposed they would fly above and behind their bombers, so RAF fighters may be able to get at them before the escorts intervene. He thought it possible that the Germans would modify some of their bombers to use as escort fighters: without bombs, they could carry more fuel and guns and lurk at the rear of enemy formations until combat was joined. Much of this was speculation, he admitted, and he was reluctant to lay down rules, 'but I want all concerned to be thinking ahead.'[389]

After 10 May, disastrous attempts were made at offering tactical air support for troops fighting in France and the Low Countries. On 4 June, Douglas penned some excellent Whitehallspeak for Portal: 'the strenuous and gallant efforts of your squadrons against objectives in collaboration with the land battle since 10 May have not always had results commensurate with the effort exerted.'

Portal's command was then required to assist the defence of Britain by attacking German airframe assembly factories, aluminium plants, airfields and stores. It was also charged to thwart a possible invasion by hammering German ports and shipping. Tragically, as Tami Davis Biddle has written, 'the gap between rhetoric and reality proved to be nothing less than an abyss' and the bombers achieved little at heavy cost to themselves. In return for 1,097 sorties against airfields, and a loss of 61 aircraft, Bomber Command destroyed five German aircraft and damaged 12.[390]

Harris, head of 5 Group, wrote to Dowding on 7 September 1940 to say that all his men were 'full of admiration for the magnificent efforts of the fighters', adding – in a light-hearted moment – that he hoped they would leave some for the bombers to destroy. Dowding responded in the same vein: 'I assure you that we shall not grudge you any Germans which you can blow up on the other side. There are still plenty left! Thank you for your appreciation of the fighter pilots; they are indeed magnificent.'

As Harris's most recent biographer has written, there was 'mutual respect' between those 'strongly contrasting personalities'. Harris would be among those who believed that Dowding was unjustly treated after the Battle of Britain: 'the only commander who won one of the decisive battles of history and got sacked for his pains.' Dowding paid his own splendid tribute to Harris and his crews at a Festival of Reunion organized by the RAF Association in the Albert Hall on 22 September 1946. 'Truly,' he said, 'if Fighter Command's calvary was measured in months, theirs was reckoned in years.'[391]

14

From Norway to Dunkirk, April to June 1940

Ignominious Failure

Norway's strategic importance in September 1939 was obvious: if she were to be brought under British control, Britain would control the sea routes from Germany to the North Sea and into the north Atlantic. Britain would also have access to the German coast and the Baltic and would be able to cut off imports of Swedish iron ore to Germany. With a campaign in France and the Low Countries pending, and his thoughts never far from an assault on the Soviet Union, Hitler preferred Norway to remain neutral. However, the British and French took so long to plan an 'occupation' of Norway that Hitler was given time, and cause, to mount his own occupation, beginning on 7 April 1940. The result, from a British point of view, was a disaster that might well have been even worse, because Chamberlain's government – described by General Ironside (head of the British Army) as 'a bewildered flock of sheep' – intended to support Finland in her conflict with the Soviet Union, but the Finns surrendered on 13 March 1940 and Britons narrowly avoided finding themselves at war with both Nazi Germany and the Soviet Union.[392]

Peirse, Deputy CAS, wrote to Dowding on 4 April about plans to stop the passage of ships carrying iron ore from Narvik, on the north coast of Norway, to German ports by laying mines in Norwegian waters from the 8th onwards. The Germans may attack Norway, Peirse continued, and if they do we – the British and French – will consider it as an attack on ourselves, but our response would not, he airily supposed, require much air support: one Gladiator squadron, he thought, would serve, plus a flight of Westland Lysanders for reconnaissance. Peirse's thinking reflected the RAF's reluctance to consider seriously any use for aircraft as other than offensive bombers or defensive fighters.[393]

This ill-conceived, badly-planned venture became an ignominious failure, 'a glaring example of what Dowding most feared,' in the words of Hough and Richards: 'having to waste his squadrons overseas in circumstances far removed from his carefully-planned scientific air defence system at home.' The fiasco, displaying 'an amateurishness and feebleness which to this day can make the reader alternately blush and shiver,'[394] ultimately cost Dowding three squadrons – two of Gladiators, one of Hurricanes – together with many well-trained pilots. However, the Scandinavian campaign was not all loss. It got rid of Chamberlain and some of his lackeys, it cost the German Navy most of its precious warships and it allowed Churchill to become prime minister: a man eager to conduct a war instead of a man hoping it would go away.

The fiasco also had an important effect on Dowding: if the Royal Navy could fail so dismally to prevent the Germans from mounting a successful seaborne invasion of Norway, how much easier would be an invasion across the Channel if Fighter Command were defeated? The evidence of crass incompetence between the British services as well as in co-operation with the French was still very much in Dowding's mind when the German assault on France and the Low Countries began on 10 May. What reliance could a prudent commander, and Dowding was certainly that, place on soldiers, sailors or politicians, British or French? It is with these questions in mind that the superficially persuasive arguments in favour of maintaining a balance between the claims of Fighter and Bomber Command, between defence and offence, collapse. As for Peirse, he went on to enjoy high command for the next four years, reaching the rank of air chief marshal, until sexual misconduct brought a timely end to his undistinguished career.[395]

When Squadron Leader Jack Donaldson, CO of 263 Squadron (equipped with Gladiators), and Flight Lieutenant Stuart Mills (one of his flight commanders) returned from Norway, they were required to report on 28 April to the Air Ministry. When we pointed out the difficulties, Mills recalled, such as 'wrong aviation spirit, wrong oil, no serviceable starter batteries, unsuitable equipment, no maps, lack of ammunition,' senior officers could only say: "You appreciate the squadron was sent to Norway as a token sacrifice."'

Donaldson and Mills were then sent to Sir Samuel Hoare (Chamberlain's last Secretary of State for Air), and warned not to tell him about the numerous mistakes made in mounting and conducting the expedition to Norway; they should offer Hoare as favourable a picture as possible. After this whitewash session, it would have been a relief to meet an RAF officer – even one widely regarded as 'stuffy' – who was both honest and capable. Dowding entertained them to dinner at Bentley Priory, read out the citations for the decorations they had been awarded – DSO for Donaldson, DFC for Mills – and listened carefully to what they had to say. At the end of their tale of woe, he told them he fully supported their actions and agreed with their criticisms. More than a year later, when writing his despatch on the Battle of Britain, Dowding found space for this tribute: 'I trust that the epic fight of 263 Squadron, under Squadron Leader J. W. Donaldson, DSO, near Aandalsnes may not be lost to history.'[396]

Immortal Letter
Dowding therefore resisted demands to allow his precious fighters, especially his few Spitfires, to cross the Channel and help to stem the German invasion of the Low Countries and France. A month earlier, on 12

158

April, *Aeroplane* magazine had opined that Britain's concentration on home and shipping defence was too much and more fighter squadrons should be sent to France. 'One can only thank God,' commented Bill Gunston on this nonsense, 'that Fighter Command was run by a chap called Dowding, and not by whoever wrote that!'[397]

On 10 May the Luftwaffe had about 2,750 aircraft ready for action in the west to support powerful land forces: 1,180 bombers, 340 dive-bombers, 970 single-engined fighters and 270 twin-engined fighters.[398] Dowding was convinced that the efforts of every modern fighter currently in service, however gallant, could not affect the issue there, whereas their absence from the home base would leave Britain dangerously vulnerable to invasion. Even so, six squadrons of Hurricanes were in France on day one of the invasion and within a week Dowding had lost the equivalent of six more. Another four were fighting over France each day and returning – if they could – to England each evening.

The pressure for yet more assistance was 'relentless and inexorable', in Dowding's words, so on the morning of 15 May he attended a Cabinet meeting at which Newall spoke up, and resisted sending any more fighters to France. Despite what he later thought had happened on that occasion, and what several historians have written, Dowding did not 'confront' Churchill all by himself. Following Newall, he spoke calmly and lucidly, making a strong case for retaining all his fighters for home defence. At that time, however, the BEF was still in position near Brussels, about to attack German lines of communication, and could not be denied reinforcement.[399]

Next day, 16 May, when the Germans were clearly sweeping all before them, Dowding set out his case, in a letter to the Air Ministry, against sending more fighters to France. We had to face the possibility, he wrote, that the Allied armies might be defeated. Should that happen, he assumed that Britain would fight on. (However, there was in fact a significant number of Britons in high places who privately doubted whether the fight should continue if France fell and Churchill found it very difficult to outface them.) If Britain were to fight on, Dowding continued, he needed to know the Air Ministry's opinion of the 'minimum strength' required to do so. He had been told 52 squadrons were needed, but he had only 36 on hand. Until the minimum strength was reached, he asked that not a single additional fighter be sent overseas, 'no matter how desperate the situation may become.'

He was sure that:

> 'If an adequate fighter force is kept in this country, if the fleet remains in being, and if home forces are suitably organized to resist invasion, we should be able to carry on the war single-handed for some time, if not indefinitely. But if the home defence force is drained away in desperate attempts to remedy the situation in France, defeat in France will involve the final, complete and irremediable defeat of this country.'

This letter has become the most famous written by any airman at any time in any country to any recipient. The framed original now hangs in an honoured place in the RAF College at Cranwell in Lincolnshire, a better resting-place for it than any office of the now defunct Air Ministry. It has been quoted in countless books, articles, radio and television documentaries, films, websites, lectures, essays and conversations on the Battle of Britain.

It is less well known that Newall attached this letter to a clear statement on air defence weakness circulated to his fellow-chiefs that same day. Fighter Command, he wrote, could give no further assistance to France, 'if we are to have any chance of protecting the United Kingdom, the Fleet, our seaborne trade, our aircraft industry, and all the vital centres throughout the country on which we must depend for our ability to continue the war.'[400]

On that same day, 16 May, the Air Ministry ordered Dowding to prepare another eight half-squadrons to send across the Channel and that was being done because no-one yet realized that the campaign was going to be lost, swiftly and completely. Dowding now had only 36 squadrons on hand. In his postwar memoirs Churchill mistakenly claimed that Dowding told him he needed only 25 squadrons for home defence, not 52.

Whatever he actually believed at the time – and he refused, after the war, to correct his mistake when it was pointed out to him – Churchill then flew to France and telegraphed to London asking for six more squadrons to be sent as well as the eight half-squadrons. They would give the French Army a last chance, he said, 'to rally its bravery and strength. It would not be good historically if their requests were denied and their ruin resulted. Also night bombardment by a strong force of heavy bombers can no doubt be arranged.'

But fighters could not prevent the French 'ruin'.

As for 'heavy bombers', the British had none and the medium bombers they did have were quite unable to hit the Germans hard with any accuracy in daylight, let alone in darkness. Despite Churchill's constant fear that any action of his might not look good 'historically', he would have looked a great deal worse if Fighter Command had collapsed and Britain with it.

This was the payoff for years of talk and little action. The War Cabinet met at 11 pm on the 16th and agreed to Churchill's request. He returned home next day and told the Cabinet that the decision to send yet more fighters to France had been 'the gravest decision that a British Cabinet had ever had to take,' and had heartened the French to a considerable degree. Newall now made another positive contribution that helped Dowding. He told the War Cabinet that there were not enough airfields in France for them, so the six squadrons remained in Kent and flew across the Channel each day.[401]

Dowding wrote to Park on 16 May, telling him of our 'notable victory on the "Home Front" this morning.' The orders to send more Hurricanes were cancelled. Appeals for help would doubtless be renewed, however, with increasing insistence and Dowding did not know 'how this morning's work will stand the test of time,' but he would never relax his efforts to prevent the dissipation of the home fighter force. He then sent 'a personal emissary' to France, to get a first-hand account of the situation there. The officer chosen was Wing Commander the Duke of Hamilton, at that time serving as a controller in 11 Group. Hamilton spent three days across the Channel (17-19 May) and confirmed Dowding's opinion that the Germans were winning and any fighters sent to help the Allied armies would be lost for no good reason.[402]

Churchill ruled on 19 May that no more fighter squadrons were to leave Britain, no matter how serious the situation became in France, and the War Cabinet formally endorsed that ruling next day. On those two days, all but three of the fighter squadrons in France returned home. Their return, Dowding told his masters on 24 May, 'converted a desperate into a serious situation.'[403]

Harold Larnder, in charge of the group from Bawdsey that became on day one of the war the 'Stanmore Research Section', was asked by Dowding on 2 June (not on 15 May) for a clear, simple graph to help him convince Churchill and the War Cabinet. Larnder and his deputy, Eric Williams, produced exactly what Dowding needed. Many years later, in 1978, Larnder wrote: 'There seems little doubt that, had Dowding not won his battle with Churchill in May [June, actually, but the point remains just as valid], he would have lost the Battle of Britain in September.' The Canadian-born Larnder was apparently something of a 'rough diamond', but Dowding always valued 'the gusto and forthrightness of his approach and his readiness to bring out home truths.' When Dowding was sacked in November, Larnder sent him a note of thanks for all his support. Dowding returned it, with this comment: 'Thanks. This war will be won by science thoughtfully applied to operational needs.'[404]

By 3 June, Dowding's fighters had flown more than 2,700 sorties over France and suffered heavy losses, because they were short-range interceptors intended to protect targets in England as the sharp point of an elaborate defensive system. Protecting ground forces far from their bases was a task for which they were not designed and their pilots not trained. Consequently, in a little more than three weeks since the German assault began, Dowding had lost more than 430 fighters, and as many of his even more precious peacetime-trained pilots.

He therefore sought and obtained permission to attend another Cabinet meeting on 3 June, and spoke forcefully. He thought he was not impressing Churchill (the only other person present who mattered). Beaverbrook, who was among those in the room, 'has since told me that he saw me throw my pencil down on the table and said to himself, "He's going to resign."' That idea had not crossed his mind, but he was desperate to convince the Prime Minister:

'Luckily, I had realized that one can often convince a person through his eyes when it is not possible to do so through his ears, and I had armed myself with a graph showing the balance of Hurricane wastage against replacements. I got up from my seat and walked round the table to the PM's chair. I laid the graph on the table before him and said, "If the present rate of wastage continues for another fortnight, we shall not have a single Hurricane left in France or in this country." That did the trick!'[405]

A. J. P. Taylor, a very popular historian and television lecturer of the 1960s, alleged that: 'When argument failed, Dowding laid down his pencil on the cabinet table. This gentle gesture was a warning of immeasurable significance. The War Cabinet cringed, and Dowding's pencil won the Battle of Britain.'[406] 'Taylor's remark,' wrote Dowding to Wright (his second biographer) on 9 June 1966, 'about the Cabinet cringing is really rather absurd.' He had no intention of resigning, then or later, and it was the graph which won over Churchill. Dowding came to believe that neither Sinclair nor Newall supported him at that meeting. He was mistaken: the facts – of fighter losses, the collapse of resistance on the ground to advancing German forces – were self-evident, but Newall again spoke up. More than 250 fighters had been sent to France, 'against the advice' of Dowding, whose graph showed the strength of his Hurricane force after 11 days of intense operations, 8-18 May: 250 had been 'permanently lost' and only four received from new production.

Had this rate continued throughout May, Dowding said, he would have lost *all* his Hurricanes by the end of the month. The fighting over Dunkirk, he added, had imposed 'a tremendous strain' on fighter resources. If the Germans were to begin a heavy attack on Britain at this moment, 3 June, he could not guarantee air superiority for more than 48 hours. He had about 500 fighters on hand, including those needing repair or service, but a good many pilots were not yet ready for operations.

A Bastardized Air Force
The failure of the French Air Force to offer effective resistance to the German invasion is a vital, and under-emphasised, factor during these critical days. Oceans of ink, plus millions of keyboard taps, have been devoted to debating how much or how little the RAF contributed to resisting that invasion, but it is surely important to consider what efforts were made by the French Air Force in support of Allied ground forces to defend their own homeland.

At the end of the Great War, France had a large, powerful air force, but it was – and remained – under Army and Navy control until it became nominally independent in 1933. For the next several years it tried to follow the RAF's example of favouring the creation of a strategic bomber force at the expense of all other forms of air power, but the result was even more of a muddle than in Britain. No fewer than 60 different aircraft types were flying in 1940, among them a twin-engined 'aesthetic monstrosity', the Amiot 143, designed in 1928, put into production in 1933 and still flying for no good reason when the Germans came. Worse still, the French had nothing approaching the British defence system, based on radar, radio, and observer posts.

From 1937, however, although there was an increasing focus on fighters, those produced proved to be markedly inferior to the latest German and British types. For example, the Bloch MB-152. Like so many French aircraft of the time, the Bloch story 'began badly, got into its stride just in time for the capitulation and eventually produced outstanding aircraft which were unable to be used.' Although the Bloch was outclassed in aerial combat, it was a sturdy and quite well-armed warplane, suitable for strafing German troops and armour. Unfortunately, it was only used in the former role and never in the latter.[408]

The French had one excellent twin-engined bomber, the Sud Est LeO 451, which first flew in 1937 and was superior in every measurable way to two of Germany's three major bombers (the Heinkel and the Dornier) and comparable to the Junkers Ju 88. As with the fighters, there were too few of them, too few spares, too few trained crews and too little effort was made during the 'practice war' to combine their attacks with fighter cover.[409]

The Bréguet 691, a promising twin-engined fighter-bomber, was ready to fly in March 1937, but had to wait almost a year for engines because Bréguet had not joined the newly-nationalized aviation industry and few were in service in May 1940. The Dewoitine D 520 single-seat fighter had an even sadder history. First flown in December 1938, it was an excellent design: fast, well-armed, a match for the best German fighters and deadly to German bombers, but there were too few of them. The only French fighter built in quantity was the Morane-Saulnier MS 406, which equipped 19 of the 26 combat-ready groups in May 1940. According to one of its former pilots, the fighter was 'free from vices, but too slow to catch German aircraft and too badly armed [one cannon, two machine guns] to shoot them down.' When the French authorities belatedly realized that a strong, modern air force might be of value, they bought an American fighter, the Curtiss P-36 (known as Hawk 75A in its export version). Like the MS 406, it was robust, vice-free, too slow, too lightly-armed – and there were too few of them where they were needed.[410]

In short, the French designed a number of highly promising fighters and bombers, but they were neither produced in quantity, nor delivered to squadrons, nor located in the battle areas, nor provided with sufficient air or ground crews, nor properly equipped (some even lacked propellers in May 1940).

Constant changes in the government – nine ministers of aviation between 1935 and 1939 – were a handicap, both politically and in relations with industry. Even so, there were plenty of aircraft. Guy la Chambre, air minister in 1940, would tell a parliamentary enquiry after the war that in May 1940 France had 3,289 modern aircraft, of which no fewer than 2,122 were fighters. But only one-third of them, 790, were actually available on the combat fronts, and only 418 were serviceable, because of 'mechanical difficulties'. Large numbers of fighters were evenly spread throughout France and its overseas colonies, at the behest of local Army or Navy commanders. Procedures for concentrating them where they were needed were so complicated, by red tape and a shortage of pilots, that most of them made no contribution whatever to the defence of France.

From every point of view – doctrine, equipment, personnel, training, logistics, command and control arrangements, morale – the French Air Force was inadequate. There were, of course, many occasions when individual pilots or even squadrons behaved with great courage and skill, but in the overall picture they were merely tragic gestures.[411] For 20 years, wrote Robert Young, the Army insisted that it was preparing 'a tactically formidable air force'; it was not. The air command no less vociferously insisted that it was designing 'a truly formidable strategic strike force'; it was not. 'France thus entered the Second World War with a bastardized air force, the offspring of a couple which had never been well married.' Pascal Vennesson was equally unimpressed. 'In May and June,' he wrote, 'many ground commanders had no clear idea of what they could do with aviation in the battle, and many air force officers were more convinced by long-range reconnaissance than any other mission.'[412]

If Dowding thought he had problems with Whitehall – and he had – he would quickly have realized they were insignificant if he had commanded fighters in France or, for that matter, in Germany. As for Italy, he would either have been driven into an early grave or taken his skis up some mountain and stayed there.

Co-operation between the French and British air forces was practically non-existent before and after the war began in September 1939. The RAF had given no thought to tactical support of ground forces and remained doggedly committed to planning and even occasionally carrying out raids on 'strategic' targets in Germany, rather than attacking those forces currently overwhelming British and French soldiers.

This abstinence was justified by the fact that many RAF commanders in 1940 had spent the best years of their lives as students or teachers in staff colleges, and subsequently served in Whitehall or in subordinate headquarters, where they told each other so often that the battlefield was no place for bombers that they came to believe it. Such aerial reconnaissance as was carried out either by French or British aircraft was so inept that it failed to spot thousands of Germans massing in the Ardennes on the eve of the invasion. Finally and perhaps most depressing of all facets of the Allied defeat is the fact well established in recent years that France and Britain had the resources on the ground and even in the air to withstand the invasion. German soldiers and airmen were not supermen, led unerringly by brilliant commanders; most of them were astonished (if delighted) by the speed and completeness of their victory, despite all the cockups usual in conducting a massive invasion of a powerful enemy.[413]

Salmond has the Answers

Meanwhile, John Salmond, who had been head of the RAF at the end of its 'best flying club in the world' days (1930-3) was recalled to serious service, in his 60th year. He went to Harrogate, in the West Riding of Yorkshire, as head of armament production in Beaverbrook's newly-created Ministry of Aircraft Production. Although Salmond had reached the top of what was then a small service, there is much to be said for David Omissi's opinion that he 'was not an especially studious man, even by the unexacting standards of the Royal Air Force, but he was quick-witted and energetic.'[414] He also had a high opinion of his own merits, but whether he was any longer sensible, let alone wise, is another matter.

For example, this is what he wrote to Trenchard on 11 May 1940: 'will the government,' he asked, 'now make up its mind that it is essential to bomb the sources of supply of German aircraft *in Germany*?' Hitler will not shrink from bombing anything and everything in this country, when it suits him. 'That must be his plan and if we don't bomb his sources of supply now, when we are in a favourable position to do so and he is not, being immersed in operations in Belgium and Holland, then it may be too late.'

Salmond's 'great hope', he added, was that Trenchard would be rescued from his long retirement and appointed Secretary of State for Air. Andrew Boyle, who published a biography of Trenchard in 1962, praised him as 'the man who prepared victory in the Battle of Britain.' A. J. P. Taylor was among those who disagreed. He wrote:

'The Battle of Britain was won by Fighter Command and radar. Trenchard had despised the one and knew nothing of the other. What Trenchard prepared was the strategical air offensive of 1940-41, which was a total failure.... Like Haig, his hero, Trenchard was an extremely resolute and dogged commander, whose weapons did not come up to expectations and whose plans did not correspond to the facts.'[415]

Salmond's 'great hope' would be dashed, though he and Trenchard, conniving together, played an important part in getting Dowding out of Bentley Priory, but mercifully not until late in November 1940.

Salmond then outlined his thoughts, combining his usual massive self-confidence with alarming ignorance of Germany's likely approach to the problem of conquering the British Isles. The Germans, he wrote, will use troop-carriers and parachutists. They 'are prepared to sacrifice machines to any extent so long as they effect a landing, and will land even in places where great risk is entailed to the personnel they are carrying.' All open spaces must be 'under suspicion' because parachutists 'land on a concerted plan and frequently in large numbers. They are very highly trained in self-concealment before attacking their objective. They are normally dropped at night.'

Pause here to reflect that German troop-carriers (Junkers Ju 52s) were virtually defenceless. See them trundling slowly across the Channel, in daylight or darkness, each with 16 lightly-armed soldiers aboard. Recall that the Germans lost 150 of these machines in the Norwegian campaign and 167 over Holland. Conclude that if used in operations against Britain, escort would have been more difficult, air and ground defences would have offered a stronger challenge than was possible in Norway or Holland, and it does seem likely that losses would have been even heavier.[416]

Salmond, who knew little about Dowding's defensive system, 'understood' that the Observer Corps network covered the whole country, 'but the difficulty of seeing parachutists, etc., at night is always very great.' It followed therefore that use must be made of 'an enormous untapped reserve of watchers in the youth of the country of non-military age, e.g., boy scouts, National Cadet Organization, Air Defence Cadets, etc.' These stout lads can quickly be made into a force of 'first-class protective value':

'It is a simple matter and does not require much organization as the majority of boy scouts have their own bivouacs – make each unit responsible for watching the country around their own locality by day and night. These boys in a bivouac – one on duty at a time – could watch many miles of country from a hill-top.'

As for the defence of aerodromes, 'I am not in the picture', he admitted, but he did wonder if Army units would arrive quickly enough in the event of enemy landings; if satellite airfields not actually required were obstructed; and if 'crows nests' had been erected on hangar roofs, where men could watch for approaching enemy bombers and shoot them down as they attempted to land or passed overhead. 'I believe there is an enormous number of holes in our defence,' he wrote, 'which could be filled from our own RAF resources.' Readers might like to compare this nonsense with Dowding's letter to General Kirke on 12 November 1939 (see Chapter 13) and to note, as we shall see presently, that Salmond was selected to chair an enquiry into Dowding's conduct of night defence.

Ludlow-Hewitt, a particular friend of Trenchard and Salmond, had recently been sacked and found a new job: reporting to the Air Ministry on aerodrome defence, but he had no 'executive status'. Salmond thought it essential that an officer of high rank be appointed at once, provided with a suitable staff, and given 'over-riding authority' in regard to all RAF establishments. He mentions neither Dowding nor Fighter Command in these lengthy notes.[417]

While great events were in progress at Dunkirk, Salmond wrote again to Trenchard on 4 June 1940. He had been in touch with Ludlow-Hewitt about his new job. Unfortunately, Ludlow did not, in Salmond's opinion, realize how acute the dangers were. 'For instance, he told me that aerodromes in this part of the world were out of the range of troop-carrying German aircraft. I pointed out to him that they were quite prepared to crash their machines on landing with no idea of returning home. This had not occurred to him before.'

It did not occur to Ludlow-Hewitt, nor to Salmond, that the troops emerging from crashed transports, even if neither injured nor widely scattered, would be lightly armed, would shortly run out of ammunition, and find their thoughts turning to the absence of all the good things so readily available in the French campaign: tanks, trucks, artillery, reinforcements, food, water and medical services, to say nothing of the need to deal with (or evade) British defenders.[418]

From this time on, Trenchard and Salmond brooded and plotted to get rid of Dowding. They also opposed Newall, who earned their displeasure by wavering from the true faith in a bomber offensive, ignoring the fact – as they had done throughout their careers – that British bombers were inadequate in every measurable way: number of machines, navigational skill of crews, range, altitude, speed, weight and quality of bombs carried, defensive armour and armament.

A Possible but Unlikely Evacuation

Meanwhile, back in the real world, Dowding got the shocking news that his nephew, Denis, only son of Admiral Arthur, had died of wounds on 22 May, while serving with the Royal Tank Regiment in France. He was buried at

Wormhoudt, some 20 kilometres south of Dunkirk. Like so many men and women in the English-speaking world of his generation, Dowding had lost friends and relatives in the Great War. Now, not much more than 20 years later, he would suffer the premature loss of yet more friends and relatives. His only son, Derek, was at great risk as a pilot in Fighter Command. Despite all his other worries throughout 1940, concern for the young man's safety can never have been far from Dowding's thoughts.

Churchill asked the Chiefs of Staff on 27 May to report on Britain's prospects of continuing the war 'alone against Germany and probably Italy'. They replied that for as long as Fighter Command remained 'in being' the RAF and the Royal Navy together should be able to prevent a German invasion. But if Germany obtained air superiority, the Navy could only prevent an invasion 'for a time'; not 'for an indefinite period'.[419]

On that day, 27 May, and for many to come, fear of invasion filled many British minds. A meeting at the War Office on 19 May had discussed the problem of 'the possible but unlikely evacuation of a very large force in hazardous circumstances' through the ports of Dunkirk, Calais and Boulogne. Unlikely as the need may then have seemed in Whitehall, plans were made to effect just such an evacuation – which was wise, because those plans were implemented as soon as formulated. Anglo-French armies were being driven back to the Channel ports and when Calais and Boulogne fell into German hands on 25 and 26 May, Dunkirk became the only hope of escape.[420]

From 23 May onwards, as they tried to help troops escape across the Channel, Dowding's pilots suffered from 'friendly fire' incidents. British warships fired indiscriminately at all aircraft and the Admiralty informed Dowding, with a callous disregard for the lives of gallant young men trying to help them, that 'our destroyers fire at any aircraft that comes within range whether they make our recognition signals or not.' So much for Dowding's several detailed discussions with naval officers during the past year on how to prevent Britons from killing each other. That evening, he received three Admiralty messages complaining that fighter defences over Boulogne were inadequate, this after two fighters had been shot down and two damaged earlier in the day by fire from ships of the Royal Navy. British bombers were also prevented from attacking German forces by British naval gunners. Neither then nor later came either apology from the Admiralty or any serious attempt to prevent such tragedies.[421]

The Allied armies had disintegrated or fallen back so rapidly in the face of a powerful enemy advance that Vice-Admiral Bertram Ramsay, commanding the naval base at Dover, was ordered to implement Operation Dynamo, 'with a view to lifting up to 45,000 of the BEF within two days, at the end of which it was probable that evacuation would be terminated by enemy action.' During three critical days, 26-28 May, Churchill seriously considered seeking peace: 'if we could get out of this jam,' he said on the 26th, 'by giving up Malta and Gibraltar and some African colonies, I would jump at it.' On the 28th, he told his ministers that we should be able to get 50,000 men away from Dunkirk; 100,000 'would be a wonderful performance'. One week later, when nearly 340,000 men (two-thirds of them British) had been rescued, he concluded that this 'transformed Britain's prospects'.[422]

Ramsay was in charge of the embarkation of troops and Park had tactical control of the fighter cover. Co-ordination between fighters, bombers and reconnaissance aircraft was handled at Hawkinge, conveniently close to Ramsay's base at Dover and with good communications to Park's headquarters at Uxbridge.[423]

Dunkirk was the first major encounter between the home-based fighter force and the Luftwaffe, but Dowding could not regard it as a chance for a decisive victory, despite the obvious importance of helping to get as many soldiers home as possible. Dunkirk was at maximum range for his single-engined fighters and the Blenheims could not be used. To give continuous cover in strength would have required Dowding to concentrate virtually all his Hurricanes and Spitfires in the few airfields from which they could reach Dunkirk, and that would have meant exposing the rest of Britain to attack.

As it was, Park could offer only two-squadron patrols for much of the day or four-squadron patrols for some of the day. Fighter Command managed a daily average of 300 sorties over Dunkirk: not many, but the losses of aircraft and experienced pilots over France before the Dunkirk evacuation began had been heavy and Dowding was acutely aware of an even more serious challenge still to come. The Air Ministry claimed that 260 German aircraft were destroyed in return for 106 British fighters, though only 52 pilots were killed. In fact, the Luftwaffe lost 132 aircraft: 'evidence enough, as was the campaign in France and the Low Countries, that without the ground control organization to help them, Fighter Command equipment was only just a match for the Luftwaffe.'[424]

For his efforts to protect the evacuation, Park was assigned 16 squadrons (some 200 aircraft, including Spitfires, fighting for the first time across the Channel) out of Dowding's home defence force. The remaining 20 squadrons were used as a reserve to keep up the strength of Park's force, to protect vital targets in England, and also coastal shipping and the fleet. Although only three fighter squadrons were never engaged over Dunkirk, Park was short of men and machines for so desperate a task. The area to be protected lay at least 50 miles from his nearest bases. Fighters operating outside their planned defensive system could receive no help from radar and were obliged to rely on wasteful, exhausting standing patrols. The limited fuel capacity of fighters permitted only 40 minutes at most on the actual patrol lines. Even when resistance in Calais and Boulogne ended, Park was unable to cover Dunkirk properly because the area defended by Allied troops had a perimeter extending for ten miles, and the shipping taking part in the rescue attempt was liable to attack anywhere on the Channel crossing.[425]

Consequently, although fighters were present throughout 27 May, the first full day of withdrawal, they were seriously outnumbered. They could not prevent the Luftwaffe from reducing Dunkirk town to rubble, but they did prevent a concentration on the targets that mattered most: the harbour moles and ships. Despite the damage done, the port never became untenable.

At 2 am on the 28th, Newall told Dowding that that day was 'likely to be the most critical ever experienced by the British Army.' An hour later, he ordered him to ensure the protection of Dunkirk and its beaches from first light until darkness by continuous fighter patrols in strength. It was impossible for Dowding to obey this order because the twin demands of *continuity and strength* could not be met. Experience had already shown that weak patrols were ineffective and neither the aircraft nor the pilots were available for constant patrols – not if Dowding conserved men and machines, as he must, to counter the even greater danger of an invasion of England.[426]

At the height of this crisis, on 30 May, Peirse found time to write to Dowding. Sinclair, newly-appointed Secretary of State for Air, had asked Balfour, newly-appointed Under-Secretary, to visit some fighter stations on the 29th. These politicians now wished to know, reported Peirse, how Dowding proposed to mitigate the conditions of fatigue observed by Balfour. Dowding's long experience of Air Ministry idiocy helped him to pen a civil reply. He refrained from pointing out that there would be no fatigue if only the Germans would go home, but since they seemed unwilling to do this, Britain must accept the unpleasant fact that she was facing perhaps the gravest crisis in her long history. Those in the front line were not only hard pressed today, they would be even harder pressed tomorrow, and for the foreseeable future. The fatigue which apparently distressed Balfour arose from the unavoidable necessity, explained Dowding, of fighting a battle far from base while at the same time preparing for attacks on that base. Rest and leave would be granted, as and when possible.

There the matter ended, but it graphically illustrated the gulf between those who realized that a war to the death had begun and senior Whitehall Warriors who seemed to regard it as a tedious interlude in public affairs that was going on for too long. That gulf was only slowly narrowed during the rest of 1940. Nearly 50 years later, however, Balfour – as a veteran politician – had had time to sense that the Air Ministry's views were now as dead as it was. He therefore recalled in 1988 that Dowding was still in 1940, as he had been in 1916, an outstanding officer. He worked hard to win the confidence of his pilots, especially when they were learning to fight as well as fly their modern fighters.

> 'Far from being the old Stuffy Dowding of World War One, he set out to learn from his men about any faults which could be put right both in the aircraft and their operation. He would gather round him groups of pilots, encouraging them to speak out frankly.'[427]

Rain and low cloud hindered all aircraft, British and German, on 30 May, but during the next two days Allied troops were heavily bombed. These attacks, as well as German artillery fire, obliged the British to suspend daylight evacuation on 2 June. From then until the operation ended on the morning of the 4th, evacuation was restricted to dawn and dusk and Park was able to concentrate his forces more effectively. The very last Hurricane to fly over Dunkirk was Park's.

He later reported to Dowding that enemy formation leaders seemed very capable, and although British fighters were superior to German fighters, our pilots were less skilled either in tactics or accurate shooting, thanks to a lack of realistic peacetime training and casualties suffered since September 1939. Dowding seconded Park's angry complaint about the conduct of some Whitehall mandarins:

> 'The Air Ministry throughout the operations failed to appreciate the difficulties of operating large numbers of squadrons from forward aerodromes, resulting in frequent hasteners for patrol reports and advance combat reports. This continual flow of enquiries from higher authority was a great embarrassment throughout the operations and at times so blocked the landlines that urgent operations orders were seriously delayed between the group headquarters and squadrons at forward aerodromes.'[428]

For once, however, Dowding's usual exasperation with Air Ministry officials was offset by his delight in the courage and skill shown by the command's pilots. 'My dear fighter boys,' he wrote on 2 June in a message to them all:

> 'I don't send out many congratulatory letters and signals, but I feel that I must take this occasion, when the intensive fighting in northern France is for the time being over, to tell you how proud I am of you and the way in which you have fought since the "blitzkrieg" started. I wish I could have spent my time visiting you and hearing your accounts of the fighting, but I have occupied myself working for you in other ways. I want you to know that my thoughts are always with you, and that it is you and your fighting spirit which will crack the morale of the German Air Force and preserve our country through the trials which yet lie ahead. Good luck to you.'

Nothing stuffy about those words. They help us to understand the inspiration that gave him the strength to carry on managing his vast empire throughout the rest of a critical year.

Without the courage of numerous seamen, amateur as well as professional, who crossed the Channel time and time again in over a thousand vessels to carry soldiers to safety, there could have been no 'miracle' at Dunkirk. There were, in fact, three miracles.

One was the amazing evacuation, lovingly described, year after year, by English patriots. No fewer than 340,000 Allied troops would be rescued, a figure to compare with 'up to 45,000' hoped for when the operation began.

A second miracle was the hardly less amazing performance of French and British soldiers before that evacuation began. They were very poorly trained, many of their leaders were inept and much of their equipment was inadequate, thanks to the decision of successive governments between the wars to think mainly of air and sea power in Britain or static defence in France. There had been no effective co-ordination between the reluctant allies before September 1939 and precious little was attempted thereafter. The French and British air forces were neither trained nor equipped to support land forces. And yet many of these unlucky soldiers fought bravely and doggedly against Germans who had numerous advantages over them, especially in training, self-confidence and air support.

And the third miracle was the rescue, by 18 June, of 192,000 men (144,000 of them British soldiers) from France's Atlantic ports: a splendid feat that, for some reason, has never attracted anything like the same attention as Dunkirk. Altogether, 558,000 men – a third of them not British – were evacuated and included thousands who would serve in later campaigns, some of them better managed than this one.[429]

The bravery and determination of units of the French First Army, holding the perimeter of Dunkirk, was vital. So too was the fact that the German advance was halted for three days, partly to allow recovery from the effects on men and machines of heavy fighting, partly to preserve precious tanks for the next phase of the battle for France, and partly because Hitler was persuaded by Goering to entrust the major assault to his air force. In fact, the Luftwaffe's offensive was as much an improvisation as the RAF's defence. Close support units had been disordered by days of headlong advance and both air and ground units were exhausted. Also, German bombers were now operating at extreme range from their bases and many were withdrawn from the assault to prepare for the next stage of the campaign.

The generally cloudy weather on most of the nine days of the evacuation, together with the huge pillars of smoke arising from burning oil tanks and warehouses in Dunkirk hindered the Luftwaffe. Nevertheless, the part played by Fighter Command, assisted by the crews of Bomber and Coastal Commands, in denying the Germans supremacy over the target area was essential to the operation's success. It should not be forgotten, however, that the BEF left behind 68,000 men (40,000 of them taken prisoner), together with most of its weapons and trucks, and over 200 ships of all sizes had been sunk.[430]

Ramsay's Report

No doubt these severe losses were in Ramsay's mind when he criticized the RAF's efforts in a report to the Admiralty submitted on 18 June.[431] 'Rightly or wrongly,' Ramsay wrote, 'full air protection was expected', though even a little reflection should have suggested to him that that was not a realistic expectation, given Dunkirk's distance from the nearest airfields in south-eastern England. He might also have understood Fighter Command's obligation, like the Navy's, was to regard protection of the homeland as the first charge on its resources.[432]

Ramsay had sent a signal to Dowding, copied to the heads of Bomber and Coastal Commands, on 29 May in which he said: 'Your assistance has been invaluable. I am most grateful for your splendid co-operation. It alone has given us a chance of success and I trust you will be able to keep it up.'[433]

Only three weeks later, however, in reporting to his own masters, Ramsay sang a different tune. According to Ramsay, many ships' captains, while giving credit to airmen 'for gallantry in such combats as were observed from the ships,' expressed 'disappointment and surprise at the seemingly puny efforts made to provide air protection during the height of the operation.' Perhaps he was thinking of an hysterical signal he received from the destroyer *Vimy* on 30 May: 'Request continuous fighter action in the air;' otherwise, 'a scandal, repetition scandal, reflecting on the British Cabinet for ever, will pass to history.'[434]

Ramsay had nothing to say about British destroyers firing on British aircraft nor, in his haste to get his own version of events into the Admiralty record, did he find time to check his assertions with Dowding. Many combats had taken place out of sight of soldiers and sailors, as Ramsay could easily have discovered. Sadly, it suited him to exacerbate traditional inter-service rivalry even at a time of grave national crisis.

The Admiralty published Ramsay's report after the war, in July 1947. He was dead by then and the Admiralty, although admitting that some parts of his report were 'necessarily distorted' [*sic*], refused to correct them on the pathetic ground that they represented naval feeling at the time, 'when many of the true facts about the general RAF operations were not known to the Flag Officer Dover.' The fact that he could have discovered them, had he been in less of a hurry to record a partisan account, was quietly ignored.

The Air Ministry was, however, allowed to add a few points to Ramsay's report. For example, many enemy raids were disrupted and raiders destroyed; air action often took place out of sight of naval officers; the Luftwaffe had the initiative and could attack where and when it pleased; and operations were conducted far outside the range of radar-controlled interception.[435]

Dowding could have told the admiral, had he enquired, that more than a quarter of Britain's fighter force had been lost over France even before the evacuation began. When it ended, he had only 331 Spitfires and Hurricanes available for operations and all his squadrons were disorganized. 'There can be no doubt,' Churchill told the War Cabinet on 1 June, 'that this constituted a signal victory for the RAF, which gave cause for high hopes for our success in the future.'

Perhaps; but the fact remained, as the Prime Minister admitted in the Commons on the 4th that we had suffered 'a colossal military disaster'. In helping to make the Dunkirk miracle, 106 fighters were lost, together with 80 pilots, in exchange for perhaps 130 enemy aircraft. During the six weeks of the French campaign, the RAF lost well over 900 aircraft (453 of them fighters) and nearly 1,400 personnel, including 915 aircrew, of whom 534 were pilots, many of them experienced regulars or men trained in peacetime. These losses were hardly offset by the transfer to Fighter Command of 68 pilots from naval service during June. Quite apart from a grievous loss of men and material, most of Dowding's squadrons had been 'disarranged', to put it mildly, during the past six weeks. Ground crews returned to England, and reached their units 'in dribs and drabs', having been left to make their way home by sea. The relatively quiet weeks after

Dunkirk, while the Nazi leaders relished their victory and pondered the prospect of peace, were a godsend to Dowding and every member of his command: they re-grouped, rested and did their best to re-equip.[436]

Although the cost to Fighter Command of the French campaign has often been noted, Luftwaffe casualties have received less attention (at least in English-language accounts). By the end of June 1940, the Luftwaffe had fought its way through four campaigns (in Poland, Norway, the Low Countries and France), all victorious, but all costly in aircrews and aircraft, though 400 aircrew prisoners were released after the French surrender on 22 June. Here we come to an important reason for Britain's survival: both the training system and aircraft production were already operating at a far higher pressure than in Germany, and continued to do so for the rest of the war. Meanwhile, Luftwaffe units in France, like their opponents across the Channel, welcomed an opportunity to re-group, rest and re-equip.[437]

The Dunkirk evacuation did not end the possibility of Fighter Command's commitment across the Channel. Arthur Barratt, head of British Air Forces in France, advised the Air Ministry on 4 June that in his opinion France was rallying, and that German losses were greater than had been supposed. It was essential, he urged, that many fighters be sent to France as soon as possible. He enclosed with his letter one signed on 3 June by General Joseph Vuillemin, head of the French Air Force, who went further even than Barratt in his appeal for help: at least half the fighters presently in England, he wrote, should immediately be sent across the Channel.

After consulting Dowding, Churchill signalled Premier Reynaud on 5 June: 'You don't seem to understand at all that British fighter aviation has been worn to a shred and frightfully mixed up' by the demands of Dunkirk. Even so, he still hoped to use British fighters to support a French rally. As late as 8 June he told Reynaud that: 'We are giving you all the support we can in this great battle short of ruining the capacity of this country to continue the war.' On the 12th, however, Dowding advised Barratt that the game was practically up and he should prepare to get out. Not surprisingly, Barratt's account of this disastrous campaign was never published. More than a year later, on 9 July 1941, Churchill and Sinclair reflected on these dramatic days. France, they agreed, 'had acted shamefully in demanding more fighter squadrons after they knew the battle was lost.'[438]

In May 1942, Liddell Hart asked Dowding whether he thought a German invasion of Britain in June or early July 1940 would have succeeded. Until his despatch could be published, he could only say that he was 'extremely glad that the Germans did not start the Battle of Britain directly Dunkirk was finished with.... Fighter Command had only partially recovered from the French bleeding, and from Dunkirk, when the real Battle started.'[439]

15

The Day Battle,
June to August 1940

A Strategically Simple Task

After Dunkirk and aware that a serious attempt to wreck Fighter Command was imminent, Dowding realized more clearly than ever that the task facing him was strategically simple, even though the Luftwaffe was well equipped, carefully trained and full of confidence. All he had to do was avoid defeat until bad weather made an invasion impossible in 1940. When good weather returned, six months later, the British Army should be re-organized and re-equipped, coastal defences improved, and the whole air force – not only Fighter Command – would be stronger. Precious combat experience had already been gained, there would have been time for intensive training, more and better aircraft would be on hand.

As John Colville, one of Churchill's secretaries, put it in his diary for 14 June: 'If we can hold on until November, we shall have won the war. But holding on is going to be a grim business.' Grimmer than Colville thought, because he expected Franklin D. Roosevelt to be re-elected president of the United States in that month and to declare war on Germany immediately. 'Well! Now it is England against Germany,' wrote Dowding to Churchill on 17 June, 'and I don't envy them their job.' The great wordsmith made the same point rather more elegantly next day: 'What General Weygand called "the Battle of France" is over. I expect that the Battle of Britain is about to begin.... Upon this battle depends the survival of Christian civilization.... Let us act so that future generations will say, "This was their finest hour."'440

Stirring words, but neither Churchill nor Dowding, nor indeed the brave airmen and devoted ground crews on both sides of the Channel knew that Hitler had no idea what to do at this glorious moment, after his rapid conquest of Poland, Denmark, Norway, France and the Low Countries. Many states in all parts of the world were eagerly offering benevolent neutrality, if not active alliance. These were victories on a scale that astonished everyone, Germany's many friends and few enemies alike. Hitler, quite reasonably, awarded himself a holiday, touring with old buddies places where they had fought and suffered during the Great War. His soldiers and airmen also deserved a rest and time to recover from heavy losses in men and material.

If the war were to continue, the Luftwaffe would need time to set up the essential ground organization: stocks of fuel, weapons and spares had to be gathered, workshops and billets prepared, and a labour force (skilled and unskilled) assembled. Meanwhile, Hitler had good reason to suppose that a peace with Britain on his terms was likely because Chamberlain and his numerous supporters remained influential.

If the British continued to resist, Hitler had several options. A blockade of imports, perhaps, using U-boats and aircraft? A Spanish alliance, perhaps also one with Portugal, leading to seizure of key points in the Mediterranean and the Atlantic islands? Overthrow of Stalin's rotten régime in the Soviet Union? Encouragement of anti-British sentiment in the Middle East and Asia, pleasing his friends in Tokyo? No doubt more could be done to strengthen isolationist sentiment in the United States. The world, in those happy days, was his oyster.

As for Goering, he too awarded himself a holiday and put out peace feelers via Swedish contacts. On 23 June, Josef Goebbels (Hitler's propaganda minister) declared that Churchill would soon fall and a 'compromise government' be set up. 'We are very close,' he said, 'to the end of the war.' But a month later, on 22 July, he told his staff: 'With their totally different, un-European mentality the British are unable to believe that the offer made [to end the war] in the Fuehrer's speech was not just bluff, but was meant seriously.'[441]

The Luftwaffe, despite the hard knocks it had already taken and the problems of re-organizing for a new campaign, had every reason to feel confident of success, if the war continued. It had destroyed the air forces of Poland, Holland, Belgium and France, as well as overwhelming the RAF aircraft supporting the BEF. It had helped to conquer Norway despite the best efforts of British and French soldiers and the mighty Royal Navy.

The three air fleets facing Fighter Command by mid-July 1940 numbered some 2,800 aircraft: an apparently huge advantage over the 700 Hurricanes and Spitfires then at Dowding's disposal, but only 760 of the German aircraft were single-seat fighters, Messerschmitt Bf 109s.[442] They were marginally superior to their British equivalents, but what really mattered was the fact that most of their pilots were more thoroughly trained and more experienced in combat than were most of Dowding's surviving pilots by July 1940. In addition, the Germans had about 250 twin-engined fighters. These Messerschmitt Bf 110s carried a devastating nose armament and much was expected of them. Soon, however, it would be realized that they lacked the agility and acceleration to compete successfully with Hurricanes or Spitfires.[443]

It was not until 21 July that Goering called a meeting of his senior commanders to consider how to get air superiority in preparation for a proposed invasion of Britain, 'Operation Sealion'. Ten days later, Hitler directed that a major air assault – codenamed 'Eagle Day' – be launched from 5 August onwards and 15 September be considered the target date for Sealion to go ashore, but meanwhile his thoughts were turning towards overthrowing Stalin. 'The defeat of Russia,' he believed, 'was the prerequisite for the collapse of British resistance.'[444]

General Alfred Jodl, chief of the operations staff of the German Armed Forces Supreme Command, expected Britain to make peace before then. If not, the Luftwaffe would destroy her fighter force, aircraft industry, ports and supply depots. A landing should only be carried out 'to deal a death-blow to Britain when her war economy has been paralysed and her air force destroyed.'

The British, however, had made good use of the time granted between the fall of France and the decision to invade England. On 30 June, for example, Dowding had only 587 fighters and 1,200 pilots available for operations, but on 3 August he had 750 fighters and 1,400 pilots. Bad weather further delayed Eagle Day until 13 August and even then the assault got off to a muddled start. As Telford Taylor put it, 'the eagle did not swoop to the kill; rather, he fell off the perch.'[445]

The official dates for the day battle are 10 July to 31 October 1940. There were many changes of strength in the respective forces over such a long period, changes caused by efforts to increase rates of production and repair as well as by destruction, damage and accidents. There were also marked differences between the numbers of aircraft available on station or combat ready or unserviceable at any one time on both sides of the Channel. That is why historians find it difficult to agree on statistics, let alone agree about what, if anything, the battle achieved.[446]

In round figures, however, it seems that the Luftwaffe had about 2,350 aircraft combat-ready in July: over 1,300 bombers (including over 300 dive-bombers) and 1,050 fighters (250 of them twin-engined). Opposing this force, Dowding had in July 750 effective fighters (450 Hurricanes, 300 Spitfires, although Blenheims and Defiants were used), of which 600 were combat-ready.[447] These forces increased, on both sides, by about 10% during August and September.

Over the whole campaign, it now seems that Fighter Command suffered more than 1,000 casualties (537 pilots or aircrew certainly killed and over 500 wounded or injured) out of nearly 3,000 men who made at least one sortie.[448] At least one-third, then, became casualties: a rate of loss so heavy that Dowding and anyone else privy to these figures had good cause to fear a second battle beginning in the spring of 1941. The attack would surely be better planned; it would certainly last longer; and Fighter Command's casualties must be even heavier. Dowding never considered withdrawing his squadrons north of the Thames because this would have exposed vital targets, military and civilian, to unimpeded attack, quite apart from costing him the benefit of radar warning. There was a plan to withdraw, but only if an invasion force got safely ashore.[449]

That second battle was likely to begin in March 1941, as soon as good weather made it possible, and would certainly be more thoughtfully prepared on the German side. It would need to be, because Luftwaffe losses during the battle were very heavy: 8,700 men killed, wounded or captured – sickening losses for an air force as young as the Luftwaffe, following so closely upon the numerous casualties suffered in 10 months of almost constant operations between September 1939 and June 1940. For what raw statistics are worth, Dowding's command could fairly claim a victory: 10 fighters lost for every 19 German machines destroyed: 1,023 for 1,887 in total. But many other British aircraft were destroyed, in the air or on the ground.[450]

A Campaign, not a Battle

The Luftwaffe could spread or concentrate attacks to suit itself and by July 1940 was within close range of many important British targets. Dowding, however, was untroubled. He had lunch with Churchill at Chequers on 13 July and told the Prime Minister: 'the only thing that worried him in life was the ridiculous dreams he had every night: last night he dreamt that there was only one man in England who could use a Bofors gun and his name was William Shakespeare. It was, he said, most disturbing.'[451] Churchill, for once, was lost for words. The defenders were carefully organized and becoming more skilful by the day, but they were still unsure of the height at which enemies were approaching and there were numerous examples of poor R/T communication.[452]

The Battle of Britain was actually a prolonged campaign, in which the challenges posed were varied and unprecedented. It was fought, moreover, on the British side by a force that had little opportunity for realistic combat training in peacetime and had then lost a great many experienced pilots in France: men trained slowly and carefully to handle high-performance aircraft competently. Their replacements during 1940 were not merely green in combat, but much less competent as pilots.[453]

One important reason for Dowding's success was his use of tactical reserves, what an American historian later described as an 'air reserve doctrine', to ensure that there was always a challenge offered to the Luftwaffe, whatever force it sent across the Channel and whenever it arrived during the long daylight hours of summer. His decision, made before the war, that the squadron would be 'the largest tactical unit which it will be practically expedient to employ' preserved his resources and denied German fighters the opportunity to engage and destroy large numbers of British fighters in any particular engagement on any particular day. It also weakened the morale of German bomber crews who found themselves challenged whenever and wherever they raided. By September, those who survived often spoke with a droll gallows humour about facing yet again the RAF's last 50 fighters. As Dowding put it on 7 September:

> 'It was absolutely essential that the enemy should not become aware that he had materially damaged us; it was imperative that an undiminished front exist in the south-east, because the enemy was undoubtedly feeling the strain very much at the same time, and nothing should be afforded them in the nature of encouragement.[454]

Although Dowding regarded the policy as correct, he was led into it by the fact that his fighter force was smaller and less experienced than he thought desirable. He was also acutely aware that survival – not victory – was the name of the game. In other words, Dowding looked forward to the short, dark days of November, to the blessed interval that winter weather would provide, and always had in mind the nagging fear that the day battle must resume once the longer, lighter days of March 1941 arrived.

The joint strength of the three German air fleets based in France, Belgium, Denmark and Norway on Eagle Day (13 August 1940) had increased to 1,370 long-range bombers, about 400 dive-bombers, over 800 single-engined, short-range fighters and more than 300 twin-engined, long-range fighters: some 2,900 aircraft in total. Of these, at least 2,250 were serviceable on the day itself: 1,000 bombers, 300 dive-bombers, 700 short-range fighters and 250 long-range fighters. Dowding's 'active' strength on that day, apart from his 'passive' guns, balloons, radar staff, Observer Corps personnel and searchlights, amounted to 48 squadrons of single-engined fighters, plus six of twin-engined Blenheims and two of Defiants. His front line strength, including reserves immediately available, was now over 1,100 aircraft.[455]

The initiative did indeed lie with the enemy, able to attack from various directions at any time during the long days of summer. Dowding had been instructed to give priority to the protection of factories manufacturing aircraft. In fact, the Luftwaffe often targetted aerodromes, including some that were not part of Fighter Command. He allotted nearly half his force to Park, who controlled 21 squadrons, increased to 23 in August, distributed around seven sectors. Sir Quintin Brand, commanding 10 Group (operational from 17 July), had 10 squadrons in four sectors to cover an area from the Solent westward to southern Wales. In the Midlands and East Anglia, Leigh-Mallory (head of 12 Group) had 14 squadrons in six sectors. In the north, Richard Saul of 13 Group had 14 squadrons (not all capable of operations) in six sectors to protect Tyneside, Clydeside, Scapa Flow and Northern Ireland (see map page 192).[456]

Dowding had delegated the actual conduct of operations to his four group commanders. The most important of these was Keith Park, his deputy at Bentley Priory from July 1938 until April 1940, when he went to Uxbridge as head of 11 Group, responsible for the defence of London and south-eastern England. It could be said, wrote Terraine, 'for literary effect, but without straining the truth, that Dowding controlled the battle from day to day, Park controlled it from hour to hour, and the 11 Group sector controllers from minute to minute.'[457]

Until April 1940, it was not obvious that 11 Group, rather than 12 Group, would shortly bear the brunt of national defence. Western Europe had not been invaded, let along conquered, and until that disaster occurred, air attacks on England would have to be mounted from German bases, and the territory of Leigh-Mallory's group (the Midlands and East Anglia) would be their natural target.

Radar the Key
No-one doubts the excellence of the Hurricane and the Spitfire, or the courage and determination of their pilots, but the battle would have been lost without a radar-based defence system. An early warning and tracking

system, plus a sophisticated command and control apparatus created to get its information quickly to pilots in their cockpits was vital. 'If this system had suffered a complete failure,' wrote Zimmerman, 'either through its own inadequacies or enemy action, then surely the RAF would have been defeated.'

Although the system never failed completely, it often behaved 'just like a young lady,' in Park's words, 'as fickle as can be.' (Born in 1892, he could say things like that.) On 24 July, for example, he cited a recent occasion when a raid was reported as at most nine-plus. His controller suspected it might be a larger attack and despatched 18 fighters to tackle it: they found themselves facing about 80 hostiles, bombers and fighters. 'This sort of thing makes economical fighting very difficult,' wrote Park, with admirable self-restraint, but he was particularly anxious that radar should not be discredited, because he understood that the system, and its operators, were barely ready for a major challenge.[458]

The system, however, proved to be sufficiently flexible to meet challenges quite different from those Dowding and his advisers had planned and practised for. When France and the Low Countries were occupied, for example, the Luftwaffe was able to occupy bases far closer to Britain than Dowding had expected, and this faced his radar operators – many of whom were only partly trained and using equipment that was being improved 'on the hoof' – with even more daunting problems. Worse still, Dowding had supposed that German bombers would reach Britain unescorted, which would have been the case if they had taken off from German bases. Now, they not only had less distance to travel, and so could carry heavier loads, but they could also be escorted by fighters. This set Dowding a problem as difficult to solve as any that he faced throughout the battle: how to separate German bombers from their fighter escorts, and how to prevent his pilots from being drawn into desperate dog-fights with those escorts and thereby allow the bombers time and space to hit their targets accurately. Dowding's fighters could deal with bombers well enough, but would they be able to do so when constantly harassed by first-class German fighters?

After the day battle was long over, on 21 December 1940, Watson-Watt told Sinclair that it had been won by radar and the eight-gun fighter: 'Our old statement that RDF would multiply by three, and perhaps by five, the value of our fighter force, has been justified.' Park wrote that radar 'at its worse is most valuable to my fighter group, and at its best, it is quite invaluable and a great boon.' Dowding agreed, in his official despatch written in 1941. After outlining the many failings in the system, he concluded: 'it is not too much to say that the warning which it gave could have been obtained by no other means, and constituted a vital factor in the air defence of Great Britain.'

We must also remember that just as Fighter Command became stronger, at least in numbers, during the second half of 1940, soo too did the radar chain grow and improve. On 1 July, there were 54 stations in service; by 30 September, there were 76. Better still, constant practice helped its operators to become more and more adroit at coping with their 'fickle young lady'.[459]

Ultra and Other Intelligence

Dowding was also helped by intelligence information from several sources. Ever since 1974, when its existence was first revealed, the Ultra operation at Bletchley Park in Buckinghamshire has become the most famous intelligence source available to British (and later American) commanders in the Second World War. German wireless signals that had been enciphered by an Enigma machine were intercepted and translated at Bletchley. Enigma provided Dowding with valuable information about the Luftwaffe's organization, order of battle and equipment. But its information about the timing, size and proposed targets for particular raids usually arrived in Dowding's hands too late to be of help in meeting raids that had already been and gone. Also, the information was unreliable because the Air Fleets made last-minute changes of plan as weather worsened or improved, or units were found to have more or fewer aircraft immediately available than had been supposed.

Ultra was unable to tell whether Fighter Command would outlast the Luftwaffe because it was silent on the losses and effective strength of German units and the size of its reserves, nor could it forecast changes in German methods and objectives because communications between Berlin and the formations in France were by landline. 'For all his major decisions,' concluded the official historians of British intelligence during the Second World War, Dowding 'depended on his own strategic judgement, with no direct assistance from the Enigma.' One of those historians, Edward Thomas, as well as a distinguished German scholar, Horst Boog, later confirmed that conclusion. In fact, Dowding was not allowed into the Ultra secret until late in October.[460]

As for the Air Ministry's own intelligence organization, Dowding gave it little credence because the information gathered or received remained patchy throughout his time at Bentley Priory. By September 1939, the Air Intelligence Branch had a staff of some 40 officers, half of them 'retreads' (retired officers now re-employed) and many had been army officers in their fully-active days. Several were incompetents whose only qualification was an alleged knowledge of German, Italian or French. Nothing was learned to challenge the Air Staff's opinion that the Luftwaffe would be capable of an immediate knock-out blow because there was no continuous, systematic study of Germany's actual capabilities for an air offensive against British targets.[461]

Of far more value to Dowding (and to his peers in the other services) were the efforts of Sidney Cotton, an Australian-born naval pilot during the Great War, who kept up his flying thereafter and was employed by the British secret service from 1938 to take high level photographs over the Mediterranean and later over Germany and France. The work of Cotton and his small team of experts proved so invaluable that Dowding allowed him some Spitfires. By June 1940, however, a photo-reconnaissance unit had been created and Cotton's services were dispensed with. He had undermined an Air Ministry doctrine that reconnaissance could only be carried out by armed raiders; fast, high-flying, unarmed Spitfires were the answer.[462]

Ever since 1936, 'experts' had pictured German air power as massive, growing day by day, and poised to be hurled at Britain on the first day of a new war. Air Intelligence, reflecting a common British assumption that Britain was Hitler's main target, took it for granted that a German move westward would be intended 'to seize airfields for an air assault on Britain, rather than an attempt to outflank the Maginot Line and invade France.' The notion that Hitler was 'half-hearted about attacking Great Britain' would have bewildered most adult Britons in 1940. He preferred short, sharp campaigns with an obvious end in view, but fighting the British – and their imperial allies – seemed likely to be a long and costly business.[463]

The experts lacked technical details of German bombers, even though these were available. In October 1936, for example, two exceptional RAF officers – Squadron Leader Herbert Rowley and Flight Lieutenant Dick Atcherley – flew privately, but not at all secretly, to Germany to see what they could discover about the Luftwaffe. They were well received everywhere and permitted to fly on their own over Berlin. They examined and even flew the latest bombers. They had long conversations with men in influential positions: Heinrich Koppenberg, managing director of Junkers; with Heinkel's chief designers, the Günter twins, Walter and Siegfried; with Ernst Udet, Germany's most famous air hero of the Great War (shortly to be given a vital position in the Luftwaffe); and with members of the revived Richthofen squadron. Unfortunately, their detailed report to the Air Ministry attracted no known comment, although it was used by Churchill in his efforts to alert the British government to the danger of aerial attack.[464]

Even setting aside ignorance about basic facts of German air power, Air Ministry intelligence officers had ready access to full information about British bombers. Realistic estimates could have been made by simple analogy to calculate what weight of bombs a twin-engined aircraft could carry to a British target from bases in north-west Germany, allowing for the weight of its crew, fuel, defensive weapons, ammunition and armour. Even more reprehensible than their failure to test alarming notions is the fact that Victor Goddard, head of the European Section of Air Intelligence was 'discouraged' from expressing his objections to them.[465]

In October 1937, Swinton had circulated an Air Staff note to the Cabinet which estimated that by December 1939 Germany would have nearly twice as many first-line aircraft as the RAF: about 3,200 against about 1,700. In November 1938, Swinton's successor informed the Cabinet that the latest forecast was even more alarming. By August 1939, he said, the RAF might have nearly 3,400 aircraft (including reserves), but by then the Luftwaffe would have more than twice as many: some 7,000. Actually, when war began as we have seen, German air strength was nothing like so great: about 3,500 aircraft, including obsolete types, of which about 2,900 were serviceable.[466]

The Air Ministry admitted on 6 July 1940, following Lindemann's scrutiny of Enigma decrypts, that Air Intelligence had grossly over-estimated German bomber strength. In June, this had been reckoned at

2,500 bombers able to deliver each day 4,800 tons of bombs on British targets; these figures had now been drastically scaled down to 1,250 bombers capable of dropping 1,800 tons per day.[467]

On 13 October 1940, Churchill was 'astounded' to learn of 'the vast congregation' allowed to know the Enigma secret. 'The Air Ministry is the worst offender and I have marked [on the circulation list] a number who should be struck off at once.' He added A. V. Alexander (political head of the Royal Navy), Anthony Eden (Secretary of State for War), Peirse (head of Bomber Command) and Dowding.[468]

Quite apart from Ultra, however, Dowding benefitted from the 'Y' Service, a system of radio traffic analysis and direction-finding, which with other sources, like prisoner interrogation and the study of captured documents, gradually built up a detailed knowledge of the Luftwaffe's order of battle. Several unexpected bonuses came Dowding's way once the battle began. For example, German airmen proved surprisingly talkative both in the air (so that wireless traffic analysis gave him valuable information) and on the ground (when those who survived a crash or parachute landing, doubtless grateful to be still alive and not shot out of hand, gossipped freely with their captors and were frequently found to have useful papers on them). Also, direction-finding pinpointed the location of Luftwaffe bases more easily than Dowding expected when those bases were moved close to the Channel coast.[469]

Fighter Controllers

Dowding always regarded the squadron as the fighting unit. From the moment that orders were given by group controllers to sector controllers, they were to be executed by squadrons ordered off singly or in pairs, sometimes in larger formations, from adjoining stations. Once airborne, they were to be told what to do and where to go from the ground by direct contact with their sector controller and guided towards incoming raiders. When squadrons operated together from different sectors, each remained the responsibility of its own sector. As soon as raiders were sighted, squadron commanders took charge and no further attempts were made to contact pilots from the ground until it was reported to sector controllers that the action was over.

Group controllers tried to distinguish between major raids and feints to keep as many aircraft as possible ready for an unexpected crisis. Major raids had to be met with 'sufficient' opposition (bearing in mind the command's limited resources) and aircraft should neither waste their fuel on mere patrol nor be caught on or near the ground. When the battle began and the Germans attempted to eliminate British fighters as a prelude to invasion, several balances had to be struck every day. The reward for successful guessing would only be to delay once more the penalty for unsuccessful guessing. Within minutes of the appearance of incoming aircraft on the cathode ray tubes at coastal radar stations, group controllers saw displayed on their operations tables all the information coming from Bentley Priory.[470]

Air Raid Warnings

From the day war began the vexing question of air raid warnings had exercised many minds, civilian and military. Responsibility for sounding them (and the all-clear) lay with Dowding. 'I am of course ready to carry out any directions which I may receive,' he assured the Under-Secretary of State for Air on 10 November 1939, 'but if the matter were left to my own judgement,' he would not have sirens sound whenever a single aircraft came over. It could not cause great harm and might be one of ours anyway. There the matter rested until the prospect of heavy raids loomed in June 1940 and he wrote to the Air Ministry on the 27th:

'My personal opinion is that the public will consider that they have a right to be warned when enemy aircraft are approaching. Factory workers may be enjoined to remain at their posts, and the public may be advised to remain quietly in their homes instead of rushing for air raid shelters; but the latter may feel that they should be given some choice in the matter and this feeling may become vocal if serious raids are made on populous areas.'

He summarized the situation for Churchill two days later. A serious loss of production would follow if warnings were given too freely and over too great an area. Also, people would be angered if frequently woken up at night 'by the existing rather terrifying sirens and made to go into air raid shelters' to take refuge from raiders who never turned up or dropped nothing if they did. His system allowed five minutes for taking cover, then an appreciable delay before an all-clear, and he was well aware that it wasted a huge number of working hours. Roof watchers, he insisted, were not the answer. The warning they gave was too local and came too late. Many factories asked for direct access to Observer Corps information, but were there enough fully-staffed posts to cope and was their warning accurate enough? There were many places, however, such as docks and marshalling yards where lights were essential and serious casualties and damage would follow a failure to give early warning. 'Whatever we do,' Dowding told the Prime Minister, 'many people are irritated.' He wished it were possible to produce 'a less melancholy and terrifying warning', and to sound an 'all-clear' sooner, but these were crosses everyone had to bear.[471]

Dowding wrote to Balfour on 8 September to say that the Air Ministry was asking for a 'red warning' (raiders may shortly appear) to be given to London, so permitting parliament to continue sitting until a warning of 'imminent' danger came. He refused to agree. At Stanmore, he had no precise knowledge of what might be happening over Westminster – about 12 miles to the south – and if the parliamentary authorities chose to ignore a red warning, they must bear the same responsibility as port authorities or factory owners.[472]

A solution to the warning problem was sought through the familiar means of setting up a committee of enquiry. At its first meeting, on 24 September 1940, Dowding was asked if he would allow a 'blackable out' system, rather than a blanket 'blackout', so that life and work could go on more easily in darkness when enemy aircraft were not nearby. It would depend, he replied, on accurate early warning, a task which must fall to the Observer Corps, but it was largely ineffective at night despite its best efforts. We ought to be able to single out high-risk areas and allow lighting in low-risk areas, though it was precisely in the former that most lighting was needed. Committee members had hoped to relieve Dowding of this burden, but that was impossible:

> 'There exists a very expensive organization for producing intelligence about approaching raids, from the fighting point of view, and it seemed very reasonable that this system should be put at the disposal of the country for warning. He did not jib at all at the responsibility, although he did not deny that it was irksome at times.'[473]

Beaverbrook

Lord Beaverbrook, Minister of Aircraft Production, asked Dowding on 4 July 1940 if he would release a few more Spitfires for photo-reconnaissance duties. 'Of course I grudge every Spitfire which is taken from the Fighter Command until the supply situation has improved,' he replied, 'but I must take a broad view of the question,' because Spitfires could take more photographs more safely than other types.[474]

He therefore agreed to Beaverbrook's request and found a valuable ally in that famous newspaper owner, political wheeler-dealer and long-time crony of Churchill's. At first sight, it seemed that Dowding and Beaverbrook had little in common. A 'tall, unforthcoming Wykhamist, frugal in habit, grave of mien, innately distrustful of politicians' seemed not to be a natural friend of a 'diminutive, big-hearted but unpredictable apostle of Empire Free Trade,' mischievous and devious. Moreover, Beaverbrook had insisted that his mass-selling newspapers vehemently back appeasement of Hitler and deny the possibility of war until the last possible moment. And yet they did become close because Dowding agreed with Churchill's assessment of the Beaver's efforts during May 1940: he 'made a surprising improvement in the supply and repair of aeroplanes,' Churchill told Sinclair on 3 June, 'and in clearing up the muddle and scandal of the aircraft production branch.' And the Beaver never numbered Dowding among 'the bloody air marshals' whom he regarded with contempt.

Beaverbrook used to ring up Dowding and Pile every day to ask what more he could do for them. 'On many occasions,' Pile recalled, 'I was in Dowding's room when the call came through, and always there was a string of requests, and sometimes even of grouses. Dowding's cry was always for more and more speed. I can hear him now saying: "What we want is more revs."' Eventually, the Beaver sent him a note: 'Revolutions have always been achieved by intense pressure from below.' This response delighted Dowding and the friendship between the two became very close.[475]

A year later, Dowding warmly praised him in his despatch on the battle and did so again in a letter to *The Times* published on 1 June 1945. Everyone who played a part in victory over Germany had been praised, he wrote, but not Beaverbrook. 'We had the organization, we had the men, and we had the spirit which could bring us victory in the air,' but not the machines needed to withstand the drain of continuous battle. He gave us those machines and Dowding wanted to honour 'the indomitable spirit of one little man', who achieved what 'no other man in England' could have done. The 'little man' responded on 5 June. 'You know of my faith in the commander of the Battle of Britain. So you will understand in part my joy and satisfaction in words of praise from you.' That battle, Beaverbrook thought, 'was the greatest event in the war.'[476]

It is often said that we are attracted to persons unlike ourselves. Beaverbrook, like Arnold Lunn (Dowding's other close friend), had an exuberant personality; he knew hundreds of people, with all of whom he was happy to gossip or argue far into the night. He was difficult to dislike, if he chose to make himself agreeable. Except on a skifield, no-one has ever described Dowding in such terms.

Rod Banks, an outstanding engineer who was made Director General of Engine Production and then of Research and Development in Beaverbrook's ministry, thought he 'did a great service in getting the contracts procedure cleaned up so that firms could go ahead with the minimum of delay and paperwork;' his other great service 'was when he got the repair facilities further removed from RAF control and distributed more widely among the industry.' Overall, he created a vital sense of 'urgency and enthusiasm' that woke up some dozy persons, in or out of uniform, who had not realized that Britain was facing a desperate crisis.[477]

For what it is worth, however, the weight of opinion among serving officers – Freeman, Slessor, Tedder – plus that of most serious historians (among them Robertson and Ritchie), is that the Beaver's achievement in 1940 was much exaggerated by Churchill, the Beaver himself and Dowding. The 'established way of doing things', wrote Robertson, inherited from the Air Ministry's production branch, was not wholly broken down until Dowding left Bentley Priory. But Beaverbrook's decision in September 1940 to disperse work in aircraft factories reduced the risk of serious disruption and also reduced production. The dilemma had no easy solution, but Dowding had nothing to say, at the time or later, on this important subject. Nor did he ever criticize the Beaver's insistence on using scarce materials and skilled labour to build Blenheim and Whitley bombers during 1940, at a time when it was already clear that neither type had any serious value.

It is generally agreed, however, that Beaverbrook's initial impact in May and June was galvanic and in Dowding's opinion his energy, urgency and readiness to make decisions contrasted refreshingly with the Air Ministry's stately procedures. Beaverbrook's famous stunts – which both he and Dowding knew to be stunts – such as 'saucepans for Spitfires' and 'buy a Spitfire' were valuable in that they were popular: appealing to ordinary citizens and killing the lingering 'business as usual' attitude of Chamberlain's government.[478]

That was the positive side; 'frenetic, hand-to-mouth improvision' was the negative side. Balfour, Under-Secretary of State, was as well placed as any of the air marshals to assess the Beaver's impact. He later wrote, 'from my first-hand knowledge, even though on the Air Ministry side of the fence,' the narrow margin between defeat and victory would not 'have been tipped in our favour' without Beaverbrook.[479] On the other hand, his production priorities for Spitfires and 'his ruthless unorthodox enforcement' of those priorities gave the RAF 4,000 of these very short-range interceptors in its front line by 1943 at a time when low-level, more heavily-armed ground attackers with a longer range were needed.[480]

Reflecting on his friend's activities in 1956, Dowding remembered an incident not recorded in his despatch. It was clear to Dowding as soon as the war began that the 0.303-inch machine guns with which his fighters were equipped would only be able to down German bombers with great difficulty. The only practical alternatives were the 0.5-inch Browning machine gun or the 20-mm cannon. He wanted tests to be carried out on a German fuselage, 'but as usual the Air Ministry staff preferred to sit round a table and argue.' Beaverbrook, however, backed Dowding and made a realistic trial possible, which was 'boycotted by all Air Ministry officers. Nobody turned up to see it except myself and two junior army officers who had somehow heard what was to be done.' As Dowding expected, cannon shells caused more damage than machine-gun bullets. 'Once again,' he concluded, 'the value of the practical trial over theoretical argument was demonstrated.'[481]

Dowding's admiration for Beaverbrook was unreserved and never weakened, but crucial to his success was the fact that a large factory built to produce Spitfires at Castle Bromwich, near Birmingham, was failing to do so. Spitfires should have been rolling out from January 1940 to meet orders for 1,500 machines. In fact, not a single Spitfire had emerged by May. That failure explains why Dowding could not allow the few Spitfires he had on hand to take part in the French campaign. Using powers granted to him by Churchill, which were not available to the Air Ministry's production department, Beaverbrook transferred the management of the factory from Lord Nuffield to Vickers-Armstrong, who used their own staff as well as experts from Supermarine to get production started. Credit should be given to Swinton and Freeman who decided, before the war began, to build and equip that factory – and no credit to Wood, who had assigned it to Nuffield. Their wisdom was confirmed on 28 September 1940, when the Luftwaffe wrecked the only other factory making Spitfires, at Woolston, Southampton.[482]

Freeman had succeeded Dowding as Air Member for Research and Development in April 1936, adding production as well from June 1938 until November 1940, when he became Portal's vice-CAS and spent the rest of the war in positions of critical importance. He did much to see that Fighter and Bomber Commands eventually got plenty of modern, efficient aircraft for defence and offence. He bravely accepted the fact that in the hurly-burly of urgent re-armament some of the types produced would fail.[483]

Noble Frankland thought Beaverbrook's greatest contribution to the Battle was his son, Max Aitken, 'one of the bravest and most brilliant of our most brave and brilliant fighter pilots.' A stronger case can be made for the

Civilian Repair Organization, created in October 1939 and transferred from Air Ministry control to Beaverbrook's ministry in May 1940. Thanks to that organization, more than one-third of the fighters serving with squadrons during the Battle of Britain were repaired machines. Neither the 'bloody air marshals' nor their subsequent supporters can deny Beaverbrook some credit for that vital achievement.

Dowding was not alone in understanding that design and production were the glamorous aspects of aviation and needed plenty of unglamorous support, if a nation were to survive – let alone win – a prolonged campaign. For example, a large, ever-growing training system for ground as well as air crews was essential; so too the manufacture of millions of spare parts; the provision of several large storage depots (safe, one hoped, from enemy bombers); ample facilities for speedy routine maintenance; and by no means least a huge and highly-skilled repair organization prepared to work long hours. Neither Dowding nor Beaverbrook created any of these, though they encouraged them to a degree far in advance of anything available to the Luftwaffe.[484]

Channel War

The so-called 'Channel War' during July 1940, like the Dunkirk evacuation, posed insoluble problems for Dowding.[485] Whenever a convoy was at sea, the Luftwaffe attacked at its own convenience and obliged him to do what he most hated: order his squadrons to mount standing patrols. At one time in early July, as many as seven convoys were in passage around British coasts between Swanage in Dorset and the Firth of Forth in Scotland. All were open to attack and all were difficult to defend, given the short range of Dowding's fighters and the brief warning provided by radar.

Although unescorted bombers were easily driven away, patrol work from primitive forward airfields continued during many a long summer day. On 3 July, Dowding asked for these convoys to be routed along the west coast, but on 9 August Churchill accepted an Admiralty opinion that they should remain on the east coast for purposes of prestige and also to serve as 'bait' for the Luftwaffe. Dowding disagreed, but was ordered by the Air Ministry to meet attacks with large formations. Casualties caused by fatigue rather than combat were already alarming and Dowding was acutely conscious of a problem that would perplex him until he left the command: when should he withdraw experienced but tired men from the front line and replace them with pilots who were fresher, but novices in a savage aerial war?[486]

Operations over water soon revealed the need for a properly organized system of rescuing ditched airmen. They were at first entirely dependent on any ships which happened to be nearby. Specially equipped search aircraft and high-speed launches were essential, as well as aids to help pilots stay afloat and mark their positions. In this respect, the Luftwaffe was better prepared than the RAF: surprisingly so, given that the Luftwaffe was designed to support land campaigns and crossing the Channel had been part of countless British airmen's lives since 1914. Unlike the RAF, the Luftwaffe had float planes for rescue work, combat aircraft carried inflatable rubber dinghies, and airmen were provided with a chemical which stained the sea around them bright green. Gradually, but not until August 1941, when the Battle of Britain was long over, the Air Ministry creaked into gear and organized a comprehensive air-sea rescue organization.[487]

The Channel War was more wearing than decisive for airmen on both sides of the water. Better targets were left untouched elsewhere. On the English side of the Channel, Fighter Command had up to 30 aircraft deployed on each of its forward airfields, while important aircraft factories were within bomber range. Yet these prime targets were never systematically and persistently attacked. Conversely, on the German side of the Channel, there were some 50 airfields within fighter range, each with about 50 German aircraft parked on them. Bomber Command could have attempted low-level strikes, using the Blenheims of 2 Group. Such attacks, on both sides of the Channel, would have required wider dispersal and greater measures of local protection (ground and air), thus weakening the Luftwaffe's offensive power and Dowding's concern to engage bombers as far from their targets as possible.

The proper use of Bomber Command during the Battle should have been in making continuous attack on Luftwaffe airfields in France and the Low Countries. The Germans had their Freya radar, but neither their low-level radar nor their night fighter defences were better than those in Britain. The Germans would have had to employ more men and aircraft on local defence and the wear and tear on their airfields and aircraft would have been worth the cost to the RAF's attackers. Blenheim bombers, keeping in a tight vee of three, and escorted by Blenheim fighters, might have done useful service in the desperate summer of 1940.

The low standard of navigational skill in the RAF would have been a major problem, however, especially if raids had been sent across the Channel on cloudy days, and the Blenheim, in either its fighter or bomber version, was a feeble weapon, and yet they were often ordered out *singly* to wander about, looking hopefully and/or desperately for such 'strategic' targets as oil refineries and factories – all further inland than the airfields used by the Luftwaffe.[488]

During the Channel War, between 10 July and 11 August, German airmen claimed the destruction of 381 British aircraft. They actually shot down 178 (114 fighters, 64 bombers): a serious loss indeed to both Fighter and Bomber Commands, but nothing like as serious as the Germans believed. Of even greater concern, from Dowding's point of view, was the fact that 18% of his aircraft were wrecked in accidents during those 33 days. Of the 107 pilots killed in that period, 18 lost their lives in accidents; another five were injured. 'At this rate, were it not for replacements, Fighter Command would cease to exist by the end of 1940 through its own efforts, without any help from the Luftwaffe.'[489]

Dowding thought these losses were a result of cutting corners, unavoidable in wartime. Many pilots were inexperienced: they made taxying mistakes, mishandled their engines, misjudged take-offs and landing, and even forgot to lower their undercarriages. Their seniors had little time to pass on what lessons they themselves had learned; fighters were far more powerful and less forgiving than trainers; there were mechanical failures; and operations took place in marginal weather that would have caused flying to be cancelled in peacetime. But the biggest single cause of accidents was the command's desperate effort to fly and fight in darkness.

What made these losses all the more distressful was the fact that single-engined day fighters, without airborne radar, could never – repeat, never – become effective night fighters. The point deserves particular emphasis because Douglas and other Whitehall Warriors would later insist that these fighters be used at night. As a result, several pilots were killed or injured for no useful purpose. The twin-engined Bristol Beaufighter, with a crew of two (pilot and radar-operator) was the essential weapon, but it would not be able to play a full part, despite the efforts of Dowding, technicians and scientists, before 1941.

The Channel War taught Dowding and his pilots that the Messerschmitt Bf 109 was a formidable opponent: not only fast and agile, but firing cannon shells that were far more lethal than the rifle-calibre bullets of British fighters. Dowding also learned that the fabric-covered airframes of his Hurricanes burned, whereas his all-metal Spitfires did not. As for tactics, despite the emphasis placed by Dowding and especially by Park on flexibility, many squadrons stuck rigidly to the vic of three fighters drummed into them in prewar exercises. These vics were not nearly as effective as the 'finger four' (of two pairs of fighters) used by the Germans.

Even so, Luftwaffe losses of fighters as well as bombers were severe. During July, it lost 301 aircraft from all causes and another 196 were damaged: a casualty rate that did not auger well for the proposed Eagle Day. Bombers were alarmingly vulnerable, especially the Junkers Ju 87 dive-bomber, but so too was the Luftwaffe's much-vaunted Messerschmitt Bf 110. Overall, then, for both sides the Channel War was far more than a minor sideshow before the main battle began. Both took harder knocks than they expected and were taught lessons that they must learn if the knocks were not to be harder still in August and September.[490]

Foreign Pilots

During July, Dowding was told that a number of pilots from Occupied Europe, mostly Polish or Czechoslovakian, were available. A meeting was held on the 14th to discuss how to integrate them into the squadrons. Dowding expressed strong reservations about 'the infiltration of foreign pilots into British squadrons'. Pilot morale was for him a matter of constant concern, and unless he could be assured that these pilots had the proper fighting spirit, he did not want them. He was using the term 'foreign pilots' as a euphemism for Poles and Czechs, because he had no objection to finding places for French, Belgian, Dutch or Norwegian pilots.

If he was pressed to take East Europeans, he intended to use them as far as possible from the front line in south-east England, but a desperate shortage of pilots who had both flying skill and combat experience forced his hand. His objections, which he never explained, were perhaps rooted in a belief – transmitted from France – that East Europeans lacked true grit, were unskilled airmen, anti-Semitic, and tainted (if not worse) with Fascism or Communism. In August, all Polish airmen became members of a new

'Polish Air Force' and two squadrons were formed. Two bomber squadrons were also formed and helped to raid Channel ports. Many Poles, however, opted to remain with British squadrons.

By September, Dowding had learned that Polish and Czech pilots were among the ablest and bravest in his command and there were many of them: 145 Poles, 88 Czechs. Dowding and Lord Gort dined with Churchill at Chequers on 21 September and Dowding said the Poles were magnificent fighters. 'When we have abolished Germany,' said Churchill, 'we will certainly establish Poland – and make them a permanent thing in Europe.' He thought one Pole was worth three Frenchmen: Gort and Dowding disagreed – ten was nearer the mark.[491]

By the time the battle ended, Dowding had been fully converted: had it not been for the 'unsurpassed gallantry' of Polish and Czech pilots, 'I hesitate to say that the outcome of the battle would have been the same.' Their superior training, combat experience and fervent hatred of Germans, ensured that they destroyed more than their fair share of enemy aircraft.[492]

16

The Day Battle, August to October 1940

First Phase

From 8-18 August, the Germans used massed formations of bombers with escort fighters flying much higher. To face this challenge, Park's guiding principle – agreed with Dowding – was to engage the enemy before he reached his targets. Radar stations on the south coast hoped to 'see' aircraft assembling over the Pas de Calais or the Cotentin Peninsula, which would give them about 20 minutes to work out how many raiders were involved and where they were heading. But detection at that range was still uncertain and often inaccurate. If the radar operators felt sure that they had an identifiable plot, they would 'tell' it through to Bentley Priory's filter room. There it would be combined with plots from other radar stations. If the filter officer had confidence in the information, he gave the raid a number and 'told' it to the operations room next door, where it would appear on the table. All this took about four minutes. It took 13-14 minutes for a Spitfire to climb to 20,000 feet and a Hurricane three minutes longer, but it took only five or six minutes for a German formation to get from Cap Gris Nez to Dover. So airfields at Manston and Hawkinge in east Kent suffered regularly and severely.[493]

As a rule, Park sent Spitfires against escort fighters, Hurricanes against bombers. He thought the proportion of enemy aircraft destroyed to British losses had been about four to one during those August days, but in fact it was less than two to one, although German aircrew losses, given that bombers carried four or five crew members, were more than five times as heavy as those of Fighter Command. The defence had proven too strong for the offence, and a break of five days followed a major effort on the 18th, 'the hardest day', as Alfred Price called it, because casualties on both sides were greater than on any other day of the entire battle. At least 100 aircraft were wrecked, 67 German, 33 Fighter Command; and many other British aircraft were destroyed or damaged.[494]

The Luftwaffe should have concentrated on knocking out radar stations and Dowding's coastal aerodromes. Well-directed attacks, boldly pressed home, might well have wrecked the early warning system. Sector aero-

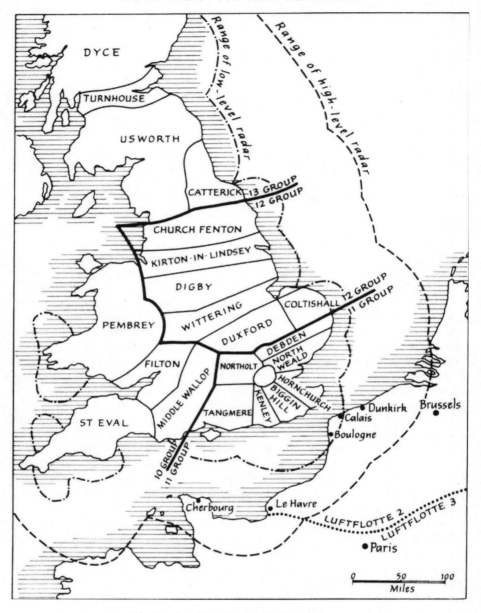

The Battle of Britain: Air Defence sectors

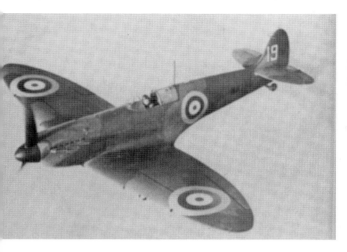

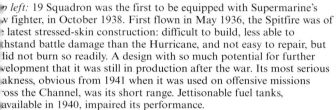

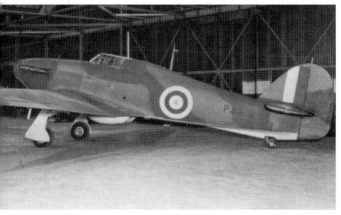

₀ left: 19 Squadron was the first to be equipped with Supermarine's ₋w fighter, in October 1938. First flown in May 1936, the Spitfire was of ₋ latest stressed-skin construction: difficult to build, less able to ₋thstand battle damage than the Hurricane, and not easy to repair, but ₋lid not burn so readily. A design with so much potential for further ₋velopment that it was still in production after the war. Its most serious ₋akness, obvious from 1941 when it was used on offensive missions ₋oss the Channel, was its short range. Jettisonable fuel tanks, ₋available in 1940, impaired its performance.

Top right: Sir John Salmond (CAS, 1930-3) was recalled to service in the Ministry of Aircraft Production at Harrogate in 1940. A devout Trenchardist, he hoped that his master would be recalled from a long retirement and appointed Secretary of State for Air. While awaiting that happy day, he vehemently advocated an all-out bombing campaign against Germany, even though the bombers then available were inadequate for such a task. He knew even less about fighters, but in September 1940 was appointed to chair an enquiry into Britain's night defences. He invited Churchill to dismiss Dowding and threatened to visit Buckingham Palace and demand that King George do so. *RAF Museum, Hendon, PC 71-19-86.*

Middle and *Bottom:* A Civilian Repair Organization was created in October 1939 and transferred from Air Ministry control to Lord Beaverbrook's Ministry of Aircraft Production in May 1940. Thanks to that organization, more than one-third of the fighters serving with squadrons during the Battle of Britain were repaired machines. The Luftwaffe had nothing comparable in France or Belgium, and there can be no doubt that these 're-treads' were of vital importance to Dowding. This Hurricane, wrecked on 28 August, was re-built and back in service within days.

Dowding looks on, as benignly as his stern face will allow, while King George VI decorates Flight Lieutenant Alan Deere with a Distinguished Flying Cross at Hornchurch, Essex, on 27 June 1940. Deere, born in New Zealand, went on to become one of the RAF's greatest fighter pilots in the Second World War.
Air Historical Branch, Ministry of Defence, CH430.

Top: In *Twelve Legions of Angels* (written in 1941, published in 1946), Dowding asked why officers over the age of 45 were so mentally paralysed. The process began, he thought, at public schools, 'where the individualist is suppressed and the good citizen mass-produced.' And yet he spoke of 'the deep-seated love' he had for his own school, even though 'I spent some of the most miserable years of my life' there. *Winchester College brochure.*

Bottom left: Dowding's last and difficult job, undertaken at Churchill's specific request, in 1941, was to see whether the RAF was making sufficient use of its men and women. Sir Wilfrid Freeman (centre) was Vice-CAS at the time and shared Portal's reluctance to co-operate with his enquiry. By June 1942, Dowding had had enough of their obstruction. He made a typically rude message from Freeman 'an excuse for a show of injured dignity' and resigned. *RAF Museum, Hendon, PC 72-95/6.*

Bottom right: Dowding added 'of Bentley Priory' to his name; appropriate enough, but the broader title 'of Fighter Command' would be even more fitting, for no subsequent head of that command, now extinct, had either his authority or bore anything like his weight of responsibility for Britain's safety. His coat of arms featured three white pillars supporting a crown above a blue fleur-de-lis. He chose as his motto *Laborare est Orare*, to work is to pray.

Top left: Churchill asked Dowding in May 1943 if he might put his name forward for a barony in recognition of 'your ever-memorable services to the country during the Battle of Britain'. Dowding gladly agreed and became the first RAF officer since Trenchard in 1919 to be so honoured. This photograph appeared on the front page of the *Illustrated London News*, on 12 June 1943. *via Nicholas Peacock.*

Top right: Harold Balfour, a pilot in 60 Squadron in 1916, found Dowding 'a silent, forbidding figure', but fair-minded and even-tempered. In 1940, Balfour became Under-Secretary of State for Air and was no uncritical admirer of Dowding, but he recorded in his memoirs that 'the great man' had been 'monstrously treated by the Air Ministry' and 'shamefully served by successive Chiefs of the Air Staff'.

Right: Sir Archibald Sinclair (left), Secretary of State for Air, and Sir Charles ('Peter') Portal, CAS, both men in office 1940-5. Sinclair was rebuked by Churchill in July and August 1940 for trying to get Dowding out of Bentley Priory. A weak, untrustworthy man, he played a major part in ensuring that Dowding was not promoted to Marshal of the RAF. Portal, a fellow-Wykehamist, came to believe that Sholto Douglas deserved his chance at Fighter Command, but he should not have accepted the opinion of Sinclair, even though it was backed by Trenchard, Salmond and Freeman, that Dowding should not be promoted. *RAF Museum, Hendon, PC 71-19-355.*

Top left: Dowding married Muriel, widow of Pilot Officer Max Whiting, a flight engineer in Bomber Command, killed in May 1944. They were married in Caxton Hall, St. James's Park, Westminster, on 25 September 1951; he was then 69, Muriel 43. They spent their honeymoon in Grindelwald, Switzerland, one of Dowding's favourite places. *Whiting Collection.*

Top right: On 11 September 1947, together with a guard of honour and the RAF band, Dowding (standing left of the name plate) presided over a ceremony on Platform 11 at Waterloo Railway Station to reveal the name plates of three magnificent steam locomotives, *Winston Churchill, Fighter Command* and *Lord Dowding,* all part of a class designed by the New Zealand-born Oliver Bulleid. *Winston Churchill* is now safe in the National Railway Museum at York, but *Fighter Command* and *Lord Dowding* are long gone. *Whiting Collection.*

Middle: Dowding and Muriel lived with many animals in exceptional content at her home, 'Oakgates', in Darnley Drive, Tunbridge Wells, from 1951 until 1967, when Dowding could no longer manage stairs, so they moved to 1, Calverley Park, also in Tunbridge Wells. During the last 20 years of his life, Dowding came to share Muriel's passionate hatred of cruelty to animals, either by killing them for food or, still more vehemently, destroying them to make cosmetics or even for research into human illnesses. *Whiting Collection.*

Bottom: All passion spent – at least it was by 1952, when Dowding and Muriel chatted with Trenchard during a reception at the United Services Club in London. In 1940, however, Trenchard had done his best, in a secret alliance with Sir John Salmond, to get Dowding out of Bentley Priory. *Whiting Collection.*

Top left: Dowding greeted by Queen Elizabeth on the occasion of his last public appearance, at the London premiere in September 1969 of a film about the Battle of Britain. He was given a standing ovation by some 350 persons, many of them former pilots: 'Dowding's chicks', as Churchill called them. *Whiting Collection.*

Top right: Dowding and Muriel leaving Westminster Abbey after a Battle of Britain service in September 1962, followed by Hilda. As he told Robert Wright, his second biographer, he always regarded that day as one for remembering, not celebrating: 'a time for remembering all those bright lads whose earthly existence was cut short in our defence.' *Whiting Collection.*

Middle: During the summer of 1968, Dowding was taken to Hawkinge airfield, near Folkestone, where scenes for a film about the Battle of Britain were being shot. Dowding was portrayed by Laurence Olivier, Sir Keith Park by Trevor Howard, seen here talking to Dowding with a Hurricane in the background. *Whiting Collection.*

Bottom: Dowding and Muriel in 1969. They met in 1946, married in 1951, and their love for each other was so deep that it more than compensated for old griefs over Air Ministry pettiness. *Whiting Collection.*

AIR CHIEF MARSHAL
LORD DOWDING
1882-1970
Commander-in-Chief,
RAF Fighter Command 1936-1940
and during the Battle of Britain

lived here
1968-1970

Left: This may be the last picture taken of Dowding, at home in Tunbridge Wells in January 1970.

ight: On 20 October 1988, a statue of Dowding, set up utside St. Clement Dane's Church in the Strand, ondon, was unveiled by Queen Elizabeth the Queen Mother. The initiative came not from the Ministry of Defence, into which the Air Ministry had long been uried, but from men and women who actually fought in the Battle of Britain. Made by Faith Winter, the expression on his face nicely blends, as John Ray wrote, surprise, severity and faint disapproval'. On 31 May 992, a statue of Sir Arthur Harris was unveiled nearby. *Whiting Collection.*

elow left: Moffat's fine memorial to its famous son. *Whiting Collection.*

Below right: Dowding was born in Moffat, 50 miles south of Edinburgh, in April 1882. Moffat's ram, erected in 1875 and standing proudly on a rock, honours the importance of sheep-farming in the area. The image of that ram – immovable, unwilling to stand down from any challenge – might also stand for Dowding.

Top left: The War Cloister at Winchester College, a memorial to Wykehamists killed in the two world wars. Dowding, Portal and Field Marshal Lord Wavell, three exceptional Wykehamists, are commemorated there. *Winchester College brochure.*

Top right: Prominently placed on the blank wall of the War Cloister is a portrait bust of Dowding. It is certainly impressive, indeed frightening, as one who knew him recalls, 'in a certain mood'; but it lacks that 'twinkle in the eye' which was more often there. *Winchester College archives.*

Middle: Dowding died at home on 15 February 1970, two months short of his 88th birthday and was cremated in a private ceremony. A memorial service was held in Westminster Abbey on 12 March. His ashes were interred below the Battle of Britain window in a chapel which honours all those who died during that battle. Denis Healey, Minister of Defence, delivered an address in which he described Dowding as 'one of those great men whom this country miraculously produces in times of peril'. *Whiting Collection.*

Bottom: The only portrait of Dowding that Muriel could look at with any pleasure. Made by Faith Kenworthy-Browne, Muriel thought it captured very well his readiness to smile behind the usual stern visage. The fact that he was not required to wear 'the world's silliest hat', which sits on the table beside him, helped to keep him in a good temper. *Whiting Collection.*

dromes could then have been attacked at leisure and landline communications disrupted. The way would thus be eased for subsequent attacks
on London's warehouses, factories, government offices and citizens. Park
later told Johnnie Johnson, the top-scoring Allied fighter pilot of the war in
Europe, that he dreaded more than anything a persistent attack on his
sector airfields. There were plenty of other airfields in southern England,
but they were not equipped to communicate direct with his headquarters.
'Without signals,' Park said, 'the only thing I commanded was my desk at
Uxbridge.'[495]

Northern Diversion

The effective resistance offered in south-eastern England led Goering to
believe that fighters must have been drawn in substantial numbers from the
north. Accordingly, Air Fleet 5 sent large formations from bases in Norway
and Denmark towards north-eastern England on 15 August. The crews
were faced with an exhaustingly long flight – out and home of about 1,100
miles – and were only able to carry light bomb loads. Worse still, they could
not be escorted by single-engined fighters and were spotted by British radar
while still far from their targets.

Thanks to Dowding's prudence, 13 Group had plenty of fighters on hand
to challenge them. Consequently, the bombers were beaten back with heavy
losses. Churchill spent part of 15 August at Bentley Priory, 'one of the
greatest days in history', he called it. Dowding's foresight, he thought,
'deserves high praise, but even more remarkable has been the restraint and
the exact measurement of formidable stresses which had reserved a fighter
force in the north through all these long weeks of mortal conflict in the
south. We must regard the generalship here shown as an example of genius
in the art of war.' It was on leaving Park's headquarters on the following
evening, 16 August, that Churchill uttered his immortal words: 'Never in
the field of human conflict has so much been owed by so many to so
few.'[496]

Claasen thought the failure of the Luftwaffe's attack on the north-east
revealed its fatal lack of an efficient fleet of long-range, high-flying, well-
armed four-engined bombers capable of delivering a heavy load of bombs,
but it may be that without a more agile long-range escort fighter than the
Bf 110 such a fleet would have been as vulnerable to Dowding's fighters as
the twin-engined bombers actually used.[497]

The failure of Air Fleet 5 was vital to Dowding. Had its attack succeeded,
his defences would have been dangerously stretched from then on. When a
crisis came in September, he could not know that the attempt on the north-
east would not be repeated, with greater skill this time, and so he was
obliged to retain a strong force there and in the Midlands. It was a matter
of striking a balance between real and potential dangers. As it happened,
some pilots in 12 Group felt themselves under-employed and it was there
that the notorious 'big wings' controversy originated.[498]

The German attack on 15 August severely damaged a Bomber Command
airfield at Great Driffield in the East Riding of Yorkshire. Arthur
Coningham (then head of 4 Group, who later became one of the war's

outstanding tactical air commanders) recalled that day in a letter to command headquarters on 10 February 1941. About 50 bombers and long-range fighters made landfall at Flamborough Head, a prominent point on the east Yorkshire coast, and there divided, 20 making north-west for Catterick, near Darlington in County Durham, the rest south-west for Great Driffield. British fighters destroyed most of the former, but none of the latter. They 'spent just over half an hour at lunch time,' Coningham recalled, 'indulging in most effective target practice.'

During all that time, a squadron of Hurricanes was kept airborne at Leconfield, no more than nine miles away, and another squadron was held ready in reserve at Church Fenton. There was no interference with the attack on Great Driffield, however, and after destroying 12 Whitleys, four hangars and causing other damage, the enemy flew off unmolested. Coningham, deeply upset, asked Leigh-Mallory for an explanation and was given the feeble reply that the Germans were expected to penetrate deeper into Yorkshire and the two squadrons were waiting for that to happen. He was angered by Leigh-Mallory's answer, and had not forgotten it when obliged to work with him for some months in 1944.[499]

Second Phase

From 24 August, after the five-day lull, smaller formations of bombers were employed, escorted by fighters ordered to stay close to their charges. These tactics made it harder for Park's pilots to obey his orders to attack bombers and avoid fighters. Worse still, the use of a larger number of smaller formations muddled the radar warning. Plots were more complicated and British fighters were liable to be dispersed in several directions, leaving dangerous gaps in the defences. As the Luftwaffe raided further inland, Park called upon 10 and 12 Groups to provide cover for aerodromes and aircraft factories near London. He was thus able to meet the enemy further forward in greater strength, while his neighbours protected vital targets behind his fighters.[500]

During the 18 days of the second phase, the Luftwaffe lost more than three aircraft for every two British aircraft destroyed, and nearly five times as many German airmen were killed, wounded or captured. Between 8 August and 6 September, Fighter Command lost 480 fighters and 124 were damaged; 186 pilots were dead and 163 wounded. The Luftwaffe lost 743 aircraft and 208 were damaged; 1,367 aircrew were dead or missing and 281 wounded. Statistically, Fighter Command still had the edge in a fierce contest. Not only were Luftwaffe casualties much heavier, but British fighter production and repair work made good most of Dowding's losses. At that rate of exchange, however, his command would collapse for want of pilots while the Luftwaffe remained in being. The output from the British training system was not filling the gaps.[501]

Churchill invited Dowding and Portal to dine with him at Chequers on 31 August. John Colville wrote in his diary:

'Dowding is splendid, he stands up to the P.M., refuses to be particularly unpleasant about the Germans, and is the very antithesis of the complacency with which so many Englishmen are infected. He told me that he could not understand why the Germans kept on coming in waves instead of concentrating on one mass raid a day which could not be effectively parried.'

These 'scattergun' tactics would not have been followed had Dowding been in command on the other side of the Channel. It seemed obvious to him that one should use maximum force against targets of maximum value – as well-led European armies had often done in the past. The talk after dinner raised the question of shooting at German airmen baling out and descending by parachute. Dowding thought it should be done, but Churchill disagreed: an escaping pilot was like a drowning sailor. But airmen landing in Britain were not 'escaping'. They were quickly captured and in some instances had useful information to give.[502]

Going Downhill

On 7 September Dowding called a meeting at Bentley Priory with Strath Evill (senior air staff officer, his right-hand man), Park and Douglas, who seems by that date to have become *de facto* CAS as Newall quietly faded away. Dowding had a high opinion of the Australian-born Evill. 'I could not have had a sounder or more reliable man supporting me,' he later wrote. 'He was always there, always on the job, and always so pleasant in that quiet way of his.'[503]

Dowding had summoned them to help him decide what steps to take in order to 'go downhill' as slowly as possible. He assumed a 'worst case' situation arising in which efforts to keep fully-trained and equipped squadrons in the battle would fail. His policy had been to concentrate a large number of squadrons in the south-east, with those on the fringes brought in at Park's request to meet crises. As squadrons became tired, they were replaced by fresh ones from the three supporting groups.

But if the present scale of attack continued, this policy would become impossible, so Dowding wanted to make a plan now to meet that situation, if it arose. Although he would not amalgamate squadrons except as a last resort, he might have to rob rear squadrons of their operationally-qualified pilots. Enough *pilots* were available, but not enough *combat ready* pilots. The point is crucial. As Patrick Bishop wrote, in words supported by several examples, 'flying skill alone did not guarantee success as a fighter pilot, nor necessarily improved chances of survival.'[504]

The Germans must not be allowed to realize how hard hit the command had been, and Dowding would therefore keep 11 Group up to its present strength, come what may, but for compelling logistic reasons – space and facilities for men and machines – he could not increase the number of squadrons in that group.[505]

Douglas had been warming various seats in the Air Ministry ever since January 1936 and consequently, through no fault of his own, his knowledge of actual operations ended with the Great War. He wondered if Dowding were not being pessimistic in talking about going downhill. In later years, Douglas liked to think of himself as an operational commander and he did in fact get to the top in several theatres, but only after the Lord Mayor's Show had passed by:

> 'The Battle of Britain was won before he reached Fighter Command, El Alamein was over just prior to his arrival in the Middle East, the crisis point in the Battle of the Atlantic was past when he reached Coastal Command, and the war was won when he went to Germany.'[506]

At this time, September 1940, he had spent more than two years (January 1936 to February 1938) as Director of Staff Duties, responsible for framing and amending the tasks assigned to those senior officers whose duty it was to carry them out. He was then appointed Assistant CAS until April 1940, when his daily concerns were weapons and equipment, including the possibility of devising radar sets small enough to fit into the coming generation of fighters and bombers. Currently, he was Deputy CAS, involved in operational policy at the highest level.[507]

Dowding had often been at odds with Douglas and now disagreed with him again. Park, he told Douglas, was at this moment calling for reinforcements to five squadrons that had themselves just come into the front line. But there was no shortage of pilots, Douglas replied. Dowding began to explain the skills needed of a *fighter* pilot, but Douglas – evidently not listening – assured him that his command would be kept up to strength. Douglas's inability to grasp such an elementary point baffled Dowding, so Evill now spoke up. Total casualties for the four weeks ending 4 September were 348, he told Douglas, and since the three operational training units (OTUs) had turned out only 280 pilots in that period, a net loss of 68 resulted, quite apart from losses caused by accidents or illness. The OTU course had been reduced from four to two weeks, which meant that some pilots were going into combat with as few as ten hours on fighters and never having fired their machine guns in anger. For the moment, Douglas fell silent.[508]

Park then pointed out to him that casualty figures in 11 Group were near 100 a week and there was indeed, no question, a pilot shortage. That very day, he said, nine squadrons had started with fewer than 15 pilots and the previous day squadrons had been put together as composite units, a practice detested by Dowding, Park, pilots and ground crews. Dowding interrupted Park. 'You must realize,' he said, speaking directly to Douglas, 'that we *are* going downhill.' Douglas, unusually, had nothing to say.

After a tense silence, Park resumed. It was better to have 23 squadrons in 11 Group with no fewer than 21 pilots in each than to have a greater number of under-strength squadrons. Some squadrons were doing 50 hours' flying a day and while they were flying and fighting their aerodromes were being bombed. While they were on the ground, they could not get proper meals or rest because of the disorganization, and now night raids were beginning.

Douglas suggested opening another OTU. This would be done if casualties remained heavy, although if the whole of August was considered the command's strength was being maintained. Dowding told him that the true picture only emerged from the figures after 8 August, when serious attacks began. Dowding had to assume that the present scale of attack, and casualties to his pilots, would continue. Another OTU, Douglas repeated, would ensure that pilot strength was kept up. An exasperated Dowding then made a point that had evidently been lost on Douglas: another OTU would itself be a drain on the command's strength as pilots and ground crews were found to staff it.[509]

An important point, apparently not raised by anyone at this meeting, emerges here. Dowding could have eased his pilot shortage by grounding all his Blenheims and Defiants. True, they would have needed re-training in order to handle Hurricanes and Spitfires, but these pilots were likely to prove of more immediate value than young men fresh out of training schools. He could also have given stronger support to the creation of OTUs, but he preferred to see pilots given the essential final stages of their training in operational squadrons – which in 1940 simply lacked the time to do so. That said, the very real shortage faced by Dowding in September 1940 was brought about largely by the Air Ministry's determination to maintain a large bomber force, and also by its failure to expand the training system urgently. It failed, in short, to anticipate the heavy casualties inevitable in wartime.[510]

Douglas returned to his comfort zone in Whitehall, aware that he had cut a poor figure at Bentley Priory, partly because the reality of life in Fighter Command was unknown to him, partly because he had not prepared properly for the meeting. Newall having virtually disappeared during his last weeks in office, Douglas was doubtless overworked. But he was also an adroit bureaucrat and a determined climber up the greasy pole to high office, as his subsequent career demonstrated.

Douglas replied to the draft minutes of the meeting, sent to him by Evill, on 14 September. Neatly evading the actual issues raised, he claimed that the minutes misrepresented his contribution. They reminded him, he told Evill, of a music-hall turn between two knockabout comedians in which one, usually called 'Mutt', asked foolish questions. He had been cast in that role. 'However, life is too strenuous in these days,' he grandly asserted, 'to bother about the wording of minutes.' The next meeting which Dowding, Park and Douglas all attended took place six weeks later – at the Air Ministry, with Douglas in the chair (Newall being indisposed) – and he did not then find life too strenuous to bother about the wording of minutes, as Dowding and Park learned to their cost.[511]

Dowding had neither taste nor time for Air Ministry politics: for coping with what Probert called a 'fearsome bureaucracy'. Douglas, however, had its intricate webs thoroughly mastered and Dowding failed to recognize that his long-standing contempt for Douglas's conduct, confirmed by his inept contributions to the meeting on 7 September placed him in grave danger. Douglas would attend no more meetings at Bentley Priory.[512]

Park's Report

In early September, Park reported to Dowding on recent operations. Dowding approved the report: Park and his staff, he wrote in a covering letter to the Air Ministry on 22 September, 'have dealt most successfully with the rapidly changing phases of the tactical situation described in this report.' He agreed with Park about the value of supplementing radar and the Observer Corps by using reconnaissance aircraft to observe the approach of enemy formations and report directly to group headquarters. This had already been tried with some success, but it needed a separate unit of specially-trained pilots with properly-equipped aircraft and he had neither. Dowding also agreed that serious damage had been done to airfields, but only Manston and Lympne were out of action for more than a few hours. The works organization was doing well, but he needed more repair and maintenance crews. Although he was anxious to move vulnerable sector control rooms away from airfields, problems regarding the re-routing of communications, security, accommodation, meals and transport were ongoing headaches.

When Douglas minuted Newall about the report he found grounds for criticism, especially of Park's brief comments on night fighting. Hardly surprising, for there had been very little night fighting up to 10 September, when the report ended. Douglas was chairman of a committee set up to consider how to deal with German bombers in darkness, but neither he nor its members ever consulted Park.[513]

In Park's mind, 7 September – when the Luftwaffe switched its main attacks from sector airfields to London – was always the turning point. Not 15 September, later designated as 'Battle of Britain Day', when his fighters achieved a spectacular success. Luftwaffe losses on the 15th, wrote Alfred Price, were 175 aircrew killed, wounded or captured; Fighter Command lost only 12 pilots killed, though 12 more were wounded. Goering was at last compelled to recognize that reports of Fighter Command's death, like those of Mark Twain's, had been much exaggerated. Two days later, on 17 September, Hitler ordered that Operation Sealion be postponed until further notice. The 'decisive factor', in Hitler's decision, according to the British official history, 'was the series of actions fought by Air Vice-Marshal Park on the 15th of that month.'[514]

Big Wings

11 Group had always been considered the senior group and treated accordingly, receiving the latest aircraft, ablest pilots and most experienced ground staffs. Park was junior to Leigh-Mallory in terms of commissioned service, although he had a far superior record during the Great War as a combat pilot, and subsequently in experience with fighters. The Air Ministry accepted Dowding's opinion that Park was the better man. The point is worth emphasis because Dowding has been rightly criticized for not getting rid of the incompetent Leigh-Mallory, but he did Britain a signal service in advocating the elevation of Park, who would prove to be one of the war's outstanding fighter commanders.[515]

One day in February 1940, while Park was still at Bentley Priory, Leigh-Mallory 'came out of Dowding's office, paused in mine and said in my presence that he would move heaven and earth to get Dowding removed from Fighter Command.' At that time, this was the mere bluster of a man perhaps privately aware that his capacity did not match his ambition.

Dowding's fall, when it came, was brought about mainly by events beyond his control, helped along by influential Whitehall Warriors for whom Leigh-Mallory was a convenient pawn. Dowding did not hear about his bluster until 1968, when Park revealed it to the New Zealand press. 'I had no idea,' said Dowding, 'that there was such a feeling of enmity towards me on Leigh-Mallory's part,' and regretted that Park had said nothing in 1940. In fact, Dowding had many opportunities to observe Leigh-Mallory's faulty handling of his group even before the war began, and Park regularly drew Dowding's attention to his sins of omission and commission.[516]

Throughout the summer of 1940, Leigh-Mallory found it increasingly difficult to accept his place in the rear, behind the front line. Then, at the very end of August, he suddenly found salvation in the 'big wings' idea of Douglas Bader, one of his squadron commanders. It was an idea that would scratch his itch to be more directly involved in the great battle, and one that would certainly be well received in the Air Ministry by Dowding's critics.[517]

Most historians as well as most pilots who fought in the battle agree that big wings were unsuitable for defensive fighting. Why? Because they took so long to assemble and move into action. They were also difficult to control, either from the ground or in the air. Park objected vehemently to them and Dowding, who agreed with him, failed to check Leigh-Mallory. This failure, surprising in a man of authoritarian temperament who had a perfect grasp of the arguments for and against, is a severe indictment of his powers of command.

Bader was a Cranwell graduate who had lost part of both legs when he crashed an aircraft, while fooling about, back in December 1931. Obliged to leave the RAF, he returned when war broke out, demonstrating the courage and skill needed to become an exceptional pilot despite his severe handicap. In February 1940 he was posted to a squadron in 12 Group and by June had been given command of a squadron that moved to Duxford on 30 August. Everyone who served with him was impressed by his forceful personality and soon became familiar with his trenchant criticism of British fighter tactics.

According to Bader, a wing of three or more squadrons should take off from airfields in 12 Group as soon as news was received that a raid was building up over France. Having had time to gain vital height, the wing would intercept the enemy as he crossed the English coast. Park's squadrons should then join in to harry the departing raiders. Bader quite understood that a wing could not operate from 11 Group airfields because there would not be enough time to climb to an effective height.[518]

Like Leigh-Mallory, Bader was irked by his place in the rear. His frustration sharpened his advocacy of a means by which he could play a prominent part in the battle. He could, and should, have served his turn in 11 Group, but Leigh-Mallory refused to part with him, and it is surprising that he himself did not agitate for a transfer south.

For Douglas and other devout Trenchardists, Bader was exactly their kind of man: educated at a good school in Oxford, a top Cranwell graduate, constantly aggressive in the air, damned good company in the mess. He had learned to fly in simpler days and had been away from the service when the air defence system was being created. His head was full of the exploits of Great War fighter pilots and he had no patience with, or understanding of, Dowding's strict ground-to-air control system. He was a natural leader and could not bear to be led.

Park wrote to Evill on 27 August about the difficulty of getting support from 12 Group when and where he wanted it. The need was already serious, as Dowding well knew, because Evill had sent him a table on the 17th showing the command's desperate pilot situation: 'replacements available at the moment are barely 50% of the casualties suffered in the last fortnight.' Park asked for support to be arranged through Bentley Priory in future. This arrangement could not have been made without Dowding's knowledge or approval and as head of the command it was his duty to settle a dispute between two of his group commanders.[519]

Then, on 30 August, Bader claimed an astonishing victory in an air battle west of Enfield on the northern outskirts of London. Ten Hurricanes attacked no fewer than 100 enemy aircraft and routed them: 12 destroyed, several more damaged, and not so much as a bullet-hole suffered in exchange. These claims were not supported by any evidence, but Leigh-Mallory gleefully accepted them and agreed with Bader that wing tactics were the answer.[520]

On 17 September Leigh-Mallory reported to Dowding on wing patrols carried out by his squadrons. Five had now taken place. All told, they claimed 105 German aircraft destroyed, another 40 probably destroyed and 18 damaged. These causes for celebration, 163 of one kind or another, were offset by the loss of only 11 pilots killed, missing or wounded and 14 fighters lost. Again, evidence to support such spectacular triumphs was absent. Victory claims by Bader's wing were notoriously high: twice as many for each squadron as were claimed by other squadrons and it is now well known that *their* claims were also greatly exaggerated.

It is easy to see why. German aircraft did indeed spin or dive away when fired on; there was usually plenty of thick smoke, black or white, drifting about and it seemed likely that the attacked aircraft were about to crash. Ground officers – often not pilots themselves – were reluctant to challenge boisterous young men who cheerfully backed what each other thought he had seen or done. Whatever private reservations a pilot might have were easily swept away by group euphoria. And no-one could deny that all the surviving German aircraft had high-tailed it for home, leaving some – perhaps many – of their number wrecked and burning all over southern England or swallowed up in the Channel.

Dowding admired his pilots only just this side of idolatry, but he did not believe everything they said, least of all those inspired by Bader. 'I read a great many combat reports,' he told Leigh-Mallory on 23 September, 'and I think I am beginning to pick out those which can be relied on and those which throw in claims at the end for good measure.' This blunt rebuke made no impression on Leigh-Mallory because it was not supported by any important person in the Air Ministry, and both the press and the BBC were encouraged to accept even the wildest claims. Perhaps there was a case for boosting Fighter Command at a time of national crisis, even though a moment's cool reflection suggests that the backlash would – and did – embarrass the Air Ministry after the war, if Germany and her allies were defeated, when captured German records showed that the claims were grossly exaggerated.

Douglas must have known that Bader's claims were fantastic, but it evidently suited him to accept them at face value. Himself a pilot in the previous war, he knew perfectly well that a gulf lay between what honest pilots *believed* they had done and what they had *actually* done. He also knew, though few airmen or writers have dared to say it, that not every pilot, in either war, was honest. Douglas also ignored a point made by Park on his copy of Leigh-Mallory's report: 'Did these Wings engage before targets were *bombed*?'[521]

Unlike Leigh-Mallory, Douglas had been a fighter pilot during the Great War, although he had had nothing to do with modern fighters. As early as 11 August 1938 he had told Stevenson that he thought it 'immaterial in the long view whether the enemy bomber is shot down before or after he has dropped his bombs on his objective,' a shocking opinion that he would later qualify as best he could. Leigh-Mallory agreed. Targets should be left to their ground defences, he thought, and a concentrated attack made on the enemy: if necessary, after he had bombed those targets. Douglas and Leigh-Mallory received useful assistance from a Member of Parliament, one Peter Macdonald, adjutant of Bader's squadron. 'Boozy Mac', as he was known, busied himself in the House of Commons in support of big wing ideas and at the suggestion of Balfour (Under-Secretary of State for Air) saw the Prime Minister himself. Churchill listened to what he had to say, but for the moment continued his support for Dowding.[522]

Months later, on 29 January 1941, after Dowding and Park had been sacked, Leigh-Mallory – now commanding 11 Group – conducted a paper exercise using the circumstances of an actual raid in September 1940. His intention was to prove correct his opinion on the use of big wings. The exercise was carefully set up and Leigh-Mallory totally mismanaged it. The 'raid' was not intercepted while approaching its targets and both Kenley and Biggin Hill were 'bombed' while their aircraft were still on the ground. When his several mistakes were pointed out to him, he replied that he would do better next time. Luckily for Britain, there was no next time, on paper or in fact. Needless to say, Leigh-Mallory received no reproof either from Bentley Priory or the Air Ministry.[523]

The experience of Myles Duke-Woolley illustrated some practical problems with wing tactics that were lost on its Whitehall advocates as well as on Bader and those pilots who enthusiastically backed him. One day, in late September, Duke-Woolley was leading his Hurricane squadron (based at Kenley in 11 Group) on a standing patrol over Canterbury in Kent, near the south-east coast. Looking north, he saw a black mass far below coming from the direction of London and recognised it as the 12 Group wing. He had spotted it miles away and had a decisive height advantage even as far south as Canterbury. This contradicted Leigh-Mallory's advocacy of Duxford as a base from which to gain a safe altitude before flying into Park's area. The wing looked so determined that Duke-Woolley decided to

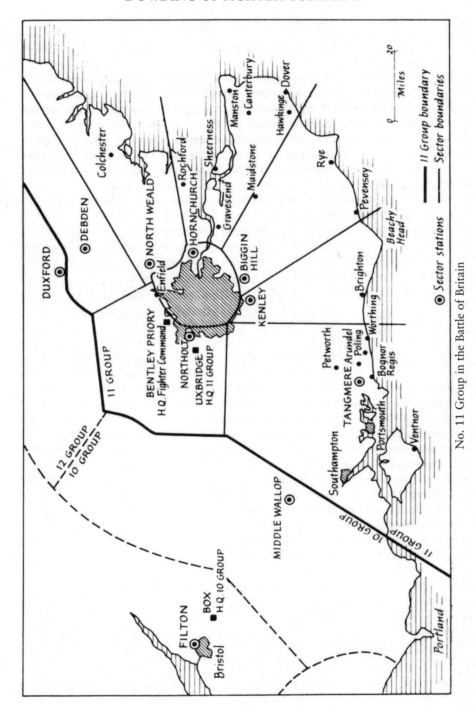

No. 11 Group in the Battle of Britain

act as its top cover. The wing leader, failing to identify fellow-Hurricanes and thinking he was about to be attacked, ordered his followers to orbit. Duke-Woolley, thinking the wing was preparing to intercept a raid that he had not spotted, followed suit. For some minutes there was complete stalemate until the wing began to run short of fuel, having taken so long to assemble, and retired in good formation northwards. At least on this occasion it made few victory claims. The whole ludicrous business also underlined the fact that wireless communication between unaffiliated squadrons was impossible at that time.[524]

An Infamous Conference

Park agreed with Evill that he could at times make better use of Leigh-Mallory's strength and outlined his intention in a letter to Dowding on 10 October. Effective sector control, he wrote, required squadrons to live and work in a sector for weeks in order to develop understanding between formation leaders and sector controllers. To achieve this, 12 Group squadrons should be exchanged with squadrons presently in 11 Group.[525]

While Park was working out a method of co-operating with 12 Group, Donald Stevenson, Director of Home Operations in the Air Ministry, was preparing a critique of his tactics, based on Leigh-Mallory's astonishing report of 17 September. Stevenson recommended that the minimum unit used to meet large formations should be a wing of three squadrons. When necessary, a force of two wings should be used, to be known as a 'Balbo', in honour of an Italian politician and airman who had led large forces of Italian aircraft – though not in combat – during the 1920s. It would frequently happen, thought Stevenson, that Balbos would pass out of radio range of their sectors. When that happened, something that he called 'Esprit de Wing' would guide them.

Dowding and his group commanders were invited to attend a conference on 17 October, 'to discuss major tactics by fighter formations, and to hear a report on the progress of night interception.' Douglas actually presided because Newall, who was to be replaced as CAS by Portal a week later, felt poorly. Portal was present, but only in his capacity as CAS-Designate, for he had no knowledge of fighters. Although a devout Trenchardist, he had never quarrelled with Dowding, a fellow-Wykehamist, and both men had once commanded 16 Squadron. But the careworn appearance of Dowding and Park contrasted sharply with the smooth eloquence and confident manner of their Air Ministry critics. The worries of Whitehall Warriors, though real enough, do not compare with the life and death responsibilities of a field commander in wartime.

Leigh-Mallory brought Bader with him and the appearance of so junior an officer at so senior a meeting was unprecedented and certainly surprised Dowding, among others. Although Leigh-Mallory was surely right to bring with him the most vocal advocate of big wings to put his case, a pilot with regular frontline experience should also have been invited to attend and comment on Bader's arguments. Neither Dowding nor Park thought of doing this and naturally Douglas, who was sure that Bader had found the secret of success, did not suggest that they do so.

Douglas invited the meeting to consider three propositions. One, that enemy formations should be outnumbered when encountered; two, that fighters should go into action with a plan to engage both escorts and bombers; and three, that fighters should seek a height advantage before tackling the enemy. These resounding glimpses of the obvious gradually emerged out of a long harangue which showed no sign of being informed by a reading of Park's many detailed reports and instructions in which these and other matters of daily concern had been carefully analysed. At least he spared Dowding an analysis of 'Esprit de Wing', which might have been good for a laugh on an otherwise tense occasion. Eventually he stopped talking and invited comments.[526]

Park spoke first, but he was wasting his breath. All those present knew which way the wind was blowing and had their own careers to think of, among them Slessor – at that time Director of Plans in the Air Ministry – who criticized this 'unhappy and wholly unnecessary' meeting, but only after his retirement. Alan Deere, one of the battle's outstanding pilots, published a study in 1970 of the tactics employed in which he came down strongly on Park's side. He sent a copy to Slessor who thought it 'an extremely interesting and absolutely sound' memorandum.

Slessor, widely regarded as an outstanding student of the proper use of air power, had only one criticism to make of Dowding's handling of the battle: Leigh-Mallory 'should never have been allowed to take the line he did.' Had he been in Dowding's place, Slessor would have told Leigh-Mallory 'to shut up and get on with commanding his group in accordance with what he knew quite well was my policy.' He would also have refused to attend that conference. If Douglas and his allies disliked what he was doing, 'they could bloody well find someone else to command. To my mind it was intolerable that a C-in-C should have been subjected to it – and I was there and heard the whole thing.' Strath Evill, one of the RAF's most highly regarded officers, both for ability and good manners, agreed. It was a 'stupid controversy' and the treatment of Dowding was 'deplorable'.[527]

Everyone present at that meeting knew, or ought to have known, that resisting, let alone defeating, the Luftwaffe was a more complex task than Leigh-Mallory supposed. The argument that his fighters, based in the rear, had time to get into position and make the initial interception while Park's fighters pursued retreating raiders, was not practicable for several reasons. Radar could not yet give accurate information about the number and height of approaching aircraft; the Germans did not select a single target for each raid and head straight for it; Park's squadrons would have been in even greater danger of being caught on the ground and less able to gain combat height once German aircraft were actually overhead; and, not least, it was not certain that an all-out fighter-to-fighter contest would end in British favour. Nor did it. In that contest, despite its escort duties and despite operating at extreme range, the Luftwaffe had a marked advantage: it lost 845 fighters (including 235 twin-engined Bf 110s) in exchange for destroying 1,172 British fighters (631 Hurricanes, 403 Spitfires, 115 Blenheim fighters and 23 Defiants).[528]

Both Park and Brand sent a list of proposed amendments to the draft minutes of the meeting, but Douglas – still smarting from his embarrassment at Bentley Priory in September – enjoyed the satisfaction of rejecting them all. Nor did he answer Dowding's rebuke on 22 October: 'Please do not say that I agree, reluctantly or otherwise,' to the decision to divert a Hurricane squadron to night fighting. 'I am carrying out orders which I believe to be dangerous and unsound with our present strength of fighter squadrons.'[529]

Leigh-Mallory asserted at that meeting that he could get a wing of five squadrons into the air in six minutes and that it would be over Hornchurch in Essex at 20,000 feet in 25 minutes. Not so. On 29 October, long after this meeting ended and while his Air Ministry admirers were still applauding him, the Duxford Wing was to take 17 minutes to leave the ground and a further 20 before it set course from base: this after two months of constant practice. Moreover, because the wing absorbed five squadrons from a relatively weak group, important targets in East Anglia and the Midlands were left short of fighter cover.[530]

There is no reliable evidence that the Duxford Wing ever achieved significant results. In fact, on 32 occasions when a wing was ordered, there were nine instances when it failed to form up at all, and only seven resulted in combat. Only once did Bader's men get to incoming aircraft before other defenders and on that occasion they shot down eight bombers; not the 57 claimed. All that is well enough known these days. At the time, however, there seemed no doubt in the minds of either Air Ministry officials or those pilots who followed Bader that he and Leigh-Mallory had jointly found a Holy Grail: a certain method of knocking down scores of Huns, many more than were being destroyed by the methods advocated by Dowding and Park.[531]

17

The Night Battle, September to November 1940

Assault on London

Horst Boog argued that from 8 August (when he believes the Battle of Britain began) until 6 September, the Luftwaffe aimed at military targets, but turned to an attack on civilian morale from 7 September onwards. That decision may well have saved Dowding. By that date, 11 Group was close to collapse: six of its seven sector stations had been badly damaged and pilot losses were very heavy.

About 5 pm on 7 September, while Dowding was still discussing how best to manage his declining resources with Evill, Park and Douglas at Bentley Priory, the Luftwaffe launched a massive attack on London. During the next hour and a half, 348 bombers (escorted by 617 fighters) set fire to docks, oil tanks and warehouses along both banks of the Thames east of the city. They also blasted numerous densely populated streets. It was by far the most powerful attack yet launched by any air force against any target. The fact that the Luftwaffe chose a new target, one not hitherto attacked in daylight, contributed to the surprise achieved.

Although the eventual challenge was vigorous, costing the Germans more than 60 aircraft destroyed or damaged, London was hit hard and Fighter Command lost 24 pilots killed or injured. Dowding knew how helpless his command was at night and, as he feared, the Luftwaffe returned at about 8.30 pm. For the next seven hours, wave after wave of bombers flew over London, finding fresh targets in the light of fires started by their comrades in daylight. They bombed at leisure, unhindered either by anti-aircraft fire (of which there was little and that ill-directed) or by night fighters (of which there were few and those ill-equipped).[532]

On 8 September, the day after the meeting at Bentley Priory and the first assault on London, Dowding had divided all squadrons into three classes. Class A were those in 11 Group, to be maintained at a minimum strength of 16 pilots. Some squadrons in 10 and 12 Groups were also designated Class A, but their pilot strength might include non-operational pilots. As for Class B squadrons, they might include up to six non-operational pilots in their quota of 16, and Class C squadrons would retain at least three operational pilots. Dowding himself would inform the three supporting groups each day of the number of pilots they must transfer to 11 Group.

Starting on 7 September, about 5,300 tons of bombs were aimed at the London region during the rest of that month. This was more than four times the load dropped in daylight in the same period. In early September, the Luftwaffe had over 700 serviceable bombers in France and Belgium, each capable of carrying about one ton of bombs across the Channel. So many airfields were available to them that attacks could be launched from several directions, and bad weather was unlikely to close all these airfields at any one time, either for departure or return. The Germans also made use of several beacons, beam transmitters and other aids to night-flying and target-finding. These made attacks possible in conditions of low cloud and heavy rain that would hinder the defences as much as darkness.

During the 68 nights between 7 September and 12 November, there were only 10 on which the Luftwaffe did not mount what it regarded as a 'major' raid (dropping at least 100 tons of high explosive). 'This was an ordeal that, for its continuity (though not for the severity of the destruction) was never to be approached by either side for the rest of the war.'[533]

At that time, Britain's night defences were not nearly as effective as the day defences. Few heavy anti-aircraft guns were available and all lacked radar assistance to direct fire accurately. Like the barrage balloons and searchlights, they served mainly to keep aircraft high. Radio counter-measures effectively upset German beams, but London was an easy target to find without them. It was so large, so close to the Luftwaffe's bases, and from the coast a broad river positively invited pilots to the city centre. Decoys such as large fires started in open country might sometimes divert bombers from other targets, but never from London.[534]

As for night fighters, there were in September eight squadrons assigned to that duty, six of Blenheims, two of Defiants, all close to useless. A fighter specifically designed for night work was urgently required and had begun life as long ago as November 1938 when the Air Ministry learned of Bristol's intention to re-design its Beaufort torpedo-bomber. But it would not be until the end of March 1941 that the new machine, a twin-engined, two-seater named 'Beaufighter', was in regular squadron service. It had very powerful Bristol Hercules engines, offering 1,650 hp for take-off and the unheard-of armament of four 20-mm nose-mounted cannons and six wing-mounted machine guns. It could also stay airborne far longer than any single-engined fighter; it offered an excellent view forward for the pilot, and had a top speed of over 300 mph, much faster than any German bomber.[535]

Of equal importance was the fact that its airborne radar was gradually becoming reliable. No aircraft was much use at night without the help of two radar sets, one aboard the aircraft and the other on the ground. Airborne radar had many teething problems. It was in any case useless without some means of bringing a night fighter within three miles of its quarry, because that was the maximum range at which an airborne radar could 'see'. British radar stations, such an essential help to Dowding in the day battle, were all sited on the coast and looked out to sea. Once an aircraft had crossed the coast, radar could no longer track it. The Observer

Corps, Dowding's other vital aid in daylight, was of no help at night.

A new network of radar stations was needed, to reveal the course and height of enemy bombers over land. The War Office had been developing radars to assist anti-aircraft guns and Dowding borrowed a few of those GL (gun-laying) radars to help his so-called night fighters. He installed them at searchlight posts in Kenley sector (stretching south of London as far as the coast). Direct communication with Kenley airfield enabled these posts to keep the sector controller informed of the position of bombers in his area. He knew the position of his own fighters, and tried to bring one or more of them within range of a particular bomber. He did this partly by radio telephone and partly by ordering a searchlight to point towards the bombers. This method would be the basis of that used when GCI (ground control interception) came into service.[536]

Defence in Darkness

Douglas sent Newall a very long minute on 28 August 1940 about night interception problems. We must tackle them, he urged, 'rather more vigorously than at present'. Dowding was 'pinning his faith almost entirely on the Beaufighter plus AI' (airborne interception), but the Beaufighter was not yet ready for operational service and neither was AI. In Douglas's opinion, we must therefore specialize more Defiant, Blenheim and Hurricane squadrons for night work. Dowding was not putting up enough fighters at night, he thought, and we must arrange for standing patrols over major targets. We should remove the Blenheim's mid-upper turret, which would improve its speed, according to Douglas's information, by 15 mph and modify its engines to use 100 octane fuel, hitherto reserved for the Hurricane and Spitfire.

As usual by this date, Newall seems to have had nothing to say, but Dowding replied to Douglas on 7 September, raising – again, as usual – several practical points. How long would it take to remove the Blenheim's turret and install a blister? What effect would this have on its centre of gravity? How much time would it take to modify the Blenheim's Mercury engines to take the improved fuel? He went on to remind Douglas that standing patrols were already employed over specially vulnerable potential targets and that the Defiants – advocated so strenuously by Douglas and some of his colleagues – had failed totally as day fighters and its crews were not yet trained in night flying, let alone fighting.

He was rather too busy with a constant day battle being waged over south-east England to worry unduly about a night offensive which had not yet begun, but he would be prepared to discuss the subject with Douglas when next he visited Bentley Priory. He had in fact already written to Douglas on 28 August about his reluctance to employ Hurricanes at night; and emphasized, not for the first time, that the Beaufighter was Britain's only realistic hope for an effective night fighter. Park issued sensible instructions for the operation of night fighter wings on 27 October 1940. The tactics to be employed, he wrote, 'once the enemy has been seen, are those of a cat stalking a mouse rather than a greyhound chasing a hare.'[537]

Solving a Problem

Committees being the usual British method of tackling (or at least discussing) problems, Douglas had set up a 'Night Interception Committee' in March 1940. That committee, together with the Fighter Interception Unit formed in April, gave good value during the rest of the year in testing AI equipment and devising techniques for making effective use of it against intruders.

Several versions of AI equipment were produced, some of them poorly made and all them failing to perform adequately. The root of the problem lay in the failure to find some means of bridging the gap between the research done at Bawdsey and the practicalities of devising equipment that would fit into aeroplanes; the gap between scientists on the one hand and technicians and companies capable of mass production on the other. None of this was the fault of either the Air Ministry or Dowding, but the result was a total shambles in the second half of 1939 that could not be put right in time to meet the German blitz from September 1940 onwards. Not for six months was the Beaufighter ready for large-scale operations, with the help of a ground-based radar and an airborne radar that, between them, gave it a fair chance of destroying enemy bombers.[538]

Solving the problems of night radar had been handicapped by the more immediate problem of setting up an effective day radar system. There simply were not enough skilled men available for the latter task, let alone the former. Moreover, progress was impeded by personality clashes, muddle and indecision in the Air Ministry, a reluctance to involve the electronics industry and the incredible decision, taken shortly before the outbreak of war, to allow Watson-Watt to shift all the Bawdsey experts some 350 miles north to his old college in Dundee, where facilities were primitive and there was no airfield within 20 miles. Dowding had been unable to prevent this 'unmitigated disaster' to the radar research programme, but it was he who agreed with Tizard in January 1940 to involve EMI, a leading electronics firm, in solving night-radar problems: the vital turning-point, 'for it would be EMI that would eventually make the improvements that would turn the radar device into an effective weapon system.'[539]

Overwhelmed by alarm at the success of German night bombers and anxious to be seen by Whitehall's other authorities, civilian as well as military, to be taking positive action, Salmond was chosen on 14 September to chair a meeting of senior officers – among them Freeman, Tedder and Douglas – who swiftly produced resounding proposals. It was easy for them to do so, for like Salmond they knew little about the subject. More Beaufighters were needed with AI Mark IV radar sets, more information from ground radars, more radio aids for night fighters and more night flying training. All these were matters that Dowding and his staff had long had under anxious consideration.

On 17 September, after two days of deliberation, Salmond's committee produced a long list of conclusions. Only after these instant experts had decided what should be done was Dowding asked for his opinions: this on the morning of the 18th. In the opinion of the committee members, control of aircraft at night should be shifted from group to sector commanders;

filtering should be transferred from Bentley Priory to group headquarters; a night fighter training unit should be combined with a tactical development section; and Dowding should make more use of single-engined fighters at night. But Dowding insisted that fighters without airborne radar, which they could not then carry, served no useful purpose at night. He was overruled. It was believed, perhaps rightly, by officers more politically aware than Dowding that 'something must be done'; a visible gesture was needed to console concerned politicians and citizens.

In short, Dowding was as unimpressed by the committee's recommendations as its members were by his blunt rejection of most of them. Their exchanges ran on into October. It now seems that Dowding was wrong on some points at issue and unwise, at least, to correspond directly with Churchill about them. It was sensible, despite Dowding's opposition, to decentralize filtering from Bentley Priory to groups and work at GCI, whereby one radar station controlled one night fighter in an orbit round a particular area.

The greatest tribute to the overall performance of the air defence system is the fact that only one aspect of it came under constant criticism: Dowding's refusal to decentralize filtering to group level. Salmond's committee eventually won this battle, but only after Dowding's authority had been eroded by his failure to counter night bombing.[540]

Removing Dowding: Round Three

Salmond told Sinclair, Beaverbrook and Churchill that Dowding must go and felt so hotly opposed to him that he even considered the bizarre step of making his way to Buckingham Palace and demanding that King George VI personally sack him. Presumably wiser heads reminded him that it was now some years since British sovereigns lost the power to act like that. On 25 September he wrote to Trenchard: 'as you and I know,' Dowding 'has not got the qualifications of a commander in the field, as he lacks humanity and imagination.' Newall should also be sacked, thought Salmond, because 'his strategic judgement is completely at fault.' Although Trenchard agreed wholeheartedly, he preferred more devious methods of working. 'I never mention that you and I are working in agreement on the matter,' he told Salmond on 4 October, 'as I feel it is more use our apparently being independent but working for the same cause.' One may reasonably doubt, however, whether many Whitehall Warriors, long familiar with the personalities and opinions of two well-seasoned wheelers and dealers, were deceived. Salmond wrote to Churchill next day, 5 October:

> 'I am most anxious to put to you the case for a change in the holder of the important position of C-in-C Fighter Command. Recently, on Lord Beaverbrook's instructions, I have carried out an enquiry into night air defence, the result of which, together with what has since occurred, makes a change, in my opinion, imperative. This opinion is also very strongly held by most, if not all, service members of the Air Council.'[541]

Churchill, however, was not yet ready to sacrifice a commander whom he greatly admired. Trenchard and Salmond were motivated – perhaps mainly motivated – by a sincere concern for the management of Britain's air power, but ignorance, prejudice and malice also played their parts. Two nights later, on 7 October, Churchill and Dowding – accompanied by Tim Pile – dined at No. 10 and then drove to a gun site in Richmond Park. Despite an air raid warning, they then drove on to Biggin Hill. It proved to be a miserable evening: nothing worked properly and everyone got thoroughly wet and frozen. Yet Churchill bore up cheerfully, treating Pile to Bovril and sardines when they returned to No. 10 (Dowding, perhaps wisely, forewent this treat). The Prime Minister understood more clearly than a couple of retired air marshals, who were becoming more eccentric by the month, that Dowding and Pile knew what they were about and that the difficulties facing them had no easy solution. On 13 October, Churchill again had Dowding as his guest at Chequers, this time with Portal. He told them that he was sure Britain would win the war, although just at this moment he could not quite see how.[542]

Almost every evening from September onwards, Dowding would be driven to Kenley or to Redhill (about five miles farther south) to observe experiments with airborne radar. He would return via Uxbridge to talk with Park, his driver picking his way 'through streets littered with masonry and assorted wreckage, every ravaged house a reminder of the shortcomings of the air defences.' Back at Bentley Priory, where he often worked far into the night, 'naked electric bulbs showed a neglected building, bare, damp, dirty and freezingly cold.' A WAAF plotter met him leaving the building one night, his face grey with fatigue, 'but he did not fail to hold the door open for her, and his hand went up to his cap as he said good night.'[543]

He was acutely aware that night bombers were causing many casualties and severe damage, and that both the government and the Air Ministry needed a remedy. This was indeed a time of crisis, as grave as that endured in daylight during the summer, but even so it seems unwise that Dowding should have taken the whole burden on his own shoulders; no-one can work all day and all night too, at least not for long.[544]

Dowding pushed himself beyond reasonable limits during 1940 and expected everyone under his command to do likewise. He took a hard line on honours and awards, even for gallant actions. Park would complain to his senior staff officers on 10 December that his recommendations to Dowding were forwarded to the Air Ministry only after 'considerable delay' and 'after having been pruned'. Continuous, demanding effort under unprecedented strain did not, in Dowding's view, justify public recognition, although he privately honoured most of the men and women who helped to defend Britain in that memorable year – and in later years was unstinting in their public praise.[545]

Admiral Tom Phillips, Vice-Chief of the Naval Staff, poked in his oar on 16 October 1940. The interception of night bombers was now, he told Churchill, the most important problem facing Britain's defenders. He went on with more trite comments: as yet, neither an effective airborne radar nor a fighter to carry it was available. His solution, echoing that of Douglas and several other Air Ministry luminaries, was to use day fighters on patrol over London.

Churchill invited Dowding to respond, which he did the same day. We have been trying to carry on as we did at the end of the last war, he told the Prime Minister, but it has not worked, 'although a great deal of latitude has been given to various commanders to develop theories and variations in conjunction with searchlights.' But German bombers flew too high and too fast to be picked up by searchlights and as for patrolling over cities in the hope of spotting a bomber it was not feasible, even on clear moonlit nights. Only an airborne radar set that works will help us. 'You will note,' he ended, 'that Admiral Phillips suggests no method of employment of fighters, but would merely revert to a Micawber-like method of ordering them to fly about and wait for something to turn up.'[546]

On several occasions in October and November, Dowding composed long and detailed letters on the difficulties of achieving interceptions in darkness which he circulated widely. He outlined the problems faced by everyone concerned with getting airborne radar to work consistently, with GCI equipment that was still under development, with the most effective use of searchlights – singly or in clusters? – with improving the Beaufighter's cockpit layout and solving its seemingly endless engine troubles.

But the Germans were not doing as well as they should, in his opinion. Too many raids did not concentrate on a single target, hitting it first with incendiaries and then with high explosives. Even so, wrote Dowding on 28 October, he was concerned that the Germans were able to reach London and bomb accurately in weather so bad that his fighters could not even leave the ground.

His command needed blind-flying apparatus and pilots needed more practice at taking off and landing in the dark. The question of de-icing the Beaufighter had not yet been looked at, but would become serious once winter set in. The task would not be complete until we could 'locate, pursue, and shoot down the enemy in cloud by day and night;' airborne radar 'must become a gun sight.' We were not yet even approaching this ideal, but every night that he spent watching attempts at interception confirmed his opinion that 'haphazard methods' will never succeed in producing more than an occasional lucky encounter. The only answer was that 'night interception depends on the laborious development of a system the defects of which are eliminated one by one by means of practical trials and thoughtful analysis of the results.'[547]

No doubt true, but dull stuff for men in Whitehall, in or out of uniform, who felt that something dramatic must be possible, to lift everyone's spirits. A German pilot wrote that the raids had become 'routine, like running a bus service'. Ground gunners 'put on a good show', but few aircraft were hit. His own bomber 'never collected so much as a shell fragment', and the few night fighters spotted by the Germans caused no harm. During September, the Luftwaffe flew 6,135 sorties over Britain, and only four bombers were shot down; 3,200 civilians were killed in the last two weeks of that month.

There were even heavier losses during the last three months of 1940 and it was clearly necessary for the head of the man responsible for defending

Britain in darkness to roll. The fact that Salmond and his advisers were wrong and Dowding was right about how to defeat night bombers was beside the point. The lack of an effective, radar-equipped night fighter from September onwards sealed his fate.[548]

Dowding forwarded another report from Park to the Air Ministry on 15 November. He thought Park wrong to exclude wounded and injured airmen from his statistics, which made the command's situation look better than it was. He accepted losing pilots as instructors at newly-opened training schools as 'a wise and necessary investment', but not sending them overseas: that was 'a pure dissipation of capital'. No vital British interests, in his view, lay east of the Third Reich, nowhere in the Mediterranean, and certainly nowhere east of Suez. Dowding then assured his Air Ministry readers that he did not consider forming big wings a practical proposition and endorsed Park's preference for using fighters in sections of four, not three: two pairs could look after each other better.[549]

A System that Worked

What gradually became 'The Dowding System' withstood the German challenge in daylight splendidly. 'No other country had such a defence mechanism,' wrote Air Marshal Sir Peter Wykeham, author of an excellent history of Fighter Command, 'and at its zenith it was to be a marvel of what human ingenuity could devise.'[550]

It obviously depended on pilots, ground crews, radar operators, monitors of wireless transmissions, anti-aircraft gunners and those who manned Observer Corps posts, barrage balloons and searchlights. But they all received essential help from many other men and women, in and out of uniform. These included the medical personnel who attended casualties, the heavy rescue teams (who dug out survivors from collapsed buildings), firemen, policemen and members of the Women's Voluntary Service, who were active everywhere, doing whatever no-one else had time for. There were the heroes who dealt with unexploded bombs, those who repaired damaged runways, hangars and offices; post office, gas and electricity workers; those who serviced and repaired the elaborate defence teleprinter network; the Civilian Repair Organization, which rebuilt hundreds of fighters and the 'Ancient and Tattered Airmen' (officially known as the Air Transport Auxiliary, including women pilots) who flew replacement aircraft every day from factories for final fitting out to maintenance units, on to airfields and then, when time and conditions permitted, flew them back to maintenance units for major servicing.

It was, wrote Wood, 'a very large system involving tens of thousands of people, quite apart from all the squadrons themselves.' Dowding understood it perfectly. He was the man 'who knew when the system was going wrong and what it needed, and he got it.'[551]

The creation of Fighter Command, as an effective defence force 'was due almost entirely to Dowding'. If genius really is an infinite capacity for taking pains, Dowding was a genius. Slessor had argued in 1936 that the RAF needed only a few single-seat fighters for air defence because the two-seater was a better bet. It took Dowding's 'spirited objections' to the Defiant in June 1938 to ensure a high level of Hurricane and Spitfire production. In short, as Murray has written, Dowding's conduct of the Battle of Britain was 'surely as great a conceptual triumph as the creation of the German panzer force.'[552]

Before and after he became prime minister, Churchill often praised Dowding personally and the conduct of Fighter Command under his direction. In Churchill's opinion, it was the only effective part of the RAF. For years he had observed, with contempt turning to anger, the words and deeds of the Air Ministry. Its senior officers had tried hard to get rid of Dowding, and yet their long-standing focus on the bomber had not produced a weapon that worked when it was needed. Churchill's anger was all the greater because he was so keenly aware, as he said on 3 September, that: 'The fighters are our salvation, but the bombers alone provide the means of victory.' On 1 November 1940, he therefore rebuked both Sinclair and Portal for the 'pitifully small' number of bombs dropped on Germany; it was 'a scandal... deplorable... a serious reproach to the organization of the RAF that only such limited results can be shown for so much money and material.'

No doubt these savage words encouraged the Air Ministry's masters to press Dowding to attempt some sort of an offensive. As Harold Nicolson (diplomat, Member of Parliament, author and critic) wrote in November 1940, 'I think we have managed to avoid losing this war, but when I think how on earth we are going to win it, my imagination quails.'[553]

The failure of the Luftwaffe to eliminate Fighter Command meant that its forces available to attack the Soviet Union in June 1941 were actually weaker than in the attack on western Europe in May 1940. Belief in German military invincibility was shaken, which encouraged the stirring of resistance movements in the occupied territories and persuaded many doubters in the United States that Britain would survive. Spain did not join the Axis: had she done so, Gibraltar and probably Malta would also have fallen into enemy hands.[554]

Throughout the battle, Dowding and Park were 'steadfast and wise'. They displayed the alleged Teutonic virtues, trusting grimly to a meticulously-planned defence and making ruthless demands on the skill and spirit of their men. Goering, in contrast, had the alleged British virtues: refusing to plan seriously, dabbling with one expedient after another, convinced that the personal appeal – to honour, loyalty, patriotism, whatever – more than compensated for technical or administrative deficiencies. Dowding would turn from the cares of daytime defence only to study the problems of night-time defence, while Park took what chances he could to pilot his own Hurricane around the combat zone.

Goering, meanwhile, gave close attention to his numerous costumes (medieval hunting, comic opera military), his fabulous art collection, his magnificent train set, the finest wines and food, drugs, perfumes and jewels available anywhere in Europe. Above all, to thwarting anyone in or out of uniform who might threaten his standing at Hitler's court. Unlike Dowding and Park, conducting an air battle was for Goering only one of many interests and, not surprisingly, his intermittent interventions were often ill-advised.

The vital difference in military performance between Britain and Germany was not in pilots, but in leadership. 'The Germans,' Bungay wrote, 'were out-generaled.' He went on to identify ten men who made the critical decisions or had the essential insights; in Bungay's opinion, they were truly 'the few' who should be most honoured.[555]

Number one, in chronological order, was Ashmore, head of London's air defences in the Great War, who created the system which Dowding resurrected and developed. Then came the scientists, numbers two and three, led by Tizard and Watson-Watt. Fourth, fifth and sixth were the aircraft designers Mitchell and Camm, with Ernest Hives, responsible for developing and producing the excellent Rolls-Royce Merlin engine. Number seven was Sorley: without his pressure, the Hurricane and Spitfire might well have been equipped with only four machine guns. Even with eight guns, pilots found it difficult to bring down German aircraft.

At number eight came Dowding:

'He built on and supported all the efforts of others, drew them together and created a weapons system which was not only unique in its ability to create clarity out of a mass of constantly changing data without using computers, but was also extremely robust.... He made resistance possible and laid the foundations of victory.'

In ninth place Bungay placed Churchill, who 'conducted the nearest-run campaign of the summer against the peace lobby': a group that adroitly ducked for cover after the Battle made it clear to everyone – friend, enemy, neutral – that Britain would fight on.

And finally Bungay honoured Park:

'He wielded the weapon that Dowding created and Churchill decided to use. Had he failed, as he could have done, the efforts of all the others would have come to nought. Throughout the long months of strain, Park hardly put a foot wrong, making all the major tactical decisions, attending to relevant details, visiting pilots and airfields himself, and fighting an internal political battle. Tedder was right: if ever any one man won the Battle of Britain, he did.'[556]

18

What Happened Next:
After November 1940

End of a Reign
Readers who have followed to this point the saga of the Air Ministry's efforts to prise Dowding out of Bentley Priory will not be surprised to learn that there was one last muddle before he went. Sinclair had told Dowding, privately and civilly, on 13 November that he had been selected to head a mission to the United States to assist with equipment purchases and to get closer to American leaders: politicians as well as military men. Near the end of his life, when severely crippled and with his memory failing, Dowding told Robert Wright, his second biographer, that Sinclair sacked him in a brief telephone call. That is not so.[557]

Sinclair confirmed at another meeting on the 17th that he was to leave Bentley Priory immediately, but then discovered that Douglas – his designated successor – could not take over until the 25th, so Portal was obliged to write to Dowding, asking him if he would stay on until then. Dowding replied at once: 'I have been out on night operations and your letter reached me at 1.20 am. Certainly I will carry on till the 25th if that will be convenient to you.' On the 24th, he sent this signal to all squadrons:

> 'My dear Fighter Boys:
> 'In sending you this my last message, I wish I could say all that is in my heart. I cannot hope to surpass the simple eloquence of the Prime Minister's words. "Never before has so much been owed by so many to so few." The debt remains and will increase. In saying goodbye to you, I want you to know how continually you have been in my thoughts, and that, though our direct connection may be severed, I may yet be able to help in your gallant fight. Goodbye to you and God bless you all.'[558]

Charles Willett, a member of his clerical staff, recalled Dowding calling in at each office to say: 'I think you know that I am going, thank you very much.' On his last morning, Douglas arrived while Dowding was still at his desk: 'he finished what he was doing, looked up at Sholto Douglas and simply said, "Good morning", and was away.'[559]

The departure of Dowding was 'a sad day' for the Observer Corps, wrote its historian. He had fostered the organization since 1936 and valued it highly. Churchill referred to it as 'stone age', but Dowding knew better. He had proposed on 2 December 1939 that the work of the corps merited the distinction 'Royal' and after due process had been laboriously followed, that title was awarded on 9 April 1941.[560]

Did Dowding suffer in his last years 'the unhingeing bitterness of one who was scurvily treated in the moment of victory?' John Terraine thought so. He wrote a massive history of the RAF in the European War that has influenced most writers and readers since it first appeared in 1985, so his opinion is widely known and probably widely accepted. On this point, however, Terraine was mistaken. When reflecting, at Wright's request, on his years at Bentley Priory, Dowding did indeed recall – not always accurately – bitter moments. But they certainly did not 'unhinge' him. As we shall see, the last 20 years of his life were filled with interests far removed from the daily hurly-burly of Bentley Priory and Whitehall. These interests, shared with his beloved second wife, gave him such lasting joys that old woes were but clouds passing swiftly across the sun.

Dowding had learned on 8 October 1940 that he was to receive the rare honour of being made a Knight Grand Cross of the Order of the Bath (GCB): a public recognition by influential persons in the Air Ministry and Whitehall of his exceptional merits. His response, so typical, was to regard it as an award for his pilots. 'If I could,' he wrote to Balfour, 'I should like to cut the decoration up into a thousand pieces and distribute it to the fighter boys, who are the ones who have really earned it.'[561]

We shall see presently that he was awarded an even higher honour in 1943 and during the years before he died in 1970 he was well aware of the fact that nearly every book or article published on any aspect of the battle praised him and criticized – fairly or otherwise – the conduct of those who opposed him, in particular, the decision not to promote him to the RAF's highest rank. As early as 1956, the official historian of the defence of Britain had concluded that: 'Not many men in British history have shouldered such a burden of responsibility as he had borne and few have been privileged to shield their fellow-citizens from so grave a danger.'[562]

He lived just long enough to write a foreword to what is still regarded as an outstanding account of the battle: 'it is a pleasure for me to be able to say that I agree so much with the opinions that are expressed and the verdicts that have been reached' in this 'perceptive and moving book.' A magnificent steam locomotive was given his name in 1947 and there must be many Britons of a certain age who spent their youths on railway platforms for whom no greater accolade is conceivable.[563]

Nor was he 'scurvily treated in the moment of victory', as Terraine wrote. Neither Dowding, nor anyone else in Britain, thought 'victory' had been achieved in November 1940. The case for relieving him of his command at that time was a strong one. There was also, of course, a case for leaving well alone, but the decision to remove him made sense. Right or wrong, it should not be castigated simply because it pleased some vocal and crafty opponents (such as Trenchard and Salmond) and satisfied some ambitious men (such as Douglas and Leigh-Mallory).

Ronald Lewin, a fine historian, once wrote that Britain survived 'for all the other glorious reasons, but mainly, and quite simply, because Dowding got it right.' There is a great deal of truth in these words, but Lewin went on to say: 'Then we besmirched the glory, and sacked him.' There was no 'glory' about for Britons in November 1940, only daily labour, nightly fear, and the realization that 1941 was likely to bring total disaster. Portal, more assertive and astute than his predecessor, may have been mistaken in removing him from Bentley Priory, but he was fully justified in accepting a very strongly expressed opinion, civilian as well as military, that it was time for a change.[564]

Dowding's 'true monument', wrote Lyall, is the command he created before the battle. 'Others might have handled it as well or better – the Air Staff certainly believed so – but that is a tribute to what he built; nobody has suggested who else might have built so well.' Zimmerman, in his magisterial study of the part played by radar in Britain's ability to withstand the Luftwaffe, thought Dowding must be singled out for special praise. His support for the Bawdsey scientists never wavered after the Daventry experiments, despite several setbacks and failures. He and Tizard were solely responsible for promoting the crucial work done at Biggin Hill and Dowding oversaw virtually every aspect of fitting the new devices into his ever-growing system. He may have been wrong about centralized filtering, but if so this error does not offset his massive contribution. 'His dismissal from Fighter Command was caused by both political and personal factors which came together only when the scientists were unable to deliver in time the technology needed to defeat the Blitz.'[565]

It was Tizard who had first identified the need for an airborne radar set, but it was Dowding who sponsored the development and helped define its military needs. 'Without these men of the highest calibre,' wrote White, 'airborne radar in Britain would not have progressed at the rate it did, nor would an AI set have been available at the time when the country needed it most.' Although Dowding had gone by then, during and after 1941 the scientists whom he encouraged perfected one of the war's most valuable devices.[566]

Was he to blame for the misery inflicted on Park (replaced by Leigh-Mallory in December 1940)? Should he have realized that the disagreement between his two senior group commanders was acute and acted decisively to end it? Many writers have thought so, but Wykeham (himself an air marshal) reminded his readers that Dowding carried heavier burdens than most of us can even imagine. Apart from constant worry over pilots and aircraft, 'The Prime Minister was never far from his elbow; the Air Council, though doing their best to sit on their hands, could not stay off the telephone for long' and seeking an effective answer to night bombing was an exhausting and dispiriting task. His burdens were immense and it is perhaps not surprising that he paid less attention to arguments between two group commanders than do subsequent historians, sitting at their ease and well aware that Hitler is long dead and gone.[567]

It was 'hard luck' on Park, commented Lyall, but 'hesitancy in command can cause casualties other than those in battle.' Dowding had held his command for more than four years, a very long time as appointments go in any of Britain's armed forces, but Park had only been at Uxbridge for seven months. 'To my dying day,' he said in 1968, 'I shall feel bitter at the base intrigue which was used to remove Dowding and myself as soon as we had won the battle.' Leigh-Mallory, recalled Park, showed no generosity in victory: 'He did not even bother to attend to the usual formality of taking over from me, so I handed over to my senior staff officer.'[568]

In a preface to Collier's biography, published in 1957, Dowding declared that he had 'no sense of grievance' over his removal from Fighter Command. He commented on 'the apparent ingratitude of the nation' towards him, adding – as few writers did in those days – that 'the attacks of our bombing aircraft upon the barges massed along the coast of Flanders exercised an important influence upon the outcome, and were not effected without heavy losses.' A fair point, given that Bomber Command destroyed at least 10% of those barges.[569]

He went on to say, showing a pleasing breadth of understanding, that few people in Britain could possibly realize in late 1940 that a significant victory had in fact been achieved. The night raids dislocated everyone's lives, causing severe damage and heavy casualties. Had they gone on much longer, they would have had a serious effect upon trade and industry. They had little connection with the invasion threat, but who could say what the long summer months of 1941 might have brought? In sum, wrote Dowding, 'Laurel wreaths are awarded to a victorious commander generally in response to an outburst of national gratitude, but the nation did not know at the time that it had anything in particular for which to be grateful.'[570]

The notorious bombing of Coventry came a few days before Dowding was required to leave Bentley Priory. Coventry's many factories produced machine tools, vehicles, aircraft and synthetic fibres. As a centre of 'industrial excellence', the Germans regarded it as an important target in their attempt to ruin Britain's economy. Over 300 bombers attacked that city on the night of 14 November, 119 patrols were made by night fighters who claimed to have seen seven bombers but intercepted none of them. Although around the city were five times as many guns per head of population as ringed London, neither they nor aircraft prevented some 1,800 civilians from being killed or injured.[571] The decision to sack Dowding had already been taken, but this disaster confirmed the opinion of those responsible that they had made a necessary change.

The Battle's Significance

Frankland, who sharply criticized Deighton's book *Fighter*, nevertheless warmly approved his summary of the battle's significance:

'Had the Luftwaffe eliminated Fighter Command, its bombers could have knocked out all the other dangers one by one. Given the sort of command of the air that the Luftwaffe had achieved in Poland in only three days, German bombers, guided by radio beams, could have destroyed everything from Whitehall to the units of the Home Fleet. There would have been no insurmountable problem for invasion fleets and airborne units if the air was entirely German.'

Here, in a few words, thought Frankland, 'is why the Battle of Britain must rank directly with Drake's defeat of the Armada and, though less directly, with Nelson's victory at Trafalgar, as being among the handful of decisive battles in British history.' One wonders, however, if Frankland would have been able to write so triumphantly if the Luftwaffe had resumed its offensive over southern and eastern England from March 1941 onwards.[572]

In June 1945, Francesca Wilson, a Quaker who spent her life trying to help war victims, met a German scientist ('Dr X', she calls him) whom she asked: 'When did you know the war was lost?' 'Stalingrad was a landmark,' he replied. 'But in reality it was lost after Dunkirk and the Battle of Britain. We had miscalculated the huge build-up of air power in Britain and the United States and started putting factories underground too late.'[573] At about the same time, Russian journalists asked Field Marshal Gerd von Rundstedt, the most senior surviving commander, which battle of the war he regarded as most decisive. They expected him to say 'Stalingrad'. Instead, he answered: 'The Battle of Britain'. This not being what they wanted to hear, they put away their notebooks and left. On a first reading of this opinion, one sympathizes with the Russians. Far larger 'butchers' bills' were presented after many other battles – especially on the Eastern Front – during the most horrendous war that mankind has yet inflicted on itself. And the British, as Dowding and Park knew better than anyone else, did not even win the battle: they avoided defeat, which had been their goal since the first German bomber took off in a westerly direction. But if Fighter Command had been eliminated, it is difficult to see how the Royal Navy, deprived of air cover, could have prevented an invasion.

Such, in fact, had been the opinion of the Chiefs of Staff on 25 May 1940: if the Germans gained air superiority, they declared, the navy would be unable to stop enemy landings over 'an indefinite period'; and the British Army – poorly-trained, ill-equipped and also without air cover – would be 'insufficient to deal with a serious invasion'. But before either of those disasters occurred, it seems likely that the peace party, headed by Halifax, Hoare and Simon, with such persons as Butler and Douglas-Home hovering on the sidelines, would have raised its head again and uttered thousands of smooth words in favour of a realistic, peaceful settlement.[574]

The Luftwaffe's failure over south-east England in the summer of 1940, and the decision to turn eastward in an attempt to overthrow Stalin's rule of the Soviet Union before Britain was defeated, mark a decisive turning point not only in the fortunes of the Luftwaffe but in those of the Third Reich. A defiant Britain was left unconquered in the German rear and became a base for an Anglo-American bomber offensive, followed by a massive invasion. Those few summer weeks, wrote Cooper, were perhaps the most important in the entire war.[575]

Dowding nearly ended his time at Bentley Priory long before the Battle of Britain began, and if his appointment had not been extended – an exceptional decision – would his successor have fostered and operated the defence system with anything like the same skill? Here we come to the *schwerpunkt* (the centre of gravity, the crucial point) of a battle, a campaign or a biography.

Although Dowding had completed three years as head of Fighter Command, the ever-escalating crises with Germany, Italy and Japan resulted in Air Ministry dithering. There were other ambitious officers waiting in the wings, and an easily understandable desire to see the back of Dowding. He was notoriously intolerant of the slackness normal in the comfortable pre-war Whitehall world, in which he had served for six years. He was abstemious and unsmiling even on social occasions. He was damnably eloquent on paper and an untiring critic in meetings, a man who had actually read all the papers.

But there was a recognition – genuine, if reluctant – in some quarters of the Air Ministry that Dowding's understanding of the air defence system, as yet by no means fully functioning, made him the best man to continue working it. Not until November 1940 was there irresistible pressure to remove him, when he seemed to have no answer to the dreadful night blitz and Churchill was at last persuaded that another man must have his chance to find that answer. Park, who had carried the immense burden of the day-by-day conduct of a unique battle, was also sacked.

A hard word, 'sacked'. Richards, an official historian, found a much nicer word: 'translation'. The translation of Dowding and Park, he wrote, 'though doubtless wise in itself,' as of course Air Ministry decisions usually were, in the opinion of in-house writers, 'was not perhaps the most impressive immediate reward that might have been devised for the victors of one of the world's decisive battles.' Sir Humphrey Appleby, immortal master of words used to conceal meaning in television's *Yes Minister*, could not have put it better.

Sir Humphrey would also have approved of the Air Ministry's best-selling pamphlet on the battle, published in March 1941, that carefully avoided mentioning even the names 'Dowding' and 'Park'. Written, anonymously, by one Hilary St. George Saunders (a librarian in the House of Commons), it sold 300,000 copies on publication day and perhaps 15 million all told. Saunders later acted as diarist for Leigh-Mallory in 1944 and shared with Richards in writing a three-volume history of the RAF, published in 1953-4 and re-printed in 1974-5.[577]

Not for the first time, Churchill was angered by the Air Ministry's inept conduct of its business and asked Sinclair to explain. It was a time of serious crises in the progress of the war, but Churchill made time, as Gilbert recorded, to protest on Dowding's behalf. He wrote to Sinclair on 12 April:

'The jealousies and cliquism which have led to the committing of this offence are a discredit to the Air Ministry and I do not think any other service department would have been guilty of such a piece of work. What would have been said if the War Office had produced the story of the Battle of Libya and had managed to exclude General Wavell's name, or if the Admiralty had told the tale of Trafalgar and left Lord Nelson out of it! It grieves me very much that you should associate yourself with such behaviour.'[578]

Sinclair waffled away in the best Sir Humphrey tradition, with the help of material supplied by Richard Peck, Assistant CAS (General): we wanted 'to tell a simple story of the fighting from the human side and present it rather as the "soldiers' battle", which it very largely was.' This is absolute nonsense. It is difficult to think of any other *campaign* (it was not a *battle*) in recorded history that was more closely directed from the top, often hour by hour, for months. If Dowding and Park had been named, Sinclair went on, everyone else who fought in the battle would also have deserved a mention and so on. Churchill disagreed and eventually, in August 1943, Sinclair – who is generally regarded as an honourable man, for a politician – accepted that such a petty attitude would not do, and saw to the production of an illustrated edition of the pamphlet that not only named Dowding and Park but even used photographs of them.

And yet the criticism remains that Dowding failed to prevent the Luftwaffe bombing where and when it liked in darkness from September onwards. Ray and some other historians have suggested that a more outgoing man would have shared his worries about night defence with at least some senior members of the Salmond committee, but Dowding was not that kind of man and in any case no member of that committee knew more about night defence than he did and they all – even Salmond – had their own important jobs to look after.

There was a strong belief in the Air Ministry that Fighter Command could have acted more aggressively even during the day battle, and that it must do so in 1941. That proved to be a disastrous policy, but it accorded well with the RAF's Trenchardist tradition. In short, it was not unreasonable for Churchill and Beaverbrook, such staunch allies of Dowding throughout the summer, to accept that he was no longer the man for the job and to suppose that Douglas and Leigh-Mallory, with strong backing inside and outside the Air Ministry, could do better.

Douglas in Command

With Dowding's reluctant agreement, Park had spoken on 21 October 1940 about 'taking a more aggressive role than the defensive attitude forced upon us recently.' And Douglas, within a week of taking over from Dowding, had been told by Portal – advised by Trenchard from his privileged back seat – that the fighter force should 'lean forward into France' and there take on 'the Hun', just as British airmen had done so gallantly and at such heavy cost to themselves during the Great War. Actually, Bomber and Coastal Commands had been the first to attempt this offensive. Their aircraft made a number of night attacks on airfields in France and the Low Countries from mid-1940 onwards, but Dowding had no strength to spare for such operations. During 1941, night intrusions were not given a high priority by Fighter Command's new manager, who preferred daylight sweeps even though they achieved little and proved very costly.[579]

One German bomber was brought down on the night of 19/20

November, but none at all in December, when Douglas was in charge. Portal told him on the 7th that 'mere numbers of night fighters will do no good until the problem of intercepting and shooting down the bomber is solved.' Dowding had made that point on numerous occasions and Douglas was already realizing what a gulf lay between easy criticism from a Whitehall office and actual responsibility in a command headquarters.

Countless trees have perished in the great cause of informing readers about the Battle of Britain, but much less has appeared on what Fighter Command attempted and achieved under its new management by the two men who replaced Dowding and Park. If there had been a second daylight battle in 1941, as was widely expected by Britons, by Germans, by conquered Europeans, by hesitant allies and by apprehensive neutrals, and if Douglas and Leigh-Mallory had remained in charge of Britain's air defences, that battle might well have been lost. Unlike the battle in 1940, it would have begun in March, with six months of generally good weather stretching ahead and one may suppose that it would have been more intelligently conducted on the German side.

Neither before nor after he became head of Fighter Command did Douglas recognize a distinction between *flying* a modern fighter competently and using it as an *effective weapon*. On 31 October 1940, for instance, he would write that the pilot position had undergone a 'kaleidoscopic change' during the last week or two and Fighter Command in fact had a surplus. Two days later, Evill reported more realistically on the situation as at 31 October. At the end of July, he wrote, there had been 62 squadrons and 1,046 operational pilots. At the end of October, there were four and a half more squadrons but only 1,042 pilots. Total 'wastage' during the past three months was 1,151 pilots: an appalling loss rate of 25 every two days. Many of these casualties were a result of inexperience and the Air Ministry must shoulder the blame for a shortage of competent pilots because of its failure to expand the training schools early enough and maintain an adequate course length.[580]

Douglas replied on 9 December to Portal's comment on the defence's failure in darkness to say that Freeman – greatest of Whitehall Warriors – advocated putting *all* the day fighter squadrons on to night fighting. This suggestion reveals Freeman's alarming ignorance of issues that had been anxiously debated, sometimes in his presence, during Dowding's time as head of Fighter Command. Douglas, fortunately, was wiser than Freeman: 'I am sure this is not the answer,' he told Portal, and then echoed the arguments Park had advanced about the need for different techniques and training to meet this crisis. 'It is vital,' Douglas concluded, echoing Dowding's words, 'to defeat the enemy night bomber – we may even lose the war if we don't.'[581]

Douglas was then responsible for what an official historian would later call 'an oddly conceived' experiment on 11 December. He ordered 24 Hampden bombers to patrol over Birmingham during a raid. They reported sighting some German bombers, but were unable to catch them. Had they done so, it is unlikely that they could have inflicted significant damage because they were armed only with two forward-firing machine guns.

Worse still, the Hampdens, when glimpsed by searchlights, looked exactly like German bombers and were therefore in real danger from friendly fire. The experiment's only value was to show Douglas's colleagues in the Air Ministry and his admirers in the government that 'something was being done'.[582]

By mid-December, according to Douglas's postwar despatch, the Luftwaffe had virtually ceased raiding England in daylight, having suffered so heavily since September 1939. The time therefore seemed ripe for Fighter Command to take the offensive, for the sake of British morale and to prevent the Luftwaffe from recuperating at leisure. Sadly, the proportion of battle-hardened pilots was not high; many had been killed or wounded and all were very tired; others had been sent to OTUs or to the Mediterranean theatre. Their replacements were not only untried but incompletely trained, as a result of the desperate need for pilots by the autumn of 1940 and the onset of bad weather since then. Even in raw numbers, despite what Douglas asserted in September, the command was short-handed. The average squadron strength was down to about 21 pilots, compared with the original establishment of 26. Nevertheless, a small offensive was begun.[583]

On 18 December Hitler issued Directive No. 21, 'Barbarossa', which turned the thoughts of his military planners towards the Soviet Union. Night bombing of British targets continued, however, in order to deceive both Churchill and Stalin as to his intentions for 1941. Thanks to Barbarossa, there would be no resumption of the day battle over Britain in that year.[584]

A few days later, on 29 December 1940, came one of the most destructive of all German raids, aimed at the City of London and Whitehall. 'Nearly 1,300 separate fires were started,' recalled Douglas after the war, 'some of them of vast dimensions. The weather was poor and the night fighter force had no success.' The new men, for all their talk, were achieving no better results than the old. In some respects, the results were worse because Douglas clung stubbornly to his belief in the use of Hurricanes at night in spite of everything Dowding and Park had told him. British pilots remained as brave and determined as ever, but they brought down no bombers and continued to suffer death and injury themselves.[585]

It was not until effective radar ground control equipment came into use in early 1941 that interceptions began to be achieved: and yet only one bomber was destroyed and one damaged by AI night fighters in the whole of January. An increasing number of victories was achieved from February onwards, but not enough to deter the Luftwaffe. In April, 150 bombers were withdrawn from the west for the campaign in the Balkans and more left in May to rest before the Russian offensive. Even with greatly reduced forces, the Luftwaffe was able to carry out a very heavy attack on London during the night of 10-11 May.

This attack proved to be the most damaging London suffered throughout the war. The defences claimed 28 bombers destroyed and Douglas considered this performance 'eminently satisfactory'. So it was, from a German viewpoint, because the Luftwaffe actually lost only seven of the 550 aircraft employed to British defences. Over 3,000 Londoners were killed or injured that night, one-third of its streets were rendered impassable, every mainline railway station but one was blocked, and some fires were not extinguished for days. That raid indicated what a *maximum* effort by the Luftwaffe, in daylight and darkness, might have achieved during the summer of 1941 even with Douglas commanding numerically stronger forces (but weaker in flying skill and combat experience) than Dowding did during his time at Bentley Priory. No-one in Britain could know, on the morning of 11 May, that the worst was over. From a German point of view, the worst should just have been beginning.[586]

Trenchard, Salmond and Freeman manfully forebore to mount a campaign seeking the dismissal of Douglas and Leigh-Mallory for their failure. However, by May 1941 that trio of wise men may have begun to realize that the problems of dealing with night raiders were less easily solved than they had so blithely supposed in September 1940. They may also have begun to notice that Fighter Command's much-vaunted offensive was also a dismal failure.

In December 1940, as soon as he succeeded Park at Uxbridge, Leigh-Mallory wrote to Douglas urging a formation of no fewer than 108 fighters. Either to defend over England or offend over France, he saw a mighty aerial armada, thundering along in Bader's wake and ready at his call to hack down Huns by the score, but Hurricanes and Spitfires were short-range defensive fighters, needing all the help they could get from radar and the Observer Corps if they were to match the latest Messerschmitt Bf 109 on its home ground or the even more deadly Focke-Wulf Fw 190, introduced in July 1941.

Alan Deere, a New Zealander who became one of the war's outstanding fighter pilots, wrote that Fighter Command's aim in 1941 was the same as the Luftwaffe's in 1940: to entice enemy fighters into the air where they could be destroyed. British bombers sent across the Channel in daylight were in effect bait – and not a very attractive bait either, because they were too few and too lightly armed to threaten seriously any target the Luftwaffe wished to protect. Johnnie Johnson, another exceptional fighter pilot, found when leading big wings over northern France in 1941 that they were difficult to control in action because pilots got in one another's way. When he climbed his wing through cloud, more time was spent looking for friendly aircraft than seeking targets in the air or on the ground.

As early as 12 February Douglas was unhappy. 'Our idea,' he reminded Leigh-Mallory, 'was to go over the other side and leap on the enemy from a great height in superior numbers; instead of which it looks as though we ourselves are being leapt on.' As Douglas should have foreseen, the Germans merely waited for the short-range British fighters to turn for home and then picked off the inevitable stragglers.

The level of training in Fighter Command during 1941, when there was time for it – unlike in the previous summer – was very low, but Douglas was fixated, as a devout Trenchardist, on ceaseless offensive operations even with pilots who were not ready for combat. 'Esprit de Wing', though exhilarating in Whitehall, lacked zest when exported to France. Those airmen who fought in the campaigns of 1940 caused serious damage to the

Luftwaffe and significant political damage to the Nazi régime, but those who carried out forays across the Channel in 1941 achieved nothing comparable. They were as brave and determined as the men of 1940, but they should not have been there. The words 'advance' and 'morale' never ceased to thrill Trenchardists. As Portal, a devout disciple of the master, put it on 13 February 1941: 'I regard the exercise of the initiative as in itself an extremely important factor in morale, and I would willingly accept equal loss or even more in order to throw the enemy onto the defensive.'[587]

It may be that many of the pilots so 'willingly' sacrificed – by commanders, sitting safely in offices – should have spent some part of 1941 in training, rather than on nit-picking operations, pending posting to theatres overseas where their services were really needed. The failure of an offensive that kept at most some 2-300 German fighter pilots from either the eastern front or the Mediterranean was disguised by extravagant estimates of German losses. Between 14 June and the end of the year, fighter pilots on daylight sorties claimed the destruction of 731 enemy aircraft, nearly all of them fighters. In fact, the Germans lost no more than 103 fighters over France and the Low Countries in combat during the whole of 1941; another 51 were destroyed in accidents or on training flights.

Collier, an official historian, did what he could to put a good face on these appalling figures. They do not, he wrote, 'reflect the moral value of the operations. Many British fighter pilots gained from the raids experience which served them well in later years.' But many more died or were injured or captured who might have survived to take part in operations of actual, as opposed to moral, value if they had been better trained. Douglas and his advisers were gravely at fault. Instead of devising 'a realistic method' of assessing claims, wrote Cox, Fighter Command went on accepting exaggerated claims, believing 'it was winning a battle of attrition when it was in fact suffering severely.'[588]

As Evill told Douglas on 7 March 1941, the amount of training in 10 Group was too little and the situation was even worse in 11 Group. Too high a state of readiness was being maintained; squadrons standing by on the ground were neither fighting nor training and the command was wasting a quiet period before the expected renewal of heavy fighting in the spring. 'It is out of all proportion,' he protested, 'that we should be imposing such a serious handicap upon ourselves.'[589]

Another aspect of this fighter offensive concerns casualties inflicted on the French. On 27 December 1940, a wing commander responsible for intelligence at Bentley Priory minuted the group captain in charge of operations about an attack made by two Spitfires on buildings at Le Touquet occupied by French civilians. Given that we hope to win this war partly by an uprising of the local population, such actions do not help, he noted drily. Known as 'Rhubarb' operations, they were as unpopular with pilots (save for a maniacal minority) as they were with French civilians, not to mention their horses, cattle and sheep, pigs and chickens. Douglas said that their main target was enemy aircraft on the ground or in the air, but these were rarely found. Pilots were not given specific targets and were insufficiently discouraged from simply blazing away at random.

Rhubarb is an appropriately inglorious name for such antics.

Another kind of venture involved several squadrons of fighters sweeping over northern France. Sometimes they were accompanied by Blenheim light bombers, except for a few weeks in July when the new Short Stirling heavy bomber was used. When bombers were present, the venture was code-named 'Circus', another suitably inglorious name. Hundreds of bombers – and their crews – were lost in attacks that probably caused at least as much harm to the French, their livestock and property as they did to the Germans. In short, wrote Bishop, under Douglas and Leigh-Mallory there began 'a phase of fighting which killed hundreds of pilots for negligible results. Between November 1940 and the end of 1941, nearly 470 pilots who had survived the Battle of Britain were killed.'[590]

On a less grim note, one may turn to the second volume of Douglas's memoirs, *Years of Command*, written with the help of Robert Wright, and due to be published in 1966. When Wright told Dowding about it, he replied on 20 September 1965:

> 'I am glad to hear that he wishes to put the record straight because, of course, he was one of my principal opponents at the Air Ministry before and during the Battle. Once the battle was over, any animosity which I might ever have felt against him very quickly evaporated.'

In fact, all references to Dowding in what is a disappointingly bland outline of Douglas's highly coloured life are favourable and no reader would ever guess that they often differed on important matters, or that a cross word ever passed between them. Dowding wrote to 'My dear Sholto' on 1 June 1966, to thank him for sending him a copy of the book, 'and for the kindly things which you have said about me.'

When writing to Wright on 9 June, Dowding asked him to tell Douglas 'how much I sympathize with the cavalier treatment to which he was subjected at the end of his time in Egypt', when the Americans vetoed his appointment as Allied Commander in South-east Asia: an appointment prematurely offered to him by Sinclair with Churchill's approval. 'The authorities,' he wrote, with personal knowledge, 'can be astonishingly brusque on occasion.'[591]

19

American Interlude, November 1940 to May 1941

Reluctant Envoy

While still at Bentley Priory, Dowding had an interview with Sinclair on 13 November 1940. Sinclair told him that the government was well aware of the need to strengthen Britain's organization in the United States for selecting, modifying and purchasing aircraft and air armament. The task would call for 'the driving force of a strong personality and unless there was at its head a man whose influence on American production engineers, staff officers and members of the American government would carry weight, we could not expect satisfactory results.'

The United States, said Sinclair, had the world's finest production engineers with huge resources at their disposal, but they lacked war experience, 'and needed to be told what to do.' Under a good leader, Britain could get what she needed and help the United States to shape her own air force (to use against Germany, Italy and Japan, if she ever found herself at war). Henry Morgenthau, Secretary of the US Treasury, had asked for Portal – recently appointed CAS in succession to Newall – to carry out this important task, but Sinclair argued that his current job was even more important.

The position lay within Beaverbrook's control, as Minister of Aircraft Production; he wanted Dowding to have it and Sinclair agreed. But Dowding was reluctant to take it on. Would it be a temporary mission and would he return to Fighter Command after it was over? No, Sinclair replied: Douglas was to have that appointment. Could he think it over and see the Prime Minister? Certainly, said Sinclair. Churchill spoke to Dowding next morning, 14 November, explaining the importance of getting American war aviation to develop along the right lines, in step with that of Britain. Although he remained reluctant to accept the task, Churchill told him that the 'public interest, of which I am the judge' required his consent. 'Personally,' Churchill assured Sinclair, 'I think he will perform the task very well, and I will give him a letter to the President. I have a very great regard for this officer and admiration for his qualities and achievements.'[592]

Henry Tizard sent Dowding some notes on 21 November about the

American scene. 'All members of my mission, including particularly the service members, were quite definitely of the opinion that even in those directions where the Americans were technically efficient, they had not thought out operational problems, and it is on that side that you may be able to help them most.' He was authorized to discuss radar matters with very senior officers and Tizard was sure he would find the Americans keen to listen and learn. 'I believe that the only way of getting sufficient production for ourselves,' wrote Tizard, 'is to persuade the Americans that what is best for us is also best for them.'

Dowding was to have an assistant, Flight Lieutenant Frederick Hillary Ximenes Gwynne, who kept a diary of their time in the United States. He and Gwynne quickly became good friends and on 28 March 1941 Dowding would write a warm recommendation for him. Gwynne's knowledge of America and Canada had proved most valuable. So too had his string of Christian names: 'very suitable for a gentleman's gentleman among colonials', remarked Dowding (but only in private). Gwynne was by profession an engineer – just the sort of man with whom Dowding felt most comfortable – and handled all the paper work most efficiently. This posting, Dowding emphasized, cost Gwynne a promotion to squadron leader in Coastal Command and Dowding now urged his case.[593]

They sailed from Glasgow aboard the *Leopoldville*, a Belgian vessel with a Belgian crew, on 18 December. The voyage, Dowding's first to the New World, 'must have run Columbus's close for duration,' he recalled. The ship was capable of 19 knots, but the first part of the voyage was made in a convoy that progressed at no more than seven. Even when they joined their naval escort, bad weather kept the pace down to twelve. Numerous depth-charges were dropped and Dowding wondered why no information was given out about lifeboat stations and no boat-drills were organized. He was told there was no room in the boats except for 'invalids': Canadians, 'most of whom,' said Dowding, 'were malingerers working their passage back home.' The rest of the passengers 'consisted of the flower of our youth going out to be trained as pilots in Canada.' Had the ship been torpedoed, all the non-invalids were to jump into the sea and swim to the nearest raft: 'an unpleasing prospect in the North Atlantic in January', for a man nearly 60 who did not swim.

Impressing North Americans
However, they arrived safely at Halifax, Nova Scotia, on the 28th. There they were met by two Canadian officers and travelled by rail to Ottawa via Montreal. En route, he managed to get in two days of very indifferent skiing at a millionaires' club. 'Undismayed by reports that central London was a mass of flames,' he assured Canadian journalists that 'by spring we shall have taken the sting out of night bombing.' He hinted at new methods and weapons. 'I do not mean to say,' he went on, 'that enemy machines will not be able to make single raids in bad weather,' but mass raids would be dealt with. These were unduly optimistic words, but by March 1941 night fighters were at last finding and destroying an increasing number of enemy bombers.

Dowding now began to earn his pay, chatting to selected local worthies, meeting the press and taking lunch with the Prime Minister, MacKenzie King. He then went on to Washington DC, also by rail, where he was provided with a luxurious office and warmly welcomed by everyone who mattered in early January 1941: Sir Henry Self and Arthur Purvis, responsible for Britain's dealings with the United States government in matters of supply, particularly of aircraft; and important American civilians (Morganthau and Henry L. Stimson, Secretary of War) as well as military men, George C. Marshall (head of the army) and Henry H. Arnold (head of the air forces). 'We want to get the best products of both countries,' he said at every opportunity in public and private, 'and to assure co-ordination in some essentials.'

American journalists asked him what he thought of an American aircraft, the twin-engined Lockheed Hudson. He actually knew little about it, for the Hudson served in Coastal Command, but he readily praised it. The Lockheed Corporation, as he really did know, had good reason to be grateful to the British purchasing mission that had begun to visit the United States from April 1938 onwards. At that time, Lockheed had not built a single military aircraft and was struggling to stay alive. 'The transformation of Lockheed can be pinned down to a day in June 1938', according to the historians Green and Swanborough, when the Air Ministry ordered up to 250 aircraft: it was the largest order yet received by an American manufacturer. As Dowding rightly said, it is 'the best type we have in Coastal Command,' far superior to the fragile, low-powered, short-ranged, poorly-armed and inadequately-armoured Avro Anson which it replaced. He then went on to praise the twin-engined Douglas DB-7 Boston, which would also serve the RAF with distinction, and a variant named Havoc which, Dowding said, 'has been modified for certain specific purposes,' as a night intruder across the Channel. Finally, he told Americans that their navigation instruments were 'by far the best in the world'.[594]

He was well received partly because he represented Britain at a time when many Americans were becoming convinced that with American help she might very well resist Hitler successfully. Partly also because his reputation had gone before him: he was the man whose leadership had done so much to bring about that encouraging result. And most of all because everyone who heard him speak or read what he wrote rightly took him for a man who knew his stuff and said what he thought. They had enough of their own smiling smoothies not to need one from the old country (although those were the people they too often got). To a journalist who asked him for his impressions of the United States he said: 'Your Sunday papers are too thick and your lavatory paper too thin.' The journalist was delighted. Dowding 'went over big with the boys,' he told Arnold Lunn. 'He sure is a great guy.'[595]

On 7 January Dowding again seized the opportunity to praise the Boston, Hudson and also the Martin A-22 Maryland, a twin-engined reconnaissance bomber that would give valuable service in the Mediterranean theatre. A single-engined Curtiss fighter, later developed into the robust P-40 in many variants, was not yet – he said, diplomatically –

quite up to the required standard. He quickly went on to commend again American navigation instruments, plane controls and bomb sights. 'He revealed,' according to the *New York Times*, 'that the Eagle Squadron, made up of American volunteer pilots, was going into active service, having finished preliminary and combat training.' Unlike many British officials in the United States, Dowding refused to be seen as a beggar, so he went on to say that the Eagle Squadron was 'valuable more as an example than for its strength, since Great Britain does not need manpower.'[596]

Old Punctuality
It was also on 7 January that Dowding spoke to Edward T. Folliard of the *Washington Post* and other newsmen for 90 minutes in the headquarters of the British Purchasing Mission on the 9th floor of the Willard Building. He was, wrote Folliard, 'the tall, blue-eyed Scotsman who headed the RAF fighter force in the days of the "all-out" battle last September' and was quite sure that the Germans would never conquer Britain. According to Folliard, he was known in the RAF not only as 'Stuffy', but also as 'Old Punctuality', and represented the 'cold anger and steady determination' of the British people, whose only fear 'is a patched-up peace.' These last words suggest that Folliard, an acute journalist, had heard that Lord Halifax (recently sent by Churchill to Washington as ambassador) and members of his entourage still hankered for that 'peace' which they tried so hard to secure in 1940.[597]

Joseph Alsop and Robert Kintner, two widely-read columnists, wrote about Dowding at length in the *Washington Post* on 23 January. Two influences had 'startlingly altered expert opinion' on Britain's chances of surviving Germany's attack. One was a stream of encouraging reports from American observers in Britain who reckoned that bombing had done surprisingly little damage to essential facilities. The second was Dowding's visit – and this was the more important. This fact, they wrote, was both welcome and surprising because 'he was said to be,' presumably by Halifax and his more determined Whitehall opponents, 'the least promising envoy to America in the entire fighting services of Britain.' During the past three weeks, however, he had spoken with generals (army and air) and senior officials. 'And although some of our air experts consider him somewhat optimistic, he has both made a good impression and carried conviction.'

'Dowding's most dramatic report,' continued Alsop and Kintner, 'concerned progress made on the British device for combatting night air attacks.' This was airborne radar, now showing promising results in the Beaufighter. 'The nature and even the effects of the device are closely-guarded military secrets, revealed only to the chiefs of our air forces, who are adapting it for our use.' He assured American airmen that the spectacular raid on Coventry caused only minor damage to the vital aviation industry, thanks to a wide dispersal of manufacturing and assembly plants. Dowding was making a good impression, these journalists emphasized, and had now gone to Dayton, Ohio, with a delegation of aviation experts.[598]

Throughout January and into February, when he succumbed to influenza, he was fully engaged on non-stop visits to factories and airfields. 'It was extremely interesting to me,' he wrote, some 15 years later, 'but I did not flatter myself that I was doing anything of value.' No doubt that was so, in terms of deals struck and implemented. But there can also be no doubt that those aviation experts and senior politicians who met him – and they included the highest in the land – were impressed by what they knew of his splendid achievement at Fighter Command, the depth of his professional knowledge and, not least, his straight-shooting, no-nonsense words in public and private. He was no ambassador, but he was a fine representative of Britain at a time when she needed every ounce of help that the New World could provide.

Once or twice he escaped to ski fields and 'in his leisure moments here [in Washington DC] dances around the rink with various partners',[599] but otherwise it was a punishing routine of inspections, talks with senior officers, balls, cocktail parties and formal dinners: not at all the kind of life in which he felt at ease, though his powerful sense of duty – together with good manners and obvious expertise in anything to do with aviation, skiing and skating – got him through. He had the whole day of 25 February with President Roosevelt, Harry Hopkins (his most trusted assistant), his principal secretaries – Cordell Hull (State), Henry L. Stimson (War), James V. Forrestall (Navy) and Henry Morgenthau (Treasury); and General George C. Marshall (Army), Admiral Harold R. Stark (Navy) and John G. Winant, soon to go to London as ambassador instead of the pro-German Joseph P. Kennedy, recalled in disgrace to Washington.

'Today's was the first definite move,' reported Frank L. Kluckhohn in the *New York Times*, that 'the President or anyone else in the government has made' to get American war supplies moving to Britain. He did so because Senate and House leaders had assured him that the Lease-Lend Bill would be passed without further substantial amendment. After the meeting, some reporters tried to get a comment from Dowding. He silenced them in his frostiest manner: 'I don't talk to the President and then come out and tell you what was discussed.'[600] Other days, other manners. He had in fact asked Roosevelt to consider having the Napier Sabre aero-engine built under licence in the United States to power the Hawker Typhoon, intended to replace the Hurricane as a frontline fighter. Hopkins assured him that the Americans would build it, but they never did.

His itinerary took him to Los Angeles and Seattle as well as numerous factories and offices in the eastern states, but he did manage to include a four-day break at Sun Valley, near Boise, Idaho, where he got in some serious skiing as a guest of Averill Harriman, a member of Roosevelt's inner circle who served him as a special envoy to Britain and then as ambassador to the Soviet Union. For a man nearing 60 his skill and energy, not only on the ski fields, greatly impressed all who met him. For his part, Dowding 'was much struck by the high average skill of the American skiers as well as by their friendliness to a stranger.'

Although he was an expert on air defence, his thoughts were not systematically tapped at any time during his stay in the New World. He visited the Army's Air Defense School at Mitchel Field, Long Island, on 4

April, to be briefed on efforts to use radar to get warning of raiders approaching a navy/army base at Pearl Harbor in Hawaii. Sensible plans were discussed, but no serious action was taken. The system was neither complete nor efficient and the operators were poorly trained and carelessly supervised, as would be graphically demonstrated on 7 December 1941 when Japanese aircraft attacked that base.[601]

For England and St George

Dowding gave an unusually passionate speech on 23 April at the Waldorf in New York. He had been asked to speak on war in the air and readily agreed, though telling his audience, in his usual direct way, that he was yesterday's man, already out-of-date. Before doing that, however, he wanted to say a few words about England and the English on this St George's Day.

> 'On the other 364 days we have to be very careful to use portmanteau words which shall include all the inhabitants of Great Britain and the Empire; but today let us be free to talk of England and the English.'

He praised Churchill and the spirit of England during the past year of crisis, recounting the tale of an elderly general who stopped at the entrance to his club shortly after Dunkirk and said to the porter, 'this is very serious, isn't it?' To which the man replied, 'Oh, I don't know sir: we're in the final and we're on our own ground.'

A few days later, on 29 April, Dowding was obliged to turn his thoughts once again to the problems of defence in darkness that had so deeply concerned him in 1940. The Americans were using a Douglas B-18 twin-engined bomber to test an airborne radar. Dowding was invited to take a flight in the bomber and judge for himself how well the radar (and its operator) performed. Before leaving the US, Dowding wrote to Major-General James E. Chaney to recommend urgent production of that radar. He repeated that opinion to Beaverbrook on his return to Britain and asked him to order sets: he did so, and this became 'the first order for American radar placed in that country by Britain' and the start of a partnership proving of great value to both countries.[602]

Dowding had often been asked, especially here in the United States, why Hitler failed. His answer was that he needed command of the air and never got it. The Germans were beaten by brave fighter boys and good equipment. At this point, Dowding's next words exactly caught the mood of many Britons in 1940, a mood that no-one who did not live through that year can capture, though he or she may accurately describe it: 'they were beaten because it was not ordained that they should win. In those days, the nation prayed to God for victory and their prayers were answered.'

Having guarded against the danger of losing the war, and having made the base secure – a message he had constantly urged upon his colleagues and masters – it was now becoming possible to consider how to win the war. He thought that could be achieved without a massive invasion of the continent, presumably by a combination of bombing and blockade. As it happened, he was mistaken on this point, but his foresight was working properly when he said that submarines would soon prove to be a greater menace to Britain than night bombers. He had no idea how to counter that menace: 'and if I knew what was being done I could not tell you.' Dowding then concluded with praise of his hosts: he had not been a stranger in a strange land and believed there was a bond between the British and American peoples that could never be broken.

He gave several other lectures. One was on the practicalities of air fighting in which he emphasized the need for fighters to be at least 30 mph faster than any bombers they opposed. He spoke about the need for a fast rate of climb as well as speed in level flight, and the advantages of easy manoevrability at all speeds and altitudes. Pilots needed protective armour, he said, and good radios, cockpits offering all-round visibility, anti-icing devices and bullet-proof windscreens. He discussed the performance of machine guns and cannons and stressed the need for pilots to become skilled at deflection shooting whatever weapons they were using. All these practical matters were very well received by air force men in his audiences, who noticed, but politely refrained from commenting on, his silence – at least in public – about the help radar could give to pilots.

Another of his more general lectures considered the war in general. After Dunkirk, he said, the Germans had a choice: either to finish off the French armies, which were in no condition to continue effective resistance, or to use their whole strength against the British Isles. One must remember that at that time their so-called 'heavy' bombers had not been seriously employed:

> 'I do not know what would have happened if the Germans had decided to turn the whole weight of their air force on England at this stage as a preliminary to invasion. I believe that we should have beaten them off, but I am very glad that it did not turn out like that and we were able to secure a breathing space and to re-organize our defences and take advantage of the immediate improvement in the supply situation which came about directly Lord Beaverbrook took charge of the situation.'

Drones Abounding

On 20 April Dowding set down for Beaverbrook his general impressions of aircraft plants in the United States and Canada. Construction, design and equipment were all, he thought, excellent. But the Americans knew little about 'actual war requirements of aircraft', especially in armour, pressure cabins and limiting the effect of gunfire. They have not yet used all the essential information we have given them, free of charge, based on our practical experience. The aircraft industry was the only one not suffering from strikes, so far; the average age of employees was low, strong unions limited the pace of work and there was infiltration by persons of communist or anti-British sentiment. Dowding was also struck by the very slow pace at which manufacturers got government permission to proceed with orders and wondered at the readiness of the press to reveal information about bases and equipment that should be secret.

As for 'us overseas experts', Dowding wrote, we are soon out of date and a 'lackadaisical feeling' seems to develop after a few months. He thought it no exaggeration to say that many Britons in the United States were not earning their pay. There were far too many assistants enjoying pleasant, danger-free lives, too much delegation to juniors and the easy option of referring difficult issues back to London for decision was routinely taken. They failed to check the lists of items shipped to England and consequently there were many serious deficiencies. As for ATFERO, the Atlantic Ferry Organization, whereby American-built aircraft were supposed to be flown to England, the 'muddle, lack of organization and complete unprepared-ness' were shameful.[603]

Removing Dowding: Round Four

While in Washington, Dowding learned of a campaign urging Americans to subscribe to the RAF Benevolent Fund. He was himself a member of the fund-raising committee, but he thought the British should finance it themselves: it was 'wrong and humiliating' to press Americans for help. Dowding said so, at a public lunch, and was summoned to the British embassy to be rebuked. The newly-appointed ambassador was none other than Lord Halifax, Chamberlain's closest ally and the man most members of the British 'establishment' would have preferred as prime minister. Churchill, however, took advantage of the unexpected death on 12 December 1940 of Lord Lothian to pack him off to Washington in January 1941 as his replacement. He went reluctantly and his unconcealed disdain for all things American caused offence. Dowding's blunt ways, in tune with those of his hosts, added to Halifax's unhappiness. 'However, I was quite unrepentant,' Dowding recalled, 'and said that my position on the committee entitled me to object to this barefaced panhandling.'

To accuse a noble lord – ex-viceroy of India, ex-foreign secretary, nearly a prime minister – of 'panhandling', of behaving like a dropout begging for money in the street, was a dreadful insult. Protected against unkindness since his Eton days, deeply infected by Victorian 'highmindedness and humbug', Halifax felt deeply wounded; he needed, and got, revenge. But Dowding, a man of integrity (as well as outstanding ability), was incapable of bowing to a man who was notable, on his best days, for no quality higher than a 'puzzled rectitude'.[604]

Halifax disagreed even more strongly with Dowding's public support for a number of British nationals in Canada and the United States who were in dire financial straits because they were forbidden to convert their sterling income into dollars. Dowding thought the embassy view that such persons should return to Britain was wrong: their homes, families and friends were in the New World and he could see no good reason for uprooting them. 'America is doing so much for us,' wrote Dowding, 'and is giving us so much for which we can never pay materially, that this price [allowing conversion of sterling into dollars] would be a small one to save our prestige.'[605] Halifax also took it amiss that Dowding spoke out on behalf of the wives and families of American airmen who had volunteered to serve with the RAF. Some made only a trivial allowance out of their pay for their dependants, others none at all. 'I thought of all the dollars which were crossing the Atlantic in gifts for the Benevolent Fund and in "Bundles for Britain", while these poor American wives were left to starve. I gave what evidence I had to the American Army authorities.'

Slessor, Director of Plans in the Air Ministry, had been sent to Washington in November 1940 to set out the RAF's needs and do what he could to get American help. Although an able officer, he could never resist the urge to offer unsolicited advice on any subject to anyone; he was also a devout Trenchardist, a seasoned Whitehall Warrior and dazzled by Halifax's noble rank. Consequently, he did not believe Dowding's presence in Canada or the United States would advance the British cause. As early as 5 December, before Dowding had even begun his journey across the Atlantic, Slessor rightly feared that he would speak candidly to influential Americans (civilian and military) as well as to press and radio reporters. He himself, of course, could be trusted to address them appropriately. He therefore took it upon himself to advise Portal to see that Dowding was provided with a carefully-worded handout on his arrival and a minder from the embassy to vet all his statements.

Portal, wiser than Slessor, took no action. Only recently appointed CAS, Portal saw no reason to suppose that a fellow-Wykehamist, far superior in rank and experience to Slessor, could not handle a mission for which he had been selected at the particular request of Churchill and Beaverbrook. Portal soon learned that most Americans liked what Dowding had to say. As Beaverbrook told Dowding on 26 January, 'The immense success you are having in the US makes the most favourable impression here.'[606]

However, on 25 March Halifax asked Churchill to summon Dowding home because he was expressing personal views that contradicted official policy, as interpreted by Halifax. Beaverbrook stood up for Dowding, but he himself did not wish to create a new career in the United States and Churchill eventually agreed that he should come home: better for Halifax to stay there, far from Whitehall, publicly supported and privately by-passed. He was allowed no significant role in the constant and vitally important questions arising between Churchill, Roosevelt and their principal advisers.

Dowding remained in the United States during April and then went to Montreal, where he helped to sort out plans for ferrying American bombers to Britain. Finding pilots and other crew members for a hazardous journey across the Atlantic was one problem; returning these men to Canada or the United States was another. Could they survive in the converted bomb bays of Consolidated B-24 Liberator bombers? Typically, even though he was nearly 59, Dowding asked to return home in a bomb bay, to see if the journey was feasible. He did so, in early May, in a bomber flown by the Australian-born Don Bennett, already a famous airman who later became head of Pathfinder Force in Bomber Command.

The flight nearly killed Dowding, partly because the heating system failed to work, partly because the oxygen supply to the pilot's cabin also failed, meaning that oxygen had to be diverted from the passengers to the pilots, and partly because the nose wheel refused to retract, allowing a continuous blast of icy air to sweep through the fuselage:

'I have never spent such a night. I was in such a condition that in the morning the news that all the electrics had failed and that we could neither send nor receive a signal nor get a radio bearing, left me quite unmoved: misery had reached its limits. I did vaguely wonder if the landing wheels would come down and if we should have to land on the nose wheel, which had never come up, but I didn't really care very much. However, Bennett was dead on course and we made our landfall on the Donegal coast, after which we landed at Prestwick without further adventure.'

This American interlude in Dowding's career has usually been lightly dismissed (by the present author, among others), but in fact he performed an important service at a critical time. Dowding was one of the few Britons of indisputable military quality and personal merit whom Americans had met in recent years. He offered a refreshing contrast to the aloof nonentity Halifax and those of like stamp who attended upon him. Dowding, unlike them, had indeed 'been there and done that'. His visit was brief and produced no resounding declarations, but it did help American leaders, civilian and military, to realize that Churchill was not entirely alone in his fight against Hitler. He had Dowding to help offset the erstwhile Chamberlain supporters. From then until the end of the European war, some four years later, they would meet other exceptional Britons. Dowding, in this sense, might well be considered among 'the first of the few'.

20

End of a Career, May 1941 to July 1942

An Important Despatch

On 22 May 1941 Sinclair told Churchill that Moore-Brabazon, Minister of Aircraft Production in succession to Beaverbrook, no longer wished to employ Dowding and Sinclair wondered what to do with him. Would he serve with Ludlow-Hewitt as Inspector-General? He could be very useful in dealing with maintenance and servicing problems, given his background in supply and research.

If not, could he be appointed Governor of Southern Rhodesia (later Zimbabwe)? 'While gratefully conscious of the honour', not forgetting the pay and prestige, Dowding refused the offer: he 'had seen too many governors and high commissioners in action to covet their jobs [and] had no hesitation in declining.' He knew nothing about Southern Rhodesia, had no interest in imperial politics, had no need of starting a round of mutual hassle with a different set of Whitehall policy-makers, and had sufficient money to live as he wished. He also refused to sit on the board of any city companies: in his witty phrase it would be dishonourable 'guinea pigging'.[607]

Longmore, head of Middle East Air Command, was sacked in May 1941 and Churchill recommended Dowding to replace him, but Sinclair and Portal objected, preferring – very wisely – to promote Tedder, Longmore's deputy. In early September, when Tedder fell out of favour with the Prime Minister, he again urged the appointment of Dowding, but Sinclair and Portal, backed by Freeman, again objected – even more wisely this time because Tedder was already proving to be an outstanding commander. Meanwhile, in early June, Churchill wanted Dowding to take over Army Co-operation Command from Barratt. 'I hope you will be able to do this,' he said to Sinclair, 'as I am sure nothing but good will come of it.' Sinclair, backed by Portal, refused, even though Churchill thought the appointment would 'give confidence to the Army.'[608] Although the Air Ministry was right to reject Dowding for these commands, Churchill's advocacy shows the strength of his regard. Incidentally, the fact that Churchill accepted his rebuffs also shows a critical difference between his use of power and Hitler's.

On 29 June 1941 Dowding was asked to take on a job he could not refuse: to write a despatch on the Battle of Britain. He would have to work quickly, for he was to be retired as from 1 October – nearly seven months before his 60th birthday on 24 April 1942, the date on which he had earlier been told he must retire. No doubt that piece of information had been misfiled somewhere in the Air Ministry's bowels. As one would expect, he submitted his report well ahead of the deadline, on 20 August 1941. He had used the Air Ministry's 'admirable account' of the Battle and also a book on Fighter Command by Wing Commander A. B. Austin (published by Gollancz in 1941). Only two points in the Air Ministry's pamphlet really bothered Dowding: the Hurricane was a good 30 mph slower than that pamphlet claimed, and the command was by no means stronger at the end of the Battle than before it.

'The Battle may be said to have started,' wrote Dowding, 'when the Germans had disposed of the French resistance in the summer of 1940, and turned their attention to this country.' But in his opinion, it really began in the autumn of 1939. The report is lucid, perceptive and the tone throughout is temperate. There is no re-fighting of old battles, but the report is far from bland. His arguments, and those of others, are not passed over silently, they are calmly summarized. He here repeats what was for him the 'fundamental principle' of national defence. Fighter needs should not be compared with the needs for other types of aircraft. 'An adequate and efficient fighter force ensures the security of the base, without which continuous operations are impossible.' He made this point for the umpteenth time in a letter to Liddell Hart on 27 February 1942: 'Fighter strength is the basis of every successful operation by air, land or sea. You can't win a war with fighters, but you can't do anything at all without them.'[609]

As for German attacks in darkness, 'I had long been apprehensive of the effect of night attacks, when they should begin, and of the efficacy of our defensive measures.' He outlined the difficulties clearly: bringing into service a suitable night-fighter, getting airborne radar to work adequately, training personnel on the ground and in the air and – not least – trying to do all this in bad weather when German raids were constant.

> 'I had to leave the development of night interception at a very interesting stage; but it is perhaps not too much to say that although much remained to be done, the back of the problem had been broken.'

Meanwhile, his retired pay would be £1,300 per annum until further notice and the Air Council sent him a letter expressing:

> 'High appreciation of the valuable services which you have rendered during your long and distinguished career in the RFC and the RAF. The Air Council have most particularly in mind the ability and tenacity with which, over a period of more than four years, you discharged the onerous responsibilities, both in peace and war, of Air Officer Commanding-in-Chief, Fighter Command.'[610]

The house his father had bought in Wimbledon had been leased to a London firm needing alternative accommodation should it be bombed out, so he leased a smaller house nearby and his sister Hilda came to share it with him.

After he completed his despatch, Dowding published a brief summary of the Battle in the *Sunday Chronicle* on 26 October 1941. He had had no hand in the production of the Air Ministry's pamphlet, was not even consulted by its anonymous author, but he had read it and thought it tended 'to exaggerate the ease with which the most dangerous assault which has ever been made on this country was beaten off.' Park's contribution, he added, should be more widely known. 'His initiative and resource in countering each new move on the part of the enemy, and his leadership of the gallant men whom he commanded, were beyond all praise.' A generous, unsolicited tribute: one that earns Dowding credit, for commanders do not always praise subordinates. 'It was Park,' said Dowding, 'who bore the main burden of responsibility' in the actual battle. 'Indeed, so completely did Park fight the tactical battle,' wrote Hough and Richards, 'that Dowding was not even aware, in many respects, of how he was doing it.'[611]

Dowding had sent a cutting of his article to Park, then head of 23 Training Group in South Cerney, near Cirencester, Gloucestershire. Park replied at once. The article was 'the more gratifying' since he had recently heard from John Babington (head of Technical Training Command) that Leigh-Mallory 'is still relating with relish his own account of a certain Air Council meeting after the Battle was won.' As a matter of fact, it was a meeting in the Air Ministry, not an Air Council meeting, but Park correctly recalled that Sinclair – who knew nothing about aircraft, let alone aerial combat – decided that Leigh-Mallory was correct in his claim that he could have won the battle more easily than Park had: 'these tales are rather amusing, though they might be taken seriously by the uninformed.'[612]

Once the war was over, the question arose of publishing Dowding's account of the battle, completed as long ago as August 1941. In general, the Air Ministry was concerned lest a detailed account of his defence system might be of assistance to any future enemy. More seriously, several senior officials rightly feared the bad publicity bound to follow when readers learned that a wide gap lay between the number of enemy aircraft *claimed* as destroyed by Fighter Command – a number quoted by Dowding in his despatch – and the number now *known*, from captured German records, to have actually been shot down.

Richards, the Air Ministry's 'senior narrator', was asked for his opinion of the claims issue and replied on 3 October 1945. It would be unwise, he thought, to conceal the figures from the public. The Americans or some nosey British journalist would be bound to get hold of them, sooner or later, and the Air Ministry would receive even worse publicity. The fact is, RAF pilots *did* over-claim. Various officials had their say on this issue and were obliged to accept that German figures for their own losses were accurate whereas the RAF's claims were not. They also noted that nowhere in his despatch did Dowding state that his figures were exact, but we need not be too apologetic, these officials thought: German victory claims were far greater than ours and they did not invade. For example, in an assessment of 20 August 1940, German intelligence claimed 644 British aircraft destroyed in the period 12-19 August, when the true figure was only 141.[613]

The matter hung fire for months until 10 August 1946 when Tedder, now CAS, wrote to the man who had once tried to have him severely disciplined, with whom he had later worked to solve training problems and was now one of his fellow peers of the realm. He told Dowding that the Air Ministry had decided against adding a foreword to the despatch in which the claims issue would be summarized and would publish it, as is, 'naked and unashamed'. A despatch, said Tedder, should reflect the author's opinions at the time and it was for subsequent historians to tell a fuller and perhaps more accurate story.

Tedder wrote again on 13 May 1947 to tell Dowding that there was going to be a question in the House of Commons next day on the subject of German aircraft losses during the Battle of Britain. The Secretary of State (Philip Noel-Baker) would announce that the figures now available to the Air Ministry were lower than those quoted in the despatch. Dowding replied on the 15th: 'I can think of no reason why the Air Ministry should not publish the most accurate figures of Battle of Britain casualties to which they have access.'[614]

One Last Job
As anyone who has followed the saga of Dowding's employment this far may readily guess, his departure from active service was confused. Although his retirement was duly gazetted and reported in the press, it did not take effect. At least, not for long: he had only been on the retired list for a month when Beaverbrook wrote on 31 October 1941 to say Churchill had told him that Dowding was required for another important job from which 'immeasurable benefits will flow'.[615] Sinclair, instructed by Churchill, asked him to examine the RAF's establishments and suggest reductions. He would remain on full pay with a bonus of 25%, plus ordinary expenses. Sinclair put this deal to Dowding on 28 October and reported to Churchill next day. The new job, he had told Dowding, was 'one of extreme delicacy as well as urgency,' given the immense strain on human and material resources in wartime. Sinclair was relieved to find Dowding 'most agreeable and even friendly' at their meeting and assured him that he was the right man for this demanding task, but it was no use.

Dowding had written to 'Dear Sir Archibald Sinclair' on the 28th. He began by referring Sinclair to the saga of his retirement up to 29 June 1941, when he was told, for the eighth time (including twice by Trenchard after the Great War) that he must retire:

'I readjusted my whole life and ideas; took this house [3, St Mary's Road, Wimbledon] and furnished it; brought my sister up from the country to keep house for me and wrote a small book. I have in fact been completely happy as my own master for the first time in my life. You may imagine then with what distaste I view the prospect of returning to harness under the same yoke which has galled me so deeply.'

If he thought the country needed his services, and this need did not exist a month ago and could not have been foreseen, 'I should not hesitate to put all personal considerations aside and do what you ask,' but he doubted that very much. He recommended Sir Lawrence Pattinson, recently retired, for the job. Dowding 'had always looked on him as one of the most promising of the next "wave" of senior officers, and he has served for some time in the organization branch.'

Dowding ended this letter by assuring Sinclair that he had nothing to do with press criticism of the Air Ministry's decision to retire him. He would be quite prepared to say so publicly, if Sinclair thought it would help. 'If you don't like the suggestion, please forget that I have made it.' He did not remind Sinclair that he had been promised employment until his 60th birthday, in April 1942.[616]

But Churchill summoned Dowding to his presence on 30 October and told him he had a right to demand his service. When Dowding asked why he did not ask 'someone like Salmond' (who had resigned from the Ministry of Aircraft Production in March 1941) to take on the task, Churchill replied: 'because I want you to do it.' He went on to say that he had only learned of his retirement from the newspapers and said it again when Dowding expressed astonishment. Dowding then told the Prime Minister that he was very reluctant to work with Sinclair because he disliked and distrusted him. Churchill said he was one of his oldest friends 'and had never said a word against you, though others may have.' Dowding asked to return to the active list, although he knew perfectly well that it would be greatly to his financial advantage to be called upon from the retired list. 'I am not doing this for the money,' he snapped.

Dowding spent the night of 14-15 November 1941 at Chequers with Churchill ostensibly to discuss possible methods of saving manpower in the RAF. One says 'ostensibly' because Dowding was obliged to sit through a tedious Russian film. Before, during and after it, Churchill, who was relaxing nicely with the help of a drink or three, gave him the benefit of random reflections on various subjects. On world harmony, for instance. He did not believe it could be other than a mess, like mixing together all the colours in a paintbox. On the future. He thought the English-speaking peoples might work only a four-hour day after the war and enjoy themselves more than they had in the past, though struggle was necessary to avoid decadence. But the future – after his own time – did not interest him. He would not agree to the publication of a 'little book' that Dowding had written until at least the end of the war because certain passages might be useful to the enemy. All this blather came with a phonograph in the background belting out songs from Victorian musicals and the Prime Minister regularly broke off from his reflections to join in the choruses. In short, the abstemious, non-smoking Dowding was no fit companion for an off-duty Churchill. As he later recalled in his driest manner, the evening 'was not suitable for serious conversation.'[617]

Trimming the Fat

Portal had already assured Churchill that he ran a lean machine, there was no fat anywhere and so cuts in RAF manpower were quite impossible. As long ago as November 1940, when Harris was moved from 5 Group to the Air Ministry, as Deputy CAS, he had observed that its staffs were 'fantastically bloated' with officers sure of their own importance. Harris did what he could to begin 'an enormous and very suitable clear-out'. Both Churchill and Dowding knew that Portal's opinion was nonsense. No doubt he and Freeman (his *alter ego*) privately agreed, but they were shrewd operators. They judged, perhaps correctly, that any attempt to trim the fat would face determined resistance, overt and covert, from every level of command; better to let sleeping dogs lie. But Churchill had no regard for the RAF as an institution. He was also acutely aware of Britain's need to make efficient use of all its men and women in a war that, at that time, was a desperate struggle for survival with no prospect yet of ultimate victory. He saw in Dowding one of the RAF's few strong men, and one able and willing to wield a sharp knife.

Dowding was well aware that this job 'was certain to revive all the smouldering animosity which had existed between the Air Ministry and myself for the past five years.' Nevertheless, he gave it his full attention from a new headquarters, in Room 207 of Bush House, central London. He again had Frederick Gwynne (now promoted to squadron leader) as his personal assistant and wisely stipulated that he be allowed to send one copy of each report direct to Churchill, 'so that they could not be completely ignored' by persons in the RAF who regarded current staff numbers at all headquarters and bases as an essential minimum, pending equally essential increases.[618]

Dowding travelled extensively throughout Britain – that in itself was a wearisome business in wartime – and enquired closely into manning levels. He responded constructively to arguments put to him in defence of those levels, but he did uncover many examples of men and women neither fully nor usefully employed. As early as 20 November 1941 he outlined for Portal and other Air Ministry luminaries the procedure he proposed to follow. There are, he wrote, about 2,000 units in the RAF and it would take years to inspect them all. He was reluctant to create a large staff of assistants and thought existing machinery could well check and revise establishments, but he was handicapped by a lack of sufficient expert assistance: a lack that Portal and Freeman were in no hurry to remedy.

One immediately obvious candidate for substantial saving, in his view, would be to reduce the number of barrage balloons: they all required a great deal of labour to operate and many were flying in areas either adequately defended by other means or unlikely to be seriously threatened. In general, he advocated a 'geographical principle': large staffs in units likely to be heavily engaged, smaller ones in quiet areas. He resisted a proposal to form an 'aerodrome defence corps' and recommended that that duty should remain with the army, but opinion in both the Air Ministry and the War Office was against him on this point and proposals to form what became the RAF Regiment went ahead.

He thought re-arming and re-fuelling parties at all airfields could safely be reduced. Savings could also be made in the training system. A pupil might well pass through as many as ten separate units before reaching a service station:

> 'Every move involves a posting, and postings involve personnel staff; and each time a pupil moves he becomes a "new boy" again, with a fresh lot of instructors. Operational Training Units have been misused as Flying Training Units because pupils have not been adequately taught at Service Flying Training Schools. Their numbers could be reduced. There is an unhealthy plethora of minor specialist instructional units.'

Officers and men assigned to interrogate prisoners of war often had little to do. So too had bomb disposal units. Many cypher officers 'vegetate at stations and forget what they had previously learned about cyphering.' He found a motor transport company in Cambridge that enjoyed the use of valuable vehicles for no useful purpose that Dowding could find. He came across numerous cases where units had invented non-jobs, resented his enquiries and did their best to deceive him. But the enquiry that caused the loudest – and most powerful – complaints came when he claimed that there were far too many officers in Portal's department. Some of these men, of combat age, could well be replaced by women or civilians. Overall, Dowding concluded, investigations similar to his own should be carried out at all stations overseas.

An examination of strength against establishment figures revealed that 26,000 skilled fitters above the authorized establishment had been recruited. Most of them had no work to do, nor even living accommodation, except at otherwise unoccupied stations. Dowding recommended that they return to civilian industry unless or until they were needed. He also revealed that no fewer than 70,000 aircraft hands above establishment had been recruited. 'Either *post hoc* or *propter hoc*, the RAF Regiment came into existence and the surplus was absorbed.'

Removing Dowding: Round Five and Knockout
On 2 June 1942 Dowding circulated a memorandum to senior Air Ministry officials. He was, he said, near the end of his useful work. The 'Establishments Directorate', over which he presided, was being slowly strengthened and should be capable of keeping an eye on the manpower situation in all units. His departure would have a 'positive advantage', if the task was taken out of the hands of 'an individual exercising the function of criticism without responsibility.' However, although he was one of the RAF's most senior officers, appointed at the direction of the Prime Minister himself and with ready access to the Secretary of State, he had had 'the greatest difficulty in overcoming the objections of some senior officers to accepting any reductions' in their own staffs. An Assistant CAS was needed who had no other duties and the authority to make decisions.

By the middle of June, Dowding had had more than enough of his 'very invidious and unpleasant position', which he had accepted 'only with extreme reluctance'. Most of his proposed economies were 'hotly opposed by the Air Ministry and I resumed my position as Public Enemy No. 1.' He heard a rumour that he was to be sent to Cairo to continue his 'witch hunt' there. He made a typically rude message from Freeman 'an excuse for a show of injured dignity' and sent Sinclair a short, blunt note of resignation on 18 June.

Freeman was Vice-CAS at the time, Portal's only confidant and an exceptional Whitehall Warrior in that he had plenty of managerial experience, none in command of fighting men, and was precisely the kind of man with whom Dowding had wrestled throughout his years at Bentley Priory. Freeman regarded most senior officers, including Dowding whom he had known since before the Great War, with unconcealed contempt. Although Portal was usually shrewd enough to ignore his advice about postings or promotions, the fact that he was never rebuked even for his wildest assertions encouraged Freeman to blast away throughout his time at Portal's side and later when he moved to the Ministry of Aircraft Production.

One example, among many possible, was his disdain for Stevenson, Director of Home Operations (1938-41), head of 2 Group, Bomber Command (1941), then of RAF Burma in 1942. Although he and Dowding had frequently differed, Dowding respected Stevenson for his hard work in a difficult job and Portal agreed. He regarded Stevenson, so he wrote in December 1941, as a 'thoroughly up-to-date officer of proved ability'. But in January 1942 Freeman was reluctant to recommend his promotion to temporary air vice-marshal. He proposed to write to him, pointing out what were, in Freeman's opinion, 'some of his more obvious defects' and adding for good measure that Stevenson was notoriously unpopular. Clearly, either Portal or Freeman misjudged him. However, Stevenson's skilful handling of a losing situation in Burma suggests that Freeman, as usual, was not merely rude but a poor judge of merit as well as character.[619]

Dowding had made detailed suggestions for a re-organization of air staff duties. Instead of a reasoned response, he got only a curt rebuke from Freeman: 'The matter rests in the hands of the CAS and Permanent Under-Secretary who are in a better position than yourself to judge what is necessary.' As Dowding told Sinclair:

'Apathy and obstruction must be expected by anyone who, like myself, is introduced into a government department on an economy mission; this I have been prepared for: but I am not prepared indefinitely to tolerate gratuitous impertinence from an officer junior to myself.'

A few days later, on 23 June 1942, Sinclair received a note from his private secretary on the fat squeezed by Dowding out of the RAF's bloated body during the few short months of his enquiries in spite of determined resistance from those comfortable with the *status quo*. Sinclair learned that no fewer than 733 officers and 24,145 other ranks were now available for productive work. While ruminating on these figures, displeasing to those who liked to think of the RAF running a lean machine before Dowding came along to upset everyone, Sinclair received another letter from him:

> 'Throughout the period of my present appointment, staff officers of various grades have been guilty of obstruction, inertia, and of supplying incorrect information. Yet I have not been apprised of a single instance in which blame has been imputed or reproof administered; and in the code and cypher case, Freeman explicitly supports his staff. You support Freeman in supporting his staff, and imply that I am unreasonable in resenting his impertinence.'

In conclusion, he refused to accept Sinclair's disgraceful opinion that it was 'an act of disloyalty' to bring Air Ministry 'defects' to the Prime Minister's attention.[620]

Sinclair replied on 27 June. As an experienced politician, knowing that he had strong Air Ministry backing, he avoided dealing with Dowding's points of substance and contented himself with amiabilities about resolving problems with 'patience and good humour'. Nothing, of course, was done to reduce the number of able-bodied men filling offices in Portal's department. Dowding was placed on the retired list with effect from 15 July 1942. It may have amused him in later years to reflect that he served for 81 days beyond his 60th birthday.

Unpromotable

Two days later, on the 17th, Alexander Hardinge (King George's private secretary) forwarded to the Air Ministry George's suggestion that Dowding be promoted to the rank of Marshal of the Royal Air Force: 'it has always seemed to him that Dowding performed a really wonderful service to this country in creating, and putting into practice, the defence system which proved so effective in the Battle of Britain.' This unprecedented suggestion from the king himself was considered by Philip Babington, Air Member for Personnel. He noted on the same day, 17 July, that marshals are never retired; they remain on half pay, which was currently at the rate of £1,629 per annum, whereas a retired air chief marshal was on £1,300. The proposal would need Treasury sanction, 'but should cause no great difficulty as the net difference to the Exchequer would be in the region of £150 a year.' Sinclair, however, decided that it could not be done. Presumably he consulted Portal and Freeman, perhaps also Trenchard and Salmond. In any case, he and/or they settled Dowding's hash for what they hoped would be the last time.

All clever men, with a sure grasp of bureaucratic niceties, they found a way of doing it that could be presented, with sincere regret, as the only possible solution. As far as the RAF's reputation is concerned, however, perhaps they were too clever by half. Sinclair wrote to Hardinge on 21 July 1942. Dowding had not been promoted at the end of the battle, and nearly two years had now passed since then. Also, he had already retired once – for one month before he was recalled to active service by the Prime Minister personally – and were he now to be promoted, 'in lieu of reversion to the retired list, it would be a matter for comment.' One wonders by whom. One also wonders why Sinclair thought the 'comment' would not be favourable, at least outside some Air Ministry offices. Perhaps, he continued, something might be done at the end of the war. King George, well able to read between the lines on such matters, understood that the Air Ministry did not intend to promote Dowding and backed down.[621]

Three years passed, the war in Europe ended, and more praise came Dowding's way. Sinclair wrote on 9 May 1945 to commend his 'inspiring leadership' [that] helped to save 'our island citadel.... The whole nation, indeed freedom-loving men and women the world over will always gratefully remember you and the gallant "few" who fought and flew under your command.' They might well 'gratefully remember' him, but it remained quite impossible for the Air Ministry to recognize his 'inspiring leadership' by promoting him to its highest rank; fine words would have to serve instead. As far as Sinclair was concerned, they were not even sincere words. Three weeks later, he wrote more honestly to Douglas: 'I felt as though I had won a battle when I got Fighter Command into your hands, and, looking back, how right I was.'[622] Those pilots killed on pointless operations over France in 1941 may not have agreed.

Despite an alleged prohibition against promotion to the highest rank for officers who had not served as chiefs of the Air Staff, that rule was waived for two officers whose undoubted merits may well be considered to fall below those of Dowding. These officers were Harris, whose conduct of Bomber Command during the years 1942 to 1945 has attracted, with good reason, severe criticism as well as praise for devotion to duty as he understood it; and Douglas, who held several high commands but none at a critical time. Nevertheless, both were elevated above Dowding in January 1946.[623]

'The British can be generous to heroes,' reflected Ray. 'In their day, Marlborough, Nelson, Wellington and Haig were all adorned with honour and rewarded with wealth and high rank by a grateful nation.' But Dowding, 'victim of a vendetta', got less than most other high commanders in all three services. At this point, one might reflect, as Zimmerman has, that most of the scientists whose efforts underpinned Dowding's achievement, 'were poorly treated by their country after the war.... Not one radar scientist was invited to participate in the Victory Parade.' Watson-Watt and Tizard were knighted, but no particular mark of favour was bestowed at that time on the other heroes: Wimperis, Rowe, Larnder, Bowen, Hill, Blackett, Wilkins.[624]

Balfour was well placed as Under-Secretary of State for Air in Churchill's government, to know what went on in the Air Ministry's smoke-filled back rooms, and even to be present behind firmly closed doors. He was also more in sympathy, to put it no stronger, with Douglas, Leigh-Mallory and other 'Big Wing' advocates than were most pilots or historians. Consequently, Balfour has usually been ranked among Dowding's opponents. If he was, he had changed his opinion by 1973, when his memoirs were published. Dowding, whom he had known since 1915, 'was a great man,' he wrote, 'monstrously treated by the Air Ministry' from 1937 to 1941; he was 'shamefully served by successive chiefs of the Air Staff over his personal career' and was never, 'as he should have been,' promoted to Marshal of the Royal Air Force.[625]

A distinction needs to be drawn here. On the one hand, we have the cold discourtesy so often shown to Dowding in regard to his continuing employment, including the determination never to allow his promotion. For this misconduct, the Air Ministry's senior officers – including Sinclair and Balfour – deserve all the opprobrium heaped on their petty heads for so many years. Their only excuse, a poor one, is the muddle and incompetence endemic in that ministry, as Churchill and others so often observed. Perhaps that 'muddle and incompetence' spilled over into the mind of Hoare, a notable appeaser in the 1930s who occupied many senior government offices, among them, Secretary of State for Air (1924-9 and again from March to May 1940) before Churchill banished him to Spain. In the index to his memoirs, *Nine Troubled Years* (published in 1954) Dowding appears as 'Marshal of the Royal Air Force'.

On the other hand, we have the decision to remove Dowding from Bentley Priory. It may not have been the right decision, but it was made for several reasons that seemed sensible at the time. Five men share the responsibility for both decisions. Trenchard, Salmond and Freeman never made any secret of their opposition to many of Dowding's words and actions, and Sinclair went along with stronger men on all issues throughout his five years in office. Portal was a match for all of them and had never been at odds with Dowding until his fat-trimming days, but he chose not to intervene.

21

Out of Office,
After July 1942

Typhoon

In early July 1942, Dowding drafted an article on the Hawker Typhoon fighter and its Napier Sabre engine which he sent to Beaverbrook for his comments. He was then admitted to hospital, exhausted in body and mind by long hours of travelling, enquiring and arguing; also perhaps by reaction to finding himself no longer on active duty. Beaverbrook was sorry to learn that Dowding was out of sorts, but Hilda had assured him that he would soon be out and about again. 'You will have seen the paragraph in the *Evening Standard* tonight [21 July] regretting your retirement,' wrote the Beaver. 'I hope it will not last long.' He recalled that the decision to go ahead with the Sabre was almost his first decision as Minister for Aircraft Production, and made with Dowding's agreement. The Typhoon depended on successful development of the Sabre and neither the airframe nor the engine was yet ready for production.[626]

Dowding then wrote to Churchill on 10 August 1942, telling him that 'I am desperately uneasy about our day fighter situation.' He enclosed a copy of the article he had revised in the light of Beaverbrook's comments which the censor had rejected. The Prime Minister might wonder, wrote Dowding, why he did not send his article to the Air Ministry:

> 'My opinions are known, but they are not accepted, and my despatch on the Battle of Britain has been withheld even from Commanders-in-Chief and service members of the Air Council... the clear lead in the performance and hitting power of our day fighters has been allowed by slovenly thinking and slack development work to degenerate into a state of inferiority in both respects.'[627]

Churchill, then in Egypt, asked Tedder (head of RAF Middle East) for his thoughts on Dowding's article. His brief, unhelpful reply on 21 August avoided comment on Dowding's unease about fighter development, offering instead general reflections on finding for fighters the right mix between machine guns and cannon, and ending with the suggestion that Dowding submit his queries to Portal.[628]

249

Tedder's 'dead bat' response gave Churchill no help in framing a reply to Dowding on the 25th. It would have been a 'reckless step' to publish such an article, said the Prime Minister, which would have given valuable information to the enemy: 'you knew well from our relations that you had only to write to me to ensure that immediate attention would be given to what you said.'

Dowding had encouraged Hawker's to plan a replacement for the Hurricane as early as 1937 and had hoped to see it in squadron service during 1941. He believed that the Typhoon was the only fighter in prospect that could match the Luftwaffe's deadly Focke-Wulf Fw 190: the Hurricane was now obsolete and even the Spitfire 'has been moribund as a home defence fighter for two years, and died when the Focke-Wulf made its appearance' in July 1941. Churchill, relying on Portal's advice, assured Dowding that improved versions of the Spitfire could match this German fighter. Dowding was not convinced. 'Look what happened to the Italians who drew a false lesson from the Spanish war and put manoeuvrability first!... One may conjure a quart out of pint pot, but one can't get a gallon.' The Typhoon may not be the ideal successor to the Spitfire, but in Dowding's opinion it was the best available.

He was mistaken. The Typhoon did not fly until February 1940 and a production model was not ready until May 1941. That long delay was caused in part by Beaverbrook's prohibition of aircraft development, other than five approved types, for several months in 1940; in part also because of problems with the Typhoon's airframe and engine. It never became an effective high-altitude interceptor, but as a ground-attack weapon, it was fast and robust enough to survive or avoid battle damage. Armed with four 20-mm cannon and eight rockets, it could destroy even the most heavily armoured targets and became a formidable weapon in 1944 and 1945.[629]

With regard to the non-circulation of Dowding's despatch, Churchill asked Portal for a report. Portal immediately claimed that Dowding was mistaken, but on 12 September 1942 he was obliged to admit that Dowding was in fact correct: due to 'an oversight', the despatch had not been circulated to all those concerned. The oversight was probably not deliberate, merely yet another example of a very large staff's inability to manage simple routines.[630]

Battle of Britain Day
Dowding agreed to speak to the press on 15 September 1942, a day set aside to remember the Battle of Britain every year from then on. Trenchard 'argued that it was wrong to commemorate a battle that had come to be so closely associated with one command.' A curious point of view, even for Trenchard, whose faith in the bomber and low regard for fighters (or, indeed, any other kind of aircraft) never wavered. Consequently, 'he found it difficult to accept that the RAF's greatest achievement was a *defensive* victory.'[631]

Dowding asked for three battle pilots to join him on the platform: Malan, Aitken (Beaverbrook's son) and one of the many sergeants, R. H. Gretton, now a warrant officer. It took time, he said, to realize that we had in fact won the Battle of Britain, largely because night bombing began during it and continued for months. Unlike some commanders, he refused to preen his own feathers: 'My own principal contribution to the defence had been made weeks and months before the battle started, and I could leave most of the tactical work to subordinate commanders and to the matchless spirit of the fighter pilots.' He went on to praise those pilots, now two years older, 'with more rings on their sleeves and more ribbons on their chests. If they had what they deserved their chests and sleeves would be completely obliterated with embroidery,' but he was anxious to remember, 'with sorrow and affection,' those who did not survive.

As always, he praised the command's ground crews and, not least, its brave and competent women. Unlike some senior officers, he never thought of them as 'some inferior substitute who might fail us in an emergency' and singled out Flight Officer Elspeth Henderson, then a corporal in the operations room at Biggin Hill, who was awarded the Military Medal. The fact that she was Scottish no doubt had nothing to do with his admiration of her. On 30 August, nine Junkers Ju 88s bombed the airfield, destroying an air raid shelter, killing 39 men and women and burying several others. Elspeth helped to dig them out and was back on duty next day when the Luftwaffe returned and made a shambles of the operations room. She and two colleagues, Sergeants Helen Turner and Elizabeth Mortimer, risked their lives to send information until it became impossible and then moved to an emergency telephone exchange and carried on from there. They were three of only six WAAFs who received the Military Medal during the Second World War.[632]

Dowding went on to praise his gunners, searchlight, balloon and Observer Corps personnel as well as the crews of Bomber and Coastal Commands and those Americans who served in the Eagle Squadron for their joint efforts in checking the enthusiasm of 'the individual Fritz':

'I have left the most important thing till the last. We are not too proud to organize National Days of Prayer, and we should not be too proud to acknowledge the results. Some people are inclined to say, "Good Lord deliver us from this grievous affliction" and afterwards to attribute their deliverance to their own efforts. I have a deep personal conviction of divine intervention in this war, which I believe we should otherwise have lost some time ago.'

Authoritative Articles
A few days later, on 20 September 1942, his review of a famous book, Alexander Seversky's *Victory through Air Power*, appeared in the *Sunday Chronicle*. From then on, Dowding would contribute a number of 'authoritative articles', as the editor described them, to that newspaper. The book, he thought, was nearly a very good one, but Seversky made too many sweeping statements. His claims for bombing accuracy from high levels were fantastic and Dowding was convinced that neither British nor American bombers could win the war by their own efforts.

He reviewed another book for the *Sunday Chronicle* on 18 October 1942 by an American author: William B. Ziff, *The Coming Battle of Germany*. Ziff was wrong, he believed, to write off Allied chances of winning air superiority if an invasion of the continent was ever mounted. As for British bombing, Dowding was sure that the Allies must decide on a few major targets and not disperse their efforts too widely. The German situation was already desperate: they had the bull by the tail and dared not let go because they had behaved so cruelly in Poland and the Soviet Union that they faced a real threat of complete extermination during and after the war.[633]

Dowding wrote a piece published in Beaverbrook's *Evening Standard* on 8 April 1943 about the government's takeover of the poorly-managed Short aviation company. When it came to state intervention in the aircraft industry, Dowding was well informed. He had spent six years at the Air Ministry in charge of research, design and development of aircraft and their equipment. Derisory sums made available to the RAF meant that Britain had engines and airframes that were behind those of other great powers. Fortunately, the industry's private ventures often produced excellence. For example, the Fairey Fox (1925). Officially a two-seater light bomber, it was not merely a handsome design, it was faster than any RAF fighter then in service, and led directly to the Hawker Fury and on to the monoplanes of the Battle of Britain.[634]

When Dowding was at the Air Ministry, he recalled, he was frequently urged by the finance department to buy the design of a successful firm and put it to open tender among its competitors for production orders. He always resisted this policy because it seemed to him that the successful firm should reap the results of its skill and initiative in the form of a production order at a liberal price. Otherwise, firms would let their design staffs degenerate and devote their energies to undercutting their competitors in tendering for production orders. 'This would be fatal for efficiency, though you would certainly get cheap aircraft – cheap and nasty.' Government designers were 'conscientious mediocrities', too ready to listen to experts, who rejected Henry Ford's opinion that 'an expert is a man who tells you something cannot be done.'

A Peer and a Knight

In April 1943 Dowding asked leave to relinquish his appointment as the King's principal ADC. He had held it for six years and thought it time for such a prestigious appointment to go to an officer on the active list. He thereby severed the last link, he thought, with his old life, but he was wrong. To his surprise and delight, Churchill wrote to him on 11 May 1943 to ask if he might put his name forward for a barony in recognition of 'your ever-memorable services to this country during the Battle of Britain. I should like you to know that when I first mooted this proposal it received the warm acclamation of your colleagues in the Royal Air Force and in the Air Ministry.'

No doubt it did, perhaps for the best of reasons; perhaps also because it reflected glory on the service, could be represented as settling unease over the refusal to promote him, and it cost the Air Ministry nothing. Dowding added 'of Bentley Priory' to his title. He was the first RAF officer since

Trenchard in 1919 to be elevated to the peerage. His coat of arms featured a falcon sitting on a catherine wheel and he chose as his motto *Laborare est Orare*: to work is to pray.

Another honour came to the Dowding family on New Year's Day 1945, when Hugh's brother Arthur was made a Knight Commander of the Order of the British Empire (KBE). He had served as superintendent of HM Naval Dockyard at Devonport since September 1938. The duties had been 'particularly exacting in time of war', according to the recommendation, 'not least during and after the serious air attacks which burnt out a large portion of the South Yard, and more recently in connection with the landings in Normandy.' The brothers had always been close and took great delight in each other's success.[635]

Twelve Legions of Angels

During the summer of 1941, Dowding had completed the manuscript of a 'small book', which he submitted to Churchill, who leafed through part of it and told Brendon Bracken, Minister of Information, to read it all. The proposed title was *Twelve Legions of Angels: an Essay in Straight Thinking*. Most of it, unlike his subsequent books, was a distillation of the thoughts of an outstanding air commander on strictly military matters. It dealt with the principles governing the design of aircraft, the case for unrestricted bombing of Germany, and the prospects for avoiding yet another war with that nation once victory in this war had been achieved. Both Churchill and Bracken thought it should not be published at present, for the excellent reason that German or Italian readers would have found it very helpful. Dowding had no choice but to agree. In February 1942, however, he did send a copy to Mabel, wife of his particular friend Arnold Lunn, who was then in the United States. 'I can't send it to Arnold for obvious reasons,' Dowding wrote, 'but of course he has read it in the proof stage.'[636]

Douglas Jarrold, whom Dowding had asked to consider publishing it, sent a copy to the famous military historian Sir Basil Liddell Hart. 'It is very stimulating in every way,' replied Liddell Hart on 20 February 1942. Dowding has 'a mind eager for new ideas, and with the genuine scientific spirit of wishing to solve problems by experimental test. If such an attitude had been more common, we should not have lost so many other battles.... I do *like* his mind and spirit,' Liddell Hart concluded, 'and can only regret that we have never made personal contact.'[637] Jarrold put them in touch and they soon became good friends.

The book was 'an inadequate effort', thought Dowding, an attempt in part 'to acknowledge the help from invisible sources which we had received during the Battle of Britain.' At the height of the crisis, a goodly number of people would have applauded these words. Afterwards, of course, most of us flinch from such notions. In any case, when it eventually appeared in 1946 (published by Jarrold), it was, in Dowding's words, 'a resounding flop'.[638]

His memorable title was taken from St Matthew's Gospel (Chapter 26, Verse 53). At Gethsemane, shortly before Jesus's arrest, a disciple wounded a servant of the high priest and Jesus rebuked him: 'Do you think I cannot now pray to my father, and he shall presently give me more than twelve legions of angels?' In other words, if violence would serve in this crisis, Jesus had access to plenty of overwhelming help, if he chose to call for it, but those, he said, who take up the sword will perish by it. An admirable sentiment, though not a common one among military men, especially not in 1941 when Hitler's legions still seemed invincible.

It is indeed a small book, only 74 pages with no index, but well worth reading. Dowding added a foreword in 1946 to say that he had finished it four years ago. Unfortunately, 'the powers that be (or rather that were) refused to pass it for publication.' He thought readers might wonder why, for it reveals no military secret – he would never commit such an indiscretion – but he did not complain: 'Those responsible for the safety, honour and welfare of the state in time of war cannot be fettered in the exercise of their judgement; and besides, a person who nurses a grievance is an object of contemptuous pity and, what is more, he is a bore.' Wise words that apply not only to his little book but even more appositely to his removal from Bentley Priory and the resentment he allowed Robert Wright to publish on that subject.

Dowding regretted the veto because he was 'conceited enough' to think that if some commanders and staff officers had read it at the time, it might have improved their thinking and thereby saved lives and expense. True enough, but some of those commanders and staff officers might have been German or Italian.

He had shuddered as long ago as 1941 to think what might happen if the energy locked up in the atom were ever released and now, by 1946, it had been. He visualized men in all three services saying: 'How little need we alter our methods, equipment and training to cope with this new menace?' But the question they should be asking is: what need have we now of armed services? Would we in Britain ever drop an atomic bomb as a regular weapon or even in self-defence? There is the probability, Dowding wrote, 'the truth of which is known to the government but not to me,' that harmful radiation emanations will last. And the fact, 'known to me, but probably not to the government,' that 'killing people by the agency of the atomic bomb has a harmful psychic effect which is likely to persist for some time after death.' Is it too much to hope that we may eschew force in the postwar world? Fear is 'the last enemy'; the basis of hatred and jealousy, suspicion and cruelty; 'nothing good or stable was ever built on a foundation of fear.'[639]

After these postwar reflections, Dowding summarized his thoughts on the wartime use of air power, in a chatty, relaxed style that would surprise any reader who knew him only through discussing military matters round an office table or reading his official correspondence. Although he was long gone from Bentley Priory when it was written, his reputation was still so high and his professional knowledge so thorough that one can easily understand why Churchill prevented publication until 'The Pact of Steel' and the Third Reich were no more.

The Italians, wrote Dowding, had placed too much emphasis on fighter agility, rather than rate of climb, level speed and hitting power. The fighter's main task must always be to shoot down bombers, not other fighters, using fixed, forward-firing guns: cannons were far more destructive than machine guns, when they can be got to work properly. The harmonizing of guns was still a moot point: which was most effective, a broad spray or a narrow cone of fire? Thought must also be given to keeping the pilot warm, comfortable, and supplied with plenty of oxygen for high-level work. Except perhaps in night fighters, turrets were useless: their weight and that of the gunner were a serious handicap. Dowding remained silent on the critical advantage that airborne radar, in a twin-engined machine able to carry much more fuel than a single-engined fighter, gave a pilot and his radar operator.

He then turned to bombers, imagining a conversation between Goering and Udet, seasoned with his own thoughts, on how best to design, equip and employ bombers. They must fly as fast and high as possible, be provided with reliable bomb sights, armour for their vital parts (crews, engines, fuel tanks) and be directed to targets of known importance. However well equipped they were, bombers needed fighter escorts and cloud cover to operate successfully in daylight and were best employed in darkness. Anti-aircraft fire upset their formations, reducing the accuracy of their bombing, but rarely destroyed them.

An invasion of Britain, wrote Dowding in 1941, could only succeed if an enemy enjoyed air superiority:

'He could then send over parachutists, gliders and transport aircraft in an unending stream; our own bombers and coastal aircraft will not be able by day to attack and sink his flotillas which carry his other troops with their guns and munitions, nor will the Navy be able even to approach the scene without shattering losses.'

Dowding did not undervalue the work done by Bomber and Coastal Commands in attacking invasion ports, 'but the outstanding point is that the crux of the battle lay in the ability of the Fighter Command to remain in effective operation.' Even now, however, in 1942, there was a danger that the Germans might produce more effective fighters, even better than the Focke-Wulf Fw 190, in unexpectedly large numbers; or they might use poison gas. Consequently, a powerful home defence fighter force remained an absolute requirement, not to be compared with fighter needs elsewhere. Night bombing might still undermine British resistance, but: 'A grimmer spectre lurks in the oceans, more insidious and more dangerous because its effects are gradual and cumulative.' The war at sea was a grave danger and despite Britain's best efforts it was difficult to deal with U-boats.

As for winning the war, the 'willing docility' of the German people had been a standing menace to European peace for 80 years. They must not only be beaten – with the help of heavy bombing – they must be made to accept that they have been beaten and then 'brought into the community'. We failed to do this after the Great War and needed to create a strong peace-keeping force, incorporating as many nations as possible. Dowding himself thought this part of his book unsatisfactory: there are 'so many unknown quantities that I am in danger of becoming woolly, and I hate woolliness.'[640]

After striking that low note, Dowding asked another question: 'Why are senior officers so stupid?' He had often wondered why some men of high rank over the age of 45 show all the symptoms of 'mental paralysis'. He feared the process began at public schools, 'where the individualist is suppressed and the good citizen is mass-produced.' It is so easy to squash junior officers. 'When I was at the Staff College in 1912, the unforgiveable heresy was to cast any doubts on the effectiveness' of cavalry because half the Army's generals were cavalrymen. Thinking was to be avoided and saying 'No' to any proposal was always better than saying 'Yes'.

Dowding then cited an actual case of senior officer stupidity. For many years, he recalled, the Air Ministry had been seeking a design for an efficient 'crash proof' fuel tank for aeroplanes. It could not be done: a self-sealing tank could be built, but the officer responsible did not see this. 'Should I conceal his name? It was me.' Also, many senior officers were reluctant to settle by controlled experiments matters that can be solved, once and for all, that way. Perhaps, then, this little book might serve as 'a gentle laxative to mental constipation'.

Wessex and Mercia

He then turned from reflecting on material things, 'The Things Which Are Caesar's', to those of the spirit, 'The Things That Are God's'. We English, he believed, are reluctant to speak of God, except with our intimates. The God he always had in mind was He of the New, not the Old, Testament. Dowding also found it almost impossible to speak of personal patriotism 'or the deep-seated love which I bear to the school [presumably Winchester, not St Ninian's] where I spent some of the most miserable years of my life.' Readers may wonder why he had so much to say about Caesar and so little about God. It was because God's things are easier to understand and he knew more about Caesar than about God. Both the miracle of the Marne in 1914 and that of Dunkirk in 1940 were brought about by prayer, as well as our own efforts:

'I pay my homage to those dear boys, those gallant boys, who gave their all that our nation might live; I pay my tribute to their leaders and commanders; but I say with absolute conviction that but for God's intervention the Battle of Britain would have been lost. Now, therefore, as I lay down my sword, I take up my pen and testify.'

Dowding then came to his main purpose in writing this book: to encourage all people on Earth to find a means of living peaceably together. He entitled this chapter 'Wessex and Mercia' and imagined a conversation between Egbert and Athelstane, two respected citizens of Winchester, who were regretting the constant fighting between Wessex and Mercia. A means of ending that conflict was eventually found and Dowding hoped all conflicts, everywhere in the world, might now be ended without fighting. The Nazis think war is a good thing, but it is 'a hateful remedy for worse evils'.

Improvements in communications should help; as Kipling wrote in his 'imaginative masterpiece', *With the Night Mail*, an aerial board of control had as its motto 'Transportation is Civilization'. A common language would also help. He himself could never think of the United States as a foreign country because he spoke its language. If only we could all understand one another's speech, as well as our own languages, it might not stop wars, but it would be a positive step in the right direction. At present, 'it is easier, in fact, for the British to maintain mental contact with New Zealand than with France.' Could we not get everyone to drive on the same side of the road and adopt the metric system? Why does 'the Chinese coolie live with a handful of millet between himself and starvation while the western workman has a car and a radio set?'[641]

22

A New Career,
From July 1942

Many Mansions
From July 1942, although he made no sharp break with his old interests, Dowding gradually became as devoted to spiritualism as he had once been to the organization and equipment of Fighter Command and the defence of Britain from German invaders. He was also attracted by Theosophy, a movement seeking some universal truth supposed to be common to all religions. Dowding commented at length in November 1942 on Liddell Hart's critical examination of the authority behind the gospel story. He wondered why Jesus chose as his apostles 'simple and ignorant working men, and not educated priests or philosophers.' If Jesus never existed, Dowding believed:

> 'It is inconceivable that these ignorant and humble men could have invented him and imposed his existence on the whole world. To a humble and ignorant person like myself, it seems to be certain that he existed, and that it was the quality of simplicity and love in his teaching (however distorted by his biographers) which has made an appeal to the wide world.'

Liddell Hart thought it possible that a fusion of Buddhist, Jewish and Greek thought might have produced a new religion without an historical Jesus,[642] but Dowding was losing patience with all exclusive creeds and becoming a devout spiritualist. He had long been interested in the writings of an Anglican vicar, the Reverend George Vale Owen (1869-1931), who was eventually required to resign his living. Encouraged by Northcliffe, Conan Doyle and others, Owen went on lecture tours throughout Britain and the United States and published five volumes of experiences, entitled *The Life Beyond the Veil* in London in 1926.

Dowding decided to set down his own thoughts on the intangible world. He deliberately avoided any personal experiences and dealt solely with 'a cross-section of the very voluminous evidence which existed on the subject.' While researching and writing:

'I succeeded in thoroughly convincing myself of the fact of the conscious survival of death and the possibility of communicating with dead people in certain circumstances. I hope that the book may have had the same effect on some of its readers. The book went the dreary round of many publishers before it was eventually accepted.'

In June 1964, Dowding wrote to an old friend, Beaverbrook, reflecting on his life at Bentley Priory. By then, he had come to believe that 'a Divine Will' had arranged for him, in partnership with Beaverbrook, to save Britain in 1940. This belief first came to him in 1943, when he recalled having been a chief in one of the Mongol tribes sweeping westward across Asia and into Europe. He was careless, however, and suffered a severe wound in battle against a well-armed tribe. As he lay dying, his second-in-command (given a message by 'one high in the hierarchy of this planet') told him he must return to life in a future age and lead his people, with Beaverbrook's help, more intelligently than he did in the 13th Century:

'I think it more than probable that your part in the Battle was laid down by the Lords of Karma as a result of some action of your own in times long past. Looking back on my own life, I can see how events conspired to put me at the head of Fighter Command at the critical time, instead of succeeding Ellington as CAS, as I had been told in 1935 that I should.... That is how two such dissimilar characters as you and I were brought together and enabled to work harmoniously for the preservation of our dear country.'[643]

His first spiritualist book, *Many Mansions*, was respectfully noticed in *The Times* on 25 November 1943. He came across as a modest, thoughtful, sincere advocate who wrote clearly and simply and made no claim to have had any personal psychic experience. At that time, he had never attended a séance, everything he knew came from reading and he laboured to reconcile the numerous opinions of spiritualists in the hope of bringing comfort to men and women who had lost relatives during the war. It was not a work that would convince sceptics, but then it was not addressed to them.

He wrote no fewer than four books on these themes: after *Many Mansions* (published in 1943), came *Lychgate: The Entrance to the Path*, *God's Magic: An Aspect of Spiritualism* and *The Dark Star*, between 1945 and 1951, all reprinted several times. He became a regular lecturer at meetings in towns throughout England: what an 'unkind journalist' called 'a peripatetic evangelist'. It often happens, Dowding believed:

'That when men have been suddenly killed in the heat of action, they have no idea that they are dead and wander about for a time in a state of great bewilderment. These were the people whom we were enabled to help by quietly explaining their condition to them and by putting them in touch with those who would be able to give them further assistance in this new stage of their life.'

He insisted that his judgement and discrimination were no less acute than they were during his service days and 'my present ideas are not based on a credulous senility.' Religion, science and philosophy were all content to continue 'without any clear idea of whence we come and whither we go, when there is available so much evidence of ante-natal and post-mortem existence, if they will take the trouble to read it.' It is surprising that he makes no mention of Conan Doyle's beliefs and experiences, perhaps the most famous of all British spiritualists: Dowding had known Conan Doyle and his own beliefs and experiences were remarkably similar.[644]

Peripatetic Evangelist

Dowding's third book was entitled *Lychgate*: a word usually meaning the roofed gateway of a churchyard where a coffin awaits the arrival of a priest. Dowding, however, used it to mean the entrance to a new path, after death in this life, leading to a wisdom that will gradually increase. The book was published in September 1945 and summarized his spiritual experiences since he completed *Many Mansions*. Both books, and the two that follow, are a world away – in every sense – from *Twelve Legions* and the life Dowding had led until his retirement.

Yet he remained in most ways the same reserved, considerate man he had always been, concerned for the welfare of all men and women who served the nation, especially those in uniform. By 1944, he and Liddell Hart were corresponding regularly and met whenever they could. One subject that agitated both men was the 'hypocritical hollowness' of the government's war-savings campaigns. These, they agreed, were primarily fund-raisers and did little to improve the pay of service men or women or provide for the dependents of those killed or wounded. They were led to wonder what sort of a world would emerge from the most destructive war in history. Would mankind learn anything of lasting value? Would stronger economic and social direction by governments help? Plus a greater emphasis on spiritual values?[645]

Dowding revealed in *Lychgate* that he was in 'constant personal communication' with his wife Clarice (who died in June 1920) and other friends and relations, as well as new friends, 'whom I have never seen on earth and yet who rank among the dearest and most intimate of my acquaintances.' Unfortunately, he could not reveal their names because it might distress relatives 'who cannot bring themselves to believe in their conscious and active survival.' Also, those whom he called 'the Great Ones' would not allow him to disclose their names. His own particular 'Guide and Guardian' (with whom he had been associated 'since before the dawn of history') explained why: 'I am not yet strong enough to face the great waves of thought which would be directed towards me if I were known by name.' So Dowding refers to him only as 'Z', and tells us that above Z there is a 'Master' who is responsible for 'the Great Plan'.

Dowding had now progressed from being no more than 'an objective student and observer of spiritualism', as he had been for many years, into a regular communicator with the spirit world and an active participant in the Great Plan 'for the illumination and edification of mankind'. He received many messages apparently from dead airmen and in May and June 1943 had a selection published in four successive issues of the *Sunday Pictorial*. Numerous readers were provoked to write to him about those letters: 'poor bereaved mothers and widows', also 'the boys themselves, whose own sorrow is lightened in proportion as the black and hopeless grief of their dear ones is dissipated.'

When Dowding first asked to meet Clarice again, he was told: 'Here is a lady, very quiet, peaceful and dignified.' He replied: 'Well, that's not *my* wife anyway; she was always full of laughter and fun and gaiety.' At these words came shouts of laughter from Clarice, who appeared to him as she had during her life. It made him so happy to be able to help the bereaved by passing on news of their loved ones. 'I don't mind if half my readers think that I ought to have my head examined, provided that the other half can glean something that will help them here and hereafter.'

The only aspect of his new life that he disliked was the obligation to make speeches all over the country. It went against the grain of his character, not helped by the discomforts of travelling in 1944 and 1945 and staying in 'provincial' hotels, but he accepted the obligation as a duty and became 'a peripatetic evangelist'. His message was that true spiritualism was not an affair of séances, mediums and phenomena, but 'a glad and happy co-operation with the saints and angels of God in their loving work of bringing His kingdom to Earth.'

He emphasized the enormous power of Thought, offering the example of great orators who could stir and unify the thoughts of his audiences either to religious exaltation, or to the heights of patriotism, or to the depths of hatred and blood-lust. He spoke not only of dead British airmen, but of a German boy, an American Red Cross nurse and many others who appeared to him from time to time. He also spoke of healing work done during sleep, that is forgotten when we awake. Clarice – whose name was 'Heartsease' on the other side – told him that one night he had worked in concentration camps, bringing blessed sleep to sufferers. Spirits, he learned, work in the 'Shadowland' between Earth and the Lower Heavens, where hundreds of young men remain voluntarily, to help their comrades still in the flesh.

Clarice also informed him that animals and birds enjoy a future life, without fear of each other or of humans. 'Some people,' she said, 'say there are no animals "Far On"; I can't believe that. Surely even in the Highest Heaven a bird must sing or a dog bark. They are part of the Creator, just as we are.'[646]

In September 1945 Dowding wrote an essay on those who died in the Battle of Britain: they live on, he believed, in a different kind of 'life'. For that reason, 15 September should never become a day of mourning. During the war, most of those killed 'fell at once into place in the existing organization of the celestial counterpart of the Air Force and took up the work of meeting those of their friends whose time had come to join them or protecting those whose sentence of imprisonment in the flesh was not yet due to expire.'

Dowding often wrote on this subject in mainstream newspapers as well as in *Psychic News* and came to believe he could prove that dead airmen live on. A message came to him, he said, from a dead fighter pilot who had been invisibly present at a lunch to commemorate the Battle of Britain. 'They'll talk one day of memorials to us,' the pilot told him.

> 'The finest memorial we could have is to see our comrades well cared for, our wives and children looked after, and the land we love so much once more free and smiling. These are the things we fought for and are still fighting for.'[647]

Tony Bartley, who made his name as a fine combat pilot during the Battle of Britain, married Deborah Kerr, a famous actress, in November 1945. Dowding was among the guests. He alarmed Bartley's father after the service by asking him if he could feel, as he could, the presence of his son's dead comrades.[648]

The Bartleys and, of course, a number of other friends and acquaintances found such conversations difficult to handle, but everyone who knew Dowding shared his delight – not quite concealed – on 11 September 1947. On that day, together with a guard of honour and the RAF Band, he presided over a ceremony on Platform 11 at Waterloo Railway Station, together with Air Marshal Sir James Robb (currently head of Fighter Command) to reveal the name plates of three magnificent steam locomotives. They were the 'Winston Churchill', 'Fighter Command' and 'Lord Dowding', all part of a class designed by the New Zealand-born Oliver Bulleid. He regarded himself as no more than the representative, he said, of 'all those lads who laid down their lives for their country and for us.' The 'Winston Churchill' was used in January 1965 to haul the special funeral train after the great man's death and is now safe in the National Railway Museum, York; 'Lord Dowding' and 'Fighter Command' are long gone, but 'Sir Keith Park' (minus his name plate) may be restored one day.[649]

Animals, Fairies, Aliens

Dowding's 'very unfashionable' retirement interests, as he himself described them, 'may appear to the orthodox as being strange, heretical and, still worse, "non-U".' The 'wall' between spiritualism and theosophy was very thin and Dowding had been a member of the Theosophical Society almost as long as he had been an avowed spiritualist. Together, their teaching had changed his views on animals in the scheme of creation and evolution. 'The evidence for the survival of physical death by animals,' he believed, 'is just as good in quality, if less massive in quantity, as that for the survival of human beings. They are but a rung behind ourselves on the great ladder of evolution, they are our younger brothers and sisters.'

Dowding had given up shooting and become a vegetarian. He believed that in the course of time, perhaps hundreds of years, civilized humanity would come to regard the eating of animals much as we regard cannibalism today. But 'I don't tilt at windmills that are out of reach, and I recognize that animals will be killed to satisfy human needs for many a long day to come.' But he did urge that the killing be done humanely and spoke several times on that subject in the House of Lords. As for the 'cruel exploitation' of animals in the interests of medical research, he was hotly opposed.

Dowding expected that many people came to regard him as 'the world's prize crank': not because of his concern for animal welfare, perhaps not even for believing that one may communicate with the departed, but certainly for his belief in fairies. There were, he said, thousands of people who claimed to have seen them, but they were usually children or uneducated peasants and therefore their testimony was not regarded seriously. 'To confess to a belief in fairies is almost tantamount to a confession of insanity. "He believes in fairies" is accepted as a polite metaphor for "He is off his head",' and yet Dowding believed 'they are essential to the growth of plants and the welfare of the vegetable kingdom and I have a good deal of evidence to support me in this belief.'

Finally, Dowding came to the 'most dreadful confession of all': he believed in the existence of vehicles known as 'flying saucers'. He found the evidence of thousands of recorded sightings totally convincing. They had been photographed at close range, tracked on radar, 'have on one occasion at least collided with an aeroplane sent up to investigate.' Their *existence*, in Dowding's opinion, was certain, but he did not know where they came from or why they visited Earth's skies. These are important questions and the answers may profoundly affect human life and progress. Flying saucers 'are certainly not a joke and it is surprising that they should be so generally regarded in that light.'[650]

Second Marriage

Dowding had married for the second time on 25 September 1951 in Caxton Hall at a corner of St James's Park, Westminster: a registry office then familiar to all followers of high society doings, as it was the most fashionable place for out-of-church weddings.[651] He was then in his 70th year and his bride was Muriel, then aged 43. She was the widow of Pilot Officer Max Whiting, a flight engineer in Bomber Command, killed in an Avro Lancaster of 630 Squadron shot down over Denmark on the night of 21-22 May 1944. Max, who was 31, had been in a 'reserved occupation', but had volunteered. He and his six companions, now lie in Esbjerg (Fourfelt) cemetery, near the Danish west coast.[652]

Muriel Albino, a very handsome and elegant woman, was a Londoner, born in Paddington, in March 1908. She had married Max in August 1935 and their son David, born in September 1938, became close to his stepfather, remains devoted to his memory and followed a career very much to Dowding's taste: an aviation engineer, later specializing in electronics and navigation.[653]

Dowding's sister Hilda, his brother Arthur and his wife were among those present. The happy couple, who had known each other since 1946, spent their honeymoon in Grindelwald, Switzerland, one of Dowding's favourite places. He skied and skated to his heart's content and Muriel found, despite her comparative youth and best efforts, that these were two of very few interests she was quite unable to share with her new husband. During their honeymoon, Dowding told her that he doubted whether he would ever write an autobiography, but after he was gone she would probably be asked about 'certain matters'. He then told her of his distress at the way he was dismissed from Fighter Command. 'Apart from this one occasion... he seldom referred to those days.'[654]

As a child, and again after Max's death, Muriel had dreamt of marrying a tall, slim soldier named Hugh. Her father-in-law, Harry Whiting, who knew about Dowding's interest in life after death, put her in touch with him. He invited her to lunch at the United Services Club in London and they took to each other immediately. They sat quietly in the club lounge for the whole afternoon. Dowding spoke mostly about the lost airmen whose families he wanted to help 'by bringing them positive news of their loved ones, through any available channel, whether by ordinary intelligence reports, or through the vehicle of a spiritualistic medium.'

In his book, *Many Mansions*, Dowding had written that he believed it was sometimes possible to communicate with the dead and as a result he received numerous letters from widows and mothers who had lost loved ones. Some years after they met, Muriel asked: 'Did you invite them all out to lunch?' 'Only you,' he replied. 'Because your husband asked me to.'[655]

Muriel converted him to her own hatred of cruelty to animals, either by killing them for food or, still more vehemently, destroying them to make cosmetics or even for research into human illnesses. She was the chief inspiration behind the creation in 1959 of 'Beauty without Cruelty', which became a registered charity, and also of a cosmetic firm with the same name from which she had withdrawn by 1980, when it became a commercial success. 'Beauty without Cruelty' has become an influential force in many countries to encourage the manufacture of cosmetics without harming any living creatures. Muriel was highly honoured for years of tireless work by the Royal Society for the Prevention of Cruelty to Animals, and Dowding gave her wholehearted support. He declared in the House of Lords in July 1957:

'I firmly believe that painful experiments on animals are morally wrong, and that it is basically immoral to do evil in order that good may come – even if it were proved that mankind benefits from the suffering inflicted on animals. I further believe that, in the vast majority of cases, mankind does not so benefit, and the results of vivisection are, in fact, misleading and harmful.'

In 1973, the National Anti-Vivisection Society set up 'The Lord Dowding Fund for Humane Research' to honour his memory and help research into methods of testing products and curing diseases that do not depend on the use of animals. He had given up hunting, became a vegetarian, tended a garden full of roses with loving care and only rarely risked blowing the house up by overheating a temperamental boiler.

Dowding left his old home at 3 St Mary's Road in Wimbledon. He had shared it for ten years, from 1941 to 1951, with his sister Hilda and it is now adorned with one of London's famous blue plaques to record his residence there. Hilda went to live nearby with her brother Arthur. Muriel's son David recalled that Dowding used to drive them to Wimbledon to collect Hilda and go ice-skating in Richmond. 'It was a wonderful sight to see these two elderly people, straight as flag staffs, gracefully weaving delicate patterns on the ice as they waltzed to the music.'

The happy couple lived with many animals in exceptional content at her home, 'Oakgates', in Darnley Drive, Tunbridge Wells: a splendid house given to her in 1946 by Harry Whiting. 'My mother,' wrote David, 'did not know the difference between a screwdriver and a tin-opener, but suddenly I had a Dad who would talk to me about mechanical things.'

He lost none of his enthusiasm for immaterial things, however. On 10 September 1960, for instance, he opened the triennial conference of the International Spiritualist Federation in London and declared: 'I believe that spiritualism may well turn out to be the salvation of the world. People find the teachings of the churches inadequate. They turn from the priests to the scientists, and the teachings of science are basically materialistic.' Two days later it was back to the material world when he was escorted round a Battle of Britain exhibition by Air Marshal Sir Arthur McDonald (Air Member for Personnel) on Horse Guards Parade. He examined a Spitfire cockpit, watched a demonstration of 'the workings of a typical operations room' during the battle, and enjoyed a Signals Command radar display.[656]

To mark their 15th wedding anniversary, in September 1966, Dowding gave Muriel a magnificent amethyst and diamond ring, together with this couplet:

'To the love of my life.
Isn't it fun – she's also my wife!'

But he had broken a hip while skiing in 1961 and four years later suffered a broken thigh on leaving his club. He recovered well from both accidents, but they caused him a great deal of pain in his last years. Consequently, he and Muriel moved in 1967 to 1, Calverley Park, also in Tunbridge Wells, but free of stairs.[657]

Revered Icon

The Battle of Britain Fighter Association was formally organized in March 1958 with Dowding as Life President (succeeded in 1970 by Park). He regularly attended its reunions, at which he was regarded as a revered icon, but his arthritis was severe and he gradually lost most of his eyesight. His handwriting, always with a pen in black ink, had been big, bold and easy to read, but in his last years he could do little more than sign his name in a wavering scrawl. For years he attended the memorial service in Westminster Abbey on Battle of Britain Day. As he told Robert Wright on 15 September 1962, he regarded it as solemn occasion for thankfulness, rather than a celebration of any kind. 'It is also a time for remembering all those bright lads whose earthly lives were cut short in our defence.'[658]

Sadly, there were influential persons in public life, in and out of uniform, for whom he was 'a serious problem', when it came to remembering the great battle. He was known to rail against 'the sporting, unimaginative, public school "hearties" who dominated the services.' Even more than his interest in spiritualism, his passionate commitment to animal rights baffled some of his 'church-parading and fox-hunting peers'.

There were also many politicians, especially on the Left, who liked to regard World War Two as a 'People's War'. They were not keen on further elevating the 'few', even though most surviving pilots were vocal in their praise of the 'many' who in countless capacities made it possible for them to fly and fight. It is, however, a disappointing fact that only aircrew, not ground crew, were eligible for membership of the association. For various reasons, then, 15 September has never been regarded with anything approaching the reverence accorded to Armistice Day.[659]

During the summer of 1968, Dowding was taken to Hawkinge airfield, near Folkestone, where scenes for a film about the battle were being shot. Dowding was portrayed by Laurence Olivier, Park by Trevor Howard. As always, Dowding refused to preen his own feathers. He told Howard: 'If it hadn't been for Keith Park's conduct in the battle, and his loyalty to me as his commander-in-chief, we should not be here today.'[660] His last public appearance was at the London première of that film in September 1969. Sadly crippled by arthritis and confined to a wheelchair, he was given a standing ovation by some 350 persons, many of them former pilots: 'Dowding's chicks', as Churchill had called them. On 3 November 1969, one of those chicks – later Wing Commander Jock Thomson – wrote to Liddell Hart.

> 'I believe that our chief was the only C-in-C of any major successful campaign in the 1939-1945 war who did not receive his fifth star. Yet his victory was critical, complete, unreversed and against near overwhelming odds. I can think of five-star commanders who could not lay such a claim.'[661]

Arnold Lunn was perhaps Dowding's closest friend. They had skied and climbed together for many years and during the summer of 1940 Lunn often visited Bentley Priory and sat with him, in his office. As a good friend, he was available for a chat or a confidence or just to be silently there. On one occasion, Dowding suddenly said, rather gruffly, 'I don't know anything about your financial position or whether you've been badly hit by the war, but as long as I've got some money in the kitty you could let me know if you were in a jam.'

In 1964 Lunn recalled Dowding saying: 'My job was to prevent the war from being lost, not to win it, and when my job is done, I shall go out like a cork from a bottle.' Lunn went on to pay him a memorable tribute: 'Hugh Dowding piloted England through a storm far more terrible than any Alpine blizzard.'[662] In June 1968, Dowding sent Lunn a *typed* letter (though he managed to sign it 'Hugh'). Now 86, he accepted that his skiing days were over. 'If I were optimistic enough to believe that heaven awaits,' he ended, 'I should join you in wishing that skiing or some other superior substitute lay await for us.'[663]

During the summer of 1969, the Air Ministry was making plans for his funeral and memorial service, keeping in regular touch with his son Derek. It was thought proper, when he died, that the letter of condolence should be signed either by the secretary of state or the minister of defence, given Dowding's reputation, 'and the recent controversy about the alleged lack of proper recognition for his services to the nation.' Denis Healey, the minister, signed the letter:

'In the years preceding the Second World War, his vision and his careful planning undoubtedly laid the foundations for the victory that lay ahead; and when the storm broke, his leadership during the Battle of Britain was an inspiration to his men and a decisive factor in the survival of this nation and indeed of the free world. He has a secure and lasting place both in the annals of the Royal Air Force and in the minds of the British people.'

One of Dowding's last letters, signed on 27 January 1970, was to Lunn. 'I am a tremendous crock now,' he wrote, what with arthritis and pains in his hands and legs, 'but I shall never forget our skiing days together, nor all that you did to help me in various ways. In spite of my ailments, I am still cheerful and young at heart.'[664]

Less than three weeks later, he died at his home on Sunday, 15 February 1970, two months short of his 88th birthday and was cremated. 'Look forward to death,' he had written in *Many Mansions*, 'as something to be infinitely welcomed when your life's work is done. Do not mourn or pity those who have gone before you, but think of them as fortunate. If you loved them here, continue to love them in your heart until you meet them again.'

According to Lord Bowden of Chesterfield, who contributed a foreword to E. G. Bowen's memoirs, *Radar Days*, in 1987, Dowding 'received a miserable pension and died in poverty.' In fact, he left a little over £22,000 when he died. One draws attention to these ridiculous words only because some readers of Bowen's important book may believe what the noble lord wrote.[665] During the weeks following Dowding's passing, Muriel received some 8,000 letters of condolence and with the help of a secretary and friends replied to all of them.[666] A private service was held at 4 pm on the 18th in Tunbridge Wells at which Father Geoffrey Nixon, a family friend, said 'he slipped peacefully out of this life into one to which, we believe, he was not a complete stranger. The manner of his going was in keeping with a man for whom fuss and pettiness were equally abhorrent.'

The numerous floral tributes were afterwards sent to the Queen Victoria Hospital at East Grinstead in Sussex, about 12 miles west of Tunbridge Wells. Dowding had been an honorary member of the group of airmen badly burned during the war and treated at that hospital.

The memorial service, attended by more than 3,000 people – including 46 air marshals of various grades – was held in Westminster Abbey on 12 March and his ashes were interred below the Battle of Britain window in a chapel dedicated on 10 July 1947, which honours all those who died during the battle. The lower lights of the window contain the badges of all the squadrons named in Dowding's despatch as well as the flags of seven nations and Shakespeare's words, 'We few, we happy few, we band of brothers'. Overall, thought Adrian Gregory, 'it is probably the strongest example of the synthesis between Christian and patriotic tradition of all British war memorials.' The Roll of Honour, written on parchment and bound in leather, contains the names of 1,494 pilots and aircrew. It deserves to be remembered that more than 1,000 of those men were not serving in Fighter Command: 718 in Bomber Command, 280 in Coastal Command, 14 in other commands, 34 in the Fleet Air Arm and no more than 448 in Fighter Command.[667]

Healey delivered an address at the memorial service in which he described Dowding as 'one of those great men whom this country miraculously produces in times of peril.' As is usual with the British, the arrangements were thorough, but there was some muddle – which no doubt vastly amused Dowding's spirit – when several important persons failed to arrive on time, did not sit where they were supposed to, and failed to depart in accordance with the operational plan.[668]

A full-page obituary appeared of the 'Victor of the Battle of Britain' in *The Times* on 16 February, as well as a news item on the front page. If he had died before the battle, 'his work in the field of technical development would place him high among his country's saviours.' His nickname, Stuffy, 'completely belied his gift of charm and accessibility.' In his summary of Dowding's career, the obituarist – anonymous in those days – singled out his six years at the Air Ministry in charge of supply, research and development. 'No better choice was ever made'; he had 'a good grasp of the practical side of airmanship and a rare understanding of the limitations of air power.'[669]

An obituary also appeared on that day in the *Daily Telegraph*, written by Air Commodore Teddy Donaldson, commander of 151 Squadron (flying Hurricanes) from North Weald in Essex during the battle.

'We admired him more than we loved him, for none of us really knew him intimately. He was too busy "rowing with the Ministries" on our behalf to get us the equipment we so desperately needed, so we saw him all too seldom to get to know him well.'

He had turned up at North Weald from time to time, where he preferred to listen rather than talk. Everyone known to Donaldson, including Bader, thought he should have been elevated to five-star rank as a Marshal of the Royal Air Force: 'Seldom in our history,' wrote Bader in the *Guardian*, 'has a man deserved so much of his fellow countrymen and wanted and received so little.... Dowding surely earned his place alongside Nelson and Wellington and other great military names in our history.' Churchill's postwar account of 1940 'follows the Air Ministry line' and 'steers clear of the controversy about Dowding', but an early draft, David Reynolds discovered, explained that he had 'reluctantly yielded to Air Ministry pressure on this, adding "I was wrong not to insist on my view."' For Churchill, the two critical moments of the war, 'when everything was at stake,' were the Battle of Britain and the Battle of the Atlantic.'[670]

There are memorials in Moffat, Tunbridge Wells and Winchester College. His old school, St Ninian's in Moffat, has been converted by the RAF Association into a home for disabled ex-airmen since 1988 and named Dowding House. That association also has a room in his honour in a home for disabled ex-airmen at Sussexdown, Storrington, in Sussex. In September 1982, Queen Elizabeth the Queen Mother sent a message to Moffat to mark a special service in St Andrews on the first Battle of Britain Day following Dowding's centenary. His 'inspired leadership was of incomparable value to our country,' she wrote. 'The King held him in the highest esteem and I am very pleased to pay my personal tribute.' Battle of Britain Day is honoured there every year. There is a pastel drawing of Dowding, made in 1939 by Sir William Rothenstein, in the Imperial War Museum, a portrait made in 1942 by Sir William Russell at Bentley Priory and one by Faith Kenworthy-Browne in the family's possession. A bronze by David Wynne was exhibited in 1968 at the National Portrait Gallery. On 16 September 1986, he was depicted on a British postage stamp, together with a Hurricane – not a Spitfire.

Dowding's son Derek said in July 1990 that he remembered him as 'a marvellous father'. There was nothing 'stuffy' about 'the papa who was all affection, the chap who wrote me entrancing letters about war and flying and polo and shooting from Iraq and Palestine,' letters that are now, it seems, all lost.[671] His medals were purchased by the RAF Museum at Hendon in March 1997 for the enormous sum of £69,000: at that time, a world record for any group of medals other than one including a Victoria Cross. The deal was negotiated by Spink of London, following an approach by Hendon on behalf of Odette, baroness Dowding, widow of Derek, who had died in July 1992. She hoped the sale would help promote the case for his posthumous promotion to the rank of Marshal of the Royal Air Force, but that had long been impossible.

Park, Camm, Mitchell and Merlin

Keith Park died in Auckland, New Zealand, in February 1975 and a memorial service in his honour was organized in London by the Battle of Britain Fighter Association on 12 September. The service was held in the RAF's own church, St Clement Dane's in the Strand, and Bader – now Sir Douglas – was invited to speak. He did his best to put an end to whatever bitter feelings remained about events in 1940. The battle, he said, 'was controlled, directed and brought to a successful conclusion by the man whose memory we honour today. The awesome responsibility for this country's survival rested squarely on Keith Park's shoulders. Had he failed, Stuffy Dowding's foresight, determination and achievements would have counted for nought.'[672]

If in fact Hugh Dowding's spirit survives, he would have welcomed Bader's generous words in praise of a man who helped to make Britain safe from defeat in 1940. He would also welcome the following tribute to two other men whose skilful, devoted efforts made a huge contribution to that triumph; and to the engine that powered their fighters.

Sir Sydney Camm's Hurricane was a lineal descendent of his excellent

Fury: in Wykeham's opinion, 'the most beautiful biplane ever flown.' The Hurricane might best be described as Dowding's right-hand punch in the Battle of Britain, with Reginald Mitchell's Spitfire as his left-hand follow-up. Between them, they ensured that Fighter Command was able to beat back a massive prolonged assault in daylight. The Hurricane was the first monoplane, eight-gun fighter in frontline service anywhere in the world; the first RAF fighter to exceed 300 mph in level flight with a full operational warload and the first to possess a retractable undercarriage. As we have seen, the Hurricane was the last of a distinguished line, the Spitfire the first of a new line, but 'if the Hurricane had encountered half the production problems met in the early Spitfire,' wrote John W. Fozard, 'we would have lost the Battle of Britain because of insufficient fighters.' There would be countless occasions in 1940 when its pilots were forced to land at satellite airfields where only primitive servicing and repair facilities were available, and yet they were often airborne again in only a few hours. The same could not be said for the Spitfire, which usually had to be dismantled and transported by road back to its sector airfield, if it had suffered more than superficial damage.

Over 1,700 Hurricanes were flown in combat during that battle – more than the total of all other RAF aircraft involved – and they claimed nearly 80% of the victories achieved. All told, about 14,000 were built between 1935 and 1945. Although not original in any way, it proved to be more than the sum of its parts: high performance, pilot-friendly, steady gun platform, easily produced and repaired, rugged in service. Camm and his small team of the mid-1930s 'working in shabby premises in a run-down Kingston backstreet, changed the course of history in 1940 and thus preserved our way of life and our civilization.'[673]

Reginald Mitchell, designer of the seaplanes which won the famous Schneider Trophy for Britain, used that expertise to produce the even more famous Spitfire. Together with the Hurricane, the Spitfire made possible the strategy devised by Dowding and the tactics employed by Park. Nearly 1,600 Mark I Spitfires flew in the Battle of Britain, although a faster and more powerful Mark II was beginning to appear in service by June 1940. All told, more than 20,000 Spitfires were built in 40 different modifications and it gave excellent service from the first day of the war until the last.

When Vickers acquired Supermarine in 1928, it was on the understanding that Mitchell, already that company's most valuable asset, was part of the deal. But Mitchell died in 1937, having been in constant pain during the last four years of his life, and for reasons that seemed compelling to officials in Whitehall and Westminster a posthumous knighthood for him has always been quite out of the question. Camm was deservedly knighted in 1953 and lived until 1966, with several more excellent designs to his credit. A letter commending Mitchell was signed by eight of the ten living secretaries of defence in September 2005, but it failed to have any effect. As with Dowding, however, his name will live for the foreseeable future and an American billionaire, Sidney Frank, has paid for a splendid statue in his honour that is now to be seen in London's Science Museum.[674]

Both fighters were powered by a marvellous Rolls-Royce engine, made more marvellous still by the fitting of a Rotol constant speed propeller, and the use of 100 octane fuel – developed by the United States – and far superior to the 87 octane fuel used throughout the war by the Luftwaffe. The particular value of this propeller and this fuel was to improve dramatically a fighter's rate of climb. Like the Hurricane, the Merlin engine was based on earlier successes, especially the liquid-cooled, in-line Kestrel engine, which became PV (Private Venture) 1200 Merlin through 'the engineering genius' of Ernest Hives, Stanley Hooker and their colleagues. The Merlin became a famous aero-engine, powering not only Dowding's fighters in the Battle of Britain, but many other frontline British aircraft of the Second World War as well as the most successful American fighter of that war, the P-51D Mustang.[675]

Surprise, Severity, Faint Disapproval

For good or ill, Dowding was not a man to compromise. Consequently, he provoked anger, exasperation, respect and devotion: sometimes all of these in a single day. He was also a man who cared deeply about casualties and always did his best to keep these down. Although well read, with a dry sense of humour, he was too abstemious, too serious, to be easy company except with his family and close friends. He did not care for small talk and did not always impress in debate across a table, preferring instead to state his case or to give instructions in writing. With pen in hand, he was cogent, often blunt, sometimes offensive.

His appearance matched his personality: upright, lean, correct, unsmiling. 'Dowding is one of those people,' wrote Lunn, 'who seldom make a pleasant remark to one's face, but who never make an unpleasant remark behind one's back.' Friendship, for him, was not expressed by pretty speeches, but if necessary, by action which cost something. When he died, Lunn wrote:

> 'We skied and climbed together for years and I knew how much he delighted in the ever-changing effects of the mountains in their many moods, for try as he would, he could not avoid sometimes dropping his mask of "stuffiness" and so I was not deceived when he wrote "Do not number me among those skiing authors who come over all holy about their personal reactions to the solitude and grandeur of the mountains."'[676]

His beloved Muriel died in November 1993, at the age of 85, and her ashes now lie next to his in Westminster Abbey, an honour she deserved in her own right and not merely as his widow. Before she died, she knew that he had been awarded, even though posthumously, a most signal honour.

On 20 October 1988, when his particular opponents were all dead or moribund, a statue of Dowding, set up in London outside St Clement Dane's was unveiled by Queen Elizabeth, the Queen Mother. The initiative came not from the Ministry of Defence, into which the Air Ministry had by then been buried, but from survivors of those who actually fought in the battle, on the ground as well as in the air. Fund raising for the statue began in 1983 and Dowding would certainly have enjoyed the delays in completing the project by bureaucratic agitation: the Fine Arts Commission (which controlled the erection of statues in London), the Department of the Environment, rival sculptors and others all had plenty to say. More than £60,000 was raised, to cover the cost of construction and subsequent cleaning. The expression on his face most appropriately blends 'surprise, severity and faint disapproval at both spectators and proceedings.'[677] If he is right about life after death, it must give him quiet satisfaction – with no element, in his elevated state, of triumphant glee – to know that his reputation remains high whereas almost all those officers and civil servants with whom he jousted so often for so many years are quite forgotten. His statue is here to stay (one presumes) whereas the Air Ministry is long gone.

An inscription on the statue's base cogently summarizes his achievements. Readers learn that he was responsible for preparing and conducting the battle, ensuring that his command was equipped with Hurricanes and Spitfires:

> 'He was among the first to appreciate the vital importance of RDF (radar) and an effective command and control system for his squadrons. They were ready when war came. In the preliminary stages of that war, he thoroughly trained his minimal forces and conserved them against strong political pressure to disperse and misuse them. His wise and prudent judgement and leadership helped to ensure victory against overwhelming odds and thus prevented the loss of the Battle of Britain and probably the whole war. To him, the people of Britain and of the Free World owe largely the way of life and the liberties they enjoy today.'

He was 'the unquestioned victor,' thought Terraine, of a battle which 'he had begun to win years before it was fought.' During the Great War, it was said that Admiral Jellicoe, commanding the Grand Fleet, could have lost the war in an afternoon. In the Battle of Britain, it is probably true that Dowding, Park and their controllers could have done the same, 'but whereas Jellicoe was put to the test only once, they were tested every day for two and a half months' and never made a serious mistake.[678]

A few weeks after his statue was unveiled, serious thought was given to erecting one of Harris nearby. Sir Michael Beetham (CAS, 1977-82) said the plan was 'to commemorate outside the RAF Church both the man who saved us from defeat in the Battle of Britain and the man who subsequently paved the way for victory.' A fair comment, if the British may overlook – as they often do – the immense contributions of the Soviet Union and the United States. Yet there remains a gulf between their respective achievements:

> 'Dowding goes down in history as the one airman with an indisputable victory in a recognizable battle of decisive importance to his name; it is a very special accolade. Harris does not possess one

like it; his one very clear victory is the Battle of Hamburg, but no-one could call that decisive.'[679]

The same sculptor, Faith Winter, was responsible for both statues. An almighty fuss was made in the media, both in Britain and abroad, from September 1991 onwards, when the news broke that Harris was to be honoured.

This is no place to summarize arguments that have raged, for and against Bomber Commmand's actions during the Second World War, but one would dearly love to hear what Dowding and Harris said to each other after the Queen Mother unveiled the Harris statue, on 31 May 1992, and everyone had gone home. They would, naturally, have been gratified at the recognition. Somewhat late in the day, perhaps, but never mind: nothing happens quickly in Whitehall. They would also have exchanged tart – *very* tart – observations on some of their fair-weather friends as well as their all-weather critics. But none of this matters much, now that the spirits of both men have moved into a new sphere (as Dowding has explained to Harris). Having nothing now to do except stand around all day, they would reflect on the part they played, in co-operation – however uneasy or even reluctantly at times – with so many men and women around the world to overthrow the vilest régime that has yet infested this planet. Is it too much to claim that Trafalgar saved the nation, but the Battle of Britain saved the world?

Endnotes

1   Orange, 'Dowding' in *Oxford DNB*, vol. 16, pp. 773-7.
2   Collier, *Leader*, p. 27.
3   'Dowding History', p. 1: an 84-page manuscript written by Hugh late in 1956 (see p. 53) to help Collier with his biography. Now held by Air Historical Branch, Ministry of Defence, London. It was also made available to Wright for his biography.
4   Davies, *The Isles*, pp. 120, 187.
5   Hornung, *Raffles* (dedicated to Conan Doyle); Booth, *Doctor, Detective*, pp. 181-2; Stashower, *Teller of Tales*, pp. 136-7.
6   AIR 76 (Kenneth's service record).
7   Collier, *Leader*, pp. 28-33, 37.
8   Joubert de la Ferté, *Third Service*, p. 129.
9   'Dowding History', p. 82.
10 Orange, 'Trenchard' in *Oxford DNB*, vol. 55, pp. 299-304.
11 Collier, *Leader*, p. 20; *The Times*, 16 February 1970, pp. 1 & 10.
12 Collier, *Leader*, p. 20; Orange, *Park* & 'Park' in *Oxford DNB*, vol. 42, pp. 633-6.
13 Collier, *Leader*, pp. 44-50.
14 Collier, *Leader*, pp. 52-60, 'Dowding History', pp. 1-9.
15 Collier, *Leader*, pp. 60-8.
16 'Dowding History', pp. 9-15, 21.
17 Collier, *Leader*, pp. 68-73; Orange, *Slessor*, p. 67 & 'Newall' in *Oxford DNB*, vol. 40, pp. 562-4; 'Dowding History', pp. 16-17.
18 'Dowding History', 19-20.
19 *The Times*, 5 September 1911, p. 12.
20 Muggleton Papers.
21 Lewis, *British Fighter*, p. 27.
22 'Dowding History', pp. 21-25.
23 Collier, *Leader*, pp. 79-83; *The Times*, 27 January 1914, pp. 15-17; 19 March 1914.
24 Burns, 'Lunn' in *Oxford DNB*, vol. 34, pp. 769-70; Wilson, *Snow Crazy*, chap. 26; Lunn, 'Man Who Won', p. 487; I am grateful to Elizabeth Hussey for references, here and elsewhere, to Dowding from the publications of the Ski Club of Great Britain.
25 *The Times*, 11 May 1914, p. 10; Taylor, *CFS*, p. 25.
26 Bridgman-Stewart, *Clouds Remember*, pp. 7-18.

27 AIR 1 758/204/4/117; 'Dowding History', pp. 25-6.
28 Collier, *Leader*, pp. 84-7; Salmond Papers, B/2638, Hendon; Ray, Battle of Britain, pp. 138-40; Meilinger, 'John Salmond' in *Oxford DNB*, vol. 48, pp. 738-40; Orange, 'Trenchard' & 'British Commanders', pp. 34-5. Laffin's biography of Salmond, *Swifter than Eagles*, is particularly inadequate here: he alludes, critically and inaccurately, to Dowding, but without naming him, pp. 236-7.
29 Collier, *Leader*, pp. 88-9; Barker, *RFC in France*, p. 60; Bridgman-Stewart, *Clouds Remember*, p. 19; Hobson, *Airmen Died*, pp. 413-6.
30 Barker, *RFC in France*, p. 60.
31 AIR 1 2163/209/9/1; Collier, *Leader*, pp. 89-93; 'Dowding History', pp. 27-9.
32 Collier, *Leader*, pp. 93-4.
33 Air Ministry, *Short History*, p. 31; Hobson, *Airmen Died*, p. 25.
34 Dye, 'Royal Flying Corps', p. 71.
35 Dye, 'Royal Air Force', pp. 71-88 & 'Major Musgrave', pp. 203-7 & 'Major Musgrave: Update', pp. 95-9; *Cross & Cockade (International)*, vol. 28, no. 1 (Spring 1997) p. 59; Dowding History', pp. 29-30; Norris, *Royal Flying Corps*, p. 113.
36 AIR 1 1232/204/6/4; 1246/204/6/72; 2163/209/10/5; 'Dowding History', pp. 30-31.
37 'Dowding History', pp. 29-30; Norris, *Royal Flying Corps*, p. 114.
38 Dye, 'Musgrave', pp. 203-6 & 'Musgrave: Update', pp. 95-102 & 'No. 9 (Wireless) Squadron', pp. 106-120.
39 Dye, 'No. 9 (Wireless) Squadron', pp. 111, 114; Smythies, 'Experiences during the War (1914-8)' in Air Ministry AP 956 (December 1923); Brabazon, *Brabazon Story*, 87-90; Barker, *RFC in France*, pp. 62-5 (James & Lewis); Wright, 'Good to Talk', pp. 210-9 (Lewis).
40 AIR 1 1241/204/6/50; AIR 2/18 (Smythies' report); Dye, 'No 9 (Wireless) Squadron', pp. 106-120.
41 Baker, *Marconi*, pp. 167-8, 170.
42 Collier, *Leader*, pp. 100-103; 'Dowding History', pp. 32-33.
43 Collier, *Leader*, pp. 107-8; Gray & Thetford, German Aircraft, pp. x-xi, 20-3 (Albatros), 59-63 (Aviatik), 82-6 (Fokker), 195-8 (Rumpler); Fitzsimons, *Purnell*, vol. 4, pp. 974-6 (Fokker); Hobson, *Airmen Died*, pp. 44-5.
44 Muggleton Papers.
45 'Dowding History', p. 37.
46 'Dowding History', pp. 34-6; Hobson, *Airmen Died*, p. 49.
47 Barker, *RFC in France*, pp. 86-7; *Cross & Cockade (International)*, vol. 20, no. 1 (Spring 1989) p. 55.
48 Harvey, 'Great War Fighter Aces', p. 121.
49 Grinnell-Milne, *Wind in the Wires*, pp. 39-41; obituary in *Cross & Cockade*, p. 144.
50 Grinnell-Milne, *Wind in the Wires*, pp. 42-3.
51 Grinnell-Milne, *Wind in the Wires*, pp. 78-9.

52 Bruce, *Aeroplanes of RFC*, pp. 381-4.
53 Grinnell-Milne, pp. 108-110; Tredrey, *Pioneer Pilot*, p. 33.
54 Grinnell-Milne, p. 163; Jones, *Tiger Squadron*, p. 30.
55 Obituary in *Cross & Cockade*, p. 144.
56 Collier, *Leader*, pp. 108-112; 'Dowding History', p. 36; Townsend, *Duel of Eagles*, p. 22.
57 Tredrey, *Pioneer Pilot*, p. 56.
58 Cole & Cheesman, *Air Defence*, p. 77.
59 AIR 1 1259/204/9/1 & 8; 1268/204/9/76; 1267/204/9/69; 1265/204/9/54; 'Dowding History', p. 38.
60 Penrose, *British Aviation*, pp. 98-102 (Sopwith), pp. 142, 151-2, 210 (RE 7); pp, 50, 70, 126 (Elephant); Bridgman-Stewart, *Clouds Remember*, pp. 38-41 (Morane Bullet).
61 Revell, *Fighter Squadrons*, p. 26.
62 Lyall, 'Dowding', p. 206.
63 Lunn, 'The Man Who Won', pp. 487-8.
64 Robertson, *Sopwith*, p. 72; Penrose, *British Aviation*, p. 210.
65 *Aeroplane Monthly*, September 1988, pp. 570-1; Balfour, *Westminster*, p. 33.
66 'Dowding History', pp. 39-40; Warne, '60 Squadron' in *Cross & Cockade*, p. 31; Douglas with Wright, *Years of Combat*, p. 143.
67 Raleigh & Jones, *War in the Air*, vol. ii, pp. 471-2; Henshaw, *Sky Their Battlefield*, p. 575.
68 Meilinger, 'Trenchard', p. 249; Higham, 'Brancker' in *Oxford DNB*, vol. 7, pp. 331-3.
69 Boyle, *Trenchard*, p. 184.
70 'Dowding History', pp. 40-41; Revell, *Fighter Units*, p. 37 & *Single-Seater*, p. 35; Orange, 'Robert Smith-Barry' in *Oxford DNB*, vol. 4, pp. 149-51.
71 'Dowding History', p. 41.
72 Hobson, *Airmen Died*, pp. 413-6.
73 AIR 76 139.
74 *The Times*, 1 October 1935, p. 9.
75 AIR 76 (Becke's service record); Collier, *Leader*, pp. 119-121, 128.
76 'Dowding History', p. 44; Collier, *Leader*, p. 123; Wright, *Dowding*, p. 46.
77 *Flight*, 8 July 1920, pp. 701-711.
78 *Flight*, 30 June 1921, pp. 432-6, 7 July 1921, pp. 451-6.
79 AIR 2/4427 & 8; *Flight*, 29 June 1922, pp. 365-73.
80 Wilson, *Snow Crazy*, chap. 26.
81 Orange, *Tedder*, 63 & 'Tedder' in *Oxford DNB*, vol. 54, 14-19.
82 Orange, *Tedder*, pp. 68-9.
83 Obituary of Higgins in *The Times*, 4 June 1948, p. 7.
84 *The Times*, 2 August & 7 August 1923, pp. 7 & 7.
85 Omissi, *Air Power*, pp. 19-20.
86 Meilinger, 'Trenchard', pp. 253-4; Beaumont, 'New Lease', p. 87.
87 Orange, *Slessor*, pp. 33-4; Biddle, Rhetoric, p. 83.
88 Omissi, *Air Power*, pp. 162-76; Beaumont, 'New Lease', p. 87;

Orange, *Slessor*, pp. 33-5.

89 Wakelam, 'Roaring Lions', pp. 61-2; Lyall, 'Dowding', p. 206; the policy was vehemently supported by Kingston-McCloughry in *Winged Warfare*, pp. 201-57, and more calmly by Portal, 'Air Force Co-operation'.

90 AIR 5/344; James, *Imperial Rearguard*.

91 'Dowding History', pp. 46-9; James, *Imperial Rearguard*, p. 79.

92 *The Times*, 27 January 1925, p. 13.

93 Wilson, *Snow Crazy*, chap. 26; papers of Ski Club of Great Britain via Elizabeth Hussey.

94 Huskinson, *Vision Ahead*, pp. 26-7.

95 Orange, *Tedder*, p. 75; *The Times*, 18 November 1927, p. 23.

96 AIR 30/69; 2/804; *The Times*, 2 January 1929, p. 14.

97 *The Times*, 12 September 1929, p. 12; Omissi, *Air Control*, pp. 44-5, 66-7.

98 Dowding Papers, AC71/17/1, Hendon; much information on this episode is to be found at Hendon in the papers of Trenchard (MFC76/1/174) & Dowding (AC71/17/2).

99 'Dowding History', p. 52.

100 *The Times*, 4 September 1929, pp. 12 & 13, 26 April 1937, p. 16 (obituary of Shaw).

101 Dowding Papers, AC71/17/3.

102 Bushby, *Air Defence*, p. 17.

103 Ferris, *Fighter Defence*, p. 853.

104 Bushby, *Air Defence*, pp. 18-22.

105 Bushby, *Air Defence*, pp. 33-4; Cole & Cheesman, *Air Defence*, p. 136.

106 Bushby, *Air Defence*, pp. 41, 47-8; Cole & Cheesman, *Air Defence*, pp. 207-9; Gray & Thetford, *German Aircraft*, pp. 128-32.

107 Bushby, *Air Defence*, pp. 49-51; Cole & Cheesman, *Air Defence*, pp. 243-72.

108 Bushby, *Air Defence*, pp. 51-3; Cole & Cheesman, *Air Defence*, p. 229; Higham, 'Ashmore' in *Oxford DNB*, vol. 2, pp. 665-6; *The Times*, 7 October 1953, p. 11.

109 Bushby, *Air Defence*, pp. 56-8.

110 Cole & Cheesman, *Air Defence*, 62-5.

111 Jones, *Strategic Air Power*, pp. 160-3.

112 Bushby, *Air Defence*, pp. 77-8.

113 Ferris, *Fighter Defence*, pp. 845-884; Collier, *Defence*, pp. 13-20 with excellent maps of Steel-Bartholomew & 52 squadron schemes; James, *Growth of Fighter Command*, pp. 1-6.

114 Bushby, *Air Defence*, pp. 120-1.

115 Orange, *Park*, pp. 45, 50 & 'Park' in *Oxford DNB*, vol. 42, pp. 633-6; Ferris, *Fighter Defence*, p. 859 & 'Achieving Air Ascendancy', pp. 31-2; Smith, 'RAF' in *Burning Blue*, p. 25.

116 Lumsden & Thetford, *Silver Wings*, pp. 52-75.

117 Orange, *Park*, pp. 67-8.

118 Orange, *Park*, pp. 50-3.

119 *The Times*, 8 & 13 August 1930, pp. 10 & 10; Sutton, *Raiders Approach!*, pp. 66-70; Penrose, *Widening Horizons*, pp. 41-2; Clark, *Rise of Boffins*, pp. 38-9.
120 *The Times*, 13 August 1930, p. 10.
121 Robinson, *Giants in the Sky*, p. 297; Lord Onslow, revised Higham, 'Thomson' in *Oxford DNB*, vol. 54, pp. 497-9; Hyde, *British Air Policy*, pp. 252-68.
122 *Flight*, 10 October 1930 (detailed account of last flight): pp. 1107-1114, 1126; *Flight*, 17 October 1930 (funerals): 1137-1141.
123 Wright, *Battle of Britain*, p. 53; Collier, *Leader*, pp. 135-40; AIR 2/444.
124 *Flight*, 24 October 1930, p. 1170; 31 October, 1187; 7 November, pp. 1228-9; 14 November, pp. 1238-9, 5 December, p. 1421 & 12 December, p. 1446; *The Times*, 14 October 1930, p. 14; 24 October, p. 15; 29 October, p. 9; 30 October, p. 20; 5 November, p. 19; 7 November, pp. 9 & 14; Collier, *Heavenly Adventurer*, pp. 220-223; Hyde, *British Air Policy*, pp. 257-62.
125 'Dowding History', pp. 56-7.
126 Robinson, *Giants in the Sky*, p. 296.
127 Hyde, *British Air Policy*, p. 257.
128 Shute, *Slide Rule*, pp. 53-7, 66, 101-115, 118-32.
129 Andrews & Morgan, *Supermarine*, pp. 56, 60, 174-202; Banks, *Diary*, pp. 85-96.
130 'Dowding History', p. 57.
131 Muggleton Papers; *Illustrated Encyclopedia*, pp. 65-73; Green, *Famous Fighters*, pp. 125-38 (Spitfire), pp. 267-76 (Hurricane).
132 Taylor, *English History*, p. 228.
133 Bialer, 'Humanization', p. 79; Bond & Murray, *British Armed Forces*, pp. 98-100.
134 Bialer, 'Humanization', pp. 80-1, 83-5, 92.
135 Bialer, 'Humanization', pp. 86-92; Overy, 'Air Power', p. 79.
136 Smith, 'RAF' in *Burning Blue*, pp. 156-7.
137 Bushby, *Air Defence*, p. 96.
138 Cranwell Papers.
139 Smith, 'RAF' in *Burning Blue*, pp. 162-3; James, *Growth of Fighter Command*, pp. 18-21.
140 Smith, 'RAF' in *Burning Blue*, p. 26.
141 Reynolds, Command, 98-9; Smith, 'RAF' in *Burning Blue*, p. 28.
142 Smith, 'Planning and Building', pp. 41-2; Higham, 'Government, Companies', pp. 335-6.
143 Bond & Murray, *British Armed Forces*, pp. 103-4; Bushby, *Air Defence*, p. 97.
144 Bushby, *Air Defence*, pp. 98-9.
145 'Dowding History', p. 57.
146 Ritchie, 'Price of Air Power', p. 89.
147 AIR 41/8, p. 71.
148 Penrose, *Widening Horizons*, p. 17.
149 Ritchie, 'Price of Air Power', pp. 82-6.

150 Ferris, *Fighter Defence*, pp. 866-7; Lumsden & Thetford, *Silver Wings*, pp. 198-221.
151 Obituary of Thomson in *The Times*, 29 August 1939, p. 15.
152 Collier, *Leader*, pp. 140-2; Hough & Richards, *Battle of Britain*, pp. 36-7; Penrose, *Ominous Skies*, p. 5; Gustin & Williams, *Flying Guns*, pp. 91-2; AIR 20/2371.
153 Lyall, 'Dowding', pp. 206-7.
154 Bushby, *Air Defence*, pp. 119-120.
155 Gustin & Williams, *Flying Guns*, pp. 94-6; Bishop, *Fighter Boys*, pp. 244-5.
156 AIR 30/101; *The Times*, 2 January 1933, p. 14.
157 Kinsey, *Orfordness*, p. 44.
158 'Dowding History', p. 59; Hogg, *Anti-Aircraft*, pp. 92-3; Gunston, *Rockets and Missiles*.
159 Ritchie, 'Wilfrid Freeman', pp. 252-3.
160 Ferris, 'Achieving Air Ascendency', p. 40.
161 AIR 2/716.
162 Reader, *Architect*, pp. 216-8, 257-8; Bond & Murray, *British Armed Forces*, p. 104; Smith, 'Planning and Building', pp. 47-8.
163 Smith, 'Planning and Building', pp. 42-3.
164 'Dowding History', p. 60; Hyde, *British Air Policy*, pp. 372-5.
165 Till, *Air Power and the Royal Navy*, pp. 100-1, 103.
166 AIR 2/1927, 1743, 8066, 3369; Gilbert, *Finest Hour*, pp. 733-4.
167 *Smith, British Air Strategy*, pp. 94-105; Hyde, *British Air Policy*, p. 402.
168 Meilinger, *Airwar*, pp. 75-85.
169 Brown, 'Skua and Roc', pp. 231-8; Fitzsimons, *Purnell*, vol. 1, p. 60 (Albacore), pp. 289-90 (Barracuda), vol. 4, pp. 1012-3 (Fulmar).
170 'Dowding History', pp. 62-3.
171 Roskill, *Naval Policy*, vol. 2, pp. 194-212 & 392-413.
172 Liddell Hart Papers. LH 1/245/32.
173 Bushby, *Air Defence*, p. 84.
174 Bushby, *Air Defence*, pp. 84-6; James, *Growth of Fighter Command*, pp. 11-17; Collier, *Defence*, pp. 28-35 with map of re-orientation scheme after p. 32.
175 Collyer, *Kent's Listening Ears*, pp. 16-17.
176 Collier, *Leader*, pp. 150-2; Bushby, *Air Defence*, pp. 99-100; Clark, *Rise of Boffins*, pp. 33-6; Hyde, *British Air Policy*, pp. 329-33; Collier, *Defence*, pp. 36-40.
177 White, *Air Intercept Radar*, p. 5.
178 Wykeham, *Fighter Command*, p. 38; Clark, *Rise of Boffins*, p. 12; White, *Air Intercept Radar*, p. 6.
179 Clark, *Rise of Boffins*, p. 41; Zimmerman, *Britain's Shield*, pp. 166-7; Edgerton, 'Prophet Militant', p. 368.
180 *The Times*, 29 July 1972, pp. 519-20; Robins, 'Cunliffe-Lister' in *Oxford DNB*, vol. 33, pp. 988-92.
181 Robert Rhodes James, *The Times*, 3 November 1977, p. 15; Hyde, *British Air Policy*, pp. 354-5.

182 Hough & Richards, *Battle of Britain*, p. 50; Reynolds, *Command*, pp. 97-8; Bushby, *Air Defence*, pp. 105-9; Clark, *Rise of Boffins*, p. 29; White, *Air Intercept Radar*, p. 7; Zuckerman, *Six Men*, pp. 18-21.

183 Frankland, review of Deighton, *Fighter*, TLS, 23 October 1977, p. 1265; Bushby, *Air Defence*, pp. 88-92.

184 Collier, *Leader*, pp. 152-3.

185 Hough & Richards, *Battle of Britain*, p. 332.

186 Smith, 'RAF' in *Burning Blue*, p. 28; Bushby, *Air Defence*, pp. 114-6.

187 *Signals*, vol. 5, p. 3.

188 *Signals*, vol. 5, pp. 14-15, 19-20.

189 Sir John Steel was first head of Bomber Command at Uxbridge, Sir Arthur Longmore of Coastal Command at Lee-on-Solent, near Gosport in Hampshire and Sir Charles Burnett of Training Command at Ternhill in Shropshire: *The Times*, 18 June 1936, p. 16; James, *Growth of Fighter Command*, pp. 22-3; Webster & Frankland, *Strategic Air Offensive*, vol. 1, p. 82.

190 Dean, *RAF and Two World Wars*, 66.

191 Lyall, 'Dowding', p. 207.

192 Ferris, 'Achieving Air Ascendancy', pp. 40-41 & 'Air Force Brats', p. 132.

193 Wykeham, *Fighter Command*, pp. 46-7.

194 Flint, *Dowding Headquarters*, pp. 37-40.

195 *The Times*, 24 August 1936, p. 6; ADM 196/50 pt. 1 (Arthur's service record).

196 Cranwell Papers.

197 Smith, 'RAF' in *Burning Blue*, pp. 26-7; Townsend, *Duel of Eagles*, pp. 144-6.

198 Lake & Schofield, 'Conservation' in *Burning Blue*, pp. 233-4.

199 AIR 2/2824; AIR 41/8, pp. 84-6; Hyde, *British Air Policy*, pp. 340-3.

200 *Flight*, 24 June 1937, p. 610.

201 Fitzsimons, *Purnell*, vol. 1, pp. 296-7 (Battle), vol. 3, pp. 698-700 (Defiant); Green, *Famous Fighters*, pp. 220-9 (Defiant); Smith, 'Planning and Building', pp. 48-51.

202 Smith, 'Planning and Building', pp. 44-5.

203 Orange, *Slessor*, p. 80; Hastings, *Bomber Command*, pp. 83-4; Hough & Richards, *Battle of Britain*, p. 29; Probert, *Bomber Harris*, pp. 88-9; Smith, 'Planning and Building', pp. 51-2, 60; Green & Swanborough, 'Hampden', pp. 244-52.

204 Wright, revised Goulter, 'Evill' in *Oxford DNB*, vol. 18, pp. 805-6. Sir Douglas Claude Strathern Evill was known, unofficially, in the service as 'Strath'.

205 Irving, *Rise and Fall*, p. 58; Hyde, *British Air Policy*, pp. 393-6.

206 AIR 41/8, pp. 72-8; Gilbert, *Churchill*, vol. 5, pp. 1017-18.

207 'Dowding History', pp. 60, 64-5; Balfour, *Westminster*, pp. 104-5.

208 Ritchie, *Industry and Air Power*.

209 James, *Growth of Fighter Command*, pp. 34-40.
210 Collier, *Leader*, pp. 165-6; Hough & Richards, *Battle of Britain*, pp. 56-7.
211 Biddle, *Rhetoric*, p. 90.
212 Biddle, *Rhetoric*, p. 125.
213 Smith, 'RAF' in *Burning Blue*, pp. 22-3; Orange, *Slessor*, pp. 49-50.
214 David Hunt, review of Deighton, *Battle of Britain*, in *Listener*, 25 September 1980, p. 407; Middlebrook & Everitt, *Bomber Command War Diaries*, pp 20-242.
215 AIR 2/1390.
216 AIR 2/1389.
217 AIR 8/214.
218 AIR 2/2615; Mason, *Hawker Hurricane*, p. 15.
219 Smith, 'Royal Air Force', 164-5.
220 Bond, *British Military Policy*, 257.
221 Greenwood, 'Caligula's Horse', pp. 17-38.
222 Smith, *British Air Strategy*, pp. 193-7.
223 Smith, 'Royal Air Force', pp. 166-171; *The Times*, 29 March 1938, p. 11.
224 Bond, *British Military Policy*, 257-64.
225 Collier, *Leader*, pp. 163-4.
226 AIR 2/3518.
227 Probert, *Bomber Harris*, p. 94.
228 Dowding Papers, AC71/17/6, Hendon.
229 Hyde, *British Air Policy*, pp. 494-5; Sweetman, 'Ellington' in *Oxford DNB*, vol. 18, pp. 158-9; Terraine, *Right of Line*, finds more merit in Ellington than other historians have: pp. 15-17, 23-36, 44-5, 682-4.
230 James, *Paladins*, p. 165.
231 Douglas with Wright, *Years of Command*, pp. 40-2, 94-5; Dean, *RAF in Two Wars*, p. 142.
232 Orange, *Slessor*, pp. 63-7; Dean, *RAF in Two Wars*, pp. 88-9.
233 Ritchie, 'A Political Intrigue'; Orange, *Slessor*, pp. 66-7. There are many papers written by Kingston-McCloughry in the Imperial War Museum, London.

In the opinion of a distinguished historian, Noble Frankland, there was more to Kingston-McCloughry, CB, CBE, DSO, DFC, than the ancient story of a disgruntled medium-rank officer convinced that his merits were under-valued and those of others over-valued. He was in fact 'a man of great ability, deep insights and ideas which were much in advance of his time.' On the other hand, added Frankland, he had 'a passion for intrigue or, as he would have put it, constructive criticism.' He reached air vice-marshal rank in 1947, but was the only officer of his promotion block still in that rank in 1953.

Whatever problems he had with his masters, he remains one of very few RAF officers to have made a significant mark as an author. His four valuable studies of aviation history, all published in

London by Jonathan Cape, seem not to have attracted the attention of RAF teachers and students that they deserve. They are *Winged Warfare: Air Problems of Peace and War* (1937), *War in Three Dimensions: The Impact of Air-Power upon the Classical Principles of War* (1949), *The Direction of War: A Critique of the Political Direction and High Command in War* (1955) and *Global Strategy* (1957).

234 Ludlow-Hewitt Papers, Air Historical Branch, Box 3.
235 Dowding Papers, AC71/17/4, Hendon.
236 Dowding Papers, AC71/17/5, Hendon.
237 Dowding Papers, AC71/17/7, Hendon; *The Times*, 25 February 1937, p. 10.
238 Dowding Papers, AC71/17/8, Hendon; AIR 2/300.
239 *Flight*, 1 July 1937, p.
240 AIR 2/2084; Lucas (ed.), *Wings of War*, pp. 183-4.
241 AIR 14/277.
242 Greenhous (& others), *Crucible of War*, vol. iii, pp. 168-9.
243 Bond, *British Armed Forces*, p. 119; AIR 2/2964.
244 AIR 2/2625.
245 Orange, 'Douglas' in *Oxford DNB*, vol. 16, pp. 713-7.
246 AIR 2/2964.
247 Orange, *Park*, pp. 69-70.
248 AIR 16/260.
249 Collier, *Leader*, pp. 167-8.
250 Collier, *Leader*, pp. 162-3.
251 Orange, *Park*, p. 94.
252 *The Times*, 19 July 1960, p. l5.
253 Obituary of Roberts in *The Times*, 7 May 1982, p. 12.
254 Orange, *Park*, p. 77; Air Ministry, *Origins*, p. 11; Hartcup, *Effect of Science*, 103.
255 Orange, *Park*, p. 76; Wykeham, *Fighter Command*, p. 52.
256 AIR 14/449.
257 *The Times*, 12 & 28 June 1937, pp. 16 & 11.
258 AIR 2/3029.
259 AIR 16/196.
260 AIR 14/449.
261 AIR 8/238.
262 AIR 16/677.
263 *The Times*, 30 June 1938, p. 4.
264 Gilbert, *Finest Hour*, pp. 554, 606, 1061.
265 AIR 2/3345.
266 AIR 2/1391, 1392.
267 AIR 2/2587; Zimmerman, *Britain's Shield*, pp. 169-70, 186-90.
268 Biddle, *Rhetoric*, pp. 89, 123; Stephens, *Knock-out Blow*, p. 28.
269 AIR 16/81; AIR 20/435.
270 Orange, *Park*, p. 73.
271 Orange, *Park*, pp. 73-4; Ludlow-Hewitt Papers, Box 3, Diaries, Air Historical Branch, Ministry of Defence.

272   Orange, *Park*, p. 74.
273   Sweetman, 'Bottomley' in *Oxford Dictionary*, vol. 6, pp. 770-2.
274   AIR 14/449; Probert, *Bomber Harris*, p. 86; obituary of Warrington-Morris in *The Times*, 26 & 30 March 1962, pp. 20 & 19.
275   Riding (ed.), *War in the Air*, no. 1, p. 2; Gilbert, *Finest Hour*, pp, 543-4; Pugh review of Parker, *Chamberlain* in *TLS*, 31 December 1993, p. 24.
276   Rowse, *All Souls*, p. 83.
277   Gilbert, *Finest Hour*, pp. 989-93; Maier, 'Luftwaffe' in *Burning Blue*, p. 17.
278   Lunn, 'The Man Who Won', p. 487.
279   Riding (ed.), *War in the Air*, vol. 3, p. 68.
280   Lumsden & Thetford, *Silver Wings*, pp. 138-221; Hough & Richards, *Battle of Britain*, pp. 58-9; Smith, *British Air Strategy*, pp. 214-5; Murray, 'German Air Power', pp. 107-117; AIR 2/2822.
281   *Illustrated Encyclopedia of Aircraft*, vols. 4 & 6, nos. 47 & 67, pp. 934-6 & 1326-32 (Blenheim), vol. 8, no. 85, pp. 1693-4 (Battle).
282   AIR 9/98; Collier, *Leader*, p. 170.
283   AIR 16/94.
284   Orange, *Park*, p. 77.
285   AIR 2/1393, 1394, 1646.
286   *The Times*, 4 & 14 August 1939, pp. 12 & 7; *Signals*, vol. 5, pp. 21-36, 71-104.
287   Orange, *Park*, pp. 68-9.
288   Orange, *Park*, pp. 148-9.
289   Zimmerman, *Britain's Shield*, pp. 191-3.
290   Bond, *British Military Policy*, pp. 274-5.
291   Hyde, *British Air Policy*, p. 422.
292   Smith, *British Air Strategy*, pp. 210-20; Ray, *Battle of Britain*, p. 23.
293   Harris & Hillmer, 'Development of the RAF', pp. 348-9.
294   AIR 41/8, 33-70.
295   Orange, *Slessor*, pp. 53-4; Smith, 'Royal Air Force', pp. 153-74; Hough & Richards, *Battle of Britain*, p. 60; Smith, 'RAF' in *Burning Blue*, p. 29.
296   Collier, *Leader*, pp. 171-3; Hough & Richards, *Battle of Britain*, p. 71.
297   AIR 16/261.
298   Orange, *Park*, p. 71.
299   Orange, *Park*, p. 72.
300   Dowding Papers, AC71/17/9, Hendon.
301   Dowding Papers, AC71/17/11-14, Hendon; Orange, *Slessor*, p. 64; obituary of Courtney in *The Times*, 25 October 1976, p. 15.
302   AIR 2/300.
303   Ray, *Battle*, p. 11; Gilbert, *Finest Hour*, pp. 657-8.
304   Ray, *Battle of Britain*, pp. 12-15; AIR 19/572; Dowding Papers, AC71/17/22, Hendon.

305 Ray, *Battle of Britain*, pp. 11-12; Orange, 'British Commanders', p. 33.

306 Dowding Papers, AC71/17/14, Hendon; AIR 19/572; Wright, *Dowding*, pp. 138-43, 158; 'Dowding History', p. 72; Townsend quoted this passage at the front of his autobiography, *Time and Chance*; Metzger & Coogan, *Companion to Bible*, pp. 697-9.

307 Wykeham, *Fighter Command*, p. 56

308 AIR 41/1, p. 204.

309 AIR 41/11, pp. 28-58, 170-1.

310 *Signals*, vol. 5, pp. 109-115; *Illustrated Encyclopedia of Aircraft*, vol. 4, no. 47, pp. 937-8 & vol. 5, no. 50, pp. 985-91; Green, *Famous Fighters*, pp. 51-6; Green & Swanborough, 'Beaufighter', pp. 25-32, 47; Flint, *Dowding and Headquarters*, p. 27; Bowen, *Radar Days*, pp. 69-72.

311 AIR 16/45.

312 Pile, *Ack Ack*, p. 11; Macksey, 'Pile' in *Oxford DNB*, vol. 44, pp. 307-8.

313 Pile, *Ack Ack*, p. 95; Bungay, *Most Dangerous Enemy*, p. 59.

314 Pile, *Ack Ack*, p. 96.

315 Pile, *London Gazette*, p. 5974.

316 Hogg, *Anti-Aircraft*, pp. 92, 99; Gilbert, *Finest Hour*, p. 191.

317 Zuckerman, *Six Men*, p. 22; Pile, *Ack Ack*, p. 100.

318 Hogg, *Anti Aircraft*, p. 103.

319 AIR 2/3518.

320 AIR 16/659.

321 Orange, *Park*, p. 80.

322 *Penguin Dictionary of Quotations*, p. 412.

323 Air Ministry, *Rise and Fall of German Air Force*, pp. 1-13.

324 Peach, *Neglected Turning Point*, pp. 147-8; Air Ministry, *Rise and Fall of German Air Force*, pp. 13-17.

325 Boog, 'Luftwaffe', in Addison & Crang (eds.), *Burning Blue*, p. 18.

326 Irving, *Göring*, p. 293; Overy, *Goering*, p. 224.

327 AIR 41/8, pp. 33-70.

328 Ray, *Battle of Britain*, pp. 44-5.

329 Price, 'Watching the Detectives', pp. 22-6; Wood with Dempster, *Narrow Margin*, pp. 10-11.

330 Zimmerman, *Britain's Shield*, pp. 205-8.

331 Irving, *Göring*, p. 279; Overy, *Goering*, pp. 102-3, 199, 241; Murray, *Luftwaffe*, pp. 13-15; Dye, 'Logistics', pp. 1-11.

332 Overy, *Goering*, pp. 106, 138.

333 Levine, 'World War II', pp. 43-6.

334 Smith, 'RAF' in Addison & Crang (eds.), *Burning Blue*, p. 35.

335 The title of an excellent account of the Battle by Wood with Dempster.

336 Irving, *Göring*, p. 291.

337 Cooper, *German Air Force*, pp. 7-23 on Goering, Wever & Milch; pp. 23-33 on Jeschonnek & Udet.

338 Irving, *Rise and Fall*, pp. 119-37.

339   Cooper, *German Air Force*, p. 33.
340   Wood with Dempster, *Narrow Margin*, pp. 20-1; Turner & Nowarra, *Junkers*, p. 109; Smith & Kay, *German Aircraft*, pp. 7 (Do 19), pp. 418-22 (Ju 89/90); Air Ministry, *Rise and Fall of German Air Force*, pp. 48-9; Murray, *Luftwaffe*, pp. 9-10, rejects the opinion of many historians that Wever's death caused the cancellation of these bombers, asserting that inadequate engine power was responsible.
341   Orange, 'Broad Margin', p. 66.
342   Irving, *Rise and Fall of the Luftwaffe*, pp. 142-3, 170-2; Cooper, *German Air Force*, pp. 66-73; Smith & Kay, pp. 200-07 (Fw 200), pp. 279-89, 305-6 (He 177/277); Brown, 'Condor', pp. 143-50.
343   Smith & Kay, *German Aircraft*, pp. 106-114 (Do 17), pp. 243-60 (He 111), pp. 370-8 (Ju 86), pp. 378-93 (Ju 87), pp. 394-417 (Ju 88); Brown, 'Ju 87', pp. 19-24.
344   Green, *Famous Fighters*, pp. 9-22 (Bf 109), pp. 261-6 (Bf 110); Smith & Kay, pp. 467-92 (Bf 109), pp. 493-505 (Bf 110); Wood, 'Emil', pp. 180-5, 196-200.
345   Orange, 'Broad Margin', pp. 68-69.
346   Smith & Kay, *German Aircraft*, pp. 162-5.
347   Mason, *Air Power*, p. 51.
348   Cox, 'Comparative Analysis', pp. 426-7, 435; Mason, *Air Power*, pp. 51-2.
349   Boog, 'Luftwaffe' in Addison & Crang (eds.), *Burning Blue*, pp. 46-8; Cox, 'Comparative Analysis', pp. 435-8.
350   Orange, 'British Commanders', pp. 1-3.
351   Boog, 'Luftwaffe', in Addison & Crang (eds.), *Burning Blue*, pp. 19-24.
352   Overy, Goering, pp. 170-2 & 'Significant' in Addison & Crang (eds.), *Burning Blue*, p. 268; Smith, 'RAF' in Addison & Crang (eds.), *Burning Blue*, p. 34.
353   Cox, 'Comparative Analysis', p. 438.
354   Zimmerman, *Britain's Shield*, p. 180.
355   Townsend, *Duel of Eagles*, p. 218.
356   Zimmerman, *Britain's Shield*, p. 175; Bishop, *Fighter Boys*, pp. 109-110.
357   Zimmerman, *Britain's Shield*, pp. 177-8.
358   AIR 16/12, 11; AIR 14/272, 273.
359   Wood, *Attack Warning Red*, pp. 69-70.
360   AIR 2/1646.
361   AIR 16/362.
362   Orange, *Park*, pp. 75-8; Orange, 'Leigh-Mallory' in *Oxford DNB*, vol. 36, pp. 345-7.
363   Orange, *Park*, pp. 80-1.
364   AIR 16/425.
365   Collier, *Leader*, pp. 183-4.
366   Smith, 'RAF' in Addison & Crang (eds.), *Burning Blue*, pp. 30-1; Penrose, *Ominous Skies*, p. 290.

367   AIR 16/677; Smith, 'RAF' in Addison & Crang (eds.), *Burning Blue*, pp. 29-30.
368   Signals, vol. 5, pp. 37-45.
369   Dean, *RAF in Two Wars*, p. 143; Hough & Richards, *Battle of Britain*, pp. 76-7; Gilbert, *Finest Hour*, p. 661.
370   James, *Growth of Fighter Command*, p. 72.
371   Irving, *Goering*, pp. 228, 280.
372   AIR 20/409.
373   James, *Growth of Fighter Command*, p. 73.
374   Smith, 'RAF' in Addison & Crang (eds.), *Burning Blue*, pp. 31-2; James, *Growth of Fighter Command*, pp. 53-5.
375   Hough & Richards, *Battle of Britain*, pp. 129-39.
376   AIR 16/30.
377   Collier, *Leader*, pp. 182-3; James, *Growth of Fighter Command*, pp. 55-9.
378   Orange, *Park*, pp. 81-2.
379   Orange, *Park*, p. 73.
380   Collier, *Leader*, pp. 184-7.
381   Dowding Papers, AC71/17/15, Hendon; Orange, *Park*, p. 82.
382   Zimmerman, *Britain's Shield*, pp. 170-2.
383   Zimmerman, *Britain's Shield*, pp. 172-3.
384   Orange, *Park*, pp. 77-8.
385   AIR 16/659.
386   AIR 14/449; Gilbert, *Finest Hour*, pp. 342-3; Webster & Frankland, *Strategic Air Offensive*, vol. 1, p. 138.
387   AIR 14/449; James, *Growth of Fighter Command*, appendix 10.
388   Murray, *Luftwaffe*, pp. 122-3; Murray & Millett (eds.), *Military Innovation*, pp. 120-1.
389   AIR 14/154.
390   Biddle, *Rhetoric*, pp. 185, 187.
391   Probert, *Bomber Harris*, pp. 98, 370.
392   Pallud, 'Norwegian Campaign', pp. 2-55; Hinsley (& others), *British Intelligence*, vol. 1, pp. 115-125; Air Ministry, *Rise and Fall of German Air Force*, pp. 57-64; Cooper, *German Air Force*, pp. 108-111.
393   AIR 16/677.
394   Terraine, *Right of Line*, p. 115.
395   Smith, 'RAF' in Addison & Crang (eds.), *Burning Blue*, p. 32; Hough & Richards, *Battle of Britain*, pp. 81-2; Claasen, *Hitler's Northern War*, pp. 62-140; Orange with Cross, *Straight and Level*, pp. 83-113; Orange, *Tedder*, p. 163; Murray, *Luftwaffe*, pp. 38-9.
396   Lucas (ed.), *Wings of War*, pp. 56-8, 61-2.
397   Riding (ed.), *War in the Air*, vol. 11, pp. 26 & 63.
398   Maier, 'Luftwaffe' in Addison & Crang (eds.), *Burning Blue*, p. 18; Air Ministry, *Rise and Fall of German Air Force*, pp. 65-73; Cooper, *German Air Force*, pp. 111-120.
399   Terraine, *Right of Line*, pp. 137-140 corrected some 'flights of fancy' regarding this meeting for which Dowding, Beaverbrook, A.

J. P. Taylor (*English History*, pp. 480, 485 & note) and Wright (*Dowding*, pp. 105-6) were jointly responsible; James, *Growth of Fighter Command*, pp. 88-9.

400 Wright, Dowding, p. 116; James, *Growth of Fighter Command*, pp. 90, 92-3, Dowding's letter is at Appendix 11, Newall's at Appendix 12.

401 Collier, *Leader*, p. 192; Gilbert, *Finest Hour*, pp. 352-4.

402 Orange, *Park*, pp. 84-5; Gilbert, *Finest Hour*, pp. 351-2; Lucas (ed.), *Wings of War*, p. 50.

403 Collier, *Leader*, pp. 192-4; Gilbert, *Finest Hour*, pp. 365-6; James, *Growth of Fighter Command*, Appendix 16.

404 *The Times*, 24 August 1981, p. 10; Hartcup, *Effect of Science*, p. 103.

405 Collier, *Leader*, pp. 190-1; Zimmerman, *Britain's Shield*, pp. 183-4.

406 Taylor, *English History*, p. 485n.

407 Ray, *Battle of Britain*, pp. 28-9; Muggleton Papers; Gilbert, *Finest Hour*, pp. 456-7.

408 Gunston, *Combat Aircraft*, p. 12 (Amiot), p. 22 (Bloch); Leyvastre, 'Bloch's Fighters', pp. 179-88, 204-5.

409 Green & Swanborough, 'Liore-et-Olivier 45', pp. 179-89.

410 Gunston, *Combat Aircraft*, p. 31 (Bréguet), 56 (Dewoitine), 166 (Morane-Saulnier); Green, *Fighters*, vol. 4, pp. 36-44 (Hawk 75A); *Illustrated Encyclopedia of Aircraft*, vols. 1-4, & 6, nos. 12, 14, 36, 37, 44, & 63, pp. 232, 264, 717-20, 734, 877-8, 1259-60.

411 May, *Strange Victory*, p. 450; Terraine, *Right of Line*, pp. 119-121; Cohen & Gooch, 'French Army and Air Force', pp. 197-230.

412 Young, *Strategic Dream*, p. 76; Robineau, 'French Inter-War Air Policy', pp. 627-57; Vennesson, 'Institution and Air Power', p. 53.

413 Millett & Murray, *Interwar Years*, vol. 2, pp. 49-53, 265; Peach, *Neglected Turning Point*, pp. 146, 149-60; May, *Strange Victory*, pp. 3-11, 357-61.

414 Omissi, *Air Power*, p. 31.

415 Taylor, *Boer War to Cold War*, pp. 372-4.

416 Smith & Kay, *German Aircraft*, pp. 357-70.

417 Salmond Papers, B/2638, Hendon.

418 Salmond Papers, Hendon, B/2638.

419 Gilbert, *Finest Hour*, pp. 407-8.

420 James, *Growth of Fighter Command*, pp. 93-5.

421 Orange, *Park*, p. 85.

422 Gilbert, *Finest Hour*, p. 419.

423 Orange, *Park*, pp. 85-6.

424 Smith, 'RAF' in Addison & Crang (eds.), *Burning Blue*, pp. 33-4; Zimmerman, *Britain's Shield*, p. 195.

425 Orange, *Park*, p. 86.

426 Orange, *Park*, p. 86.

427 Orange, *Park*, p. 87; Balfour, *Aeroplane Monthly*, September 1988, pp. 570-1.

428 AIR 16/870; AIR 2/5251.

429 Reynolds, *Command*, pp. 170-1; Terraine, *Right of Line*, p. 159; Calvocoressi (& others), *Total War*, p. 137.
430 Orange, *Park*, pp. 87-8.
431 Ramsay, *Evacuation*.
432 James, *Growth of Fighter Command*, pp. 95-6.
433 AIR 16/1170-3.
434 Gilbert, *Finest Hour*, p. 430.
435 Orange, *Park*, pp. 88-9; Ramsay, *Evacuation*, p. 3297.
436 Terraine, *Right of Line*, pp. 162-3; Bishop, *Fighter Boys*, pp. 216-8.
437 Orange, *Park*, p. 89; Gilbert, *Finest Hour*, pp. 447-8, 466; Smith, 'RAF' in Addison & Crang (eds.), *Burning Blue*, pp. 34-5; Ray, *Battle of Britain*, pp. 39-40.
438 Orange, *Park*, pp. 89-90; AIR 2/7468; Gilbert, *Finest Hour*, vol. vi, p. 1135.
439 Liddell Hart Papers, LH 1/245/6.
440 Gilbert, *Finest Hour*, pp. 548, 564, 571.
441 Overy, 'Significant' in Addison & Crang (eds.), *Burning Blue*, p. 269.
442 Zimmerman, *Britain's Shield*, pp. 195-6; Air Ministry, *Rise and Fall of German Air Force*, pp. 75-91; Cooper, *German Air Force*, pp. 121-60.
443 Green & Swanborough, 'Bf 110', pp. 26-33, 240-7, 283-9.
444 Overy, *Goering*, p. 104; Bond, 'Introduction' in Addison & Crang (eds.), *Burning Blue*, p. 2; Schenk, 'Sealion', pp. 1-19.
445 Maier, 'Luftwaffe' p. 19, Boog, 'Luftwaffe', p. 40 & Cox, 'RAF's Response', pp. 57-8, all in Addison & Crang (eds.), *Burning Blue*; Taylor, *Breaking Wave*, p. 139.
446 Collier, *Defence*, pp. 163-250 (survey from July to October 1940); see his 'Summary of Operations', 10 July-12 August, pp. 450-1 & 13 August-6 September, pp. 456-60 & 7 September-31 October, pp. 491-2.
447 Bond, 'Introduction' in Addison & Crang (eds.), *Burning Blue*, p. 3.
448 Wood with Dempster, *Narrow Margin*, p. 358; Ramsey, *Battle of Britain*, pp. 254-9.
449 Cox, 'RAF's Response' in Addison & Crang (eds.), *Burning Blue*, p. 62; Bishop, *Fighter Boys*, p. 398, but no figures, here or elsewhere, are guaranteed to be entirely accurate.
450 Orange, *Park*, pp. 118-9; figures slightly amended in Terraine, *Right of Line*, p. 219 & in Ramsey, *Battle of Britain*, pp. 706-7.
451 Colville, *Fringes of Power*, p. 194.
452 *Signals*, vol. 5, pp. 45-54.
453 Orange, 'British Commanders', p. 38.
454 Preston, *Key to Victory*, pp. 20, 27-8; Dick, *Battle of Britain*, p. 16.
455 Boog, 'Luftwaffe & Battle of Britain' in Probert & Cox (eds.), *The Battle Re-Thought*, p. 24; readers should be wary of exact figures in this or any other book on the Battle of Britain.
456 C. J. B. Joseph, 'Brand' in *Oxford DNB*, vol. 7, pp. 343-4; Collier, *Leader*, pp. 204-6; Orange, *Park*, p. 91.

457 Terraine, *Right of Line*, p. 184.
458 Zimmerman, *Britain's Shield*, pp. 199-200.
459 Zimmerman, *Britain's Shield*, pp. 196-200.
460 Orange, *Park*, p. 95; Hinsley (& others), *British Intelligence*, vol. 1, p. 178; Thomas, 'Intelligence Aspect', pp. 42, 45; Boog, 'Luftwaffe & Battle of Britain' in Probert & Cox (eds.), *Battle Re-Thought*, p. 25; Zimmerman, *Britain's Shield*, pp. 197-8; Cox, 'Sources and Organization', pp. 432-3.
461 Cox, 'Sources and Organization', p. 553 & 'A Comparative Analysis', pp. 425-6; Wark, 'British Intelligence', p. 647 & *Ultimate Enemy*, pp. 63-5; Orange, *Slessor*, pp. 54-8.
462 Hinsley (& others), *British Intelligence*, vol. 1, pp. 28-30, 136, 171, 496-9.
463 Cox, 'Comparative Analysis', p. 428; Calvocoressi (& others), *Total War*, pp. 146-7.
464 Orange, 'German Air Force', pp. 1011-28; Hinsley (& others), *British Intelligence*, vol. 1, pp. 60-1.
465 Murray, 'Appeasement', pp. 55-6; Wark, 'British Intelligence', p. 642; Hinsley (& others), *British Intelligence*, vol. 1, pp. 78-9. The four-engined Focke Wulf Fw 200 Condor was used only over the Atlantic.
466 Gilbert, *Churchill: 1922-39*, pp. 881, 635n, 556n; Wark, *Ultimate Enemy*, pp. 244-5; these are round numbers – more precise numbers are suspect.
467 Gilbert, *Finest Hour*, pp. 654-5; Cox, 'Comparative Analysis', pp. 429-30.
468 Gilbert, *Finest Hour*, pp. 848-9.
469 Orange, *Park*, pp. 94-5; Lewin, review of Deighton, *Fighter* in *The Times*, 12 October 1977, p. 20; Wood, *Attack Warning Red*, p. 73.
470 Orange, *Park*, p. 94.
471 AIR 16/21.
472 AIR 2/919, 920.
473 AIR 16/1017.
474 AIR 16/659.
475 Pile, *Ack Ack*, pp. 95-6.
476 *The Times*, 1 June 1945, p. 5; Collier, *Leader*, pp. 200-3; AIR 19/162; Muggleton Papers.
477 Banks, *Diary*, pp. 141-2.
478 Wykeham, *Fighter Command*, p. 116.
479 Orange, *Tedder*, pp. 110-115; Terraine, *Right of Line*, pp. 191-2; Balfour, *Westminster*, pp. 125-7; Robertson, 'Lord Beaverbrook', pp. 80-100.
480 Noble Frankland, review of Deighton, *Fighter*, in *TLS*, 23 October 1977, p. 1265; Terraine, *Right of Line*, pp. 190-1.
481 'Dowding History', p. 70.
482 Wood with Dempster, *Narrow Margin*, pp. 143-4.
483 Cox, 'RAF's Response' in Addison & Crang (eds.), *Burning Blue*, pp. 61-2; Ritchie, 'Wilfrid Freeman', pp. 252-63.

484 Dye, 'Logistics and the Battle of Britain', pp. 1-11.
485 *llustrated Encyclopedia of Aircraft*, surveys the day and night battle: vol. 2, nos. 21-24, pp. 401-5, 421-5, 441-5, 461-5, vol. 3, no. 25, pp. 481-5.
486 Orange, *Park*, pp. 97-8; Cox, 'RAF's Response' in Addison & Crang (eds.), *Burning Blue*, pp. 56-7; Bishop, *Fighter Boys*, pp. 233-6.
487 Orange, *Park*, p. 98.
488 Higham, 'Royal Air Force', pp. 159-64. A number of raids were made by Blenheims on air fields in France, but there was no systematic campaign, and only small numbers were so employed: Middlebrook & Everitt, *Bomber Command War Diaries*, pp 56-91.
489 Bungay, *Most Dangerous Enemy*, pp. 193-4.
490 Bungay, *Most Dangerous Enemy*, pp. 195-200.
491 Colville, *Fringes of Power*, pp. 245-6; Brown, *Airmen in Exile*, pp. 204-5, 208; Zamoyski, *Forgotten Few*, pp. 58, 66, 75, 92, 97.
492 Brown, *Airmen in Exile*, pp. 204-5, 208; Bungay, *Most Dangerous Enemy*, pp. 173-4; Bishop, *Fighter Boys*, pp. 241-2.
493 Cox, 'RAF's Response' in Addison & Crang (eds.), *Burning Blue*, pp. 58-9.
494 Orange, *Park*, pp. 99-100; Price, *Hardest Day*; Terraine, *Right of Line*, p. 189.
495 Orange, *Park*, pp. 100-1.
496 Gilbert, *Finest Hour*, pp. 735-6; Townsend, *Duel*, pp. 365-6.
497 Claasen, *Hitler's Northern War*, pp. 164-9; Levine, *World War II*, pp. 43-6.
498 Orange, *Park*, pp. 101-2.
499 Always known as 'Mary', a nickname worn down from 'Maori', given to him during the Great War even though he was an Australian-born New Zealander: Orange, *Coningham*, pp. 18, 194-210.
500 Orange, *Park*, p. 102.
501 Boog, ' Luftwaffe' in Addison & Crang (eds.), *Burning Blue*, p. 48.
502 Colville, *Fringes of Power*, p. 235.
503 Wright, revised Goulter, 'Evill' in *Oxford DNB*, vol. 18, pp. 805-6.
504 Bishop, *Fighter Boys*, p. 288.
505 Orange, *Park*, pp. 104-5.
506 Probert, *High Commanders*, p. 34.
507 Orange, 'Douglas' in *Oxford DNB*, vol. 16, pp. 713-7.
508 Cox, 'RAF's Response' in Addison & Crang (eds.), *Burning Blue*, pp. 60-1.
509 Orange, *Park*, pp. 104-6.
510 Higham, 'Royal Air Force', pp. 144-7.
511 Orange, *Park*, p. 106.
512 Probert, *Bomber Harris*, p. 109; Orange, *Park*, pp. 106-7.
513 Orange, *Park*, p. 99; AIR 16/1067, AIR 2/7355.
514 Price, 'Battle of Britain Day', pp. 5-23; Orange, *Park*, pp. 108-111; Collier, *Defence*, p. 429.

515   Orange, *Park*, p. 83.
516   Orange, *Park*, p. 120.
517   Lucas, 'Bader' in *Oxford DNB*, vol. 3, pp. 196-8 & *Flying Colours*.
518   Orange, *Park*, pp. 120-1.
519   AIR 16/903.
520   Orange, *Park*, pp. 121-2.
521   Orange, *Park*, p. 123.
522   Orange, *Park*, p. 121.
523   Orange, *Park*, p. 138
524   Orange, *Park*, pp. 125-6.
525   Orange, *Park*, p. 127.
526   Orange, *Park*, pp. 127-9.
527   Orange, *Park*, p. 149; Wright, revised by Goulter, 'Evill' in *Oxford DNB*, vol. 18, pp. 805-6.
528   Riding (ed.), *War in the Air*, vol. 11, p. 62.
529   AIR 2/7281.
530   Orange, *Park*, pp. 129-30.
531   Mason, *Battle over Britain*, p. 248; Higham, 'Royal Air Force', p. 130.
532   Orange, *Park*, pp. 107-8; Bond, 'Introduction' in Addison & Crang (eds.), *Burning Blue*, pp. 3, 4; Air Ministry, *Rise and Fall of German Air Force*, pp. 91-6; Ray, *Night Blitz*, pp. 13-20; Collier, *Defence*, pp. 261-81; see also his 'Night Attacks on London', 7 September-13 November, pp. 494-8 & 'Notable Night Attacks on United Kingdom Cities', 14 November-16 May 1941, pp. 503-5.
533   Cooper, *German Air Force*, pp. 164-5.
534   Ray, *Night Blitz*, pp.
535   AIR 2/3075; Chaz Bowyer, *Beaufighter*, pp. 38-62.
536   Orange, *Park*, pp. 115-6.
537   AIR 2/7337; Orange, *Park*, p. 116.
538   *Signals*, vol. 5, pp. 117-24; White, *Air Intercept Radar*, p. 38; Zimmerman, 'British Radar', pp. 86-106.
539   Zimmerman, *Britain's Shield*, pp. 214-224; White, *Air Intercept Radar*, p. 38.
540   AIR 16/387; AIR 2/7341; Zimmerman, *Britain's Shield*, p. 210; Ray, *Night Blitz*, pp. 114-5.
541   Salmond Papers, B/2638, Hendon; Gilbert (ed.), *Churchill Papers*, vol. 2, p. 903.
542   Gilbert (ed.), *Churchill Papers*, vol. 2, pp. 907-9, 939.
543   Wykeham, *Fighter Command*, p. 138.
544   Collier, *Leader*, pp. 216-7.
545   Orange, *Park*, p. 117.
546   AIR 16/676; Zimmerman, *Britain's Shield*, pp. 212-3.
547   Dowding Papers, AC71/17/26, Hendon; Gilbert, *Finest Hour*, pp. 841-2.
548   Zimmerman, *Britain's Shield*, pp. 213-4; Ray, *Night Blitz*, pp. 123-4.
549   AIR 16/635.

550 Wykeham, *Fighter Command*, p. 50.
551 Wood, 'The Dowding System', pp. 3-10; Hough & Richards, *Battle of Britain*, pp. 328-30.
552 Murray, *Luftwaffe*, p. 293; Bungay, *Most Dangerous Enemy*, p. 60.
553 Gilbert, *Finest Hour*, pp. 881-2; Reynolds, *Command*, p. 175; Overy, 'Significant' in Addison & Crang (eds.), *Burning Blue*, p. 278.
554 Boog, 'Luftwaffe' in Addison & Crang (eds.), *Burning Blue*, pp. 48-51.
555 Calvocoressi (& others), *Total War*, p. 158; Orange, 'British Commanders', p. 37.
556 Bungay, *Most Dangerous Enemy*, pp. 380-1.
557 Orange, *Park*, pp. 136-7, 140; Haslam, 'Dowding', pp. 175-86; Ray, *Battle of Britain*, p. 10; Balfour, *Wings over Westminster*, pp. 132-5; AIR 19/258; letters to *The Times*, 14-22 January 1970 by Slessor, Dowding, R. V. Jones, Wright and especially A. J. P Taylor.
558 Muggleton Papers; Zimmerman, *Britain's Shield*, p. 211; Wilson, *Snow Crazy*, chap. 26.
559 Flint, *Dowding Headquarters*, pp. 187-8.
560 Wood, *Attack Warning Red*, pp. 101, 110-112.
561 Wykeham, *Fighter Command*, p. 145.
562 Collier, *Defence*, p. 266.
563 Wood with Dempster, *Narrow Margin*; *The Times*, 12 September 1947, p. 7.
564 Balfour, *Westminster*, pp. 132-7; Lewin, review of Deighton, *Fighter*, in *The Times*, 13 October 1977, p. 20.
565 Zimmerman, *Britain's Shield*, p. 226.
566 White, *Air Intercept Radar*, p. 25.
567 Wykeham, *Fighter Command*, p. 131.
568 Lyall, 'Dowding', pp. 207 & 212; Orange, *Park*, pp. 135-6.
569 Cox, 'RAF's Response' in Addison & Crang (eds.), *Burning Blue*, p. 62.
570 Collier, *Leader*, pp. 11-12.
571 AIR 2/7415; Gilbert, *Finest Hour*, pp. 914-5; Ray, *Night Blitz*, pp. 150-8.
572 Frankland, review of Deighton, *Fighter*, TLS, 23 October 1977, p. 1265.
573 Stafford, *Endgame 1945*, p. 466.
574 Bungay, *Most Dangerous Enemy*, pp. 386-7; Ray, *Battle of Britain*, p. 49.
575 Cooper, *German Air Force*, pp. 162-3.
576 Richards, *Fight at Odds*, p. 195.
577 Bond, 'Introduction' in Addison & Crang (eds.), *Burning Blue*, p. 1.
578 Gilbert, *Finest Hour*, vi, pp. 1060-1.
579 Douglas, 'Air Operations', p. 5021; AIR 16/368; Terraine, *Right of Line*, pp. 283-4.
580 Higham, 'Royal Air Force', p. 138.
581 AIR 16/622.

582 Collier, *Defence of United Kingdom*, pp. 273-4.
583 Douglas, 'Air Operations', p. 5025; Collier, *Defence of United Kingdom*, p. 290.
584 Boog, 'Luftwaffe & Battle of Britain', p. 31.
585 Ray, *Night Blitz*, pp. 150-8.
586 *Signals*, pp. 125-33; Cooper, *German Air Force*, pp. 164-5, 173.
587 Orange, *Park*, pp. 138-9; Collier, *Defence of United Kingdom*, pp. 290-1; AIR 41/18, part 5, para. 120; AIR 16/373.
588 AIR 41/18, part 5, para. 120; Collier, *Defence*, pp. 294-5; Bishop, *Fighter Boys*, pp. 390-1; Cox, 'Comparative Analysis', p. 434.
589 Orange, *Park*, p. 138; AIR 16/373; AIR 41/18, part 4, paras. 93-4.
590 AIR 16/366; Collier, *Defence of United Kingdom*, p. 291; Douglas, 'Air Operations', p. 5025; Bishop, *Fighter Boys*, pp. 390-1 & 394-6; Terraine, *Right of Line*, pp. 282-8.
591 Muggleton Papers; Orange, 'Douglas', *Oxford DNB*, vol. 16, pp. 713-7.
592 AIR 19/572; Gilbert, *Finest Hour*, pp. 908-9.
593 Except where noted, information about the American trip is drawn from 'Dowding History', pp. 72-6.
594 *Washington Post*, 31 December 1940, p. 5; Green & Swanborough, 'The Handy Hudson', pp. 240-63.
595 Papers of Ski Club of Great Britain, via Elizabeth Hussey.
596 *New York Times*, 8 January 1941, p. 7.
597 *Washington Post*, 8 January 1941, p. 3.
598 *Washington Post*, 23 January 1941, p. 11.
599 *Washington Post*, 26 March 1941, p. 18.
600 *New York Times*, 27 February 1941, p. 9; *Time Magazine*, 10 March 1941, p. 1.
601 Hallion, 'American Perspective' in Addison & Crang (eds.), *Burning Blue*, pp. 100-102.
602 White, *Air Intercept Radar*, pp. 142-3; Bowen, *Radar Days*, pp. 185-6.
603 Dowding Papers, AC71/17/27, Hendon; AIR 8/348.
604 Taylor, *English History*, p. 379; Roberts, *Holy Fox*, pp. 272-90; Rowse, *All Souls*, pp. 65 & 116.
605 'Dowding History', pp. 83-4.
606 AIR 8/348.
607 'Dowding History', p. 78.
608 Gilbert, *Finest Hour*, pp. 1040, 1101.
609 Dowding, *London Gazette*; Liddell Hart Papers, LH 1/245/2.
610 Dowding Papers, AC71/17/28-30, Hendon.
611 Hough & Richards, *Battle of Britain*, p. 332.
612 Muggleton Papers; Orange, *Park*, p. 142.
613 Cox, 'Comparative Analysis', p. 439.
614 AIR 2/7772; AIR 8/863.
615 Dowding Papers, AC71/17/31-3, Hendon; Muggleton Papers.
616 AIR 19/572; Muggleton Papers.
617 Collier, *Leader*, pp. 236-8; AIR 8/609; Dowding Papers,

AC71/17/35-7, Hendon.

618 'Dowding History', pp. 76-7; for what follows, see AIR 19/313; AIR 2/5381, 4807, 5384, 5537; AIR 8/609; Probert, *Bomber Harris*, p. 109.

619 Orange, *Slessor*, p. 28; Richards, *Portal*, p. 221; Portal Papers, Oxford, Box C, Folder 4; Probert, *Forgotten Air Force*, pp. 83-94, 122.

620 AIR 19/572.

621 AIR 19/572.

622 Flint, *Dowding Headquarters*, pp. 193-4.

623 Collier, *Leader*, pp. 233-6; Dowding Papers, AC71/17/47-8.

624 Ray, *Battle of Britain*, p. 7; Zimmerman, *Britain's Shield*, pp. 229-32.

625 Balfour, *Wings over Westminster*, p. 132.

626 Dowding Papers, AC71/17/39, Hendon; Muggleton Papers; Green, *Famous Fighters*, pp. 35-41.

627 Dowding Papers, AC71/17/40.

628 PREM 3/20/8.

629 Fitzsimons, *Purnell*, vol. 8, pp. 2414-5; *Illustrated Encyclopedia of Aircraft*, vol. 2, no. 17, pp. 326-33; Green & Swanborough, 'A More Violent Hurricane', pp. 91-8; Banks, *Diary*, pp. 134-9.

630 AIR 8/863; Dowding Papers, AC71/17/40-45.

631 Gregory, 'Commemoration' in Addison & Crang (eds.), *Burning Blue*, p. 217.

632 Hough & Richards, *Battle of Britain*, p. 239; obituary of Elspeth Green, formerly Henderson, in *Weekly Telegraph*, 12 September 2004, p. 12.

633 Much of what follows, except when footnotes indicate otherwise, derives from Dowding's Papers, AC71/17/59-63.

634 Lumsden & Thetford, *Silver Wings*, pp. 138-9; *Illustrated Encyclopedia of Aircraft*, vol. 8, no. 85, pp. 1689-9.

635 ADMY 1-29524, 29479, 29877.

636 Lunn Papers, Box 2, Folder 30, Georgetown.

637 Liddell Hart Papers, LH 1/245/1.

638 'Dowding History', p. 76.

639 Dowding, *Twelve Legions*, pp. 7-12.

640 Dowding, *Twelve Legions*, pp. 13-62.

641 Some of this appeared in the *Sunday Chronicle*, 6 December 1942: Liddell Hart Papers, LH 1/245/23.

642 Liddell Hart Papers, LH 1/245/16 & 18.

643 Ray, *Battle of Britain*, pp. 189-90.

644 'Dowding History', pp. 78-80; Booth, *Doctor, Detective*, pp. 309-54; Stashower, *Teller of Tales*, pp. 333-363.

645 Liddell Hart Papers, LH 1/245/36, 37 & 38.

646 *Lychgate*, pp. 5-13, 23-4. 38-9, 57-9, 102-3.

647 'Dowding History', pp. 80-81.

648 Barclay, *Smoke Trails*, p. 204.

649 Haresnape, *Bulleid*, pp. 56, 62, 110 & 125; *The Times*, 12

September 1947, p. 7.

650 'Dowding History', p. 81.

651 *The Book of London*, p. 40.

652 Chorley, *Bomber Command Losses*, vol. 9, p. 233.

653 *Kent & Sussex Courier*, 17 June 1994.

654 Muriel's autobiography, *Beauty – Not the Beast*, pp. 102-3.

655 Muriel Dowding, *Beauty*, pp. 89-90.

656 *The Times*, 12 & 13 September 1960, pp. 4 & 12.

657 Muriel Dowding, *Beauty*, frontispiece & pp. 181-2.

658 Muggleton Papers.

659 Gregory, 'Commemorations' in Addison & Crang (eds.), *Burning Blue*, pp. 217-8, 224-5, 227.

660 Wright, Dowding, p. 281; Mosley, *Making of a Film*.

661 Liddell Hart Papers, LH 1/245/42.

662 Wilson, *Snow Crazy*, chap. 26; T. F. Burns, 'Lunn' in *Oxford Dictionary*, vol. 34, pp. 769-70; Lunn, 'The Man Who Won', pp. 487-8.

663 Lunn Papers, Box 2, Folder 30, Georgetown.

664 Lunn Papers, Box 2, Folder 30, Georgetown.

665 K. Entwistle, 'Bowden' in *Oxford DNB*, vol. 6, pp. 884-5.

666 Muriel Dowding, *Beauty*, p. 185.

667 Ramsey (ed.), *Battle of Britain*, pp. 254-9.

668 AIR 20/12214; Gregory, 'Commemoration' in Addison & Crang (eds.), *Burning Blue*, pp. 220-1, 227; Muriel Dowding, *Beauty*, p. 188; memorial service in *The Times*, 13 March 1970, pp. 10 & 12.

669 *The Times*, 16 February 1970, pp. 1 & 10.

670 Dowding Papers, 76/74/1440, Hendon; *Guardian* obituary in Liddell Hart Papers, LH 1/245/65; Reynolds, *Command*, pp. 2, 187-8.

671 *The Times*, 14 July 1990, p. 12.

672 Orange, *Park*, p. 263.

673 Fozard (ed.), *Sydney Camm*, pp. 19-20, 24; Mason, *Hawker Hurricane*, p. 63; Fitzsimons, *Purnell*, vol. 5, pp. 1337-40; Postan (& others), *Design & Development*, pp. 86-91; Wykeham, 'Camm' in *Oxford DNB*, vol. 9, pp. 671-3.

674 *Daily Telegraph*, 15 September 2005, pp. 20-1; Ritchie, 'Mitchell' in *Oxford DNB*, vol. 38, pp. 432-3.

675 Hough & Richards, *Battle of Britain*, pp. 34-5, 387; Lewis, *British Fighter*, pp. 247-9; Mason, *Hawker Hurricane*, p. 44; Lord Kings Norton, revised by Robin Higham, 'Hives' in *Oxford DNB*, vol. 27, pp. 338-9.

676 Papers of Ski Club of Great Britain via Elizabeth Hussey.

677 Ray, *Battle of Britain*, p. 7.

678 Terraine, *Right of Line*, p. 684; Wykeham, *Fighter Command*, p. 147.

679 Terraine, *Right of Line*, p. 684.

Bibliography and Sources

UNPUBLISHED

British National Archives (formerly Public Record Office, Kew, London: numerous references in AIR 1, 2, 5, 8, 14, 16, 19, 20, 23, 30, 41, 76; also ADM papers for Vice-Admiral Sir Arthur Dowding.

Churchill, Sir Winston: papers in PREM 3, British National Archives, London.

Cranwell, papers in the RAF College, Cranwell, Lincolnshire.

Dowding, ACM Lord: History, 84-page manuscript written by Lord Dowding in 1956 to assist Basil Collier with his biography and later also used by Robert Wright, now at the Air Historical Branch, Ministry of Defence, London; papers in RAF Museum, Hendon, London; papers in private possession of Simon Muggleton and David Whiting; papers in Ski Club of Great Britain, courtesy of Elizabeth Hussey.

Liddell Hart, Sir Basil: correspondence with Dowding in Liddell Hart Centre for Military Archives, King's College, London.

Ludlow-Hewitt, ACM Sir Edgar: papers in Air Historical Branch, Ministry of Defence, London.

Lunn, Sir Arnold: papers in Georgetown University Library, Washington DC.

Portal, MRAF Lord: papers in Christ Church, Oxford.

Salmond, MRAF Sir John: papers in RAF Museum, Hendon, London.

Trenchard, MRAF Lord: papers in RAF Museum, Hendon, London.

Winchester College, papers and photographs.

BOOKS AND ARTICLES

Addison, Paul & Jeremy A. Crang (eds.), *The Burning Blue* (London: Pimlico, 2000)

Andrews, C. F. & E. B. Morgan, *Supermarine Aircraft since 1914* (London: Putnam, 1981)

Air Ministry FS Publication 136, *A Short History of the Royal Air Force* (Air Historical Branch, June 1920)

Air Ministry, *The Battle of Britain: An Air Ministry Account of the Great Days from 8 August to 31 October 1940* (London: HMSO, 1941)

Air Ministry, *The Battle of Britain: Air Ministry Pamphlet 156* (Department of the Air Member for Training, August 1943)

Air Ministry Air Publication 3368, *The Origins and Development of*

Operational Research in the Royal Air Force (London: HMSO, 1963)

Air Ministry, *Signals: Fighter Control & Interception, vol. 5* (London: HMSO, 1950)

Air Ministry, *The Rise and Fall of the German Air Force, 1933-1945* (London: Arms & Armour, 1983)

Ashmore, Major-General Edward, *Air Defence* (London: Longmans, 1929)

Ashmore, Major-General Edward, in *Oxford DNB*, vol. 2, pp. 656-6 by Robin Higham

Austin, A. B., *Fighter Command* (London: Gollancz, 1941)

Bader, Group Captain Sir Douglas in *Oxford DNB*, vol. 3, pp. 196-8 by P. B. Lucas

Baker, W. J., *A History of the Marconi Company* (London: Methuen, 1970)

Balfour, Harold (Lord Balfour of Inchrye), *Wings over Westminster* (London: Hutchinson, 1973)

Banks, Air Commodore F. R. (Rod) Banks, *I Kept No Diary: 60 Years with Marine Diesels, Automobile and Aero Engines* (Shrewsbury: Airlife, 1978, revised ed., 1983)

Barclay, Anthony, *Smoke Trails in the Sky* (London: Kimber, 1984)

Barker, Ralph, *The Royal Flying Corps in France: From Mons to the Somme* (London: Constable, 1994)

Beaumont, Roger A., 'A New Lease on Empire: Air Policing, 1919-1939' in *Aerospace Historian*, vol. 26, no. 2 (Summer/June 1979) pp. 84-90

Bennett, Ralph, *Behind the Battle: Intelligence in the War with Germany, 1939-1945* (London: Pimlico, 1999)

Bialer, Uri, '"Humanization" of Air Warfare in British Foreign Policy on the Eve of the Second World War' in *Journal of Contemporary History*, vol. xiii (1978) pp. 79-86

Bialer, Uri, *The Shadow of the Bomber: The Fear of Air Attack and British Politics, 1932-1939* (London: Royal Historical Society, 1980)

Biddle, Tami Davis, *Rhetoric and Reality in Air Warfare: The Evolution of British and American Ideas about Strategic Bombing, 1914-1945* (Princeton University Press, 2002)

Bishop, Patrick, *Fighter Boys: The Battle of Britain, 1940* (London: Penguin, 2003)

Bond, Brian, 'Dunkirk: Myths and Lessons' in *RUSI Journal*, vol. 127, no. 3 (September 1982) pp. 3-7

Bond, Brian, 'Introduction' in Addison & Crang (eds.), *The Burning Blue*, pp. 1-21

Bond, Brian & Williamson Murray, 'The British Armed Forces, 1918-1939' in Millett & Murray, *Military Effectiveness*, vol. 2, pp. 98-130

Bond, Brian, *British Military Policy between the Two World Wars* (Oxford: Clarendon Press, 1980)

Boog, Horst (ed.), *The Conduct of the Air War in the Second World War: An International Comparison* [proceedings of a conference in Freiburg im Breisgau, August/September 1988] (New York/Oxford: Berg, 1992)

Boog, Horst, 'The Luftwaffe and the Battle of Britain' in Probert & Cox (eds.), *The Battle Re-Thought*, pp. 18-32

Boog, Horst, 'The Luftwaffe's Assault' in Addison & Crang (eds.), *The*

Burning Blue, pp. 39-54

Booth, Martin, *The Doctor, The Detective and Arthur Conan Doyle* (London: Hodder & Stoughton, 1997)

Bott, Alan, *An Airman's Outings with the RFC, June-December 1916* (1917; reprinted Elstree, Herts.: Greenhill Books, 1986)

Bottomley, ACM Sir Norman, in *Oxford DNB*, vol. 6, pp. 770-2 by John Sweetman

Bowden of Chesterfield, Lord, in *Oxford DNB*, vol. 6, pp. 884-5 by K. Entwistle

Bowen, E. G., *Radar Days* (Bristol: Hilger, 1987)

Bowyer, Chaz, *Beaufighter* (London: Kimber, 1987)

Boyle, Andrew, *Trenchard: Man of Vision* (London: Collins, 1962)

Brabazon of Tara, Lord, *The Brabazon Story* (London: Heinemann, 1956)

Brancker, Sir Sefton, in *Oxford DNB*, vol. 7, pp. 331-3 by Robin Higham

Brand, AVM Sir Christopher, in *Oxford DNB*, vol. 7, pp. 343-4 by C. J. B. Joseph

Bridgman, Leonard, with a commentary by Oliver Stewart, *The Clouds Remember: The Aeroplanes of World War I* (London: 1936; Arms & Armour, reprint 1972)

Brown, Alan, *Airmen in Exile: The Allied Air Forces in the Second World War* (Stroud, Gloucester: Sutton, 2000)

Brown, Captain Eric, RN, 'Ju 87: Assessing an Anachronism' in *Air International*, vol. 7, no. 1 (July 1974) pp. 19-24

Brown, Captain Eric, RN, 'Condor: An Elegant Improvisation' in *Air International*, vol. 7, no. 3 (September 1974) pp. 143-50

Brown, Captain Eric, RN, 'Blackburn's Ill-fated Duo: The Skua and Roc' in *Air International*, vol. 13, no. 5 (November 1977) pp. 231-8

Bruce, J. M., *The Aeroplanes of the Royal Flying Corps (Military Wing)* (London: Putnam, 1982)

Buckley, John, *Air Power in the Age of Total War* (Bloomington: Indiana University Press, 1999)

Bungay, Stephen, *The Most Dangerous Enemy* (London: Aurum, 2001)

Bushby, John R., *The Air Defence of Great Britain* (London: Allan, 1974)

Calvocoressi, Peter (& others), *Total War: The Causes and Course of the Second World War* (London: Viking, revised 2nd ed., 1989)

Camm, Sir Sidney, in *Oxford DNB*, vol. 9, pp. 671-3 by Peter Wykeham

Chorley, W. R., *Royal Air Force Bomber Command Losses, vol. 9* (Midland Publishing, 2007)

Claasen, Adam R. A., *Hitler's Northern War: The Luftwaffe's Ill-Fated Campaign, 1940-1945* (University of Kansas, 2001)

Clark, Ronald W., *The Rise of the Boffins* (London: Phoenix House, 1962)

Cohen, Eliot A. & John Gooch, *Military Misfortunes: The Anatomy of Failure in War* (London: Collier Macmillan, 1990)

Cohen, J. M. & M. J. Cohen (eds.), *The Penguin Dictionary of Quotations* (London: Penguin, 1967)

Cole, Christopher & E. F. Cheesman, *The Air Defence of Britain, 1914-1918* (London: Putnam, 1984)

Collier, Basil, *The Defence of the United Kingdom* (London: HMSO, 1957)

Collier, Basil, *Leader of the Few: the Authorized Biography of Air Chief Marshal the Lord Dowding of Bentley Priory* (London: Jarrolds, 1957)

Collier, Basil, *Heavenly Adventurer: Sefton Brancker and the Dawn of British Aviation* (London: Secker & Warburg, 1959)

Collyer, David, *Kent's Listening Ears: Britain's First Early Warning System* (Tonbridge: Air-Britain, 1982)

Colville, John, *The Fringes of Power: Downing Street Diaries, 1939-1955* (London: Hodder & Stoughton, 1985)

Cooper, Malcolm, *The German Air Force, 1933-1945: An Anatomy of Failure* (London: Jane's, 1981)

Cox, Sebastian, 'A Comparative Analysis of RAF and Luftwaffe Intelligence in the Battle of Britain, 1940' in *Intelligence and Military Operations*, ed. Michael I. Handel (London: Cass, 1990) pp. 425-43

Cox, Sebastian, 'The Sources and Organization of RAF Intelligence' in Boog (ed.), *Conduct of Air War*, pp. 553-79

Cox, Sebastian, 'The RAF's Response' in Addison & Crang (eds.), *The Burning Blue*, pp. 55-68

Cox, Sebastian, 'Sir Arthur Harris and the Air Ministry' in Gray & Cox (eds.), *Air Power Leadership*, pp. 210-226

Cox, Sebastian & Peter Gray (eds.) *Air Power History: Turning Points from Kitty Hawk to Kosovo* (London: Cass, 2002)

Cross, Kenneth & Vincent Orange, *Straight and Level* (London: Grub Street, 1993)

Davies, Norman, *The Isles* (London: Macmillan, corrected ed., 2000)

Dean, Maurice, *The Royal Air Force and Two World Wars* (London: Cassell, 1979)

Deere, Alan C., *Nine Lives* (London: Hodder & Stoughton, 1959)

Deighton, Len, *Fighter: The True Story of the Battle of Britain* (London: Cape, 1977)

Deighton, Len, *Battle of Britain* (London: Cape, 1980)

Dick, AVM Ron, 'The Battle of Britain' in *Air Power History* (Summer 1990) pp. 11-25

Dixon, J. E. G., *The Battle of Britain: Victory and Defeat* (Woodfield, 2003)

Douglas, Sholto (MRAF Lord Douglas of Kirtleside), 'Air Operations by Fighter Command from 25th November 1940 to 31st December 1941' in *Supplement to the London Gazette* (London: HMSO, 14 September 1948) pp. 5015-5036

Douglas, Sholto (MRAF Lord Douglas of Kirtleside) with Robert Wright, *Years of Combat and Years of Command* (London: Collins, 1963, 1966)

Douglas, Sholto (MRAF Lord Douglas of Kirtleside) in *Oxford DNB*, vol. 16, pp. 713-7 by Vincent Orange

Dowding, ACM Sir Hugh, 'The Battle of Britain' in *Supplement to the London Gazette* (written in 1941; London: HMSO, 10 September 1946), pp. 4543-4571

Dowding, ACM Lord, *Twelve Legions of Angels: An Essay on Straight Thinking* (written in 1941; London: Jarrold, 1946)

Dowding, ACM Sir Hugh, *Many Mansions* (Bath: Chivers, 1943; reprints by Spiritualist Association of Great Britain, 1973 & 1976)

Dowding, ACM Lord, *Lychgate: The Entrance to the Path* (London: Rider, 1945)

Dowding, ACM Lord, *God's Magic: An Aspect of Spiritualism* (London: Museum Press, 1946; reprint by Spiritualist Association of Great Britain, 1960)

Dowding, ACM Lord, *The Dark Star* (London: Museum Press, 1951)

Dowding, ACM Lord, in *Oxford DNB*, vol. 16, pp. 773-7 by Vincent Orange

Dowding, Muriel, the Lady Dowding, *Beauty – Not the Beast* (Jersey: Neville Spearman, 1980)

Dowding, Muriel, in *Oxford DNB*, vol. 16, p. 778 by Hilda Kean

Dye, Peter J, 'Major Herbert Musgrave, DSO, RE & RAFC: The Mad Major? in *Cross & Cockade (International)*, vol. 27, no. 4 (Winter 1996) pp. 203-7

Dye, Peter J, 'Nine Squadron, RFC-RAF: An Analysis' in *Cross & Cockade (International)*, vol. 28, no. 2 (Summer 1997) pp. 73-87

Dye, Peter J., 'Logistics and the Battle of Britain' in Air Force Journal of Logistics (Winter 2000) pp. 1-11

Dye, Peter J., 'The Royal Flying Corps & Royal Air Force at St-Omer' in *Cross & Cockade (International)*, vol. 35, no. 2 (Summer 2004) pp. 71-7.

Dye, Peter J., 'Major Herbert Musgrave, DSO, RE & RFC: An Update' in *Cross & Cockade (International)*, vol. 35, no. 2 (Summer 2004) pp. 95-9

Dye, Peter J., 'No 9 (Wireless) Squadron, 1914-1915' in *Cross & Cockade (International)*, vol. 35, no. 2 (Summer 2004) pp. 106-120

Edgerton, David, 'The Prophet Militant and Industrial: The Peculiarities of Correlli Barnett' in *Twentieth Century British History*, vol. 2, no. 3 (1991) pp. 360-79

Ellington, MRAF Sir Edward in *Oxford DNB*, vol. 18, pp. 158-9 by John Sweetman

Evill, ACM Sir Douglas (Strath) in *Oxford DNB*, vol. 18, pp. 805-6 by Robert Wright, revised by Christina Goulter

Ferris, John, 'Review Article: The Air Force Brats' View of History: Recent Writings and the Royal Air Force, 1918-1960' in *International History Review*, vol. xx, no. 1 (March 1998) pp. 119-43

Ferris, John, 'Achieving Air Ascendency: Challenge and Response in British Strategic Air Defence, 1915-40' in *Air Power History,* pp. 21-50

Ferris, John, 'Fighter Defence before Fighter Command: The Rise of Strategic Air Defence in Great Britain, 1917-1934' in *Journal of Military History*, vol. 63, no. 4 (1999) pp. 845-84

Fischer, David E., *A Summer Bright and Terrible: Winston Churchill, Lord Dowding, Radar and the Impossible Triumph of the Battle of Britain* (Emeryville, California: Shoemaker & Hoard, 2005)

Fitzsimons, B. (ed.) *Purnell's Illustrated Encyclopedia of Modern Weapons & Warfare* (London: Phoebus, 1967-78, 8 vols.)

Flight aviation magazine, re R. 101: R 101: 10 Oct 30, pp. 1107-1126; 17 Oct 30, pp. 1137-1151; 24 Oct 30, p. 1170; 31 Oct 30, p. 1187; 7 Nov 30, pp. 1228-9; 14 Nov 30, pp. 1238-9; 5 Dec 30, p. 1421; 12 Dec 30,

p. 1446. See also *The Times*.

Flint, Peter, *Dowding and Headquarters Fighter Command* (Shrewsbury: Airlife, 1996)

Fozard, John W. (ed.) *Sydney Camm and the Hurricane* (Shrewsbury: Airlife, 1991)

Furse, Anthony, Wilfrid Freeman: *The Genius Behind Allied Survival and Air Supremacy, 1939-1945* (Staplehurst: Spellmount, 1999)

Gilbert, Martin, *Winston S. Churchill, vol. 5: 1922-1939* (London: Heinemann, 1976)

Gilbert, Martin, *Finest Hour: Winston S. Churchill, vol. 6: 1939-1941* (London: Heinemann, 1983)

Gilbert, Martin (ed.), *The Churchill War Papers, vol. 2 (May-December 1940)* (New York: Norton, 1991)

Gray, Peter & Owen Thetford, *German Aircraft of the Second World War* (London: Putnam, 1962, reprinted 1987)

Gray, Peter W. and Sebastian Cox (eds.), *Air Power Leadership: Theory and Practice* (London: HMSO, 2002)

Gray, Peter, 'Dowding as Commander, Leader and Manager' in Gray & Cox (eds.), *Air Power Leadership*, pp. 199-209

Green, William, *Warplanes of the Second World War: Fighters, vol. 4* (London: Macdonald, 1961)

Green, William, *Famous Fighters of the Second World War* (London: Macdonald & Jane's, 1975)

Green, William & Gordon Swanborough, 'Typhoon: The "More Violent Hurricane"' in *Air Enthusiast*, vol. 3, no. 2 (August 1972) pp. 91-8

Green, William & Gordon Swanborough, 'Beaufighter: Innovative Improvisation by Bristol' in *Air Enthusiast International*, vol. 6, no. 1 (January 1974) pp. 25-32, 47

Green, William & Gordon Swanborough, 'Hampden: Defender of Liberty' in *Air International*, vol. 27, no. 5 (November 1984) pp. 244-52

Green, William & Gordon Swanborough, 'Liore-et-Olivier 45: A Study in Elegance' in *Air International*, vol. 29, no. 4 (October 1985) pp. 179-89

Green, William & Gordon Swanborough, 'The Handy Hudson: Lockheed's First Warplane' in *Air International*, vol. 29, no. 5 (November 1985) pp. 240-63

Green, William & Gordon Swanborough, 'Messerschmitt's Strategic Fighter: The Bf 110' in *Air International*, vol. 30, no. 5 (May 1986) pp. 240-7, no. 6 (June 1986) pp. 283-9, vol. 31, no. 1 (July 1986) pp. 26-33

Greenhous, Brereton (& others), *The Official History of the Royal Canadian Air Force, vol. 3: The Crucible of War, 1939-1945* (University of Toronto Press, 1994)

Greenwood, Sean, '"Caligula's Horse" Revisited: Sir Thomas Inskip as Minister for the Co-ordination of Defence, 1936-1939' in *Journal of Strategic Studies*, vol. 17, no. 2 (June 1994) pp. 17-38

Gregory, Adrian, 'The Commemoration of the Battle of Britain' in Addison & Crang (eds.), *The Burning Blue*, pp. 217-228

Grinnell-Milne, Duncan, *Wind in the Wires* (1933; London: Panther, 1957)

Gunston, Bill, *The Encyclopedia of the World's Combat Aircraft: A*

Technical Directory of Major Warplanes from World War One to the Present Day (London & New York: Hamlyn, 1976)

Gunston, Bill, *An Illustrated Encyclopedia of the World's Rockets and Missiles* (London: Salamander, 1979)

Gustin, Emmanuel & Anthony G. Williams, *Flying Guns: The Development of Aircraft Guns, Ammunition and Installations, 1933-45* (Shrewsbury: Airlife, 2003)

Hallion, Richard P., 'The American Perspective' in Addison & Crang (eds.), *Burning Blue*, pp. 82-107

Haresnape, Brian, *Bulleid Locomotives* (London: Ian Allan, revised ed., 1993)

Harris, Stephen & Norman Hillmer, 'The Development of the Royal Air Force, 1909-1945' in *British Military History*, a supplement to Robin Higham's *Guide to the Sources*, ed. Gerald Jordan (New York & London: Garland, 1988) pp. 345-66

Hartcup, Guy (& others), 'The Air Defence of Great Britain, 1920-1940: An Operational Research Perspective' in *Journal of Operational Research*, vol. 48, pp. 563-4

Hartcup, Guy, *The Effect of Science on the Second World War* (London: Macmillan, 2000)

Harvey, A. D., 'Great War Fighter Aces in the National Archives (PRO)' [Grinnell-Milne] in *Cross & Cockade (International)*, vol. 34, no. 2 (Summer 2003), pp. 120-1

Haslam, Eric, 'How Lord Dowding came to leave Fighter Command' in *Journal of Strategic Studies*, vol. 4, no. 2 (June 1981) pp. 175-186

Haslam, Eric, *The History of Royal Air Force Cranwell* (London: HMSO, 1983)

Hastings, Max, *Bomber Command* (London: Michael Joseph, 1979)

Heinkel, Ernst, ed. Jürgen Thorwald, *He 1000* (London: Hutchinson, 1956)

Henshaw, Trevor, *The Sky Their Battlefield: Air Fighting and the Complete List of Allied Air Casualties from Enemy Action in the First War* (London: Grub Street, 1995)

Higham, Robin, 'The Development of the Royal Air Force, 1909-45', pp. 422-51 in Robin Higham (ed.), *A Guide to the Sources of British Military History* (London: Routledge & Kegan Paul, 1972). See also Jordan, Gerald

Higham, Robin, 'Government, Companies, and National Defense: British Aeronautical Experience, 1918-1945 as the Basis for a Broad Hypothesis' in *Business History Review*, vol. 39 (1965) pp. 323-47

Hinsley, F. H. (& others), *British Intelligence in the Second World War*, vol. 1 (London: HMSO, 1979)

Hives, Lord (Sir Ernest), in *Oxford DNB*, vol. 27, pp. 338-9 by Lord Kings Norton, revised by Robin Higham

Hobson, *Airmen Died in the Great War, 1914-1918: The Roll of Honour of the British and Commonwealth Air Services of the First World War* (Suffolk: Hayward, 1995)

Hogg, Ian V., *Anti-Aircraft: A History of Air Defence* (London: Macdonald & Jane's, 1978)

Horne, Alistair, *To Lose a Battle: France 1940* (London: Penguin, 1979)

Hornung, E. W., *Raffles: The Amateur Cracksman* (1899; latest ed., Ware, Hertfordshire: Wordsworth, 1994)

Hough, Richard & Denis Richards, *The Battle of Britain: The Greatest Air Battle of World War II* (London: Hodder & Stoughton, 1989)

Huskinson, Patrick, *Vision Ahead* (London: Werner Laurie, 1949)

Hyde, H. Montgomery, *British Air Policy Between the Wars, 1918-1939* (London: Heinemann, 1976)

Illustrated Encyclopedia of Aircraft (London: Orbis, 1981)

Irving, David, *The Rise and Fall of the Luftwaffe: The Life of Luftwaffe Marshal Erhard Milch* (London: Weidenfeld & Nicolson, 1974; Futura, 1976)

Irving, David, *Göring: A Biography* (London: Macmillan, 1989)

James, John, *The Paladins: A Social History of the RAF up to the Outbreak of World War II* (London: Macdonald, 1990)

James, Lawrence, *Imperial Rearguard: Wars of Empire, 1919-1985* (London: Brassey's, 1988)

James, T. C. G., *The Growth of Fighter Command, 1936-1940* and *The Battle of Britain: The Air Defence of Great Britain* (composed c. 1942-5; edited with introduction by Sebastian Cox, London: Whitehall History/ Frank Cass, 2000, 2002)

Johnson, AVM J. E. 'Johnnie' Johnson, *The Story of Air Fighting*: revised, enlarged ed. of *Full Circle*, London: Chatto & Windus, 1964, (London: Hutchinson, 1985)

Jones, Wing Commander Ira, *Tiger Squadron* (London: Ian Allan, 1954; new ed, White Lion, 1972)

Jones, Neville, *The Beginning of Strategic Air Power: A History of the British Bomber Force, 1923-1939* (London: Frank Cass, 1987)

Jordan, Gerald (ed.) *British Military History: A Supplement to Robin Higham's Guide to the Sources* (New York & London: Garland Publishing, 1988). See also Higham, Robin

Joubert de la Ferté, Sir Philip, *The Third Service: The Story behind the Royal Air Force* (London: Thames & Hudson, 1955)

Kingston-McCloughry, Edgar J., *Winged Warfare* (London: Cape, 1937)

Kinsey, Gordon, *Orfordness – Secret Site: A History of the Establishment, 1915-1980* (Lavenham, Suffolk: Terence Dalton, 1981)

Laffin, John, *Swifter than Eagles: A Biography of MRAF Sir John Salmond* (Edinburgh & London: Blackwood, 1964)

Lake, Jeremy & John Schofield, 'Conservation and the Battle of Britain' in Addison & Crang (eds.), *Burning Blue*, pp. 229-42

Leigh-Mallory, ACM Sir Trafford in *Dictionary of National Biography*, vol. 36, pp. 345-7 by Vincent Orange

Levine, Alan J., 'Was World War II a Near-run Thing?' in *Journal of Strategic Studies*, vol. 8 (March 1985) pp. 38-63

Lewis, Peter, *The British Fighter since 1912* (London: Putnam, 1965; latest ed. 1979)

Leyvastre, Pierre, 'Bloch's Fighters: The Contentious Combatants' in *Air International*, vol. 14, no. 4 (April 1978) pp. 179-88, 204-5

London, The Book of (Basingstoke: Automobile Association, 1985)

Lucas, P. B. 'Laddie', *Flying Colours: The Epic Story of Douglas Bader* (London: Hutchinson, 1981; Granada paperback, 1983)

Lucas, P. B. 'Laddie' (ed.), *Wings of War: airmen of all nations tell their stories, 1939-1945* (London: Hutchinson, 1983)

Lumsden, Alec & Owen Thetford, *On Silver Wings: RAF Biplane Fighters between the Wars* (London: Osprey, 1993)

Lunn, Sir Arnold, 'The Man Who Won the Battle of Britain' in *National Review* (Washington, DC, 16 June 1964) pp. 487-8

Lunn, Sir Arnold, in *Oxford DNB*, vol. 34, pp. 769-70 by T. F. Burns

Lyall, Gavin, 'Dowding' in Michael Carver (ed.) *The War Lords: Military Commanders of the Twentieth Century* (London: Weidenfeld & Nicolson, 1976) pp. 202-212

Maier, Klaus A., 'The Luftwaffe' in Addison & Crang (eds.), *The Burning Blue*, pp. 15-21

Mason, Francis K., *Battle over Britain: A History of the German Air Assault on Great Britain, 1917-1918 and July-December 1940, and of the Development of Britain's Air Defences between the World Wars* (London: McWhirter Twins, 1969)

Mason, Francis K., *Hawker Hurricane* (Bourne End, Bucks.: Aston, 1987)

Mason, Tony, *Air Power: A Centennial Appraisal* (London: Brassey's, 1994)

May, Ernest R., *Strange Victory: Hitler's Conquest of France* (London: I. B. Tauris, 2000)

Meilinger, Phillip S. 'Trenchard and "Morale Bombing": The Evolution of Royal Air Force Doctrine before World War II' in *Journal of Military History*, vol. 60 (April 1996) pp. 243-70

Meilinger, Phillip S., *Airwar: Theory and Practice* (London: Frank Cass, 2003)

Metzger, Bruce M. & Michael D. Coogan (eds.), *The Oxford Companion to the Bible* (Oxford University Press, 1993)

Middlebrook, Martin and Chris Everitt, *The Bomber Command War Diaries: An Operational Reference Book, 1939-1945* (London: Viking, 1985)

Millett, Allan R. & Williamson Murray, *Military Effectiveness, vol. 2: The Interwar Period* (Boston: Allen & Unwin, 1988)

Mitchell, Reginald, in *Oxford DNB*, vol. 38, pp. 432-3 by Sebastian Ritchie

Mosley, Leonard, *The Battle of Britain: The Making of a Film* (London: Pan, 1969)

Murray, Williamson, 'German Air Power and the Munich Crisis' in *War & Society: A Yearbook of Military History*, vol, 2, ed. Brian Bond & Ian Roy (London: Croom Helm, 1977) pp. 107-117

Murray, Williamson, 'The Strategy of the "Phoney War": A Re-Evaluation' in *Military Affairs* (February 1981) pp. 13-17

Murray, Williamson, *Luftwaffe: Strategy for Defeat, 1933-1945* (London: Allen & Unwin, 1985)

Murray, Williamson & Allan R. Millett (eds.), *Military Innovation in the Interwar Period* (Cambridge University Press, 1996)

Newall, Lord Newall of Clifton-upon-Dunsmore, in *Oxford DNB*, vol. 40, pp. 562-4 by Vincent Orange

Norris, Geoffrey, *The Royal Flying Corps: A History* (London: Frederick Muller, 1965)

Omissi, D., *Air Power and Colonial Control: The Royal Air Force, 1919-1939* (University of Manchester, 1991)

Orange, Vincent, 'Fortunate Fascist Failures: The Case of the Heinkel Fighters' in *Historical News* (Christchurch, NZ), no. 47 (December 1983) pp. 7-13.

Orange, Vincent, 'The British Commanders' in *The Battle Re-Thought: A Symposium on the Battle of Britain*, ed. Henry Probert & Sebastian Cox (Shrewsbury: Airlife, 1991) pp. 33-41 & comments elsewhere

Orange, Vincent, 'A Broad Margin: The Battle of Britain North of Watford' in *Defending Northern Skies, 1915-1995* (RAF Historical Society at the University of Newcastle, 1996) pp. 56-72

Orange, Vincent, *Park* (London: Methuen, 1984; new ed., Grub Street, 2001)

Orange, Vincent, *Tedder: Quietly in Command* (London: Frank Cass, 2004)

Orange, Vincent, *Slessor: Bomber Champion* (London: Grub Street, 2006)

Orange, Vincent, 'The German Air Force is Already "The Most Powerful in Europe": Two Royal Air Force Officers Report on a Visit to Germany, 6-15 October 1936' in *Journal of Military History*, vol. 70, no. 4 (October 2006) pp. 1011-1028

Overy, Richard, *Goering: The Iron Man* (London: Routledge & Kegal Paul, 1984)

Overy, Richard, 'Air Power and the Origins of Deterrence Theory before 1939' in *Journal of Strategic Studies*, vol. 15, no. 1 (March 1992) pp. 73-101

Overy, Richard, 'How Significant was the Battle?' in Addison & Crang (eds.), *The Burning Blue*, pp. 267-280

Owen, Revd. George Vale, *The Life Beyond the Veil*, 5 vols. (London: 1926)

Oxford DNB: Dictionary of National Biography (Oxford University Press, 60 vols., 2004)

Pallud, Jean Paul, 'The Norwegian Campaign' in *After the Battle*, vol. 126, pp. 2-55

Park, ACM Sir Keith in *Oxford DNB*, vol. 42, pp. 633-6 by Vincent Orange

Peach, Stuart W., 'A Neglected Turning Point in Air Power History: Air Power and the Fall of France' in Cox & Gray (eds.), *Turning Points*, pp. 142-172

Penrose, Harald, *The Great War and the Armistice, 1915-1919* (London: HMSO, 1969)

Penrose, Harald, *Widening Horizons, 1930-4* (London: HMSO, 1984)

Penrose, Harald, *Ominous Skies, 1935-9* (London: HMSO, 1980)

Pile, General Sir Frederick, 'The Anti-Aircraft Defence of the United Kingdom from 28th July 1939 to 15th April 1945' in *Supplement to the London Gazette* (London: HMSO, 16 December 1947) pp. 5973-5994

Pile, General Sir Frederick, *Ack-Ack: Britain's Defence Against Air Attack during the Second World War* (London: Harrap, 1949; Panther, 1956)

Pile, General Sir Frederick, in *Oxford DNB*, vol. 44, pp. 307-8 by Kenneth Macksey

Portal, C. F. A., 'Air Force Co-operation in Policing the Empire' in *RUSI Journal*, vol. 82, no. 526 (May 1937)

Postan, M. M. (& others), *Design and Development of Weapons: Studies in Government and Industrial Organization* (London: HMSO, 1964)

Powers, Barry D., *Strategy without Slide-Rule: British Air Strategy, 1914-1939* (New York: Holmes & Meier, 1976)

Preston, David L., 'The Key to Victory: Fighter Command and the Tactical Air Reserves during the Battle of Britain' in *Air Power History* (Winter 1994) pp. 18-29

Price, Alfred, *Battle of Britain: The Hardest Day, 18 August 1940* (London: Granada, 1980)

Price, Alfred, *Battle of Britain* (London: Arms & Armour Press, 1990)

Price, Alfred, 'Germany's Airship Spy Flights: Watching the Detectives' in *Aeroplane* (October 2007) pp. 22-6

Probert, Henry, *High Commanders of the Royal Air Force* (London: HMSO, 1991)

Probert, Henry, *The Forgotten Air Force: The Royal Air Force in the War against Japan, 1941-1945* (London: Brassey's, 1995)

Probert, Henry, *Bomber Harris: His Life and Times* (London: Greenhill, 2001)

Probert, Henry & Sebastian Cox (eds.), *The Battle Re-Thought* (Shrewsbury: Airlife, 1990)

Pugh, Martin, review of R. A. C. Parker, *Chamberlain and Appeasement* (London: Macmillan, 1993) in *TLS*, 31 December 1993, p. 24

Raleigh, Walter & H. A. Jones, *The War in the Air*, 6 vols. (Oxford: Clarendon, 1922-37)

Ramsay, Vice-Admiral Sir Bertram, 'The Evacuation of the Allied Armies from Dunkirk and Neighbouring Beaches' in *Supplement to the London Gazette* (London: HMSO, 15 July 1947) pp. 3295-3318

Ramsey, Winston G. (ed.), *The Battle of Britain, Then and Now* (London: After the Battle Publications, 3rd ed., 1985)

Ray, John, *The Battle of Britain, New Perspectives: Behind the Scenes of the Great Air War* (London: Arms & Armour, 1994)

Ray, John, *The Night Blitz, 1940-1941* (London: Arms & Armour, 1996)

Reader, W. J., *Architect of Air Power: The Life of the First Viscount Weir of Eastwood, 1877-1959* (London: Collins, 1968)

Revell, Alex, *British Fighter Units, Western Front, 1914-16* (London: Osprey, 1978)

Revell, Alex, *British Single-Seat Fighter Squadrons on the Western Front in World War 1* (Atglen, Pennsylvania: Schiffer Military History, 2005)

Reynolds, David, *In Command of History: Churchill Fighting and Writing the Second World War* (London: Allen Lane, 2004)

Richards, Denis, *The Fight at Odds: vol. 1 of The Royal Air Force, 1939-1945* (HMSO: London, 1953, reprint 1976)

Richards, Denis, *Portal of Hungerford* (London: Heinemann, 1977)

Riding, Richard T. (ed.), *War in the Air* (Sutton, Surrey: Quadrant, nos. 1-23, 1989-91)

Ritchie, Sebastian, *Industry and Air Power: The Expansion of British Aircraft Production, 1935-1941* (London: Frank Cass, 1997)

Ritchie, Sebastian, 'The Price of Air Power: Technological Change, Industrial Policy, and Military Aircraft Contracts in the Era of British Rearmament, 1935-1939' in *Business History Review*, vol. 71 (Spring 1997) pp. 82-111

Ritchie, Sebastian, 'A Political Intrigue against the CAS: The Downfall of ACM Sir Cyril Newall' in *War and Society*, vol. 16, no. 1 (May 1998) pp. 83-105

Ritchie, Sebastian, 'Sir Wilfrid Freeman and the British Aircraft Economy, 1936-1945' in Gray & Cox, *Air Power Leadership*, pp. 252-63

Roberts, Andrew, *The "Holy Fox": A Biography of Lord Halifax* (London: Weidenfeld & Nicolson, 1991)

Robertson, A. J., 'Lord Beaverbrook and the Supply of Aircraft, 1940-1941' in *Business, Banking and Urban History: Essays in Honour of S. G. Checkland*, ed. Anthony Slaven & Derek H. Aldcroft (Edinburgh: John Donald, 1982) pp. 80-100

Robertson, Bruce, *Sopwith – The Man and his Aircraft* (Bedford: Sidney Press, 1970)

Robineau, Lucien, 'French Air Policy in the Inter-War Period and the Conduct of the Air War against Germany from September 1939 to June 1940' in Boog (ed.) *Conduct of Air War*, pp. 627-57

Robinson, Douglas H., *Giants in the Sky: A History of the Rigid Airship* (Henley-on-Thames: G. T. Foulis, 1973)

Roskill, Stephen, *Naval Policy between the Wars, vol. 2: The Period of Reluctant Rearmament, 1930-1939* (London: Collins, 1976)

Rowse, A. L., *All Souls and Appeasement: A Contribution to Contemporary History* (London: Macmillan, 1961)

Salmond, MRAF Sir John, in *Oxford DNB*, vol. 48, pp. 738-40 by Phillip S. Meilinger

Schenk, Peter, '"Sealion": The Invasion that Never Was' in *After the Battle*, no. 69 (1990) pp. 1-19

Shute, Neville, *Slide Rule: The Autobiography of an Engineer* (London: Heinemann, 1954; Pan Books, 6th Printing, 1976)

Slessor, MRAF Sir John, *The Central Blue: Recollections and Reflections* (London: Cassell, 1956)

Smith, J. R. & Antony Kay, *German Aircraft of the Second World War* (London: Putnam, 1972, 4th impression, 1982)

Smith, Malcolm, 'The Royal Air Force, Air Power and British Foreign Policy, 1932-1937' in *Journal of Contemporary History*, vol. 12 (1977) pp. 153-74

Smith, Malcolm, 'Planning and Building the British Bomber Force, 1934-1939' in *Business History Review*, vol. liv, no. 1 (Spring 1980) pp. 35-62

Smith, Malcolm, *British Air Strategy between the Wars* (Oxford: Clarendon, 1984)

Smith, Malcolm, 'The RAF' in Addison & Crang (eds.), *The Burning Blue*, pp. 22-36

Smith-Barry, Lt. Col. Robert R. in *Oxford DNB*, vol. 4, pp. 149-151 by Vincent Orange

Smythies, B. E., 'Experiences during the War (1914-8)' in Air Ministry AP 956 (December 1923)

Stafford, David, *Endgame 1945: Victory, Retribution, Liberation* (London: Little, Brown, 2007)

Stashower, Daniel, *Teller of Tales: The Life of Arthur Conan Doyle* (London: Penguin, 1999)

Stephens, Alan, *In Search of the Knock-Out Blow: The Development of Air Power Doctrine, 1911-1945* (Canberra: Air Power Studies Centre, 1998)

Sutton, Squadron Leader H. T., *Raiders Approach! The Fighting Tradition of Royal Air Force Station Hornchurch and Sutton's Farm* (Aldershot: Gale & Polden, 1956)

Swinton, Lord (Philip Cunliffe-Lister) in *Oxford DNB*, vol. 33, pp. 988-92 by Keith Robins

Taylor, A. J. P., *English History, 1914-1945* (Oxford: Clarendon, 1965)

Taylor, A. J. P., ed. with introduction by Chris Wrigley, *From the Boer War to the Cold War: Essays on Twentieth-Century Europe* (London: Hamish Hamilton, 1995)

Taylor, John W. R., *CFS: Birthplace of Air Power* (London: Putnam, 1958)

Taylor, Telford, *The Breaking Wave: The German Defeat in the Summer of 1940* (London: Weidenfeld & Nicolson, 1967)

Tedder, MRAF Lord Tedder of Glenguin in *Oxford DNB*, vol. 54, pp. 14-19 by Vincent Orange

Terraine, John, *The Right of the Line: The Royal Air Force in the European War, 1939-1945* (London: Hodder & Stoughton, 1985)

The Times newspaper, re R.101: R 101: 14 Oct 30, p. 14; 24 Oct 30, p. 15; 29 Oct 30, p. 9; 30 Oct 30, p. 20; 5 Nov 30, p. 19; 7 Nov 30, pp. 9 & 14. See also *Flight*.

Thomas, Edward, 'The Intelligence Aspect' in Probert & Cox, *Battle Re-Thought*, pp. 42-6

Thomson, Lord, of Cardington, in *Oxford DNB*, vol. 54, pp. 497-9 by Lord Onslow, revised by Robin Higham

Till, Geoffrey, 'The Strategic Interface: The Navy and the Air Force in the defence of Britain' in *Journal of Strategic Studies*, vol. 1, no. 2 (1978) pp. 179-93

Till, Geoffrey, *Air Power and the Royal Navy: A Historical Survey* (MacDonald & Jane's, 1979)

Townsend, Peter, *Duel of Eagles* (London: Corgi, 1972)

Tredrey, F. D., *Pioneer Pilot: The Great Smith-Barry Who Taught the World How to Fly* (London: Peter Davies, 1976)

Trenchard, Lord Trenchard of Wolfeton in *Oxford DNB*, vol. 55, pp. 299-304 by Vincent Orange

Turner, P. St John, *Heinkel: An Aircraft Album* (London: Ian Allan, 1970)

Turner, P. St John & Heinz J. Nowarra, *Junkers: An Aircraft Album* (London: Ian Allan, 1971)

Venneson, Pascal, 'Institution and Air Power: The Making of the French Air Force' in *Journal of Strategic Studies*, vol. 18, no. 1 (March 1995) pp. 36-67

Wakelam, Randall T., 'The Roaring Lions of the Air: Air Substitution and the RAF's Struggle for Independence after the First World War' in *Air Power History* (Fall, 1996) pp. 50-63

Wark, Wesley K., 'British Intelligence on the German Air Force and Aircraft Industry, 1933-1939' in *Historical Journal*, vol. 25, no. 3 (September 1982) pp. 627-48

Wark, Wesley K., *The Ultimate Enemy: British Intelligence and Nazi Germany, 1933-1939* (London: I. B. Tauris, 1985)

Warne, Joe, '60 Squadron: A Detailed History, Part 1' in *Cross & Cockade (GB) Journal*, vol. 11, no. 1 (Spring 1980) pp. 29-34

Webster, Sir Charles & Noble Frankland, *The Strategic Air Offensive against Germany, 1939-1945* (London: HMSO, 1961)

White, Ian, *The History of Air Intercept Radar and the British Nightfighter, 1935-1959* (Barnsley: Pen & Sword, 2007)

Winkworth, Derek, *Bulleid's Pacifics* (London: Ian Allan, 1977)

Wilson, Arnie, *Snow Crazy: A Hundred Years of Stories of Derring-Do from the Ski Club of Great Britain* (London: Metro, 2003)

Wilson, Eunice, *Dangerous Sky: A Resource Guide to the Battle of Britain* (Westport, Connecticut & London: Greenwood Press, 1995)

Wood, Derek, *Attack Warning Red: The Royal Observer Corps and the Defence of Britain, 1925-1975* (London: Macdonald & Jane's, 1976)

Wood, Derek, 'The Dowding System' in Probert & Cox (eds.), *Battle Re-Thought*, pp. 3-10

Wood, Derek with Derek Dempster, *The Narrow Margin: The Battle of Britain and the Rise of Air Power, 1930-1940* (London, 1961; latest revised ed., Tri-Service Press, 1990)

Wood, W. J. A., 'Emil Über England' in *Air International*, vol. 19, no. 4 (October 1980) pp. 196-200

Wright, Peter, 'It's Good To Talk' [Donald Lewis] in *Cross & Cockade (International)*, vol. 30, no. 4 (Winter 1999) pp. 210-9.

Wright, Robert, *Dowding and the Battle of Britain* (London: Corgi, 1970)

Wykeham, Peter, *Fighter Command: A Study of Air Defence, 1914-1960* (London: Putnam, 1960)

Young, Robert J., 'The Strategic Dream: French Air Doctrine and the Interwar Period, 1919-1939' in *Journal of Contemporary History*, vol. 9, no. 4 (1974) pp. 57-76

Zamoyski, Adam, *The Forgotten Few: The RAF in the Second World War* (London: Murray, 1995)

Zimmerman, David, 'British Radar Organization and the Failure to Stop the Night-time Blitz' in *Journal of Strategic Studies*, vol. 21, no. 3 (September 1998) pp. 86-106

Zimmerman, David, *Britain's Shield: Radar and the Defeat of the Luftwaffe* (Stroud, Gloucestershire: Sutton, 2001)

Zuckerman, Lord, *Six Men out of the Ordinary* (London: Peter Owen, 1992)

Index